Adolescent Portraits

Adolescent Portraits introduces contemporary theories and research that surround adolescent development today through eighteen first-person accounts written by young adults. The case study approach of the book illustrates the complexity of the individual experience and the interactions among an individual's needs, ideas, relationships, and context. Each case, taken alone, helps us begin to know one more adolescent and his or her experience; taken together, the cases provide a rich overview of the wide, diverse, and complex range of adolescent experiences.

This edition also includes three follow-up essays, written five or more years after their original memoir. The authors of these follow-ups reflect on their original story written in late adolescence from the more mature point of view of full-fledged adulthood. These retrospectives provide a poignant and lifespan developmental perspective on the ways in which the adolescent themes of identity and challenges transform, for better or worse, with the tasks of adulthood.

With contributions from adolescents from a range of racial, class, and family backgrounds, the book provides a diverse introduction to the adolescent experience. It is a must-read for any student of adolescent development.

Andrew C. Garrod is Professor Emeritus of Education at Dartmouth College, USA.

Robert Kilkenny is Executive Director of the Alliance for Inclusion and Prevention (AIP), and on the faculty of Simmons University, USA.

Adolescent Portraits

Identity and Challenges

Eighth Edition

Edited by Andrew C. Garrod and Robert Kilkenny

NEW YORK AND LONDON

Cover image: © Getty Images

Eighth edition published 2022
by Routledge
605 Third Avenue, New York, NY 10158

and by Routledge
4 Park Square, Milton Park, Abingdon, Oxon, OX14 4RN

Routledge is an imprint of the Taylor & Francis Group, an informa business

First edition published by Pearson 1992
Seventh edition published by Pearson 2011

Library of Congress Cataloging-in-Publication Data
A catalog record for this book has been requested

ISBN: 9780367757014 (hbk)
ISBN: 9780367757021 (pbk)
ISBN: 9781003165378 (ebk)

DOI: 10.4324/9781003165378

Typeset in Univers
by Newgen Publishing UK

Contents

Contents

Cases Categorized by Themes

Theme	Case number, Title
Child Abuse	2. The Hatred Within
	14. Quest for Peace
	15. Seeking the Best of Both Worlds
Disabilities	13. Forever an Awkward Adolescent
	16. Figuring Out My Life
Drugs/Alcohol	4. Little Woman from Lame Deer
	7. The Devils Within
	11. I Walk in Beauty
	12. An Unpredictable Journey
	17. Holding My Breath
Ethnicity/Race	1. Why Didn't You Teach Me?
	2. The Hatred Within
	3. Good Hair
	4. Little Woman from Lame Deer
	6. A Latinidad I Cannot, Will Not, Hide
	8. In My World, 1+1=3
	9. In Search of a *Sangam*
	11. I Walk in Beauty
	12. An Unpredictable Journey
	14. Quest for Peace
	15. Seeking the Best of Both Worlds
	18. Multihued

Cases Categorized by Themes

School Issues	1.	Why Didn't You Teach Me?
	3.	Good Hair
	4.	Little Woman from Lame Deer
	6.	A Latinidad I Cannot, Will Not, Hide
	8.	In My World, 1+1=3
	11.	I Walk in Beauty
	12.	An Unpredictable Journey
	13.	Forever an Awkward Adolescent
	14.	Quest for Peace
	16.	Figuring Out My Life
	17.	Holding My Breath

Sexuality	5.	Looking into the Sun
	6.	A Latinidad I Cannot, Will Not, Hide
	8.	In My World, 1+1=3
	9.	In Search of a *Sangam*
	10.	Is This My Life?
	14.	Quest for Peace
	17.	Holding My Breath

Trauma	4.	Little Woman from Lame Deer
	7.	The Devils Within
	11.	I Walk in Beauty
	12.	An Unpredictable Journey
	14.	Quest for Peace
	15.	Seeking the Best of Both Worlds
	18.	Multihued

Violence	7.	The Devils Within
	14.	Quest for Peace

Women's Identity	4.	Little Woman from Lame Deer
	8.	In My World, 1+1=3
	9.	In Search of a *Sangam*
	10.	Is This My Life?
	14.	Quest for Peace

About the Editors

Andrew C. Garrod is Professor Emeritus at Dartmouth College, where he previously chaired the Department of Education, directed the Teacher Education Program, and taught courses in adolescence, moral development, and contemporary issues in U.S. education. For a number of years, he conducted a research project in Bosnia and Herzegovina on forgiveness, faith development, and moral reasoning. He also directed six bilingual Shakespearean productions in Bosnia and Herzegovina that have played in Mostar and elsewhere in the Balkans. He has also directed a trilingual production of *Romeo and Juliet* in Kigali, Rwanda and directed numerous bilingual Shakespearean plays and Broadway musicals in the Marshall Islands in the Central Pacific. From 2000 to 2014, he directed a volunteer teaching program in the Marshall Islands. His recent publications include the coedited books *Growing Up Muslim: Muslim College Students in America Tell Their Life Stories*; *I Am Where I Come From: Native American College Students and Graduates Tell Their Life Stories*; and the chapter "Bridging the Divide with Shakespeare: Theatre as Moral Education in Bosnia and Herzegovina" in *The Reflexive Teaching Artist*. In 1991 and 2009, he was awarded Dartmouth College's Distinguished Teaching Award. He holds an Honorary Doctorate in Humane Letters from the University of New Brunswick, Canada. In 2019, he was made an Honorary Citizen of the Marshall Islands.

Robert Kilkenny is the founder and Executive Director of the Alliance for Inclusion and Prevention (AIP) in Boston, MA. AIP is a nonprofit children's mental health agency working to promote childhood behavioral health and academic achievement by increasing the use of evidence-based mental health services in schools. He is the principal investigator for AIP's federally funded Center for Trauma Care in Schools, which promotes trauma-informed schooling, and also serves unaccompanied and refugee youth. He is coeditor of *Souls Looking Back: Life Stories of Growing Up Black*; *Balancing Two Worlds: Asian American College*

Students Tell Their Life Stories; *Mi Voz, Mi Vida: Latino College Students Tell Their Life Stories*; *Mixed: Multiracial College Students Tell Their Life Stories*; *Growing Up Muslim: Muslim College Students in America Tell Their Life Stories*; and *I Am Where I Come From: Native American College Students and Graduates Tell Their Life Stories*.

Preface

The eighth edition of *Adolescent Portraits* includes eighteen cases and three reflections by earlier contributors on their lives since writing their original stories. In choosing new cases and removing others, we have considered feedback from faculty and students using the book and our own understanding of the important issues facing adolescents in the second decade of this century.

Of the eighteen cases in this anthology, eight appeared in the seventh edition of *Adolescent Portraits* published by Pearson in 2012. Other memoirs have been culled from recent publications edited by Garrod and Kilkenny for Cornell University Press—*I Am Where I Come From: Native American College Students and Graduates Tell Their Life Stories*; *Mi Voz, Mi Vida: Latino College Students Tell Their Life Stories*; *Balancing Two Worlds: Asian American College Students Tell Their Life Stories*; and *Mixed: Multiracial Students Tell Their Life Stories*. Finally, one case is drawn from *Learning Disabilities and Life Stories* and one from *Souls Looking Back: Life Stories of Growing Up Black*. While some of the cases have been developed in the last few years, many were generated five, six, or seven years ago. "In Search of a *Sangam*," for instance, was written ten years ago.

Three of our authors have provided follow-up essays written five or more years after their original memoir. In the follow-ups they reflect on their original story written in late adolescence from the more mature point of view of full-fledged adulthood. These retrospectives provide a poignant and lifespan developmental perspective on the ways in which the adolescent themes of identity and challenges transform, for better or worse, with the tasks of adulthood.

The Case Study Approach

This anthology is aimed at readers who relish engaging with autobiographical writing by adolescents and young adults that is involving, insightful, and instructive. Perhaps, though, its primary audience is composed of college/university students taking a course on adolescent development. For this audience, it may serve as a welcome ancillary text to the core adolescent development text and enrich the students' understanding of the theories and research their instructor is introducing them to.

Garrod and Kilkenny were lucky in their graduate school days to study with a celebrated teacher of adolescent development at Harvard—George Goethals. With colleague Dennis Klos, he published in 1970 a groundbreaking case study book *Experiencing Youth*, a set of first-person accounts written by undergraduate and graduate students (the latter appear primarily in the second edition) that highlight key ideas in adolescent development: challenges, relationships, identity. These cases demonstrated to us how powerful narrative can be as a way of examining lives within a framework of theory and research about adolescence. A case helps us understand the phenomenology of individual adolescent experience in a way that theory and research cannot.

By listening to the voices of individual adolescents, students, and teachers of adolescent development, we can gain a greater understanding of the issues facing some of today's adolescents. Case studies illustrate the complexity of the individual experience and the interactions among an individual's needs, ideas, relationships, and context. Each case, taken alone, helps us begin to know one more adolescent and his or her experience; taken together, the cases provide a rich overview of the wide, diverse, and complex range of adolescent experiences. Through them, we come to a greater understanding of key theories and current research findings in the field of adolescence as we examine patterns in their lives and the lives of others. We are indebted to Goethals and Klos for helping us and our students learn the value of the case study.

In this book, we build on the model provided by Goethals and Klos, bringing together the voices of students and some graduates. Each case in this book was written and revised by an undergraduate or graduate, some of whom have taken a course in adolescent development.

Although it is never possible to be completely representative, we chose students and cases with the goal of achieving a cross section of races, ethnicities, class backgrounds, and experience. The eighteen case writers include adolescents who are White, African American, Native American, Latino, Asian American, and several who are biracial. The writers included men and women who are gay and straight, and those who are questioning their sexuality. Case writers come from around the United States as well as abroad; from urban, suburban, and rural environments; from more- and less-privileged backgrounds; from single- and two-parent homes; from situations that have stimulated reflection and those that have allowed the writer to develop without thinking deeply about the implications and meanings of his or her actions and ideas. Although we have included each case under a major topic (as listed in the Contents), each case addresses a number of issues. A case that appears in the Identity section could sometimes just as well have been placed in the Challenges section. Clearly there is overlap in our two main sections in the themes that any one adolescent explores. The chart at the front of the book provides a guide to themes present in each case, as do the abstracts at the beginning of each case.

Acknowledgements

The cases in this book are the words of college students and graduates whom the first editor has taught or worked with outside of the classroom—individuals who are willing to share their life experiences with many outsiders. Although we can't thank them by name, we wish to acknowledge their personal strength as well as the time and energy they invested in the project. In addition, we want to recognize the many students who worked with us on cases that have not been included in the book; they too gave tremendously of themselves as we worked to shape the final manuscript. We are particularly grateful for the enormous contributions that two of our former colleagues made on the first seven editions of *Adolescent Portraits*—Professor Lisa Smulyan of the Department of Education Studies at Swarthmore College and Professor Emerita Sally I. Powers of the Psychology Department at the University of Massachusetts at Amherst. We must mention gratefully three remarkable friends who have been involved in editing, collating, and preparing the manuscript for submission to the publisher: Dayle Wang, Bill Levin, and Gustavo Almeida. An invaluable contributor to our book who has assisted in editing every page and line you read and deserves our special thanks is Dody Riggs. Her unerring eye and feeling for an elegant sentence have immeasurably enriched our text.

Part I

IDENTITY

DOI: 10.4324/9781003165378-1

Theoretical Overview

The eight cases in the Identity section of this book show a pattern of a struggle for meaning and a quest for wholeness. Within the categories of values and ideology, the self in social context, and sexuality, the adolescent writers wrestle with important choices—who they want to be, how to relate to others, what values should guide them, and what their place is in various spheres of their lives. Though the content of the autobiographies may differ from case to case, the reader will see that the writers share common explorations and preoccupations with the self: the self in relation to others and the self in relation to the broader society. We offer here a framework for approaching the cases in this section—the Identity section.

What are the critical elements or "ingredients" that a theory of identity development might address? Santrock (2019) observes, "when identity has been conceptualized and researched, it typically is explored in a broad sense. However, identity is a self-portrait that is composed of many pieces and domains:

- The career and work path a person wants to follow (vocational/career identity)
- Whether a person is politically conservative, liberal, or middle of the road (political identity)
- A person's spiritual beliefs (religious identity)
- Whether a person is single, married, divorced, or cohabitating (relationship identity)
- The extent to which a person is motivated to achieve and is intellectually oriented (achievement, intellectual identity)
- Whether a person is heterosexual, homosexual, or bisexual (sexual identity)
- Which part of the world or country a person is from and how intensely the person identifies with his or her cultural heritage (cultural/ethnic identity)
- The things a person likes to do, including sports, music, and hobbies (interests)
- An individual's personality characteristics—being introverted or extroverted, anxious or calm, friendly or hostile, and so on (personality)
- A person's body image (physical identity)" (p. 139).

Erik Erikson (1968), who has helped shape our understanding of identity, proposed a detailed and widely applied psychosocial theory of identity development. Convinced that the study of identity is as crucial to our time as the study of childhood sexuality was to Freud's, Erikson forged a radical rethinking among psychoanalytic theorists about ego structure and the role of culture and environment in personality development. His writings have, over the last decades, been expanded (e.g., Marcia, 1967) and debated (e.g., Gilligan, 1982) by a succession of theorists, some of whom have significantly broadened and challenged his theory's applicability.

When asked to describe his adolescence, one of our students recently wrote: "I don't know where it started and have no more idea if it's ended. Something inside of me tells me I'm in transition between something and something else, but I don't know what." In transition between two "somethings," this young man is not at all sure where he has come from and even less sure of his destination; he is Kurt Lewin's (1939) "marginal man," uncertain of his position and group belongingness. As an adolescent, he is in a stage of his life in which pressures, both internal and external, to define himself become simultaneously impossible to ignore and impossible to satisfy. He is working to establish a self-concept while at the same time realizing that this concept is changing as rapidly as he can pinpoint it. Like Lewis Carroll's Alice, he may well reply to the question "Who are you?" posed by the Caterpillar by saying "I, I hardly know Sir, just at present—at least I know who I was when I got up this morning, but I must have changed several times since then." In Erikson's terms, the adolescent has entered a psychological moratorium—a hiatus between childhood security and adult independence.

Adolescence is a critical stage in the individual's development. Adolescents are intensely aware of how they are seen by others—aware, as V.S. Pritchett (1971) observes, that "other egos with their own court of adherents invade one's privacy with theirs." It is a time in which the values and perspectives of others become clearer to the developing mind. The adolescent must first attempt to evaluate his or her different options—different ethical positions or religious beliefs, acceptance or rejections of societal norms, attitudes toward sexuality, ideological stance in relation to family, friends, and community—before he or she can choose among them. In this sense, the search for identity is not only the process of molding an image of oneself—it is also the attempt to understand the fundamental components of the clay that will be used.

The identities of childhood, strengthened by identifications with significant others and by growing mastery of the tasks of school and family life, may no longer hold; the challenge for the adolescent is a creative synthesis of past identifications, current skills and abilities, and future hopes—all within the context of the opportunities the society offers. This challenge is made immeasurably harder because of the technological society we live in, in which multiple roles and careers tantalize us with choice. Mead (1958) suggests it might be easier to live in a society in which roles are inherited through birth or decided by gender! Yet the critical task of the developing adolescent is to balance the imposition of identities provided by his or her position in the social structure, the family, and the community with an agentic sense of who one is, what one stands for, and how one relates to the world.

Theories of identity development focus on themes of separation and individuation of the emerging individual and themes of connection or relationship between the adolescent and significant others in the process of renegotiating the childhood self or selves. Theories of separation stem from the work of Freud (1953) and Erikson (1968) and focus on how the individual rejects prior identifications in the search for a separate, unique, and unified sense of self. Theories of connections (Gilligan, 1982; Miller, 1991; Stern, 1989) explore how individuals come to know themselves through relationship; adolescent identity development is a process of refiguring one's relationships to account for new psychological and social needs and expectations. More recently, studies of adolescent identity have focused on how adolescents draw on aspects of both separation and connection in negotiating the multiple identities they construct and perform in this stage of life and into adulthood.

Erikson's theory of ego identity formation focuses on the concepts of ego identity, the identity stage, and the identity crisis. He defines identity as "the capacity to see oneself as having continuity and sameness and to act accordingly. It is the consistent organization of experience." Erikson held to the epigenetic principle of development in which "anything that grows has a ground plan, and that out of this ground plan the parts arise, each part having its time of special ascendancy until all parts have risen to form a functional whole" (Erikson, 1968, p. 92). The stages are not merely passed through but instead add cumulatively to the whole personality. His psychosocial stage theory is founded on the belief that life is composed of a series of conflicts that must be partially resolved before the developing individual can move to the next stage. He proposes eight general stages of conflict: trust versus mistrust, autonomy versus shame, initiative versus guilt, industry versus inferiority, identity versus identity confusion, intimacy versus isolation, generativity versus stagnation, and integrity versus despair (Erikson, 1968). Following psychoanalytic theory, these stages appear in sequential order but are never completely resolved. Erikson saw the quest for identity and the crises that it often produces as the defining characteristics of adolescence. The formation of ego identity does not take place only in the identity stage, however; the degree to which one satisfactorily resolves the identity crisis is heavily dependent on the resolutions to the challenges of the first four stages in Erikson's eight-stage life cycle theory. Each item exists "in some form," Erikson tells us, before its decisive and critical time normally arrives (Erikson, 1968, pp. 93, 95). That is, there are identity elements in all preceding stages just as there are in the succeeding stages, and if the conflicts in these earlier stages are concluded satisfactorily, the healthy development of the ego is more probable. If the conflicts are resolved unsatisfactorily, negative qualities are crystallized in the personality structure and may impede further development.

The psychosocial moratorium—a time of deferred choice—is the period in an adolescent's or young adult's life for resolving the identity crisis. It is a time when role experimentation is encouraged and where there is little expectation that the individual will commit to permanent responsibilities or roles. The identity crisis "is precipitated both by the individual's readiness and by society's pressure" to separate from childhood identifications and find a coherent individuated identity (Erikson, 1980, p. 130). The age at which the identity crisis occurs may vary "according to such social structure factors as class, subculture, ethnic background, and gender" (Côté and Levine, 1987) or socialization factors such as child-rearing practices and identification with parents (Jordan, 1971). The moratorium must end with the experience of role experimentation complete and the achievement of a resynthesis of positive identifications. These achievements enable the individual to find "a niche in some section of society, a niche which is firmly defined yet seems to be uniquely made for him" (Erikson, 1968, p. 156). The niche is dependent on the adolescent's feeling that commitment in the areas of values, vocation, religious beliefs, political ideology, sex, gender role, and family lifestyle are accepted, settled, and expressions of personal choice. Other more critical theorists, Jackson, McCullough, and Gurin (1981) for example, have suggested that the option of having a moratorium and being in a position to choose in the area of commitment are limited by social, political, and economic structures and dominant ideologies.

Allied with Erikson's faith in ego identity is his understanding of the difficulty involved for adolescents in creating and maintaining this identity. Identity confusion, and the resulting identity crisis, results from the individual's inability to understand the "mutual fit of himself and the environment—that is, of his capacity to relate to an ever-expanding life space of people and institutions on the one hand, and, on the other, the readiness of these people and institutions to make him a part of an ongoing cultural concern" (Erikson, 1975, p. 102). Feeling pressured by society and his or her own maturation to choose between possible roles even as personal perspectives are rapidly changing, the identity-confused adolescent experiences a confusion that challenges his or her ability to form a stable identity.

Erikson believes that the success with which the adolescent resolves these crises is extremely important for the eventual achievement of intimacy with others. It is only through the commitment to sexual direction, vocational direction, and a system of values that "intimacy of sexual and affectionate love, deep friendship and personal self-abandon without fear of losing ego-identity emerge" (Muuss, 1996, p. 54). Identity achievement, as opposed to identity confusion, allows the individual to move smoothly from preoccupation with the inner core of identity to exploration of the potential roles this self will play in intimate relationships with others. When identity achievement is realized in an individual, that individual is capable of making a series of basic life commitments: occupational, ideological, social, religious, ethical, and sexual (Côté, 2019, in Steinberg, 2019, p. 231).

Erikson's construct of identify versus identity confusion has been expanded by James Marcia (1966, 1980). Marcia, whose work on the ego and identity development began with his dissertation "Development and Validation of Ego-Identity Status" (1966), establishes two concepts already mentioned by Erikson—crisis and commitment—as the determining variables in identity achievement. "Crisis refers to times during adolescence when the individual seems to be actively involved in choosing among alternative occupations and beliefs. Commitment refers to the degree of personal investment the individual expresses in an occupation of belief" (Marcia, 1967, p. 119). Using these variables as the determining standards, Marcia breaks Erikson's fifth stage down into four substages: identity diffusion, identity foreclosure, moratorium, and identity achievement.

The identity-diffused individual is characterized by having neither an active involvement in the search for identity roles nor a commitment to any of these roles. He or she is not questioning alternatives. At this point, the adolescent is, like James Joyce's Stephen Dedalus (1992), "drifting amid life like the barren shell of the moon." Identity foreclosure is characterized by commitment without crisis; that is, the individual has chosen a set of values or ideological stance, most often that of his or her parents or valued others, without examining this value or searching out alternatives. In moratorium, on the other hand, the individual is in the midst of a crisis, actively questioning and searching among alternatives, without any commitment to one option. In achievement, the individual has experienced the crises of moratorium and has successfully made a commitment. Identity achievement is most often attained in the college years, with moratorium and diffusion characteristic of earlier adolescence (Santrock, 1990). It should be pointed out that differences exist between societies and between groups and individuals within societies in the length of the sanctioned intermediary period, the psychosocial moratorium (Manaster, 1989). Also, those not afforded the time or opportunity to engage in identity seeking may well not undergo an identity crisis in adolescence or young adulthood.

Some theorists, among them Miller (1991) and Surrey (1984), have suggested that adolescent identity development (like childhood development that precedes it and adult development that follows) is more a story of connection and relationship than one of separation and autonomy. Early theorists in this field argued that adolescent boys seem concerned with separation and individuation while adolescent girls create identity more in connection to peers and members of their families. Carol Gilligan (1982) writes of her reservations about Erikson's theory in *In a Different Voice.* Gilligan points out that Erikson recognized sex differences in identity development and discussed how for men identity precedes intimacy and generativity in the optimal cycle of human separation and attachment, but for women these tasks instead seem to be fused—the woman comes to know herself through relationships with others. Erikson nevertheless retained the sequence of identity preceding intimacy. The sequencing of Erikson's second, third, fourth, and fifth stages, Gilligan suggests, little prepares the individual for the intimacy of the first adult stage. "Development itself comes to be identified with separation, and attachments appear to be developmental impediments, as is repeatedly the case in the assessment of women" (Gilligan, 1982, pp. 12–13).

In contrast, more recent theorists explore how the challenges of adolescence—brought on by puberty, a more active role in the social structure, and changing cognitive abilities—are negotiated within and through relationships by all adolescents. Both adolescent girls and boys explore who they are through interaction with families (Hill, 1987; Taylor, 1996; Ward, 1996) and peers (Chu, 2004; Savin-Williams and Berndt, 1990), and through the other social groups and networks that are important in their lives (McLaughlin and Heath, 1993). While finding a separate, unique identity is important, that process occurs within and through negotiating the self in relation to other individuals and social groups. This relational perspective also allows us to examine how adolescents form multiple identities that differ to some extent by context and need. The adolescent in school, experiencing certain demands and opportunities, may differ from the adolescent at home, where alternative relationships and expectations influence actions and values (Ferguson, 2000; Flores-Gonzáles, 2002). The adolescent must learn to balance the search for a coherent, separate identity with the multiple identities, negotiated through relationships, that characterize his or her sense of self.

The process of adolescent identity formation may also vary in accordance with the ethnic and racial background of the individual. It is hardly surprising that White youth generally have much less sense of their ethnic identity than do minority youth, though youth from some White, working-class backgrounds identify powerfully with a particular ethnic, national, or racial group (e.g., German, Scottish, Irish, Italian) (Steinberg, 2019). An area of recent study has been ethnic identity outside the majority culture (Kiang and Fuligni, 2009). Black, Latino, and Asian students in the U.S. are more likely to explore their ethnic identity than are White adolescents or to make a commitment to it (Steinberg, 2019). The trigger to questioning one's ethnic identity is often the painful experience of prejudice that alerts the individual of their differences from youth in the main culture (Hughes, Del Toro, and Way, 2017). Again, context plays a vital role in the formation of the youth's ethnic identity— the ethnic makeup of students in the youth's school and the availability of others in the individual's social group (Douglass, Yip, and Shelton, 2014). A number of theorists have presented stage theories of ethnic or racial identity development (e.g., Cross, 1991; Kim, in Ponterotto and Pedersen, 1993). These frameworks of analysis suggest that non-White adolescents tend to begin the process in a stage in which they either identify with the White majority or are unaware of the role of race or ethnicity in their experiences. They move, often as the result of a series of events or encounters in which their race or ethnicity becomes salient, into a stage of awareness. In this stage, individuals become more conscious of their position in the society and begin to question who they are in relation to their own racial or ethnic group and in relation to the dominant culture. In a third general stage, adolescents identify with their racial or ethnic group and often immerse themselves in an exploration of that group's historical, cultural, political, and social position in the society. The final stage in most of these theories is one of integration and internalization, in which the individual incorporates his or her identification with a racial or ethnic group into a more comprehensive identity. This more inclusive identity may allow individuals to identify with their group and interact successfully in the dominant (White) culture. Ponterotto and Pedersen (1993) provide a similar framework for examining White racial identity development. The stages they posit parallel those previously described and include preexposure, conflict, prominority/antiracism, retreat into White culture, and redefinition and integration. Stage theories of racial and ethnic identity development have their limitations, however. They tend to assume that all members of a particular group experience the process of identity development in the same way and that the process itself is both linear and progressive. More recent examinations of the impact of race and ethnicity on adolescent identity development focus on the various ways that individuals and groups engage in explorations of who they are in relation to racial and ethnic groups and to the dominant culture. Mary Waters (1996), for example, examines a number of ways in which Caribbean American teens respond to others' expectations of who they are and their own sense of self. Stacy Lee (1996) explores the multiple identities taken on by Asian American students in an academically demanding high school. And Nilda Flores-Gonzáles (2002) describes how Latino students from the same neighborhood develop different identities based on their relationship to school and their community.

In her examination of Black identity formation, Fordham (1988) considers the phenomenon of "racelessness." She explores the relationship between group (Black) identity and academic success and concludes that Black adolescents follow one of two paths. Some respect an "individualistic ethos," disregarding their mandatory membership in the Black group—a path that may lead to academic success. Others consider this to be "selling out" and espouse the "collectivistic ethos" of their minority group in order to avoid becoming "non-Black," although they sacrifice academic success in the process. More recent research challenges Fordham's conclusions and demonstrates, again, the multiple ways in which African American students integrate their racial, gender, and academic identities. Mickelson and Velasco (2006), Annette Hemmings (2006), and Prudence Carter (2006) provide case studies of groups of African American students who negotiate school, gender, and racial identities in a range of ways. Ward (1989) examines identity formation in academically successful Black female adolescents and discovers that racial identity formation is compatible with academic accomplishment. Considering not only the factors of beliefs, values, attitudes, and patterns of family socialization but also "the girls' own subjective understanding of the role that race plays in their lives" (p. 217), she concludes that racial identity must be considered in order to gain a complete understanding of identity formation. Cases in this edition that focus in particular on adolescents' experiences of ethnic and racial identity are 1, 2, 3, 4, 6, 8, 9, 11, 12, and 18.

Other recent areas of exploration in identity development are gender and sexuality. Gender is an aspect of identity that is socially constructed, or performed, within available discourses and institutional structures (Connell, 2000; Walkerdine, Lucey, and Melody, 2001). Adolescents explore their gender identities often within a binary framework of stereotypical masculinity and femininity (Kimmel, 1994; Martin, 1996). They make choices within these frameworks, sometimes challenging the norms and sometimes functioning, consciously or unconsciously, within them. Adolescents also begin to explore their sexuality and sexual identities. While Freud (1953) sees this as a natural part of the developmental process, Mead (1958) suggests that cultures impose a heightened sense of sexuality on adolescents. While past theorists have, again, posited developmental stages of sexuality development (e.g., Troiden, 1998), more recent researchers focus, again, on the role of relationships and interactions with others in a variety of contexts in their examination of adolescents' active construction of a sexual identity (Martin, 1996; Savin-Williams, 2005). While many cases in this book include adolescents exploring aspects of gender and sexual identity, Cases 3, 5, 10, 17, and 18 in particular allow us to examine these issues.

Other authors have explored the interactions among the multiple identities adolescents actually contend with during the process of identity formation. James Sears (1996), for example, has examined the experiences of adolescents who are both gay and African American, and Alex Wilson (1996) probes the lives of those who are gay and Native American. In Leadbeater and Way's book, *Urban Girls* (1996), researchers report on studies that investigate the experiences of male and female adolescents juggling issues of gender, race, ethnicity, and class as they figure out who they are. Maria Root (1999), Theresa Williams (1996), and others have contributed to our understanding of the complexity of racial and ethnic identity development in their studies of multiracial individuals. Their work suggests that the process of racial and ethnic identity is multifaceted and complex and an inherent part of identity development for all adolescents.

Alternative perspectives on the process of identity development in adolescence, then, focus on the examination of the

individual in context. Development is seen as a process of renegotiating relationships, redefining oneself in relation to individuals and social
groups (family, racial or ethnic groups, class, and gender) of which one
is a part. In the Identity section of this book, we include cases that
address several aspects of identity development—values and ideology,
the self in social context, and sexuality. In most cases, the writers are,
themselves, engaged in exploring multiple identities. We encourage the
reader to examine these autobiographies through a consideration of
the following questions: What roles do issues of trust, autonomy, initiative, competence, and identity play in each person's case? Within what
contexts does the author define himself or herself? What relationships
and connections contribute to his or her sense of self, and how are they
changing? Of course, the adolescent is striving to develop an identity in
a particular social context; the features of this context will have an enormous impact on how that identity develops. Identity is affected by the
cultural and social milieu in which the individual develops and the particular period of time he/she lives in (Grogen, 1993, in Steinberg, 2019).

Whatever theoretical perspective one adopts, and we suggest
an eclectic approach, the essential components are a simultaneous discovery and creation of the self leading to a deepening self-understanding.
We believe the cases in this section capture that process in both tone
and substance. In each case, there is a greater sense of understanding
and acceptance of oneself at the end than at the beginning. Each author
makes clear that the process continues, but they seem here to have
reached a plateau from which they can look back and survey their progress. Readers may do well to suspend somewhat their theoretical
assumptions while reading a case, lest they miss the sheer spectacle
of lives unfolding. Though different identity theorists provide a useful
framework for interpretation of these cases, the best of them are but a
scaffolding for understanding. We should try to listen first to each author
in his or her own terms, to see the authors' evolution through their own
eyes. In the unique and intimate details of their individual lives, we can
discern the outline of a universal struggle to identify our true selves. Your
readings here should influence your understanding of theory at least as
much as theory influences your reading.

References

Carroll, L. (2000). *Alice's Adventures in Wonderland*. Wellesley: Branden Books.
Carter, P. (2006). Intersecting identities: "Acting white," gender, and academic
    achievement. In E. Horvat & C. O'Connor (Eds.), *Beyond Acting White: Reframing*

the Debate on Black Student Achievement (pp. 111–134). Lanham: Rowman and Littlefield.

Chu, J. (2004). A relational perspective on boys' identity development. In N. Way & J. Chu (Eds.), *Adolescent Boys* (pp. 78–106). New York: NYU Press.

Connell, R.W. (2000). *The Men and the Boys*. Berkeley: University of California Press.

Côté, J.E. & Levine, C. (1987). A formulation of Erikson's theory of ego identity formation. *Developmental Review*, *7*, 273–325. https://doi.org/10.1016/0273-2297(87)90015-3.

Cross, W. (1991). *Shades of Black: Diversity in African American Identity*. Philadelphia: Temple University Press.

Douglass, S., Yip, T., & Shelton, J.N. (2014). Intragroup contact and anxiety among ethnic minority adolescents: Considering ethnic identity and school diversity transitions. *Journal of Youth and Adolescence*, *43*(10), 1628–1641. https://doi.org/10.1007/s10964-014-0144-5.

Erikson, E.H. (1968). *Identity: Youth and Crisis*. New York: W.W. Norton & Company.

Erikson, E.H. (1975). *Life History and the Historical Moment*. New York: W.W. Norton & Company.

Erikson, E.H. (1980). *Identity and the Life Cycle*. A Reissue. New York: W.W. Norton & Company.

Ferguson, A. (2000). *Bad Boys: Public Schools in the Making of Black Masculinity (Law, Meaning, And Violence)*. Michigan: University of Michigan Press.

Flores-González, N. (2002). *School Kids, Street Kids: Identity Development in Latino Students*. New York: Teachers College Press.

Fordham, S. (1988). Racelessness as a factor in Black students' school success: Pragmatic strategy or pyrrhic victory? *Harvard Educational Review*, *58*(1), 54–85. https://doi.org/10.17763/haer.58.1.c5r77323145r7831.

Freud, S. (1953). *Three Essays in Sexuality*. London: Hogarth Press.

Gilligan, C. (1982). *In a Different Voice: Psychological Theory and Women's Development*. Cambridge, MA: Harvard University Press.

Hemmings, A. (2006). Shifting images of blackness: coming of age as black students in urban and suburban high schools. In E. Horvat & C. O'Connor (Eds.), *Beyond Acting White: Reframing the Debate on Black Student Achievement* (pp. 91–110). Lanham: Rowman and Littlefield.

Hill, J.P. (1987). Research on adolescents and their families: Past and prospect. In C.E. Irwin (Ed.), *Adolescent Social Behavior and Health* (pp. 13–31). San Francisco: Jossey-Bass.

Hughes, D.L., Del Toro, J., & Way, N. (2017). Interrelations among dimensions of ethnic-racial identity during adolescence. *Developmental Psychology*, *53*(11), 2139–2153. https://doi.org/10.1037/dev0000401.

Jackson, J.S., McCullough, W.R., & Gurin, G. (1981). Group identity development within black families. In H. McAdoo (Ed.), *Black Families* (pp. 252–263). Beverly Hills: Sage.

Jordan, D. (1971). "Parental antecedents and personality characteristics of ego identity statuses." Unpublished doctoral dissertation. State University of New York at Buffalo.

Joyce, J. (1992). *A Portrait of the Artist as a Young Man*. Hertfordshire: Wordsworth Editions.

Kiang, L. & Fuligni, A.J. (2009). Ethnic identity in context: Variations in ethnic exploration and belonging within parent, same-ethnic peer, and different-ethnic peer relationships. *Journal of Youth and Adolescence*, *38*(5), 732–743. https://doi.org/10.1007/s10964-008-9278-7.

Kimmel, M. (1994). Masculinity as homophobia. In *Theorizing Masculinities* (pp. 199–241). California: Sage.

Leadbeater, B.J. & Way, N. (1996). *Urban Girls: Resisting Stereotypes, Creating Identities*. New York: NYU Press.

Lee, S. (1996). *Unraveling the "Model Minority" Stereotype: Listening to Asian American Youth*. New York: Teachers College Press.

Lewin, K. (1939). Field theory and experiment in social psychology: Concepts and methods. *American Journal of Sociology*, *44*, 868–896. https://doi.org/10.1086/218177.

Manaster, G.J. (1989). *Adolescent Development: A Psychological Interpretation*. Illinois: F E Peacock Pub.

Marcia, J.E. (1966). Development and validation of ego-identity status. *Journal of Personality and Social Psychology*, *3*, 551–558. https://doi.org/10.1037/h0023281.

Marcia, J.E. (1967). Ego identity status: Relationship to change in self-esteem, "general maladjustment," and authoritarianism. *Journal of Personality*, *35*, 118–133. https://doi.org/10.1111/j.1467-6494.1967.tb01419.x.

Marcia, J.E. (1980). Identity in adolescence. In J. Adelson (Ed.), *Handbook of Adolescent Psychology*. New York: Wiley.

Martin, K.A. (1996). *Puberty, Sexuality, and the Self: Girls and Boys at Adolescence*. New York: Routledge.

McLaughlin, M. & Heath, S. (Eds.). (1993). *Identity and Inner City Youth: Beyond Ethnicity and Gender*. New York: Teachers College Press.

Mead, M. (1958). Adolescence in primitive and modern society. In E. Maccoby, T. Newcomb, & E. Hartley (Eds.), *Readings in Social Psychology*. New York: W.W Norton & Company.

Mickelson, R. & Velasco, A. (2006). Bring it on! Diverse responses to 'acting white' among academically able Black adolescents. In E. Horvat & C. O'Connor (Eds.), *Beyond Acting White: Reframing the Debate on Black Student Achievement* (pp. 27–56). Lanham: Rowman and Littlefield.

Miller, J.B. (1991). Women's growth in connection. In J.V. Jordan, A.G. Kaplan, J. Baker Miller, I.P. Stiver, & J.L. Surrey (Eds.), *The Development of Women's Sense of Self* (pp. 11–26). New York: Guilford Press.

Muuss, R.E.H., Velder, E., & Porton, H. (1996). *Theories of Adolescence* (6th ed.). Michigan: McGraw Hill.

Ponterotto, J.G. & Pedersen, P.B. (1993). *Preventing Prejudice: A Guide for Counselors and Educators*. California: Sage.

Pritchett, V.S. (1971). *Midnight Oil*. London: Chatto & Windus.

Root, M. (1999). Multiracial Asians: Models of ethnic identity. In R. Torres, L. Mirón, & J. Inda (Eds.), *Race Identity and Citizenship* (pp. 158–168). Oxford: Blackwell Publishers.

Santrock, J.W. (1990). *Adolescence* (4th ed.). Iowa: Wm. C. Brown.

Santrock, J.W. (2019). *Adolescence* (17th ed.). New York: McGraw Hill.

Savin-Williams, R. & Berndt, T. (1990). Friendship and peer relations. In S. Feldman & G. Elliott (Eds.), *At the Threshold* (pp. 277–307). Cambridge, MA: Harvard University Press.

Savin-Williams, R.C. (2005). *The New Gay Teenager*. Cambridge, MA: Harvard University Press.

Sears, J. (1996). Black-Gay or Gay-Black? Choosing identities and identifying choices. In G. Unks (Ed.), *The Gay Teen* (pp. 135–157). New York: Routledge.

Steinberg, L. (2019). *Adolescence* (12th ed.). New York: McGraw Hill Education.

Stern, L. (1989). Conceptions of separation and connection in female adolescents. In C. Gilligan, N. Lyons, & T. Hanmer (Eds.), *Making Connections: The Relational Worlds of Adolescent Girls at Emma Willard School* (pp. 73–87). Cambridge, MA: Harvard University Press.

Surrey, J. (1984). The self in-relation. In *Work of Progress*. Wellesley: Stone Center for Developmental Services and Studies.

Taylor, J. (1996). Cultural stories: Latina and Portuguese daughters and mothers. In B. Leadbeater & N. Way (Eds.), *Urban Girls* (pp. 117–131). New York: NYU Press.

Troiden, R. (1998). A model of homosexual identity formation. In *Social Perspectives in Lesbian and Gay Studies: A Reader* (pp. 261–279). New York: Routledge.

Walkerdine, V., Lucey, H., & Melody, J. (2001). *Growing Up Girl: Psycho-Social Explorations of Class and Gender (Qualitative Studies in Psychology, 16)*. New York: NYU Press.

Ward, J. (1989). Racial identity formation and transformation. In C. Gilligan, N. Lyons, & T. Hanmer (Eds.), *Making Connections: The Relational Worlds of Adolescent Girls at Emma Willard School*. Cambridge, MA: Harvard University Press.

Ward, J. (1996). Raising resisters: The role of truth telling in the psychological development of African American girls. In B. Leadbeater & N. Way (Eds.), *Urban Girls* (pp. 85–99). New York: NYU Press.

Waters, M. (1996). The intersection of gender, race, and ethnicity in identity development of Caribbean American teens. In B. Leadbeater & N. Way (Eds.), *Urban Girls* (pp. 65–81). New York: NYU Press.

Williams, T.K. (1996). Race as a process: Reassessing the "What are you?" encounters of biracial individuals. In M. Root (Ed.), *The Multiracial Experience* (pp. 191–210). Thousand Oaks, CA: Sage.

Wilson, A. (1996). How we find ourselves: Identity development and two spirit people. *Harvard Educational Review, 66*(2), 303–318. https://doi.org/10.17763/haer.66.2.n551658577h927h4.

Case 1

WHY DIDN'T YOU TEACH ME?

BOB BENNETT

DOI: 10.4324/9781003165378-2

Bob Bennett

In a predominantly white Rapid City, South Dakota high school, Bob Bennett seemingly has it all—academic success and promise, easy acceptance in a large social circle, recognition as Homecoming King and great success as a college-recruited athlete. However, Bob Bennett wrestles with his lack of a sense of his Indian heritage and dearth of Lakota cultural identity. He describes himself as an apple—red on the outside, but white on the inside. At college, Bennett courageously discovers and embraces his "Indianness" and determines "... I am an Indian and I am alive."

Success in the white world has always been easy for me. My accomplishments never surprised me because they were enjoyable and relatively effortless. My grandmother, however, was usually more than surprised—perhaps even astounded. "And you're Indian!" she would often exclaim to express the joy, happiness, and amazement she felt for me. I did well in a white school, played varsity football, baseball, and basketball, went out with *wasicu* (white) friends, dated *wasicu* women, attended an Ivy League school, and now make a living as a professional baseball player. I was doing everything she had always hoped I would do, but because I was an Indian, she did not expect me to have so much acceptance and success in the outside world of the *wasicu*. I remember, when I was very young, going over to Gramma and Grandpa's house, only two blocks from our apartment in Rapid City, South Dakota, and listening to Gramma and her mother speak Lakota to each other. During my childhood years, she never taught me one word of Lakota; she always spoke English to me. All I knew was that they were talking "Indian" and I spoke only English.

When I came to Dartmouth as a young man, I realized that my life was not well balanced because I had never learned the Lakota language and culture from my grandmother. Before I came to New Hampshire, a former Boston schoolteacher told me that many New Englanders think that "all Indians are dead." In a frightening sense, so did I. At Dartmouth, I was shocked to realize two important truths: I am an Indian and I am indeed alive.

When I first came to New Hampshire, I was at a loss because I could not answer the questions people asked about Native American life. Hell, I could not even answer my own questions! I took a Native American Studies course my sophomore year and learned more about Indians than I had in twenty years of living as one. Yet there was something ironic and troubling about the source of my newfound knowledge: I was learning about my culture and ancestors from a white professor in a white institution. That fact disturbed me and prompted me to examine why I had ended up so ignorant. That course also reminded me of a conversation I had with my grandmother.

While at her house during Christmas break, I asked her a question that caught her off guard. "Gramma, how come you never taught my brother and me to speak Lakota?" She looked surprised and sat silent for a moment. Then, with a sad, heavy voice, she said, "Oh, I really wish I had. Mom and I always talked about teaching you grandkids. I really wanted to, but I was afraid you would get made fun of by the *wasicu*." *Wasicu* was one of the few Lakota words I understood. To me it simply meant "white people," but it can also be translated as "greedy ones who take the fat."

Her reasoning is easy to understand when you consider her childhood. My grandmother was born on April 1, 1916, in Norris, South Dakota, on the Rosebud Reservation as Clara Virginia Quick Bear, the eldest of seven children. Her blood came from the *Sicangu Oyate* (Burned Thigh People) band of Lakota. When she was 10 years old, it was decided that she should go to school. She had learned a little English from her mother, who had gone to school for a few years, but had no formal schooling. She had also learned the Lakota language and traditional tribal ways as well as Catholic spirituality from Old Gramma. The lessons she learned in Catholic mission school scarred her, and eventually those she loved, forever.

Even late in her life, many of her memories of St. Francis Mission School were still vivid. She said, "It was run by all whites. They treated us very mean and I didn't like it there much. They would punish us for speaking Indian and doing Indian things. The nuns there were really mean to us and sometimes they would lock us all in one room if someone was misbehaving. There were always a few kids who were homesick and tried to run away. It would always be just a few kids, but the nuns would take it out on all of us. My brother tried to run away a few times and they would always catch him and bring him back. One time they shaved all of his hair off. They did it so the rest of us wouldn't get any ideas of leaving."

I tried to ask her to tell more, but she did not want to continue. "No, they are all dead and gone and I don't want to talk about it anymore," she said. I never asked anything more about it. I was angry, but not at her. I understood that Gramma wanted us to learn the *wasicu* ways to keep us from experiencing her ordeal. I was angry that "civilization" had denied me the freedom to be what I was, a Lakota. I look in the mirror and there it is, my Indianness. Yet I did everything in such a "white" manner that my white friends and others would distinguish me as the "good Indian" and say, "You're not like them." This acceptance is exactly what my gramma wanted for me. According to her, being an Indian in a white world gets you "made fun of." And she was correct because I was already guilty of making fun of other Indians myself. I had fallen deep into *wasicu* ways.

I remember making fun of a Lakota boy for expressing his Indian identity. I was about 10 years old when my brothers, cousins, and I first met this boy. When I asked him for his name, he lowered his head and submissively put his hands in his pockets. Then he suddenly raised his head and proudly said, "My name is Hunkpapa." We all laughed, and I said, "What?"

"My name is Hunkpapa. It's the name of my people and my parents gave it to me so I'll never forget," he replied. At this time, I was ignorant of how many bands of Lakota there were; as far as I was concerned, we were all just Sioux. The Hunkpapa, "the Campers on the End," are a northern band of the seven bands of Teton Lakota.

"Look, guys, this kid is still trying to be Indian. Hey boy, those days are over," I said as we walked away from this proud Hunkpapa.

To all of the Hunkpapas of the world, I am sorry. My grandmother's fear became a reality long before I knew it existed. I was part of that narrow-minded and twisted attitude I have grown to despise. Now I stand as a 22-year-old Lakota who is dissatisfied with that sense of white identity.

My mother is also a product of my grandmother's hurtful mission-school ordeal. She is shy of her Indianness and the world's perception of it. This shyness affects her thoughts and behaviors in many aspects of her life. One time last fall, we both ordered the salad bar in a Rapid City Wendy's restaurant. The restaurant provided us with plastic plates so that we could serve ourselves from the food bar. When she finished eating her first portion, she wanted to go for a return trip to the salad bar, but she was embarrassed by her messy finished plate.

"Mom, just go up and ask for another one," I said.

"Can you do that? No, I'll just wipe this one off," she said.

"What are you so worried about, Mom? Do you think that because you're Indian they won't give you one? What can they tell you other than no?" I asked sarcastically.

Her face had an apprehensive look while she pondered whether or not to get a new, clean plate. She looked around and saw another customer, who happened to be a white woman, with two plates, one messy much like hers and the other clean and full of new food. She jokingly said, "Look! She did it, but she is white." She was trying to be humorous, but there was also a sense of truth in it.

"Just go up and do it, Mom. These workers are here to help you, and if you want a clean plate, they will give it to you," I said in a fatherly tone. Then I snapped, "Even if you are Indian!" She gave a fearful laugh and headed toward the counter, nervously glancing back at me several times.

She looked like a shy little girl. She had a submissive pose, with her back slightly hunched and her neck leaning forward, as she handed the messy plate to the Wendy's worker. The young worker gave my mother a new plate.

"You see, Mom, that wasn't so hard," I said as she returned. "All you had to do was ask. Do you feel better now that *wasicu* gave you a clean plate?"

"Well, I didn't know what to expect. Now shut up and let me eat!" she snapped back. These types of incidents were not uncommon, and the way my mother perceived each one of them only served to per-petuate her shyness.

Despite the stultifying effects of her self-perception, my mother still has within her the strength of my grandparents. She worked hard to be a good provider and to discipline two wild young boys. My brother and I were raised, like many other Indian children, fatherless. As a single Indian woman with two children, my mother had a tough time making ends meet, but with much help from our grandparents and other relatives, she succeeded. Our struggle was not unique. Like many poor Indian people, we survived on federal money in the form of food stamps and welfare checks. Our grandparents also directed much of their limited resources to us. Gramma always kept us fed by cooking up a casserole, a pot of chili, a meatloaf, spaghetti, or soup. Gramma and Grandpa were always there for us on our birthday and Christmas. I think every new bike I ever got came from Gramma and Grandpa. I cannot imagine how life would have been without them in our lives.

When I was young, I shared my mother's timidity. The first racial insult I can remember being directed at me happened soon after the training wheels were removed from my bike. A maintenance man, coming down the stairs of our apartment building, did not see me approaching on my bicycle. I had to swerve to avoid hitting him. I stopped to see if he was all right and to apologize, but before I could say anything he blurted out, "You fucking Indian!" That insult scared me. I must have heard many similar comments afterward, because my mother said I came to her several times and told her that I wished I were white. She would lovingly respond, "Tell them you are proud to be an Indian."

Tell them I was proud? Proud of what? I knew nothing to be proud of, just like my mother. I was on welfare and received free lunches. I was a "savage" who killed white American settlers. I was a bogeyman, a gut eater, a dog eater. I was an exile in my own land. I wasn't aware of why my *akicita* (warrior) relatives fought and died for their ways and for the land. I did not know how my people lived, and I had no pride in my *Sicangu Lakota*. I didn't know the power and strength of the old stories. I didn't know how the name-calling *wasicu* had stolen my homeland and killed my ancestors. Ignorance was at the root of their misdirected bigotry, as well as my own and my mother's sense of inferiority.

Thus, during my upbringing, I made myself acceptable to nearly every white person by being just like them, *wasicu*. It was not an entirely deliberate effort on my part to fit in. These people were my friends and we had much in common and shared a similar sense of humor. I did what made me happy and really had no idea what my Indian identity was.

During high school, I was usually the only Indian in any group I was in: football, basketball, baseball, and all my social groups. I felt overly cautious when my white friends were "causing trouble." Because I was the only Indian, I was often singled out as the troublemaker. In sports, I had to be better than the non-Native players, and in social situations, I had to be more humble than others to avoid problems. As a result of this intentional and unintentional pressure, I was just as timid as my mother.

Because many Indian high-school students felt extremely unwelcome among non-Native students and teachers, they joined together for support. I am lucky that I felt comfortable with the mainstream at Central High School, but problems came from both sides of the ever-changing racial lines.

The world "apple" is a pejorative term used to describe a Native American person who has sold out the rest of the Indians and has become "red on the outside but white on the inside." Indian students who try to do well in school are often called "apples" by those who think success in the white world means you are no longer an Indian. By this definition, I fit into the apple category.

Though my behavior, social life, and school success were reasons enough for other Indians to confront me, it never happened. Still, my grandmother warned me to be leery of the "bad Indians" from the reservation. "They are bad people who will stab you in the back. They are all so jealous and will try to bring you down because you are doing so good in this world," she said, very sternly. She loved Indian people, but she also remembered the teachings of the mission school.

High school never presented any major problems for me. Everything—classes, friends, teachers, sports, and dealing with other Indians—was easy. I was just like any other kid who was curious about drinking and crossing over the lines of authority. I often went to parties—Indian, non-Indian, or a mixture of both—and did my share of drinking and other stupid juvenile acts. I often drank until I got sick, but that behavior is fairly normal among high-school kids. I was involved in smashing a mailbox with a baseball bat, overturning a hotel ice machine, and other small-time crimes.

All of these little juvenile acts were gradually coming to a head when my baseball coach, Dave Ploof, confronted me. "Bobby, you have a lot of things going for you. I would hate to see your friends and other associates screw it up for you." This was the best advice anyone could have given me.

I was an investment for Coach Ploof. During the next three years, I pitched on his American Legion team. I owe much of my success to him because he taught me the discipline I needed to become a mature ballplayer and to always play hard. He touted my baseball skills and maturity to the college baseball scouts.

I also played basketball. My senior year on the team remains one of the best times of my life. We finished with a great record and made it to the state tournament. I was the only Native American on the team and was very vocal on the court; I was perhaps our team's biggest cheerleader. But I was also friendly toward the opponents, which surprised many of them as well as the fans; I was supposed to be a mean, vicious, and dirty basketball player because of my Indian blood. People sitting in the stands gave "war whoops" and yelled insulting names at me during games, but I still played my heart out and enjoyed it.

Throughout my high-school sports career, opponents gave me the war whoop when I was on the field. I was an Indian beating them at their own game, and some found that hard to accept. I think their hostility was a response to their feelings of guilt at having reaped the benefits of their ancestors taking everything we had. Yet their fear and hatred of Indians prevailed because they knew that Indian people would continually return to reclaim what had been taken from us. We threatened them when we became educated, voiced our opinions, lived next to them, or excelled at sports.

One event showed me the irony of my position as an Indian on the team. After a game, a white woman tapped me on the shoulder. As I turned toward her, she extended her hand and said, "I just wanted to say how enjoyable it was to watch you during the tournament. Good luck." I barely had time to thank her before she smiled and walked away. What did she mean? Could she have meant: "It was good to see an Indian play the way you did?" Or was it: "You are a symbol for other Indians to emulate?" I think she was surprised that I was even out there.

Both on and off the sports field, I was the "good Indian" to nearly everyone in my school. Being elected Homecoming King in my senior year shows how well I fit into that image at Central High. Indians normally frightened the people of Rapid City, adults and teenagers alike. The mother of one of my better friends in junior high school, for instance, had a problem with me. Kirk's family was rich, and we liked to go to his large, immaculate house to jump on his trampoline and shoot pool. One day, as we were playing billiards, Kirk's mother asked him to go with her on an errand. She told him it would take only half an hour.

"Why don't you just wait here for me until we get back?" he suggested to me. He left the room, but quickly returned with a worried expression on his face. His mother was standing right behind him. "She doesn't want you to stay here while we're gone," he said reluctantly. I will always remember his mother standing in the doorway with an intimidating look that made me feel very unwanted. She could not wait for me to leave, so I did. That was the first time I had met her, but she only saw a strange Indian person, not her son's close friend. That memory still hurts.

I not only scared parents, but also my peers. I cannot count how many times kids moved quickly out of my way while I was walking down the halls or going through the bathrooms at school. I was an Indian and we were all supposed to be mean to the *wasicu*. When I went into stores, I always felt the eyes of the clerks on me. I hated to go into a store unless I truly had to buy something. If I were only browsing, I made a show of returning whatever product I was looking at to the shelf or rack to avoid any possible problems with the store clerks. Even now, I find myself being cautious when I go into a store back in Rapid City.

For my high-school graduation, I was chosen as one of the commencement speakers by the faculty. It must have been a good speech because it made several students cry and the audience seemed to listen intently. I wondered, was their interest in my words, or were they merely surprised to see an Indian up there? Whatever their opinion was, speaking for my fellow seniors was an honor and a privilege that I had earned.

The day before the graduation ceremony, another honor— a spotted eagle tail feather—was presented to me by Sidney and Shirley Keith, a traditional Lakota couple who live in Rapid City. Sidney is a Lakota spiritual leader. He and his wife performed an eagle feather ceremony for all of the Lakota high-school graduates. They sang to the four directions and to the sky, the earth, and finally to us. I wish I could describe how they sang because it was so powerful. Sidney and Shirley's voices calling to the spirits through the wind was something I had not heard in years. We all watched and listened silently.

In Sidney's aged hand were many spotted eagle tail feathers, all about a foot long with dark brown plumes that had a milky-white area at the bottom near the quills. At the base of each of the quills was a leather loop attached by a twisted red porcupine quill. I knew these feathers were holy. He stopped singing for a moment and lit some sweetgrass. He "smudged" the feathers by circling them with the smoldering braid of grass in order to make them sacred and give them power before presenting them to us. He then began again with the same powerful, rhythmic singing. Though I had no idea what the words meant, I stood with my mother and listened out of deep respect. Or was it fear?

I am Lakota. Why should I have listened in fear to a Lakota eagle feather ceremony? Because I had no clue what was happening. I recognized the sweetgrass because I had seen my grandmother use it many times before when I was a boy. Seeing and smelling the burning sweetgrass in Sidney's hand brought back memories from my youth …

"Why are you doing that, Gramma?" I remember asking when I saw her light a thick braid of sweetgrass during a powerful thunderstorm.

"I don't want the house to get struck by lightning. This grass will help protect the house and us," she said as she walked from room to room waving the smoking braid of sweetgrass from side to side. She would mumble a prayer in Lakota at the same time. She often prayed in both sides of her life, the Lakota and the *wasicu* sides.

I remember, too, going to the Rosebud Reservation with my grandparents when I was a boy to see the powwows and hear traditional Indian songs. The constant pounding of the drums and the singing filled the air and my thoughts. I watched the "real Indians" in dance attire with their big headdresses and bustles adorned with multicolored feathers, their bells rhythmically sounding with every move, their buckskin pants and shirts with colored tassels swinging, their war clubs, eagle fans, and eagle-claw staffs in their hands, and their faces painted with red, black, and yellow clay to make them look terrifying. No one told me what any of it meant or how to learn to do it. When I was perhaps 5 years old, not knowing the meaning of a song didn't scare me, but as I got older it became a different story. At age 18, my own ignorance frightened me. I hate not knowing now, and am still frightened.

When Sidney and Shirley's song came to an end, they turned to us and he told the story of the eagle feather.

In the old days they gave these feathers to people who did a good deed. That deed could have been anything—saving a life, doing well on the hunt, doing brave things when it came time to fight, or becoming an adult. Times have changed, but the honor in accomplishing tasks has not. You kids have done a great thing in graduating from high school and that is what the feather honors. Use it in the new world you are entering for strength and guidance.

They gave each of us a feather and shook our hands. I then had something that visibly made me more Indian than I had ever been before. The feather connected me with a part of myself that I had never known about, and I was uncomfortable with it because of my lack of understanding. That day also opened my eyes and curiosity to the spiritual world—or, in American terms, the religion—of the Lakota. Next to my Lakota blood, that feather is the most significant Indian thing I possess. It changed my perspective and attitude toward everything around me. My brother recently said to me, "When you got that feather, that's when you became an Indian. You never hung out with Indians before you got that feather." That blunt truth hit me hard. But the true significance of the feather dawned slowly on me as I, indifferent to my Native American identity, searched for my true self away from my people.

Finding friends at college was fairly easy because my ability to throw a baseball made the transition from South Dakota to Dartmouth much smoother. According to the college's baseball coach and the school paper, I was the number one baseball recruit that year. That reputation made it very easy for me to meet people. The baseball team had guys in many fraternities who knew the ins and outs of Dartmouth College. "Yeah, this guy is cool. He's a good ballplayer," I frequently heard. Word quickly got around among the freshmen, and I soon had friends.

Without my baseball skills, I probably would not have met the people that I did. Most of the first people I met were *wasicu*, and my identity as Native American was never more than a passing issue to most of them. That I came from South Dakota was more of a revelation to people than my Indian heritage. Most of them had never met any Native Americans before, so they had some basic misconceptions about me. They assumed I could run silently through the forest and shoot an arrow well. They did not know enough to be intentionally racist, only ignorant.

But those harmless assumptions and jokes had another side to them that was insulting, racist, and full of stupidity. Under the shadow of such preconceptions, I had to shed my own cultural and personal ignorance. If I had known more about my heritage and culture, then I could have defended myself better and educated those with a distorted perspective on Indians. Many conservative people at Dartmouth have felt that my presence, or any other Native American's presence on the campus, is simply a big favor they are doing us—that we do not really belong here. Instead, we should stay on our reservations, out of the way of progress and intellectual enlightenment. To many students, and to the college in general, we are only as real as the old Dartmouth Indian symbol that many people claim is a tribute to all Native Americans. People see a symbol or a costume, but often fail to see the human being under the braids, buckskin, and paint. They do not know us or how we perceive the world; people only assume that we are out of our element and need special guidance. I think no white person can ever truly understand the thoughts and feelings of a Native American; we can only ask *wasicu* to respect the Native perspective. This was evident early during my freshman fall at Dartmouth.

When Coach Walsh recruited me for baseball he had informed me of Dartmouth and its fabled beginning as an institution to educate Native Americans. When I arrived at Dartmouth, Coach Walsh and I immediately became friendly, and we often talked openly in his office. Though he listened attentively as I talked about life in South Dakota and my Lakota background, he already had some preconceptions about me and Native Americans in general. Behind my back, Coach Walsh asked one of my teammates to watch out for me. "Don't let Bennett hang out in the fraternity basements, because his people have a big problem with alcoholism. I want you to watch out for him," he said. I was very angry when my teammates revealed this conversation to me after Coach Walsh had left the college. I acknowledge the problems with alcohol that many—but not all—Indian people face, but I did not appreciate being stereotyped.

Coach Walsh's successor, Bob Whalen, also assumed that I needed help to overcome the shackles of my Indian identity. I had filed a petition to get my sophomore summer course requirements waived so I could play in the Cape Cod Baseball League. I wrote in my petition that I had always wanted to play pro baseball and that taking part in the league would improve my chances of getting drafted by a Major League team. I also stated that I intended to make up the academic work the following fall. I asked Coach Whalen to write a recommendation for me.

Coach Whalen's recommendation clearly showed that he saw me as Bob, the poor, disadvantaged Indian who needed help to join mainstream American life. The first sentences of his letter read, "I am writing on behalf of Bob Bennett. Due to his poor socioeconomic background I feel it is very necessary for him to forgo his summer residence and play baseball." The implications of this well-meant statement infuriated me.

I was so angry that I was crying and could not articulate my thoughts when I confronted Coach Whalen in his office. I told him how his letter made me appear to the registrar and explained that I had wanted reinforcement of my own arguments, not another handout from the white man. Of course, he replied that he had meant no disrespect and that he was only trying to help. I believed his sincerity, but he is typical of many white people who do not expect a Native person to succeed on his or her own merits. I have grown tired of having to justify my presence and identity to people. I was granted my request and, fortunately, Coach Whalen and I have grown since that incident to become friends.

Other incidents at Dartmouth forced me to confront my Indian identity. My freshman roommate was interested in my Native background because he was taking an Environmental Studies course in which he read the journal of Lewis and Clark. Lewis and Clark passed through the territory of my ancestors, and my roommate asked me to verify one observation in the journal.

"Hey, Bob, have you ever eaten dog?" he asked. "These guys said the Sioux fed them dog meat."

I replied confidently, "No, they didn't. I haven't eaten dog and they didn't eat it either. They were buffalo hunters, and wouldn't eat dogs. They used them to pull the travois and carry packs. They weren't food."

My roommate insisted that we did and even showed me the passage in the journal. How could I refute what was right in front of me in black and white? I was confused and also embarrassed because he now doubted my Indianness. I also doubted my own Indianness. That early lesson at Dartmouth about my own cultural ignorance pushed me to know more about my ancestors.

I met some other good friends through the Native American Program, although my initial involvement in the program and in the student group Native Americans at Dartmouth (NAD) was quite limited. NAD's activities didn't interest me a great deal. I just wanted to meet some other Native Americans in this strange place. I never thought too much about the political aspects associated with NAD because I had my own agenda. I was a baseball player, and that occupied most of my time and effort each term. Then I rushed a fraternity. The combination of the two shaped who my friends were and, despite my limited interaction with NAD, I came to know many of its members as well.

Academics took up most of my time during my first three years at Dartmouth. One class really opened up new doors for me. The class, Native American Studies (NAS) 22, The Invasion of America, made me fully aware of something that I had been lacking all of my life—a Native American perspective on my own Lakota heritage. None of my previous classes had really touched my inner self.

The teacher, Professor Colin Calloway, had studied the Abenaki in Vermont and had learned much about the Crow people and their reservation while teaching at the University of Wyoming. I listened very attentively as he spoke of his experience with the Sioux people. "I have spent a lot of time among them and can recognize the sound of their language, but by no means can I speak it," he said. "I only learned this." He said a Lakota phrase that means "bullshit" in English. I laughed aloud as he finished because I recognized one word of the phrase, *cesli*, which means "shit." My chuckle was heard by the entire class and every pair of eyes was suddenly on me. Professor Calloway said, "I see we have a Lakota in here with us. Did that sound right?" I said yes, and he continued with his material.

I made myself the "real Indian" of the class by recognizing one word in the Lakota language. But the extent of my Indian abilities was quite limited. I became frightened of my ignorance once again. I became aware of how white I was during each of his lectures on some other tribe, and I was overwhelmed when we came to the Lakota section of the class. I did not know the Lakota were the *Titonwan*, "dwellers of the prairie," and the western people who spoke the Lakota dialect of the Siouan language. I did not know there were seven bands of Lakota or two other groups of people who were also Sioux. I did not know anything, yet Professor Calloway always looked to me for approval when he pronounced the names of one of the bands of Sioux, and I usually gave him a nod. Other people would look to me when he said something. If only they had known that I didn't know much more than they did.

Bob Bennett

In the grand scheme of Lakota knowledge, I knew nothing. After a year and a half at Dartmouth, I began to question my life as an Indian, which was really my life as a white guy who looked like an Indian. I was trying to be the person my well-meaning mother and gramma wanted me to be: an Indian Catholic who only knew the ways of the *wasicu*.

I was searching for a personal identity before that NAS 22 class forced me to think about the path I was treading. I was trying to find my identity, but managed only to become even more lost in the blurred world of Dartmouth College. I realized how lost I was when I tried to find myself spiritually. During my first few terms at Dartmouth, my search for spirit was centered on the Campus Crusade for Christ (CCC) and the Aquinas House.

Though these groups made a great effort to treat me as a person and respected my heritage, I found it difficult to find a comfortable niche in those institutions. I can now say that my true spiritual awakening, or journey, was just beginning, and I soon abandoned white religion.

Professor Calloway's class dealt with the issue of Native religion versus Christianity. Religion was used as a tool of destruction against all tribes in the colonization of North America, and I found it difficult to accept that I was part of an institution that had destroyed so many people's cultures and lives. I did not want to be a part of that institution anymore. I wanted to learn how to be a Lakota, not a white crusader or Catholic with an entirely different culture, spirituality, language, and history.

I made the strongest attempt to regain what had been denied to me by enrolling in a Lakota language class. The professor, Elaine Jahner, had written a Lakota language book with a Lakota woman earlier in her career. She was raised in North Dakota and had a good understanding and respect for Indian culture and thinking. She knew the sound of the language and many words and pushed us patiently.

Four students, three Sioux and one Ojibwe, met weekly with her in her office. I wanted to learn Lakota very badly because I believed the language would return some of my identity. Though I learned quite a lot, Lakota was a difficult language to pick up for a 20-year-old whose only familiarity was with Latinate languages.

In high school, I studied Spanish, and I remember writing letters to my grandmother with little Spanish phrases and sentences in them. "Gramma, I'm writing and speaking a new language," I wrote with a great sense of accomplishment. That pride now troubles me greatly because I did not even know how to speak the language of my ancestors. I could not even say "How are you?" What in the world was I doing, telling my

Lakota-speaking grandmother that I could speak Spanish well? Now I'm angry with myself for being so blind.

When I told Gramma of the Lakota class and Professor Jahner, I felt proud yet nervous. I think she may have been a bit apprehensive about my reasons for learning. "Oh, you want to be Indian so much, don't you, Bobby? But ...," she said. There was usually a "but" in everything she said regarding my search for identity. She did not want me to get distracted from learning the *wasicu* ways and playing their game of baseball.

Despite her warnings and hesitation, she opened up to me before I left for my junior year at Dartmouth, after doctors found that she had developed lung cancer. "Don't worry. I'm going to beat this," she told me before I returned to college. "I've been to ceremonies before and they helped me then. Just pray for me." I never knew she had gone to traditional healing ceremonies. She was even more traditional than I had thought.

I returned to school for my junior year and often thought of her. I called her to ask questions for the Lakota class, and she spoke more freely than she ever had in answering my questions despite her intermittent warnings. She started her chemotherapy treatments later that fall.

I knew the side effects of chemotherapy—weight and hair loss—so I was nervous and frightened when I came home for Christmas break to see my grandmother. However, she had changed very little. She wore a little turban and had lost weight, but her voice and eyes still had their familiar strength. We talked a lot about her childhood and how she met Grandpa. She truly opened up to me for the first time, and I think it was because she realized her time was limited. I talked to her several times about my Lakota class. She taught me how to pronounce the word "deer" in Lakota. I wish I could remember all of the Lakota conversations we had, because they were the first ever. I hated to leave her at the end of that Christmas break because I knew I would not be home until the end of the following summer. It was a long nine months without seeing her. When the time came to see her again in September, I knew the little time I had was going to pass quickly and then I would never see her again. That one week, those seven short days, we spoke of our lives together and said our final farewell. The chemotherapy and radiation treatment had failed to destroy the tumors in her lungs. She realized her time had come, and she just wanted to go home and stop the grueling cancer treatments. During that week in September, we had several great conversations about our lives. I was always on the verge of breaking down, and every time I did she would tell me to stop. "I'm old and I'm not afraid to die. I'm just so thankful that I got to see all of you kids grow up and do so well for yourself," she said in her strong voice as I was crying next to her.

She never wanted us to feel sorry for her. I was crying and feeling sorry for myself that night. She knew she was going on her last journey soon, and she wanted to be strong for me. One night, she made herself sit up, put her arm around me, and consoled me, the healthy grandson, with an amazing strength in her voice: "I'm not afraid; it's my time to go. Bobby, you be strong for everyone here and just use the blessings you got from God. Don't cry for me because I will be fine." She had such strength in her final months.

During one of our conversations, I asked her how the Lakota described "life" with their words. She thought for a moment and casually said the words in Lakota. Of course, I could not understand them, so I asked her what the words meant in English. She thought for another moment and said, "I have come this far." "I have come this far" is a literal English translation of the Lakota concept of "life." The old Lakota had a very insightful perspective on the world, and those were the most profound words I had ever heard from her.

"I have come this far." That phrase hit me that night. Ironically, my gramma spoke the words at the end of her Lakota life. When she left this existence, my life—"how far I had come"—was just beginning. I was shedding my *wasicu* version of life and beginning to understand why my forebears had preferred to die in battle to protect their ways rather than become puppets of the *wasicu* world. Now I wish my upbringing had been as Indian as possible. I grew up solely as a *wasicu*, and that angers me greatly. My "I have come this far" is far from over, and when it does end, I want to be as content and unafraid as my grandmother was. Though she suppressed much of her Indian identity to protect herself, her children, and her grandchildren during her life, she left this world content, ready, and unafraid as a Lakota. I will follow her example.

She had gone a long way in her seventy-six years and I am thankful that I had nearly twenty-two years to spend with her. At her funeral, I put a baseball next to her body, just as I had for my grandfather years before, so she could hold it for me on the other side. That way I can play for her and Grandpa and they can give me their strength. I feel her spirit every day and I have seen her in several dreams. In her life I found strength, and her death only enhances the power we find in each other. When they closed the casket and the shadow covered her face forever, I truly realized why she did not teach me. I have to teach myself and also those who do not understand.

I am angry that a place like Dartmouth was necessary for me to figure out my identity and direction in life. The college has educated me in the *wasicu* sense, which contradicts much of the Indian knowledge I have acquired recently. Dartmouth has only licensed me as an educated Indian in the world of the *wasicu*, but that learning will be valuable in helping me help other Indians and myself. I have found more of myself, more of my spirit, and in that discovery comes knowledge. Knowledge will come to me and it will be in control. I just need to keep that in mind, relax, and allow everything that eluded me as a boy to come to me as a man.

> *Wanbli Wanji emaciyapi na han ma wicasa Lakota yelo.*
> I am One Eagle and I am a Lakota man.

My journey is far from over, and one of my yet-to-be-attained dreams is to stand on a Major League pitcher's mound with my hair in a braid, knowing that I have accomplished everything I ever wanted. Standing there alone, standing as *Wanbli Wanji*, will be a testimony to the struggle of Native people and the individual battle waged within all of us. Stand proud, Indian people. *Mitakuye oyasin.*

Case 2

THE HATRED WITHIN

JOSÉ GARCIA

DOI: 10.4324/9781003165378-3

José Garcia

This writer wrestles with issues of family, ethnicity, and self-esteem. José, a 20-year-old Latino junior, whose parents emigrated to the United States from Central America, explores his early experiences at school and his growing belief that his academic success made him not only "different" from other Latino/Latina students, but "better." Only when he reaches college does he come to understand this attitude and his disdain for his parents' relatively humble origins as a form of internalized racism. Drawn into the major Latino organization at his college and assuming a leadership role in student government, he comes painfully to name and eschew his self-hatred and embrace his developing Latino identity.

We were always horrible to the poor old man, Mr. Connors. He was the stereotypical high school substitute teacher—scolding us in a voice that echoed off the back wall and putting us to work with boring written exercises. We would respond by acting up, throwing papers, talking back, and pulling practical jokes—tormenting him in any way we could.

"Poor old guy," I thought. No more than 5 feet tall, he was bald except for the fringe of white hair that circled his bare dome. He wore rectangular eyeglasses and always came decked out in a full gray suit. I think it was the only suit he owned because he seemed to wear it whenever he substituted.

One morning, only a few minutes into the tormenting, the national anthem began over the P.A. system. As always, we stood up while the music played. Usually we did a good job of being quiet, but this time my friend Andrew and I kept joking and chatting as the music played.

When the song was over, Mr. Connors did exactly what I expected the typical "old-timer" would do. He began to yell at us for showing disrespect to the nation, but instead of focusing his obvious anger at both of us, he looked dead at me.

"Why don't you try that in your own country?" he barked.

Silence. I was in absolute shock. Did he really just say that? Without a second's pause I responded, "Why don't you try that in yours?" I took a step forward. There was no mirror there, so I have no sure idea what I looked like. But knowing how I get, I'm sure my face turned a bright red, my eyes became narrow and angry, my eyebrows crouched down. When I'm enraged, I make it very obvious. And it usually has the desired effect of intimidation because it's such a contrast to my usual jovial expression.

"This *is* my country," he answered back without a pause.

I took a few more steps forward. Not rushing to him, but with a slow threatening pace. "Well, this is *my* country, too."

"Well, how about your parents' country?" he asked, seeming not to realize that he was pushing me more and more, and that with every comment he uttered he was becoming more and more offensive.

"How about *your* parents' country?" I snapped back in the same mocking tone.

"My parents are indigenous," he said smugly.

The word at the time was unfamiliar to me. Although I was mad at myself for not knowing it (I wanted to step above this man as his intellectual and physical superior), I shot back, "What the fuck does that mean?" I didn't know what had come over me. I didn't swear at teachers, even substitute teachers. I joked, I kidded around, but I was always as respectful as my sense of humor allowed me to be.

He answered back by saying that the word meant his family had always lived here. Since he didn't look Native American, I had to assume he meant his ancestors came aboard the Mayflower or a similar absurdity. At that point I was at the foot of his desk, an arm's length away from his gleaming dome. I had no idea what I was doing. How can you ever be prepared for a confrontation like that? What did I hope to do when I reached him? Hit him? Spit in his face? I stood there barely a second before Andrew and my other pal Dave came from behind me and pulled me away, yelling, "Come on, José, back off! He's not worth it." And I knew he wasn't worth it. But what was it? What had happened to me? What did I think I was going to do? Why was I so enraged?

I wasn't the kind of student who turned violent so quickly, not with students and especially not with teachers. But something had come over me. My shock and disbelief at his words had drawn me magnetically toward him. Did he really say that? To this day, it remains the first situation that comes to mind whenever someone asks me if I have ever encountered outright racism. It was a slap in the face. But in hindsight the incident reveals more about me than it does about Mr. Connors.

Why did he look at me and not see a student like any other, or even an annoying teenager who had little respect for his country? Why did he appear to view me as a brown-skinned foreigner who didn't belong and deserved to have his identity questioned by a high school substitute teacher? That day in my sophomore year I felt like a minority. I felt like a Latino student. I felt like I didn't belong. Every other day, however, I took pride when my friends told me, "José, you're so white."

I'm surprised that it isn't harder to admit. As I see it now, I was a sellout in high school. I was a box-checker. I was a coconut. Name the insult and I was the epitome of it. In college, a friend referred to Latino students who didn't recognize their background or culture as "those who didn't associate." That was me. I didn't associate.

My high school was pretty diverse. The students in the Honors and Advanced Placement courses I took, however, were almost entirely white. I was lost, along with a handful of other students of color, in a sea of white faces. Given the fact that my classes were full of white students, it's no surprise that my friends were all white as well. I occasionally hung out with the one other Latino student whom I had known since kindergarten, but he, too, didn't "associate." He dressed in khakis and corduroys, polo shirts and button-ups, clothes that most people considered "preppie." And in my high school, preppie was syn-onymous with smart, and smart was, with a few exceptions, white.

Daniel, my good friend from the fourth grade on, was white with blond hair and blue eyes. My two best friends at the time, Nelson and Sara, both had dirty blond hair and piercing blue eyes. The pack of a dozen or so girls I hung out with junior and senior year were, with few exceptions, white. All of them were upper middle class. Most of them owned cars when they turned 16. These were my friends and I was proud of them.

But it was more than just the fact that they were white. I don't think there's a problem with having a lot of white friends, and I don't think I sought them out because of their skin color. They were just the people I saw every day. But what *did* matter was the attitude and thoughts that grew from this valuing of whiteness. Why did Mr. Connors's comments hit me so hard? Precisely because I was in denial of the fact that I was any different from my friends. I was like them. They were like me. It hurt me to be singled out as a Latino because, deep down, I really did believe that I was better than most Latinos. I was smart. I was hard-working. I was ambitious. I was successful. I was funny. These traits, I thought, were uncharacteristic of most Latinos. Mr. Connors brought me down, and I'm sad to say that that was the biggest reason he upset me so much all those years ago. He tore me away from my misconception that I was accepted and belonged in the white world, which I saw as the embodiment of the good, happy, and successful life. He forced me to confront my own racism.

I talked to my mom about this late in my senior year of high school. I actually complimented her on her parenting skills. I pondered how she had managed to raise us in a way that made us better than most Latinos. It never occurred to me how wrong this thinking was. I would never have dared to repeat my racist thoughts out loud. But at the time, I thought them. I saw other Latinos and would often assume the worst. It was easy to convince me that one was a drug dealer or a criminal, as I was already biased against them. And I always made that distinction clear: I, and for the most part my nuclear family, was not a part of *them.*

But these were all thoughts I kept buried deep down inside. I continued to check off "Hispanic" whenever forms asked for the optional race/ethnicity classification. I took pride in it then. With so few Latinos who aren't wastes, I figured I was helping myself. They would see me as an anomaly, I told myself. I was unique and that made me very happy.

So, besides the little box that I would check off from time to time, my culture and background meant nothing. In fact, I would treat it as a joke:

"Quit stealing my money, spic."
"Hey, don't look at me, I'm just a spic."
"Ah, those spics just don't get it."
"You're such a grubby, grubby spic."

These were words I spoke, phrases that sprung out of my mouth and the mouths of my closest friends. They were always said in jest and I always approved. I found it funny, because I thought being called a spic was pretty damned ironic. I recall a white friend telling me I was more white than he: I acted white, I dressed white, I talked white. In essence, to him I was normal, and normal was white. You're not part of a gang? You must be normal; you must be white. You don't shoot up every morning or carry a gun? You must be normal; you must be white. You don't speak Spanish in school; you don't know how to Latin dance? You must be normal; you must be white. And I laughed when he said I was a spic. How funny, I told myself: me … a spic? I thought I was anything and everything but that.

Besides these occasional insults, which I then thought were perfectly fine, my days at school had nothing to do with being Latino. I was normal, I told myself, therefore my ethnicity couldn't be my prime characteristic. I considered it a contradiction. This kind of thinking—this utter disdain for who I was—is something most people will never be able to understand. I think it's natural for adolescents to question their identity, but I did more than just question: I denied everything that was natural to me.

I would avoid the sun as much as possible late in high school. Why? Because I tan pretty easily and I didn't want to get too much darker than other students. A slight tan was okay, but I didn't want to get carried away. I didn't want to stick out. Sometimes I would actually fret over my darkening summer tan. How can I remain as white as possible? I would look in the mirror each morning and wish not just that my skin and features were different, but that my whole ethnicity could be washed away. My self-hatred lay at the core of my being. And that's where I kept it.

When I brought my friends home, I would be ashamed when my mom and dad, whose English was so bad, spoke to them. I would cringe when my dad tried to crack jokes because his thick accent made him sound like some teenager in a man's body. I would be embarrassed when my dad swore without pause and told them some anecdote. I would never bring my parents to school as other children did for events or programs. Worst of all, the superiority I felt over Latinos I also felt over my parents. They were older, and more experienced, but because they couldn't communicate on the phone with their mortgage bank as well as I could, or because I understood the seven o'clock news better than they did, I felt like I stood on a higher plane. I used to look at my best qualities as traits that were somehow incompatible with the language I spoke at home, the color of my skin, and the values my parents taught me.

My story, my struggle as a Latino student in a white community, is also the story of my parents. The two cannot be separated. I now realize that much of my journey is a continuation of what they began so many years ago. They immigrated illegally from Honduras to the United States several years before I was born. In Honduras my father was on his way to becoming an engineer; my mother was a teacher in the school system. When they came here, they lost everything and were forced to take menial jobs in a country where the language confused them. Within months they were caught and sent back by *la migra*. When they came to the United States the second time, they struggled constantly but they also thrived. My oldest brother Armando, who is nine years older than me, immigrated with my parents. My other brother Steve, five years older than I, was their first born in America and therefore was given the most American name they could think of.

Until I was 7 years old we lived in the "poor" section of our city. Surrounded by black and Latino kids, the feeling I can most recall is fear. I was scared of riding the bus to school. I was scared of the other kids. I was much like the scared white boy in a black neighborhood. I was scared of the others because I saw myself as inherently different. Even in elementary school, I had begun to develop the self-hatred and racism I would carry with me throughout my adolescence. All I knew was that while I was home, I had to cover my head with my pillow to drown out the police sirens and gun shots. But when I went to school and sat with the "smart kids" in the reading and math courses, I was nestled in a peaceful, white community. When my parents were finally able to save enough money, we moved out of the poor section and into the white community I had held so dear.

My father was, and still is, a drunk. Drinking was more than just something he did; through the years it had become a part of the man. I cannot imagine him without a beer in his hand, just as I cannot separate the man from the violence he inflicted. I respected and looked up to my father when I was young, but perhaps most of that came from my fear of him—fear of what he would do if I misbehaved. He was a pretty intimidating man, with a big round beer belly and huge biceps and calves. Some of my earliest memories are of me hanging off his extended arms, like a skillful monkey swinging along the trees. He had a loud, booming voice. His Spanish was always rough and convoluted. It wasn't that he spoke poorly, it was just the slang or expressions he picked up and used like standard English: "So I told him, 'Hey guy, fuck you, okay? Fuck you.'" He seemed always to be telling a story, always swearing, and, of course, always drinking. He was in his forties, but to me he sounded like a teenager trying to be cool. But as I grew up, I came to see him as a meaner, darker character. He wasn't just big anymore, he was scary. His resonant voice, which sounded like he was yelling even when he was in a good mood, often brought me to tears.

The last time my father hit me is still vivid in my mind. I was in seventh grade. I had a paper route all through middle school, and I usually delivered the papers right after school. One weekday after school I went to a friend's house instead of delivering my papers. We hung out the whole afternoon, playing cards and telling stories. I didn't get home until a little after five o'clock. I froze when I saw my dad standing on our front steps as I rode my bike into the driveway. He stared at me, clearly angry. My dad didn't even wait until I was inside the house to start yelling. "*Que hora es esta para llegar?*" He asked why I was late. Living in front of the high school, I was aware of the crowd of students staring at me as my father scolded me. I went inside, angry that my father would embarrass me like that. As soon as I was inside he slammed the door and continued his abuse: "*Donde estabas, babosada?*" In Spanish he called me a little shit, irresponsible, no good for not calling and telling him where I was. His face was bright red as his words tore through me.

As he stormed upstairs, I knew where he was going and what he was getting. The door to my brother Steve's room, which is down the hall from the kitchen, opened up and I saw his face pop out. I clung to Steve as little brothers tend to do. "If he hits me, I'm running away." I whispered, "If he hits me, I swear, I don't care, I'm running away." Tears were already streaming down my face and I braced myself for what I knew was coming. I heard my father pound down the stairs. He swung a belt and I foolishly tried to block the blows with my hands as he screamed to me to put my hands down. Again and again he brought the belt down across my thighs. The pain spurted in quick stings. There's no pain worse to me, at least in my memory, than the feel of a belt against my skin. I just wanted him to stop. I screamed louder, begging him to stop.

Eventually he stopped, probably tired of my screaming and tears; he turned abruptly and went upstairs. I remained crying, curled up in a little ball on the kitchen floor. I wished that I had the guts to actually stand up, grab my things, and leave the house forever. I had imagined and planned it so many times before—what things I would take with me, where I would go. But it was never meant to be anything more than a product of my imagination. Instead of making my plan a reality, I cried, just as I had done so many times before.

I'm not sure if he had been drinking that day or if it was just a bad mood. I mean, why hit your son for being late? My father, and the way he made me feel that day, became the personification of Honduras and my cultural roots. He was exactly what I wanted to avoid becoming. When he drank, I saw him as a stupid, pitiful fool. And it didn't take long for me to project those feelings on to all minorities around me. Except my mother—who I saw as different.

My mother is the sweetest woman in the world. She would do anything for me, including staying married to my father. She did it for me because she knew a divorce would hurt me. She did it for me because she didn't want us to have to move out of our nice home in front of my high school. She did it for me because she needed my father to help pay for college. I guess I take it for granted that it really was all for *me*. But there's no doubt in my mind that it was.

I was born with a heart murmur, which made me vulnerable as a child. My family took extra care of me, but more than anyone my mother was anxious for my safety. It was partially because of her personality, but also due to the circumstances. The combination of my sickness at a very young age and the fact that I was her last child—forever her baby—meant I was bound to be treated differently. She poured the last of her motherly instincts and care into me. Well into high school she would tuck me in at night and wake me up in the morning. Some nights I asked her to rub my back and, though she jokingly complained, she always did it. My closeness with my mother was a contrast to my father, whom I saw as the enemy.

As I grew up, my importance in the family and in her eyes grew. Armando never finished high school and failed my parents' dream of being the first son to graduate college in America. Steve failed similarly after only two terms away at the state university. I became their last chance. Out of thirty-two cousins on my father's side, I am the fourth youngest yet only the second to go to college. When Armando got into trouble, my dad unloaded on him in the only way he knew how. My father's mother had supposedly whipped my father into submission many years ago. A rope would have been a welcome change to some of the instruments he was beaten with as a boy in Honduras. Yet somehow he grew up loving and thanking his mother for every bit of punishment she handed to him. Similarly, my brother Armando has consistently defended my father for the pain he has inflicted on us. He, out of all of us, has stood by as my father's sole defender. For that reason, among others, my brother Armando and I did not often get along. Even though he knew my dad beat me, Armando felt he had gotten it much worse and viewed me as a spoiled brat.

My mother did not defend my father for most of their marriage, nor did she fight back. She quietly withstood his verbal abuse whenever he drank too much. Over time, however, whether it was the freedom she felt now that she was in the United States or her own personal growth, she began to speak up and assert herself. When he yelled, she would yell back. Usually, though, she was the voice of reason to his temper tantrums. Most of the time he didn't listen and kept on shouting, stalking off in anger and sleeping for the next few weeks in the basement, where he had a bed. Eventually, when I was in high school, my father moved most of his clothes down there and for months at a time would not sleep in his own bed with my mother. Through it all they stayed together … although *together* is a strange word to use for two people who never spoke, never stayed in the same room together for more than a moment, and were married, it seemed to me, in name only.

José Garcia

When they argued, my dad would say anything to interrupt her, to keep her quiet, to regain the peaceful life he remembered from Honduras. Her spirit took him by surprise. This wasn't the way it was in Honduras, he must have thought to himself. This wasn't the way it should be. The wife, he felt, was supposed to cook his food, serve him his drinks and meals, clean the house, stand by him always, and never talk back. But my mom, the wonderful woman that she is, would not stand for that. She knew that she was an American woman now and that things would have to change. Sometimes, crying to myself, I would hope that my mom would just give up and stop arguing back. I respect her now for being strong, but as a little boy I just wanted the shouting to stop. But no matter what, I always blamed my father. He was exactly what I didn't want to become and yet he was also the biggest male presence in my life. In my mind he represented Latino males, therefore I had no desire to grow up and become one.

As easy as it is to blame my father, another side of him, a gentler one, surfaces in my memory. He isn't always the man who beat me and yelled at my mother; sometimes he's the man who sacrificed so much for his family. During my sophomore year in college I was profiled in the college newspaper as a campus activist. The article described every-thing I was involved in and all of my accomplishments. I referred to my mother as the "force in my life." A few days after it was published, I sent the clipping home. I was worried how my father would take it. When I finally spoke to my mom about it, she said they had read it together and they both had cried. He was not angry or jealous, as I would have expected him to be. She told me that my family had had a barbecue and invited all my family members. Sometime during the party, my father pulled out the article, which he had already taken to work to show his friends, and translated the article into Spanish for my relatives. My mom told me that everyone was so proud of me, but my thoughts were with my father. This is the man I call my dad; this is the man who, along with my mother, I strive to prove myself to each day in spite of his harshness to me. When I look back on my life, I won't see it as a success unless both of my parents see it that way as well. In the back of my mind is the knowledge that if things had gone differently twenty odd years ago—if my parents had made just a slightly different decision, or if my father hadn't worked half as hard—my life would be completely different. I owe something to them, whether I like it or not, and that knowledge drives me to achieve, even when I feel that "I have too much to do."

That's why my narrative can't be separated from my parents' story. Their journey to the United States didn't end when they arrived for good, or even when they finally became citizens. The two stories continue in tandem, and just as important is the extended family they left in Honduras and the extended family that traveled with them. Growing up, I was often surrounded by my many aunts and uncles, cousins and second cousins. Just as my father became the embodiment of the Latino man—everything I didn't want to grow to be—my extended family also represented my ethnicity, my culture, and the target of my racism.

I saw my nuclear family as different from their little clans, and as I grew up, *different* also meant *better*. We Garcias were somehow special. My aunts were either single, divorced, or remarried. My cousins were constantly being arrested, having children out of wedlock, causing their parents grief. My cousins were the only Latinos I had any close connection to, so, to me their behavior exemplified all Latinos. They got into trouble, broke the law, stole, cheated, lied, and were disobedient. Although my brothers and I occasionally exhibited some of these behaviors, I nevertheless saw us as above it all. My female cousins got pregnant, moved in with boyfriends, married and divorced early—all the kind of behavior that I considered "subwhite." To do the wrong thing, then, as I saw my cousins do the wrong things, was to be less than white, to be *not* succeeding in America.

It is true that my brothers and I were generally better behaved, better educated, and better mannered than many of my cousins. But instead of leaving the comparison there, I took it a step further and said that this was because they were Latino and were acting it, while we were Latino but we had somehow overcome our heritage. Overcome our heritage! This idea disgusts me now, and yet there was a time I didn't even question it. I didn't think of my family as successful because we were Latino or in addition to being Latino, but *in spite* of that fact.

The notion of overcoming my heritage recalls a poignant incident that occurred during a family vacation to Honduras. On the road, a small child around my age came up to our van and asked for a ride. We told him we didn't have any room, but as we started to drive we noticed that he had climbed on the back of the van and was prepared to ride with us, at fifty or sixty miles per hour, holding onto a ladder. At the time I disliked the little brat; I couldn't believe he had the nerve to try and hitch a ride from us. A dozen years later I think of that kid and can't help but see myself. If circumstances had been different, I could have been him. That notion would occur to me again and again, but at the time, and even as I packed bags for college, I still looked at that boy—at so much of my identity—with disdain.

José Garcia

My parents didn't pressure me much to succeed; I put the pressure on myself: I was the one who had to bring respect to my family after Armando dropped out of high school and Steve dropped out of college. Armando and I constantly argued, and he refused to come to my high school graduation. I think my success only highlighted his failure. My parents' pride in me was a sharp stab at him. He had been expected to be the first one to do so many things that I was now doing. Steve was more complacent, always assuming he would return to school and catch up with me. And that's how I left for college—angry with most of my family, convinced that I was better than my family and my heritage, and bearing the burden of bringing home what my parents wanted to see: a good report card and a college diploma.

For the most part, college was everything it was supposed to be: I was having the time of my life and meeting so many amazing people. It wasn't until my first meeting of La Unidad, the Latino student organization, that I had my first confrontation with the hate inside me. I had gone to the meeting because I felt an obligation to go. Despite my belief that I was better than my background, I was also confronted by the feeling that my status as a so-called box-checking Latino was what got me into college. Why else would I have identified myself as such? "Associate," "identify"—words like these meant the difference between being seen as an outsider to the Latino community or a link within it. If you identified, that basically meant you acknowledged your heritage— you went beyond your box-checking status.

I went to that first Unidad meeting because I felt an obligation, not because I felt I would gain anything from it. I didn't want to be seen as a Latino student by the mainstream but I also didn't want to be seen as a sellout by the Latino students. My self-hatred and hatred of my ethnicity were deeply buried, and I had no intention of making it known. I barely thought about it, and that's the way I liked it. But my first weeks at college were characterized by a sense of exclusion, a sense that I didn't fit in anymore. Dressed in Abercrombie and Fitch, attending their parents' alma mater, most students seemed so different from me. I was afraid someone would suddenly discover that I didn't really belong. I had an overwhelming feeling that I had to start my life over again, build myself back up, yet I didn't know who I was or how to go about it.

That first Unidad meeting we all sat in a stuffy room, the Latino students on display for one another. I was immediately hit by the feeling that I was very "unLatino." The others somehow exuded more Latino-ness. It was in their accents, the speed of their speech, the Spanish words they mixed into their English. They all talked about home cooking and dishes that they loved, and although I loved my mom's home cooking, I didn't know the correct names of the foods she prepared. But most important, they all seemed to know more about their individual cultures. They were more culturally, socially, and politically aware than I ever thought I could be. What did I know about Honduras? I couldn't even tell you what kind of government they have there, let alone how "my people" are doing. What did I know about Latino culture besides what I learned in school, which was nothing? My cultural ignorance had never even occurred to me as a problem; suddenly it became a very big one.

The worst moment was when we went around the room and introduced ourselves. One by one they spoke, pronouncing their names with a full Spanish accent. Some people I knew always did so, but a few caught me off guard. *Drew* became *Andres*, *John* became *Juan*; the speed at which people said their names increased, and as we quickly went around the circle, I didn't know what to do. Of course, I could easily have used an accent, but I never did and I didn't want to do so just to fit in. I even had a fear about doing that. What if it came out badly? What if I couldn't even say my own name right? I didn't want their eyes on me, them to snicker and know that I was only a fake. I just wanted to come to the meeting, sit back, and feel like I had made up for the fact that I checked *Hispanic/Latino* instead of *white*, which is what I wished I were, or *Other*, which is what I felt like.

When the introductions finally came around to me, I blurted out my name, *José García*, with a full accent. I felt like a sellout, not because I didn't want to be Latino, but because I was willing to hide my true self in order to be accepted as Latino. I was more confused than ever. Inside I knew that I thought poorly of Latinos and that my racism was deeply rooted, yet I was willing to act unlike myself in order to be accepted by my Latino peers. I didn't know who I was or what I wanted. I only knew that I wanted to be accepted. I wanted to please everyone, and was finding I couldn't please anyone.

My confusion got worse before it got better. I had gotten involved early freshman fall in my college's student government. Representing the student body, the organization constantly worried about whether or not they were truly being representative. So they would literally take a count based on gender and race/ethnicity. I wasn't just a normal involved student, I was the token Latino, or so it seemed to me.

The word *token* was one that I would get to know well as time went on. Token Latino, token minority, people of color versus minority, ignorance versus racism, the relationship of power in racism, prejudice, institutional racism … these were all terms and phrases that I had never been acquainted with before my first year at college. I had a crash course in being nonwhite. I'm convinced that if you asked a white person, half of those terms would draw a blank response. It's not simply because they're white, but because they have had no contact with these issues. I'm a great example. I had never considered any of these issues, yet I was that person of color; I was that token minority. I was *supposed* to know. That lesson came to me during a student government meeting when I was asked to give my opinion as a Latino. I wasn't asked to give it as a student who happens to be Latino, but to give the official Latino opinion, as if all we Latinos got together one day and took a straw poll on a number of issues, all of which came out unanimous. There is diversity among races, but there is also diversity within races. I wanted my friends to be color-blind. I didn't want to be seen as Latino or ethnic or other. In a short time I went from hating my ethnicity to not minding it, but still being grateful when people could ignore it. The inner hatred I had grown up with was gone, but something rotten remained. I still had a way to go before I would embrace and actually be proud of my culture, rather than just tolerating it.

I continued going to Unidad meetings, continued struggling through my ignorance. I heard other students of color talk about the racial issues they had confronted growing up. I began to find more and more aspects of my childhood that related to their childhoods—similarities in being the children of immigrants. Most of all, I was surrounded for the first time by students who shared my skin color and also shared my academic success. I was no longer the exception in a sea of white faces. The wall I had built up between myself and my ethnicity began to break down. Despite being 70 percent white, my college introduced me to diversity. So before I realized it was happening, that lifelong correlation between *white* and *successful* stopped making sense to me.

I recall a late-night conversation with my friend Jake who is half Latino and half white. He casually mentioned that he was against affirmative action, that he saw it as reverse discrimination against white students, and felt that it only served to emphasize racial lines more. As he put it, "Why should white people today have to suffer for what white people in the past have done?" This comment led to a passionate debate. I argued that, despite what he believed, there was a racial divide in this country. It was social, as evidenced by my high school substitute's behavior years before. It was economic, as evidenced by the poor section of my hometown that bussed me in and out when

I was younger. It was educational, as shown by all the white faces in my upper-level classes from elementary school through high school. It was cultural, as witnessed by the isolation I felt at my first Unidad meeting. "You're right," I argued. "Most white people of today have nothing to do with what happened years before. But that doesn't erase the problem. That doesn't change the fact that minorities are still suffering because of what happened years before. Furthermore, whether whites are directly at fault or not, it doesn't change the fact that whites have benefited. Because others have lost, whites have gained. It's not a question of right or wrong—it's just the way things are. But that doesn't mean we shouldn't try to change things." Jake kept arguing that minorities just needed to "stop feeling sorry for themselves."

That night I developed my own theory on this subject: "Look Jake, it's like life is this one big long-distance race. Ever since the race began, the minority runners have been oppressed, kept back, slowed by slavery, by conquest, and so on. And all this time the white runners have been getting ahead. Suddenly, all restrictions are dropped. No more slavery. No more segregation. Everything is made equal. But is it really equal, Jake? All that equalization under the law doesn't change the fact that all these white runners have had a centuries-long head start. How does that translate to real life? In economics, in educa-tion, in social attitudes? These are all big problems and they call for big solutions. I don't think affirmative action is the best long-term solution, but it is a temporary one until people are willing to make the bigger commitment."

Jake said that he used his Latino background to get him into college, just as he used his running talent (he was recruited by the college for cross-country). That was all his identity as a Latino meant to him. With my mind entrenched in issues of race and ethnicity, I was outraged at him for saying something like that. And yet just a few months before I could have said the same thing.

At college, once I began to deal with the long-suppressed issues of my ethnic identity the floodgates opened. Sometimes I got in serious arguments and found myself saying things I couldn't believe I was saying. In those moments I claimed all white people were racists or the United States border should be completely open all the time. But that was part of my learning process, of pushing forward. I was in the process of testing, trying things out, seeing where thoughts would go and then evaluating whether I still believed them or not. I was trying to find myself under years of buried ignorance, self-hate, and prejudice toward my own culture.

José Garcia

In another late-night conversation with friends, I recalled that small boy who had wanted to hitch a ride with us in Honduras, whom I had disliked so much. "What's so different from me and so many of the naked kids I see running around in Honduras, begging on the streets? Sure, I think my drive and my work ethic have been important, but I think the key difference has been the opportunities I have had—attending schools that are leaps and bounds above anything in Honduras and pursuing so many things that my parents never had the chance to. And yet it might have been completely different. It could be another kid sitting here today and me in Honduras. That's why I don't think I'll be happy in life unless I'm helping them realize their own potential. I want to give others all the opportunities that I had." And the minute I said it, I knew I believed it with all my being—I knew I would never look at my role or purpose in life in the same light again. I was never religious, and yet I felt I had found my calling. I knew then I could never be an investment banker or businessman. My place was in service, in education, in any field where I could use my skills to improve the lives of others and help them open doors.

In spite of my new insights, the same demons remained inside of me. When you look at yourself in the mirror for years and see someone who is unattractive because of his skin color, hair color, speech, and other characteristics, those negative feelings don't go away easily. I felt I had a big nose, that it was too round and not slim enough. I hated the fact that I would always be a good four inches below average height. I even came to dislike my boring brown eyes and black hair. My own insecurities about how I looked and fit in remained. Even though I was growing intellectually and emotionally, I had not yet purged many of the old thoughts that haunted me.

My self-hatred was also hatred of my background and my relatives. My perception of myself and others had been altered by all the new people I met at college. Generalizations I had held to—that all Latinos are lazy, all students of color are inferior to whites—were shattered while I was at school. My relationships with members of my family and their relationships with each other had also been forced to change as a result of my absence. My leaving home was exactly what my family needed.

Just how far the healing had progressed is evident in a radiant photo taken at Armando's new apartment, which he shared with his fiancée, Molly. In the photo, we're embracing each other tightly. My father has one arm extending far to his right to reach my brother and the other hand is tightly grasping my mother's shoulder. My mother is smiling beautifully; it's a genuine smile. She seems truly happy—happy to have her family all around her. You can almost read her thoughts: she has her family together again, different than before but together. Caught in that photo is me kissing my brother. For no other reason than because I was feeling happy and wanted a funny picture, I embraced Armando's face and kissed him on his right cheek. He remained smiling while looking at the camera, his arm tightly around me. After the photo was taken, Armando wrapped his arms around me and pulled me in for a full hug. Steve came over as well. And right there, in the kitchen of my brother's new house, with my parents and his fiancée watching, Armando began to apologize to me for mistreating me for years and years. As we embraced, Armando sobbed, "I'm so sorry, José; I'm so sorry for everything I put you through. But you know I did it because I loved you and wanted only the best from you. You're my little brother; there's nothing I wouldn't do for you." He then opened his arms to Steve, and with the three of us wrapped in each other's arms, forming a little circle, Armando continued, with tears in his eyes, "You guys are my brothers, my little men. I love you two so much. So fucking much! I'm always going to be there for you guys, whatever you might need. You fucking come to me, all right? There's nothing I won't do for my brothers." The tears were coming down my cheeks now, and Steve, usually calm and reserved, also began to cry. Our coming together in love and reconciliation was the climax to what I had slowly been developing the whole year—my acceptance by and of my brothers after years of alienation. While we hugged, I remember hearing my mother tell my father to look over at us. I sensed her deep inner happiness. She was so proud to see her sons finally come together.

Several months later I took another step forward in my journey. I interned in Washington, DC, working as a research assistant for a nonprofit organization focused on strengthening the Latino community. I found myself surrounded by people who had centered their lives around making a difference in the Latino community. Two men in particular, leaders in the organization, further altered my views on Latinos. Both had gone to Ivy League schools and their résumés were packed with incredible experiences. They could have done anything they wanted to in life, but they chose to give back to their respective communities. I met many prominent Latinos through them and my perceptions of Latinos, which had expanded exponentially since high school, were further improved. Any significant prejudices I had were eliminated by the success of these two men. I admired them *and* they were Latino. In the past, I would have joined these two facts by thinking, *in spite of* their being Latino. It's such a small detail and yet reveals so much about how I thought.

I was still working in DC when I flew home for the weekend to see the production of a musical in my high school. I saw the show with Dan, my friend since the fourth grade. I told him about my involvement in student government, my increased activism, and life in general at my small liberal arts college. But since I was in DC at the time, I also mentioned my internship and the great time I was having. With pride, I pulled out my business card. "Empowering the Latino community?" He read off the card, smiling at me and waving the card to a mutual friend from high school. "Look, Chris, José is Latino now. Look at the card. Our little brown friend's creating community!" His tone was mocking and they both began to laugh as they gazed at the card. "This is the biggest load of PC bullshit. I can't believe you're a part of this crap!" He laughed louder, staring at the card in disbelief.

I felt crushed. This had been my childhood friend? This had been the life that I had enjoyed so much? I was ashamed of who I had been and what I had believed, but I didn't think the shame ran so deep. Was there anything I could turn back to? Was there anything that didn't stink of my racism? It had been a while since I felt so uncomfortable, fidgeting in place, wanting to be anywhere but there. And right then I was struck with a realization that came just before I would have begun feeling sorry for myself. "Hey, Dan, fuck you," I said. His mouth opened in disbelief; his laugh stopped in mid-breath. I continued, "Just because you haven't grown up in the last two years, doesn't mean that I haven't."

"Hey, Mr. Latino, don't take it personally. I just think that doing this sort of thing is very unlike the José I knew in high school," Dan said, handing the card back to me.

"A lot about me is unlike the José you once knew. People change, Dan, and ya know what? I'm happy with the changes I've made." I gave both of them one last look in the eye and then returned to my seat in the theater. I don't think I was particularly articulate or eloquent, but I got across what I wanted. I didn't back off.

As the show continued, I recalled that late-night conversation with Jake and the passion with which I spoke of privilege and racism. An image of that boy from Honduras came to mind and I again imagined myself living his life. I then remembered Mr. Connors, the substitute teacher, and the anger he had made me feel. I reflected on the dozens of conversations in which I called myself a spic and spat on my culture. Finally, I thought of my mother and father and all they had given me and continue to give me. Dan, who silently took his seat next to me, had accused me of being "very unlike the José he knew in school." I smiled, happy that he was right, proud that I didn't joke along with him and deny what I had spent two years forming, what is still forming, what I hope never stops forming.

Case 3

GOOD HAIR

ANA SOFIA DE BRITO

DOI: 10.4324/9781003165378-4

Ana Sofia De Brito

Ana Sofia, an undocumented immigrant to the U.S. from Cape Verde, struggles to find a deeper understanding of her own identity and acceptance within tightly defined college racial communities and in the context of relationships. While her features, skin color, and hair suggest a racial affinity with one campus community, Ana Sofia's heart desires acceptance and permanence with another. As she experiences "... confusion in who [she is] and how [she fits] in ...," Ana Sofia endures her family's conflicting views on identity and the impact on her own perceptions and evolution.

The issue of race has always been a problem in my Cape Verdean family— and in my life. We constantly argue whether we're white or black. My dad says he stayed with my mom to *melhorar a raça*, or better his race, by lightening the color of his children, and I'd better not mess up his plan by bringing a black boy home. In my home country, being lighter is equated with having money, which is a process called *branqueamento*, where money makes you whiter and marrying lighter helps your race. Needless to say, he is proud of his light skin.

I had always wondered what my dad had against broad noses. As he realized in my late teenage years that my taste leaned toward black men, most of whom had the type of nose he despised, my dad would always advise me to think twice.

> "I hope you know what you're doing," he said one night when we went out to dinner together. "What do you mean?" I had no clue what I was doing wrong.
>
> "You're destroying the race I helped create by marrying your mom. All my hard work will go to waste after you have a child with someone with a flat nose and nappy hair. You better start learning to do black people's hair!" he replied, laughing.

Destroying his race? I was not aware that I was the product of his "hard work" to make the Cape Verdean race lighter, with finer hair and a straighter nose. For years I had heard him say he "bettered his race," but I never truly believed he was serious. He would joke about my hypothetical future husband by saying he didn't want to hurt his hand when he patted the Brillo-pad hair of his grandchildren.

It wasn't until I heard his life story that I understood my dad's sensibilities. When I was a child, my father was very evasive about his own childhood. It wasn't until I was 18 years old and away at college that I started to question him seriously about his past.

In 1965, at age 3, my father left the Cape Verde Islands with his mother, father, and two youngest brothers and moved to the African country of Mozambique, another former Portuguese colony. My grandfather had been sent by the Portuguese government to serve as mayor of a village in the interior of the country that was quickly growing into a city. It was in Mozambique that my father's views about race were formed. As the Cape Verdean son of an official in the administration of a Portuguese colony, my father led a privileged life, living in a big house with great food and many servants.

All this changed, however, when he went away to a boarding school attended almost entirely by the children of white Portuguese settlers. My dad was neither Portuguese nor white, so he was constantly bullied, beaten up, made fun of, and humiliated. He never talks about this part of his life in Mozambique, but the bullying he suffered has had an irreversible effect on him. The fact that his skin was the color of tan sand made him stand out in a sea of white, and his broad nose did not help matters. At his boarding school in Mozambique, the whiter students called him "nigger" and other epithets, the very names he now calls people who are darker than him. The white children in Mozambique equated him with the darker-skinned natives, whom their parents had taught them to look down on as inferior. Although my dad returned to Cape Verde at age 13, his notion of blackness and whiteness had been radically changed, and he still carries the mindset of the bullied child. Had my dad's family stayed in Cape Verde, where color lines are blurred and there is no outright racism, I believe my dad would not be the way he is.

My mother was born and raised in the Cape Verde Islands, including Praia, a city where slaves were sent to be sold in the time of the slave trade. On the island of Santiago, where Praia is located, there are more Africans and Afro-descended Cape Verdeans than on any other island. At age 10, my mom moved from Fogo, a volcanic island with a bigger population of whiter Cape Verdeans, to Praia for schooling. My mother is the lightest in our family, and her thin, fine hair goes with the rest of her features. She has round dark eyes and a straight European-looking nose, the thin lips associated with being white, and a pale complexion that turns tan only in the summer months. My brother and I both inherited many of her features, but our noses differ. Mine is broader and his is straighter, on account of our having different dads. And even though we have similar features and complexions, we have different mindsets. We both identify strongly as Cape Verdean; he, however, identifies with being white, whereas I identify with being black.

It gets complicated when my family talk about skin color. They believe that black is ugly, but so is being "too white"; our Cape Verdean color is just right. My father seems to place Cape Verdean people in the category of an entirely different race. The reality is that Cape Verdeans are mixed both culturally and racially and are many different shades.

Cape Verde is made up of ten islands off the west coast of Africa. The Portuguese colonized the uninhabited islands in the fifteenth century. Like other colonies, Cape Verde prospered from the transatlantic slave trade. Cape Verdean people were literally born out of the interactions between the Portuguese, Italians, Asian Indians, British, French, and African slaves. Among those who call themselves Cape Verdean are blondes with green eyes and those who are dark as ebony. In between you can find any shade and combination of features. Even within my own family, our skin hue, the texture of our hair, and our eye color vary from person to person.

Our Cape Verdean-ness became even more complicated when we tried to integrate ourselves into America. In 1996 my mom decided to move to the United States and bring my brother and me along. I was 5 and my brother was 15. My father had gone ahead a year earlier. My mom stayed behind for a year because of her career as the manager of a well-respected hotel and restaurant in the capital of Cape Verde. We led a very comfortable life before moving to America. My parents were well-off, we lived in a spacious house, and my brother and I went to private schools. Nonetheless, the educational opportunities that were offered in Cape Verde could never compare with those offered in the United States. That summer we packed our belongings, got on a spacious South African plane, and came to the United States.

Our immigrant story was not that of the "huddled masses" often perpetuated by the media. We had no reason to leave Cape Verde. Our extended family is well respected there, particularly my maternal grandparents, because my grandfather saved many lives during his medical career, and my grandmother helped thousands of women give birth. To this day, people ask me to thank my grandparents for their benevolence. My grandfather had worked himself up from nothing after his father died when he was 14, leaving his mother with thirteen young children. He became a nurse and later pursued a career in politics, in addition to his medical career. My paternal grandfather did the same. His mother was a black Cape Verdean prostitute, who was impregnated by a white Portuguese judge and bore my illegitimate grandfather. He was sent away to be taken care of by his godmother during the hard times of World War II, when there was famine in Cape Verde. He excelled at school, became a pharmacist technician, and later also pursued a political career in Mozambique, becoming a mayor. My grandparents instilled in their children a love and admiration for education, which was passed on to their grandchildren. When my father left for the United States and sent back news that he had found work, my mother decided to move to the States as well to keep our family intact, and for the sake of her children's education.

When we arrived at the airport in Boston, my mom shouted, "There he is!" I turned my head and spotted my dad. It had been a whole year since I'd last seen him, so I immediately began to run as fast as my little skinny legs could take me to his outstretched arms. "*Cuquinha*," he whispered as he gave me a hug. That was my nickname—and it had been a whole year since I'd heard the word from his lips.

When we pulled up to our new home, I was very excited. I ran up the stairs, but as my dad opened the door, a wave of disappointment hit me. For some reason I was expecting something other than what I found. Our new home was a bachelors' apartment. My father lived there with a roommate; it was gray and cold and smelled like cigarettes. I hoped with all my heart that this wasn't our home; it was so much smaller than our old house. Unfortunately, this small duplex apartment has been our home for the past fifteen years. For the first three years there, I slept on a mattress on the floor of my parents' bedroom while we waited for Nelson, my dad's roommate, to leave. We watched the years go by, and the street begin to change from white to black. As more Cape Verdean and Latino families moved to our street, more white people began to move out. The streets in our neighborhood also became less cared for, and violence increased. I watched all this through my window and from my balcony, since I've always felt uncomfortable being outside in my neighborhood.

Our first summer in the United States was a period of acclimation. Everything was still new and exciting, but limited. After six months of living here, we became undocumented after overstaying our tourist visas. Our family went from being relatively well-off to living on a tight budget. Cape Verdean currency did not translate well to American dollars. My father worked cleaning offices for a business in Providence, and my mother was unemployed. She spent her time helping me learn English so I could be enrolled in school in the upcoming fall. We spent hours every night practicing with flash cards. Because my mother was the only one in the family with any knowledge of English, she was the one who helped me learn my first words in this new language.

Ana Sofia De Brito

My elementary school was attended mostly by Cape Verdean children of all colors, who either had immigrated to the United States or were born here, some Latinos, African Americans, and a few whites. When I looked around, I saw familiar faces and heard a familiar language. I never had to answer the question "What are you?" In fact, until tenth grade I never thought of myself as a "minority." This changed, however, when I transferred from a violence-ridden, under-resourced public school to a private all-girls Quaker school attended primarily by white Jewish girls. Overnight I became not only a minority but, because of my mixed racial background, also "exotic" and very much the "other."

It was in this school that I first became aware of race relations and socioeconomic classes, and how the two are inexplicably intertwined. Until then I had never given much thought to my economic situation or race. I knew I wasn't rich, but even though my mom was a domestic servant and my dad worked in a factory during this time, we were able to go on vacations to Hawaii and Florida, so I deduced that we weren't poor either. I wasn't very conscious of the various racial heritages that made up my Cape Verdean self, nor did I care. But then, suddenly, my school peer group consisted of seemingly rich white kids almost completely ignorant of people unlike themselves. I recall my mom's advice to me on the first day at my new school: "Remember where you came from and don't let these rich kids make you think they're better than you. And also remember, you're not rich."

I definitely knew I was not rich. As an undocumented immigrant transfer student into the tenth grade, I was offered a discounted tuition of only $5,000, though tuition was normally $19,000. My parents, however, could not afford to pay even $5,000 a year, as we lived from paycheck to paycheck and continually struggled to keep up with the bills they already had. I cried every day for three weeks after being notified that I had been accepted at the school, knowing I would never get to leave my public high school with its gang fights, rapes, and restrictive atmosphere. My salvation came from a Jewish family my mom worked for as a nanny and maid. They offered to pay my tuition for three years because they believed that any intelligent child deserved the same educational opportunities their son would have. For this I will be indebted to them for the rest of my life. They allowed me to become part of their family and made sure I took advantage of every educational opportunity presented to me.

My private high school solidified my identification with being black. I came to see that in this society I wasn't just Cape Verdean—I was black. My parents had told me I was a white Cape Verdean, but being in a majority-white school made me think maybe I wasn't white enough. I soon began to analyze my life in the United States through the same lens as most Americans, who saw my family and me as black. Ever since we moved to the States, my father had been complaining that he didn't receive any respect here. He used to complain often about how disrespectfully he was treated by white people. This was especially confusing for him, because he thought of himself as white too, and therefore one of them. So he chose to assume that his poor treatment was because of his immigrant status or his limited English and thick accent, which forced him to work in low-paying factory jobs. He was never willing to consider that as far as white people in this country were concerned, his tan skin meant that he was black.

My family has long been in denial that in America we are simply seen as black. It wasn't until I participated in a majority-white world every day at high school that I realized we were highly mistaken. I was not a white American and never would be. To people who didn't know what Cape Verdeans were, we were just another group of colored people.

The rest of the world aside, within my family I am considered white. From an early age, I saw the struggle of racial identification becoming a problem even within my U.S.-based Cape Verdean family. I remember the first time I felt I was better than my cousins because I was lighter. I was 7 years old and my hair was down to my waist. I was standing in front of the mirror having my cousins detangle my hair when the "hair problem" reared its ugly head. My cousins always fought with each other over who would comb my hair, which was soft and curly and long—not "black" hair. My cousins and I had just come back from the beach, and all of us had washed and combed our hair. Mine was air-drying; theirs was being flat-ironed and pulled in every direction by their mother in order to make it straight. My young cousin asked her mother why my hair didn't need to be straightened like hers. "Because her hair is nice and is not kinky like yours," her mother replied with a sigh. I beamed. To me at age 7, those words meant I had won, that despite my African features I had one thing they didn't have—*cabelo bom*, or nicer hair—and therefore I was whiter. I was too young to understand fully how prized straight hair is within the Cape Verdean community, or that my hair being "whiter" made me less black.

Today I find myself wishing my hair were kinkier in order to qualify truly as "black."

My hair is curly and fine. I do not use chemicals to make it straight; all it needs is one good pass of the flat iron—just like a white girl's hair. Being able to walk out of the shower and let my hair air-dry into my hairstyle is a freedom that my black friends do not have. Because of my hair, the black community has identified me as not being truly black. Thus I have to prove to them that I am African, that I watch black movies and know what relaxing and perming are—that I, too, have experienced racism. It's a constant struggle for me to identify as black, and I wonder how many more years I will have to fight to amass sufficient cultural capital to be considered black by other blacks.

The privileges I supposedly receive in America because of my light skin have been detailed to me by my friends at college who are considerably darker than I. They say that white people will treat me with more respect because I am light-skinned; that if I straightened my hair more often, I could easily be taken for a "maybe" white girl; and that I will be able to get jobs a darker-skinned person will not. With each such "privilege," my separation from black people becomes increasingly clear.

When I have challenged the idea that my hair can determine the course of my life, my black college friends say, "Of course your hair matters! It's been proven by scientific research that when a black girl wears her hair straight to a job interview, then she is more likely to get hired than if she wears her hair natural." A dark-skinned Dominican friend said, "When I have my hair curly, I always get curious looks, but when I have my hair straight, I don't. Watch. Straighten your hair for one day and see the difference in the comments you get." So I decided to straighten my hair for one day and walk around campus to see what happened. Sure enough, people came up to me asking to touch my hair, and I got lots of positive comments: "Oh my god! Your hair looks so pretty." "Your hair is so long!" "Can I touch it? Wow, it's so silky!" "I wish I had hair like yours." "You're even more exotic now. You should model!" All I could think was, "Damn, my friends were right." White standards of beauty had won; my straight hair got me more attention than my curly hair. The most dramatic difference I noticed was that white boys who had never paid attention to me gave me flirty smiles and talked to me. Not once while I was wearing my hair curly had white boys struck up a conversation with me on a nonacademic topic. Despite all of the attention I get with straight hair, I still prefer my natural hairstyle, which I believe makes me appear more ethnic, more black.

I often ask myself, "If I'm not considered black, what does it mean to be black?" In my Rhode Island hometown, my ethnic and racial identities have never been questioned. I'm Cape Verdean, and so are my next-door neighbors. We consider Cape Verdean a separate race. But since I came to college, my racial identity has been ripped apart, and I have not yet been able to reassemble the pieces. The look of recognition in people's eyes at home when I tell them that I am Cape Verdean has been replaced with a look of confusion among people on campus. Few people at my college know what Cape Verdean people are or even where the small island nation is located. People often assume I'm Latina or "that mixed-race girl." Never black. Never African. And with my fine curly hair, light skin, and mixed European and African features, I can see how hard it must be for others to understand me in this polarized racial world. To them I am exotic.

I desperately cling to my Cape Verdean identity, which is like a piece of string slowly unraveling and threatening to snap. If it snaps, I fear my sense of self will be in complete disarray. I identify as black, but in the eyes of the world I am neither black nor white. When I try to affiliate with black student organizations at college, black students often don't know what to make of me. They say, "I don't know what you're doing here," implying that as a light-skinned girl, I don't know what it is to be truly black. They seem to consider themselves the arbiters of who is truly black, and I somehow get lost in the shuffle.

After three years at college, I still feel there is a divide between dark-skinned and light-skinned blacks, and between African Americans and Africans. Interestingly, I am African and I identify mostly with African American culture, yet I feel as if I'm not being taken seriously at black group events because of my light skin. This has pushed me to associate more on campus with Dominicans, who understand my racial mixture and suffer the same type of discrimination.

My conundrum often arises on the dating scene as well. When I told one black freshman boy I was from Cape Verde, he said to me, "I like light-skinned girls with curly hair. And you're different from black people. You're exotic." It's hard to figure out if a boy likes me for my light features, because I'm exotic, or because of who I am.

Although I have never had a strong preference for any particular type and have dated boys from various backgrounds and races, at college my preference has focused on men with darker skin. Someone once asked me, "Why do you only like black men?" This question irritates me; why aren't white people asked why they are attracted to other white people? Is there a law that says I must be attracted to others who look just like me?

It's so much easier for me to date men from Rhode Island than from my college, as the locals tend to be familiar with Cape Verdean people, culture, and food. They know what Cape Verde is and can locate

Ana Sofia De Brito

it on a map, so I don't have to explain my heritage and can enter the relationship knowing they will understand where I am coming from. My former boyfriend was African American with Cape Verdean ancestry. He has what would be considered black features and was completely immersed in the black community.

When my parents heard I had a black boyfriend, they had different reactions. My mom was genuinely happy I had found someone I seemed to like. Her motto has always been "It's you that has to like him, not us, and it doesn't matter what his color is." My father, however, responded, "Another black person? I can see you're stuck with that category." But when he met my boyfriend, his reaction surprised me: "Oh, I thought he'd be darker. He's just like us. I like him." It seemed my new boyfriend passed the test because his skin was lighter than my previous boyfriend's. Surprisingly, my father actually acknowledged him and spoke English with him. My previous boyfriend had hardly received a hello or a handshake.

Black men at my college are interesting. They seem to consider the dark-skinned girls more authentically black, and my light skin becomes a negative in their eyes. I remember having a conversation with a dark-skinned black student one winter night about the use of the word "nigga" and whether I was "allowed" to use it. "You're too light-skinned and you can't use the word. You're almost too white. If you were to use it, it'd be as if a white person were to call me a nigger."

I tried to explain. "No it's not. That's crazy. I'm not white—I'm black! If I want to call you a 'nigga' like you do with your friends and how you sometimes address me, I can." He replied, "It's not the same. You don't understand how hurtful it seems coming out of your mouth." I pressed on, with tears streaming down my face. "Because I'm light-skinned? Because I'm a few shades lighter than you, it removes the fact that my family was also part of slavery, that my family was also discriminated against because of their skin color, that my family also has had racial problems with the world? When *IN ALL THAT* did we lose being black and become white instead?" He chuckled. "Aww, I made you cry. You don't get it. You're still light-skinned. And you just can't use the word 'nigga.' That's it." He ended the conversation and left, as he saw that I was getting increasingly upset.

I was angry. This conversation, in the end, was not about whether the word "nigga" should be used or not. I don't condone use of the word and I don't want to use it. But the fact that he was denying my right to use it because of my lighter skin made me feel like I was being discriminated against by my own people. How could he not see that my family and I also experience discrimination? It seems that because of my light skin, I am blamed for the world's discrimination against other blacks' darker skin. It almost makes me want to heed my parents' advice and date a nice Cape Verdean boy who understands the struggle of finding an identity in America, instead of having to explain myself to every new boy I date. The "Who's blacker?" argument gets old quickly.

In America, I often feel I'm forced to choose whether I'm black or white or "other." I prefer to choose "other" because I'm neither black nor white, but being in between creates problems for others trying to classify me. So here in the United States I identify as black, which is the most comfortable category to fit myself into, but I constantly feel like the immigrant stepchild to black American culture.

To make up for the lack of recognition by my fellow black people, I tend to adopt my friends' accents and mannerisms and try to appear "more black." I've become a great actress in the role of black American. My accent changes from southern to midwestern to New Yorker, depending on where the person I'm talking to is from. I've learned to talk about black hair and leave my hair curly to keep from looking "too white." I stay out in the summer sun as much as possible in order to get a tan and appear "more black." I take classes in African American studies, where I often feel that comments from lighter-skinned and African students are delegitimized because we have not gone through the same experiences as the African American students. Once again, there is the divide between Us and Them.

By the end of college I'll be able to write a book called *How to Be Black in America*, based on my experiences of learning how to fit in. Fortunately, I think I've won over most of the student body at college. I'm now seen as black, though some people are still surprised when I announce I'm in the National Association for the Advancement of Colored People (NAACP) or part of the Afro-American Association. I wish I didn't have to mount a campaign to win people over to the identity I have chosen, that I could just be Cape Verdean and be seen as what I am instead of trying to fit into the single category of being black.

Regrettably, my family's ideas about racial identity are less evolved than mine. I don't think they are racist in terms of color, but they are against what they see as the black mentality, based on stereotypes perpetuated by the media and the poverty-stricken environment we live in. My father doesn't want me to associate with black Americans, whom he views as lazy, stupid welfare users. He's always surprised when I bring home black boyfriends who are educated, but they are never good enough for him: "He's pretty educated … for a black boy." My family and

Ana Sofia De Brito

I constantly fight over the way they address black Americans, but it's hard to change their way of thinking when they continue to see the effects of poverty on the black population. This makes it hard for me to explain to them how their words affect me and make me feel like the black sheep in our family.

It's hard to live in a world where fighting for what you want to be seen as is not supported by your family members, which is summed up in what my immediate family marked down for the census—brother: white; father: white/other; mother: other; me: black/other. It seems as if America has thoroughly confused us.

I will continue to state that I am black, despite being labeled a "nigger lover" by my family, being made fun of as the whitest person in a group of "truly black" people, and always having to fight to be accepted as black. Maybe someday these racial categories can be dissolved and I'll no longer have to choose.

Case 4

LITTLE WOMAN FROM LAME DEER

CINNAMON KILLS FIRST

DOI: 10.4324/9781003165378-5

Cinnamon Kills First was raised and educated on a reservation in Lame Deer, Montana. Despite financial hardships and constant responsibilities in assisting her siblings, Cinnamon thrives in her high-school academics and defies the many discouragers and an educational culture of indifference. Surrounded by the privileges of college and away from her culture and reservation for the first time, she experiences a deep sense of loneliness, dislocation, and economic inequality. In time, Cinnamon conquers the academic challenges and grows roots among students from other tribal communities.

Growing up on the reservation means your first thought every day is "I can't wait to leave here and never come back." We see people on TV in nice houses with green lawns going on vacation. The only escapes we know are a week or two shacked up at our snag's place across the rez. We walk from town to town along rural Montana highways in the deathly heat of summer or the frigid winter cold. Cars pass us with duct-taped bumpers, and others with no hoods. We laugh when we see those brave suckers in sunglasses driving a truck with no windshield.

There's nothing to do in the middle-of-nowhere town of Lame Deer. We're a hundred miles from anything and everyone is bored. Our parents drink and fight each other, or sometimes us, and we go to school comparing tragic stories from the night before without missing a beat. There's a belief that "getting off the reservation" is the thing to do but not many know how to leave, or where to go and what to do. Education is one way out. But white teachers lack energy and don't care enough to spark a fire in the hearts of impressionable Cheyenne youth. We hear stories of the ones who go off to school, but we never see them again. I always said I would go to college and never be that person who doesn't come back.

My parents both grew up on the reservation but their education led them to Missoula, Montana, where they connected. My dad's two-year stint at Lewis & Clark Law School meant moving their young family to Portland, Oregon. Drug use, failed coursework, and a miscarriage culminated in their premature return to Lame Deer. They knew how it felt to be far away, and in that distance, their appreciation for home grew. Every summer since I was 5, my dad sat us down under the farthest tree at the limits of our big yard. For hours on end, we had to stare at the hills behind our house while they illegally drank eighteen-packs of Budweiser on a dry rez.

"Look at that!" he would say over and over, sometimes hollering, sometimes slobbering. "My grandpa used to own all of this before the BIA (Bureau of Indian Affairs) came. These hills, the hills behind them, from here all the way to over there," he'd say, waving a fully extended arm. "Isn't it beautiful?"

Despite his excitement, he had four, sometimes five, unhappy kids sitting like bumps on a log. It wasn't long before we were whining to Mom, asking to go inside because it was too hot or it was getting cold, the grass was itchy, we were scared of spiders and wood ticks, or because the mosquitoes were biting. From the hottest parts of the day until a million stars lit the black sky, Dad would sit consuming countless sunsets. "Come. Sit with me. Come look at this." But I complained, "It's the exact same as yesterday! The same field, the same creek, the same trees, the same hills, the same sky." But this view was his breath.

Later, it became mine.

At 18, I moved from the Great Plains to the granite hills of New Hampshire, where I was suffocated by towering, claustrophobic trees. Now when I go home, the simple size of the sky leaves me speechless. My eyes skim in vast circles trying to swallow all that is above. Every time I descend the big hill into the valley of the Northern Cheyenne, I get butterflies and my heart races—that's the feeling I long for. My spirit reconnects with the land. *I'm home.*

Those nights under the trees with Dad, sitting on a log or in the grass, he fantasized about birthday parties, barbeques, and stargazing on a wraparound deck. I would imagine this freshly stained, elegant hardwood sculpture attached to our dilapidated HUD house. I laugh now when I recall these images of grandeur I had in my head about that deck. We never had the money to build such a thing, so I took note and made it a personal life goal. *Build Dad a deck* was right up there with *Take Dad to a Denver Broncos game at Mile High Stadium.*

Working toward significant milestones like this drove me to do well in school. Luckily, school came easily for me. I constantly wondered how things worked. When I was 4, I concluded that our station wagon's air conditioner was probably a huge ice cube under the hood that turned the air cold before it came inside the car. Around the age of 6, my theory was shattered when I realized the ice would melt. I was sent straight back into the world of wonder, but I enjoy it there.

Fortunately, my parents were two college-educated individuals who understood that there was a bigger world out there, and in order to maneuver it, one must be educated. My mom would start mornings with "Wake up, you've got to go to school!" More than that, going to college was an expectation in my home. In seventh grade, I made my two best friends promise me we would go to college together to try to inspire them. It didn't work.

In order to want to learn, one must know what learning is worth. Nearly every home across Indian country is riddled with distractions and discouragement; mine was no different. I will never forget the times we had to improvise when we were out of toilet paper, using coffee filters or crumpled newspaper instead; the times we slept three to a bed and cuddled in the wintertime because the largest window in our house was actually only thick plastic sheeting; or the times we put mayonnaise on bread with cheese and called it the *Cheese Deluxe* because that's all we had to eat. I carry one clear memory of my older brother looking in the bare fridge then turning around to ask me, "Do you want a *Cheese Deluxe?*" with the biggest smile, like he was about to serve me super-special ice-cream cake with extra sprinkles on my birthday. Matching his excitement, I gleamed yes.

We never had a lot but we always had each other. We definitely struggled, but we survived *together.* I made sure of that. When my parents didn't make it home from their drunk-weekend escapades, I stood on a chair to cook dinner for us and crawled on top of the dryer to reach the washer's dial so we'd have clean clothes for school. When they brought the party home, I bathed the babies and put them to bed in the room farthest from the drinking. I sang them to sleep over sounds of fighting. In the morning, I'd wake them and press on knowing one thing: I never wanted my children to someday go through what we were going through.

I joined every extracurricular activity possible so I didn't have to go home at night—student council, Indian Club, Math Club, volleyball, basketball, cheerleading, cross-country, track—the list goes on. These sanctuaries were also résumé builders that I was unknowingly racking up. My parents never attended parent–teacher conferences because, they said, "we already know you're doing good. We don't need to listen to seven teachers all tell us the same thing." A few high-school mentors claimed I could go to any college I wanted, while other teachers suggested I be more "realistic" and enlist in the military instead. I even argued with an army recruiter once. He aggressively questioned how I thought I was going to pay for school and shoved the GI Bill down my throat. Honestly, I didn't quite know how I would but I knew I'd find a way.

School was my escape from the Little Mama responsibilities I had at home, but even school had its own set of dysfunctions. My junior-high English teacher moved to the high school when we did. We were in a different building with a brand-new classroom, yet she was teaching the exact same lessons.

"A noun is a person, place, or thing."

"Ugh, but we learned this last year."

Equally irritated, "We can't move on until everyone understands the basics," she said.

This meant *I* couldn't move on until everyone absent or misbehaving had learned the lessons from last year and the year before. Math class was similar. Ms. Williams would write equations on the board. "Now solve for *x* and give me an answer." She'd turn around to face the class. "Anyone but Cinnamon." On a good day, I'd sit and silently suppress my frustration. On a bad day I'd spout, "Well, what's the point of even *being here*?"

Ms. Williams knew she would lose me if she didn't keep my interest. Algebra material typically taught in one year anywhere else was broken into two years at my school. I began in Algebra IA, but she quickly bumped me up to Algebra IB with the sophomores. The following year, I started with Algebra II before Ms. Williams transferred me into Advanced Math and doubled that with Geometry. My brother wasn't happy when his sister from two grades below was all of a sudden in his class.

Ms. Williams believed in me when I didn't believe in myself, because I didn't believe in myself. Native youth are constantly hit over the head with statistics stating we aren't going to do much in life except make babies, go to prison, get sick, or die young. I never wanted to be one of those statistics, but I didn't always believe I could defy them either. Ms. Williams knew, and her acute attentiveness to my capabilities and partnership in challenging the norm was critical in propelling my academic growth.

Similarly, my literature teacher found ways to push me ahead. Mr. Nelson suggested that in addition to my junior English class I simultaneously take his Advanced Literature course, which was reserved for seniors. He routinely pulled me aside and gave me talks. "I want you to take this book home. When you get to college, they're going to expect you to have read the classics. *Catcher in the Rye* is on that list." So while the class was trudging through *Crime and Punishment*, I was expected to discuss Dostoyevsky, with Salinger on the side (not knowing years later I would share library space with J.D. himself). Mr. Nelson's bright blue eyes held hope for me. My heart understood the seriousness of their expectations. *You can do this. You're going to do this. Not just for you, for everybody.*

These teachers walked me to the unsupportive guidance counselor's office and spoke fervently on my behalf, vouching for why it was imperative I be allowed to take their advanced courses. They went to bat for me against the oppositional counselor. They stand out because they cared enough to carve a path for me; everyone else just schlepped along and expected me to do the same. It was always a fight against a failing system.

There's the story of this girl, Monique. She earned a full-ride basketball scholarship to Minot State University. Every Indian kid dreams of playing professional ball, and those who have a head on their shoulders aspire to play college ball. Just prior to her fall arrival, the university informed her she was one lab science short. She was told if she attended a community college for a semester to earn the credit, her scholarship would be held and they'd keep her spot on the team. Unfortunately, the immediacy of life on the rez has the power to force one's aspirations for tomorrow out of sight as they are blinded by the short-lived thrill of today. As it turned out, Mo soon got pregnant. The fans at Minot State were never captivated by our amazingly talented number 23. Just like that, the potential life-changing college opportunity she had earned slipped away. From the heights of excitement we had for her, we all watched this star fall. We fell with her.

I swore I would never let this happen to me. I studied the state graduation requirements as a freshman and kept a personal, unofficial transcript. During my junior year, the school switched operating software and, in the transfer, my grades had not been entered correctly. The next consultation I had with the counselor included her pressuring me into a class I had already taken. She had no record so she ignored my word and enrolled me in a course I had already aced. I fled her office and returned with my little blue spiral-bound notebook whose opening pages listed each class I had taken, quarter by quarter, complete with grades as stated on report cards. She then began to update her digital records based off my handwritten notebook. I won.

But Indian students in underfunded, rural public schools don't always win. Basic administrative incompetence killed Monique's dream—and we all mourned because it was our dream, too. She was one of our brightest stars, a smooth ball handler with a killer three and the greatest laugh. She is still a living legend all her own, and her smile still shines, but she never got her chance to take classes at Minot, step foot on that court to play under those lights, or snap the net to make those fans go wild. *How many Moniques exist?*

The lives of our children are being determined by bitter indifference. I can count on one hand how many individuals truly believed I had a future. Betty, the Montana GEAR UP coordinator, was in the ranks with Nelson and Williams. When I was a freshman in high school, she encouraged me to attend the Montana Apprenticeship Program (MAP) at Montana State University in Bozeman. It was a six-week long laboratory research program that provided more than $1,000 in stipends. I refused to fill out the forms because I didn't think I'd get in; I wasn't technically old enough. The application only had boxes to mark if you were a sophomore, junior, or senior. Betty said, "So draw a box and check it." After eighteen years of existence, MAP accepted its first freshman.

Despite these academic successes, I was full of doubt. I had my sober parents prepping me for the "real world" and my drunk parents telling me I wasn't going to do anything with my life. In school, select mentors encouraged, "You can do it! Shoot for the moon!" But it was all a cliché. I read those words on stickers and posters for years. It meant nothing. I only thought I stood out because I did my work; that was it. I didn't believe I was smart.

The day I received my ACT test results opened my eyes. Standing there holding the paper in two hands, I learned that I scored above both the Montana state and national averages. That very moment took me out of Lame Deer High School and placed me in context with every other US high-school student. That day, I believed.

Later, I received a recruitment flyer in the mail for the Native American Fly-In Program at Dartmouth College. I was scared to visit the East Coast because I imagined that everything everywhere looked like Times Square. *What did I know?* That October, I was flown to campus, hosted by a Native student, and attended scheduled presentations regarding admissions, financial aid, and student life. I found the "College on the Hill" nestled cozily in the woods. Strangers smiled as I walked across the Green, and it made me feel welcome. I saw the Native students tease each other hard and laugh; then I thought: I could go to Dartmouth.

My college decisions narrowed down to (1) accepting a full ride at MSU–Bozeman, which I was already familiar with thanks to MAP; or (2) potentially taking loans at an Ivy League school that I knew nothing about, which was located clear across the country. Betty warned, "You're accustomed to chaos and you might gravitate toward it in life." She went on: "If you're only four hours away and something goes wrong or your mom calls you crying, you're going to do everything in your power to come home and help your siblings or save your mom. What if that's every weekend?" It was true; my heart is too big. So I intentionally made it nearly impossible for me to return home at the drop of a hat. I put more than 2,000 miles between my family and me. That was the hardest short-term but most beneficial long-term thing I've ever done for myself.

My freshman floor mates were busy exploring the world as fresh-out-of-the-house 18-year-olds, but I was constantly calling home to check on my brothers and sisters. "Do you have clothes for tomorrow? Do you guys need bread?" I often asked teachers and friends to drop off a gallon of milk or spare roll of toilet paper. I played puppet master from thousands of miles away while "schmobs" incessantly toured frat basements, chugging Keystone Light. I couldn't stand the scene because it reeked of the same stale-beer smell that plagued my childhood. More so, that "fun" didn't appeal to me because I was suffering from a reverse sort of empty-nest syndrome. Immense guilt shrouded me because Dartmouth provided a roof over my head, an open-till-2-a.m. food court, and endless water and electricity. Simple things most people don't think about. Meanwhile, I just abandoned my siblings back home and they sometimes went without.

I had real, faraway things to worry about, more important than Earth Science or Linguistics. Oftentimes while studying, I found myself staring at a light fixture that I knew cost more than my entire house. It was hard not to hate the light fixture. It was hard not to hate everything. I felt like Dartmouth carelessly threw money around and I knew so many people who could use it. I was infuriated that people were paid to bag leaves all day when the next time the wind blew, *more would fall*. Ungrateful students would brush past the quiet, gray-haired men who cleaned dorm bathrooms every week as if they weren't somebody's grandpa. They never said "excuse me" or "thank you." I immediately saw two classes of people: those who clean toilets and those who attend Dartmouth, and the latter arrogantly deemed themselves more important. Everything that was prim and proper about my college caused me pain.

I was raised looking *up* at the federal poverty line, so I experienced a unique struggle in the Ivy League. While my classmates went on skiing trips and ventured up to Montreal, I had to work anywhere from one to three jobs to sustain myself (and my family, who often called asking for large sums of money). This meant I could never start studying until after dark. When I walked through the library on my way from class to work, I absolutely despised every student who could do their homework midday and socialize at night. But really, I was just jealous.

More than socioeconomic status, though, the largest degree of difference I held was in my indigenous worldview. In an ethics workshop, each member of the team was provided a false identity including age, race, and skill set. The team's goal was to determine which individuals should be tossed over the edge of a sinking boat in order to save the lives of others. Identities included an older Chinese scientist, a middle-aged African American surgeon, an autistic Caucasian child prodigy pianist, a 2-month-old baby girl, and so forth.

The white kids in the workshop immediately assessed which individuals had the most to offer society once saved, valuing and devaluing people based on age or occupation—dare I say race unspoken. The one black student in the group was left repeatedly saying, "*Women and children?* What ever happened to *women and children*? No one runs into a burning building and starts asking what talents and education people have!" All the while, I sat in complete silence not wanting to expose the fact that this decision was easy for me: toss the baby overboard.

I was taught that we are not human beings on a spiritual journey; we are spiritual beings on a human journey. I believe that we come from the Spirit World and that our physical bodies, this flesh, is what the Creator gives us to live this life here. The spirits of the children and babies would be so new to this world that it would be easier for them to return to where they came from, as they weren't given a chance to fully learn how to live here yet. Sending the children back to their unborn state made sense to me. But saying that in the boisterous environment that was the timed ethics activity would have only served to depict me as a demented child killer, echoing the age-old Euro-American stereotype of the "Savage Indian."

My concept of life and spirit and my sense of self clashed violently with that of my peers. These fundamental differences were the hardest aspects of diversity to endure because I had few options: I could openly express my beliefs at the risk of being judged and ridiculed; I could give an anthro-history lesson every chance I got; or I could say nothing at all and remain misunderstood. At the end of the day, I just wanted to return to live among the like-minds and like-hearts in the lands where I grew up.

These moments make you miss your family, your culture, and your people. It's not the simple challenges of academia itself that makes us want to quit school and move home. It's our obligation to tolerate and educate our ignorant peers *and professors* that weighs heavily on us. I've watched Native students withdraw from Dartmouth, and I respected their courage. At the same time, I hated them for leaving us behind.

Cinnamon Kills First

During my freshman fall, I took Writing 5 and was quick to find the course filled with nicely dressed, full-pocketed city dwellers. Almost all the other Native students had been placed into the lower Writing 2–3. I was alone at this level. I was alone in the class. We read Sandra Cisneros's *The House on Mango Street*, and I was excited to discuss the similarities I found between the underprivileged protagonist, Esperanza, and myself. With every page, Cisneros handed me encouragement in the form of a Latino version of my own home. Her story of hope, using education as a ladder out of an extremely impoverished community, resonated deeply with me. To this day, my heart sings the same song as the last few lines. *They will not know I have gone away to come back. For the ones I have left behind. For the ones who cannot out.*

Professor Thum opened class for discussion, and before I could raise my hand, he called on the blonde Victoria from New York City. Bursting out of her wealthy mouth came a disgust-coated sentence that stopped me in my tracks: "First of all, I just have to say, I can't believe there are people in America that still *live* like this!" My intent to share deflated slowly and painfully. I retreated into silence as the others commented on the dire conditions of the poverty-stricken neighborhood, disadvantaged school, indigent family, and the violence and abuse present in the book. Their privileged lens of perception obstructed their view of the story. They couldn't see beyond the surface of destitution to appreciate the uniqueness of culture, the beauty of Esperanza's struggle, or the amazing triumph she achieved in the end. My triumph.

They couldn't see *me*.

Only those who come from where I'm from, or a place truly like it, can feel what I feel. Like Esperanza, I come from a special place with a unique history. Our tight-knit communities were traditionally governed by warrior societies before the Indian Reorganization Act of 1934. Now, each enrolled member is a citizen of the Northern Cheyenne Nation. Our grandmothers and grandfathers give us stories and songs, and we draw empowerment from that. They make us strong. There is a very particular love and pride that lives at home. It doesn't exist anywhere else. When you leave it, your heart aches for it. There is no money there but that doesn't mean we are poor. In fact, we are rich—rich in land, culture, and family. We are the blood of great leaders, resisters, and protectors. Expressing our inherent sovereignty and freedom was once deemed "hostile." That's us.

I will never forget the words of Professor Thum. He inquired about my lack of participation the day we covered *The House on Mango Street*. I told him I was reluctant to admit I lived in poverty like

Esperanza, but I knew my home was beautiful regardless. I was the only one who held the perspective that I did. There were no other Natives in class to have my back. He responded, "Cinnamon, if you *had* shared in class, imagine what insight you would have given your classmates. The professor's assignments can only make up half of the college education. The other half must come from *you*."

From that point forward, I did my best to speak up in class despite the sense of inadequacy that floated around me. Professors lectured with words I had to take note of and look up in a dictionary later. When other students spoke, they always sounded so important. Often, I couldn't respond in discussions because I didn't understand certain words people used.

I quickly learned: if I had a question, I must ask, and if I had a statement, I must share. What mattered was *what* I said, not *how* I said it. My words might not have been extravagant but they held power. As time went on, my classroom presence grew stronger. After years of being in this intense academic environment, I began to inhale the words of those around me. "Random," "sketchy," and "booted" were a few of the first. Later came words like "Foucauldian," "dehumanization," and "indigeneity." I was always surprised at the taste of these words when they came out of my mouth.

I've come pretty far. When I visited on the fly-in program, one of the Native students on a panel discussed the same issue. She said, "It feels like everyone here is articulate and speaks so eloquently." I focused on the word *eloquently* as it did slow-motion flips in my head, similar to a scene from *Sesame Street*. I think it was the first time I heard the word in context, which only contradicted her point: she was being articulate and eloquent while trying to explain being uncomfortable with everyone else being articulate and eloquent. Years later, I hosted a prospective student from home who was visiting campus through her fly-in program. I knew she was a shy girl but she seemed extra quiet throughout the program. When alone, she confided in me, "Errrret, I feel like I talk just purely *rezzed* out!" *A girl after my own heart.*

Lame Deer is the center of the reservation and home to the Chief Little Wolf Capitol Building. There is one high school, one post office, one grocery store, and one gas station. The only stoplight, a blinking four-way flasher, directs traffic where Montana Highway 39 meets US Highway 212. Beautiful hills colored with red shale and evergreen trees cradle my hometown, which is often splashed with vibrant sunsets and crowned with bright starry skies. In January, if we're lucky, the northern lights will share their subtle rhythms and movement. In

July, we hold our largest powwow celebration and return the favor by singing and dancing into the night.

A passerby may only be able to see the trash that is constantly blown in from the unkempt local dump. There are often plastic bags stuck in tree branches and barbed-wire fences. Graffiti splashes everything: churches, stop signs, houses, buildings, cars, and even sometimes mangy, starving dogs who wander unclaimed. Yards are not fenced and there are hardly sidewalks to speak of. Every lawn has a broken-down car or two, or ten.

The bottom concrete porch step to my house has disintegrated, the front door doesn't fit the frame, and our toilet bowl—rigged with a toothbrush—leaks through the rotting floor into the basement. Like many, we have holes in our walls and mice problems in the wintertime. It gets so cold that pipes freeze unless you keep water dripping all through the night. We have our share of substance-abusing homeless people; the difference is they're our family. That was my grandpa asleep by the side of the chicken coop cuddling Black Velvet in a paper bag. Despite everything, I *love* my beautiful home because that is where my people exist.

Home is shy Native girls approaching their prime with unbridled beauty eating sunflower seeds or pickles or sucking lemons while walking uptown. Home is little Indian boys riding horses bareback down the way to Grandma's house while their rez dogs run alongside them. Home is a tin hall full of pros, double-fisting bingo daubers with six cards in front of them, just waiting for the announcer to call out B-6. Home is a high-school gym full of screaming Indians watching a basketball game as if it meant life or death for *everyone*. Home is the spring flowing fresh and sacred surrounded by prayer flags tied to tree branches honoring that *water is life*. Home is the heartbeat of the drum alive in the same place it's always been—from back when we had everything on into when we had nothing—still strong, even now. Home is in my heart because I couldn't live without it.

I assumed the other Natives at Dartmouth were all going to be rez kids like me. I was quick to learn otherwise. At Native student events, we would begin with introductions. While standing in a circle, one by one, each person would share their name, tribe, hometown, and major. "Hello! My name is Cinnamon Spear. I'm Northern Cheyenne from Lame Deer, Montana, and I'm a Native American Studies major." But then you'd get these kids who would say, "I am so-and-so and I'm *part* Cherokee" or "I am *part* Choctaw." Part this or part that, and that confused me. I thought either you *were* or you weren't. Parts didn't make sense to me. I am from a community that is 99 percent Native and there is no other identity. It was simple: the border towns were full of whites and the rez was all Native. Sure, you'd have those two kids in school who were black or white, but even *they* were Cheyenne.

Then you'd get, "I'm so-and-so and I'm this tribe and this tribe and this tribe and this tribe and this tribe and ..." until the list was ten nations long. I never understood that either. I wondered to myself, "So which *one* are you? Whose *traditions* did you grow up with? Who are the *people* you come from? Where do you call *home*?" But a lot of these students do not know their traditional lands as home and their people have never made up their community. Sometimes these kids have never even *visited* their homelands or even *met* other Natives. I didn't understand them and they didn't understand me.

One time another student asked me, "What are you?" I responded, "Northern Cheyenne." Evidently, this wasn't enough. "Well, Northern Cheyenne and what?" My answer remained, "Just Cheyenne." Then, while scoffing, he saw fit to comment on my complexion: "Well obviously you're like white, so Cheyenne and *what*?" Unfazed but irritated, "*Just Cheyenne.*" I know what I look like, but my appearance leaves only others confused. I know who I am.

My identity is solidly rooted in the hills of the homeland I come from. My blood flows fierce and everlasting like the fresh water from Crazy Heads. My feet can walk among ivy walls, brick, and concrete only because they first ran red-shale roads, played in the dirt at Ice Wells, and stood on Morning Star Peak. My fingers can dance across this keyboard only because they first picked buffalo berries and plums with my grandma, hooked worms to catch fish at Green Leaf or Tongue River with Dad, and even made a million of my sister's favorite mud pies.

I know what I come from, and that drove me to do well. My success is everyone's success. When I felt like giving up on this foreign academic world, my motivation was the many smiling faces and open arms that welcome me home when I return; the little girls that run across the gym plowing into me, excited to see me and giving me a hug; the aunties and cousins who love to hear my stories of travel and adventure; the young ballers and recent graduates who now know college is a possibility for them because they've watched me do it; the cars that pull over crazily on the street to say hi and show me their babies because they never know how long I'll be home.

It is them. They are me.

This community-as-self identity is the source of both my strength *and* my loneliness. College retention rates for Native students are lower than most and it has absolutely nothing to do with our academic capability, interest, or passion. In addition to the systemic racism and institutionalized inequality, it's the simple distance and heartache of being removed from the people, homelands, and love that we were born into that makes higher education difficult for us.

The ruthless individualism and singular success of the "American Dream" directly clashes with the Cheyenne values I was raised to respect. Giveaways are embedded in our social structure to ensure that when one person does well, they share their success with other members of the tribe. Our society functions communally; everyone celebrates and struggles together. There is a profound sense of isolation associated with being more than 2,000 miles away, in the Abenaki people's original homeland, surrounded by a variety of personalities from all parts of the globe. But if you're not connected to a people or tribal community, you don't fully understand the impact of this separation.

Indian country revolves around basketball games, babies being born, funerals, ceremonies, rodeos, and powwows. My first year away, I called a friend who laid the phone by her stereo so I could listen to my little brother play his senior-year basketball tournament over the radio, over the phone. I wanted to welcome my firstborn niece into this world but I missed her Cheyenne naming ceremony by ten days that term. My family has mourned the passing of one uncle, two grandmas, and three grandpas without me there. My education kept me from the 4th of July Chief's Powwow when Northern Cree was our host drum and the Indian National Finals Rodeo where my little cousin was titled the bull-riding champion of the world! Each of these instances causes a degree of social separation. You can't retell those stories if you don't have the memories to share. Missing the highs and lows from home broke my heart, but no matter how bad I wanted to leave Dartmouth, I wasn't going to drop out. That would mean failing everyone.

I had to learn to bloom where I was now planted. I grew to find value and be thankful for the extensive diversity among the students that actually came from other tribal communities. My first friend at Dartmouth was Quinault from the state of Washington. Her grandpa was a generous man, their family's totem was the whale, and she had a beautiful traditional cape in her room decorated with abalone buttons. My Great Plains sisters and I kept each other close because we were *home* for one another. We helped each other bless our dorm rooms at move-in and smudge off during stressed-out finals. My lacrosse player friend invited me up to Akwesasne Mohawk Territory in New York for a game, and his family showed us around their beautiful river waters on a pontoon. My Navajo friend from Tuba City, Arizona, used Mountain Smoke to pray and taught me the importance of their four sacred mountains. My bear clan, Anishinaabe friend kept birch bark in her room, told me Nanaboozhoo stories, and cooked *manoomin* for me often. My Iñupiaq friends from the North Slope of Alaska told stories of seal hunting and whaling; they even had me eating *tuttu* and *uunaalik*. My friend from the Pueblo of Acoma in New Mexico invited me to his Pueblo's feast day, where I watched him participate in traditional dances atop their 300-foot-tall mesa and was teased for having to eat from the "kids pot" because the chili was too hot for me.

Those of us who come from the depths of Indian country have an instant respect for one another based on the shared struggle of everyday life. We understand the intense longing for the beauty that exists back home. We also know how it feels to hear our classmate presume, "Wait, doesn't *everyone's* parents have a 401(k)?" Yet you're not even sure what a 401(k) *is* and your family still lives hand to mouth. Shooting a quick glance in class and locking eyes with another rez kid provides an unspoken comfort in a moment like this. We hold an undying support for one another because our hearts are made heavy, often with good and bad news from home. The stories we catch over the phone range from the most beautiful doctoring ceremony, full of song and prayer, that healed a 3-year-old boy and rid him of cancer to two teenage relatives who partied together, but one woke up bloody in a jail cell not remembering he stabbed his little brother to death while blackout drunk the night before. Everything echoes in our ear and rattles us from afar. But we stay on the grind and push ourselves to thrive in the environment that is Dartmouth—even if only to prove wrong every single person who ever told us, or silently thought to themselves, that we would never become anything more than a teen-pregnancy, prison, or suicide statistic.

When you bring Native students directly from tribal communities together, we provide each other with a unique support system that no institutional office can recreate. Administrative officers hardly understand its depth. You can offer "Speed Reading" classes and tutoring, but no sponsored activity will ensure our success. We need each other. We grow from the cultural exchanges that take place, often around food. We learn of each other's jokes, arts, languages, taboos, traditions, tribal politics, governance structures, environmental issues, and more. There is a real beauty in creating this Native network and it makes each of us stronger.

Families in Indian country encourage their relatives to go to Dartmouth because it has the largest Native student population out of any of the Ivies. Unfortunately, students who came from tribal communities were few and far between. For every rez kid there were nearly twenty box-checkers who merely "identified" as Native American on their college application. There's an injustice done when nearly 200 of Dartmouth's 4,000 students are listed on the books as Native American but maybe only fifty make up the on-campus community on a good day, while the other 350 float around not even understanding the depth of the box they checked.

Being Native American is more than claiming an ethnicity because your great-grandmother was this or that type Indian. It is more than carrying a piece of government-issued paper with a number on it. It's more than teasing about living in tipis or loving commodity cheese. Being Native American is more than throwing on a jingle dress and dancing at every powwow, or using social media to take a stand on trending hot issues, because you can and you think it looks cool.

Being indigenous means knowing you're alive because your ancestors fought and died for you. It means understanding you're the inherent recipient of blood memory, and the carrier of your people's past *and* future. Being Indian means you belong to a tribe. It means loving the living collective of which you are a part, not just knowing its name. It means voting for your tribal president and investing in contemporary local issues.

When I was growing up, my dad would always say, "We are a nation within a nation!" Then I got to Dartmouth and heard Professor Dale Turner echo, "Identifying as an American Indian college student is an intrinsically political act." So I learned early on and had reaffirmed that it's not about "race" or "ethnicity." It's about legal rights and sovereignty, and there's a responsibility in that.

Not everyone even realizes this. Furthermore, not every Native student at Dartmouth has basic familiarity with commonplace cultural and social standards. I knew students who weren't comfortable around the Native community until their senior year. They explained their distance was due to "not feeling Native enough." A girl once told me, "When I first met you, I was intimidated by you. My freshman fall, I heard you speak. You were *so* Native, and I was so *not*." I didn't get what she meant when she said it then. Now, I do.

Dartmouth is in the business of manufacturing Natives. These kids come to dinners and learn to make frybread and *wojape*. They learn how to smudge and pray, and they feel so sacred doing it. They listen to stories of rez life and learn that Indian jokes are really the funniest on earth—even though they don't get them at first. *Ayyyye.* Their friends teach them to bead and how to feel about Indian mascots. They take Native American Studies courses on history and culture to arm themselves with an identity fed to them from books. They read *The State of Native Nations* to find out what Indian country looks like and lives like. They hug the older, wise, and intellectual Tuscarora professor at the end of class, and that makes them feel more human because through her and the love she emanates they feel connected to something real.

It's one thing to know who your people are but it's an entirely different thing when your people know who *you* are. During our Mother's Day Powwow, I sat on the Green in the sunlight at my vendor booth full of beadwork. I had my hustle going. This Choctaw boy excitedly dragged this girl by the arm and stood her in front of me. "Cinnamon, this is so-and-so. She's Northern Cheyenne!" *Oh?* I've never seen her before. "Where did you grow up?" I ask. "California." Per usual, "Who's your family?" She offered a name I didn't recognize. Curiously I question, "Have you ever gone home?" She said no, but added that her father was attending a college reunion somewhere in the state of Montana that summer, as if that was somehow relevant. "You should really try to visit home sometime," I encouraged, for I don't know what it means to be Northern Cheyenne and to never have stepped foot on our homelands. I don't know if she knows either but I didn't feel it was my place to teach her.

The other kids made me uncomfortable by asking questions and wanting to hear my stories while offering nothing in return. I shared, but grew protective of the knowledge I have after I watched one girl steal another girl's story about her grandmother. I was there when the first girl told her story and I was in the same room a time later when the second girl regurgitated it nearly verbatim to unknowing underclassmen acting as if it were her own, but *she* never knew her grandma! I couldn't believe it. I sat in conflicted silence putting walls up toward the culture vultures who took a little of this and a little of that to create their own pan-Indian identity. Exposure to this crazy amalgamation of nations perhaps made them feel more connected, but I was always left thinking they were just still so clueless.

Others read tales of government boarding schools while I've spent my whole life catching my mother's tears as she recounted her traumas, knowing full well that her mother was a survivor of the same destruction. Assigned readings on congressional policy and federal Indian law made me angry and sad because I saw how the government did it all, in writing. It wasn't Amnesty International's report "Maze of Injustice" that taught me that one in three Native women will be raped or sexually abused in their lifetime—my mother has three daughters. Students who come straight from Indian country have lived among the truth that these skewed statistics are reflecting only *reported* cases. This is our reality. Our Dartmouth education only supplements lived experience. So when we read our homework, we are not learning so much as we are reliving, and that takes a deep emotional toll on us.

No one can take college courses or spend a few years around other adolescent Natives and graduate knowing what it's like to *truly* be part of a tribal community. Our homes are made up of elders and babies, dancers and veterans, artists and philosophers, medicine men and drunks. There is a certain way you carry yourself around each member of your community. Culture is composed of social roles and unspoken cues. Living on the land and having a connection to earth, sky, water, and stars are important. Being raised within this structure is what helps fully shape a Native person and with over 565 different feder- ally recognized tribes today, there isn't one set of rules. There is no one Native experience; even *this* is only *one* Native's experience.

Admittedly, it's like I'm writing on eggshells. Reflecting on my ignorant (albeit very visceral and real) reactions to many aspects of Dartmouth is not an easy thing for me to do. It took me years to dispel discomfort, set aside judgment, and actually listen to and learn from the different and difficult experiences of my peers. I eventually felt compas- sion for them—many of them are the living result of the forced assimi- lation policies of Indian removal, boarding schools, relocation, or their parents just moving away to give their children more opportunities, a better life. At the end of the day, it's not their fault.

So while we strive to find balance along the vast spectrum of indigenous identity that exists in the world, Dartmouth should make sincere efforts to recruit, admit, and support not just "Native American" college applicants who likely come from urban prep schools and are sure to do well and make great numbers, but those students in rural tribal communities who are empowered by their cultural connection and draw from that strength to challenge their failed education system for a fair chance. There are standout, drug-and-alcohol-free young leaders who are currently enduring ridiculously unfair circumstances but con- tinue to make good choices, therefore inspiring the younger generations who look up to them. They are fighting, right now, to create a better life for themselves and their siblings or unborn children. They are brilliant individuals, their families cherish them, their communities love them, and they are remarkable ambassadors for their tribal nations.

Dartmouth, as a historically wealthy institution, has both a great obligation and an amazing opportunity in its founding for the purpose of Native education. We are depicted in the college seal as naked savages, complete with feathers in our hair, being guided out of the wilderness toward civilization under the rays of the "Good Book." To this day, the weather-vane scene of founder Eleazer Wheelock towering above an unidentified "Indian" sitting cross-legged on the ground eerily overshadows our entire Dartmouth existence. For four years, we live under images of colonization that sit atop the beloved Baker Tower. A feeling of inferiority can reverberate deeply within us because of this, but students from tribal communities come from and have access to arts, medicines, languages, songs, philosophies, entire *worlds* of knowledge that others do not. We have the power to reverse the roles and sit the colonizer and his descendants on the ground to teach above them. *I think I'm doing that right now.*

Dartmouth took me from my people in order to educate me about many different things. After a while, I decided, "You know what, Dartmouth? Let me take *you* home and teach you something." I spent seven months during graduate school on the rez and used my master's thesis project to produce a documentary. I took the beauty from home and put it on screen for others to see, hear, and feel. My film, *Pride & Basketball*, explores the theory that, in the postcolonial era, the basketball court has transformed into a modern-day battlefield where historic tribal rivalries are relived and non-Native race relations are played out. Since our young warriors are no longer riding up and down across the open plains stealing horses, earning war honors, or protecting our homelands, the court is one of the few places where our young people are acknowledged for their bouts of bravery and leadership. A sense of individual, familial, and communal pride is derived from what a person can do with a basketball in their hands.

While filmmaking, I was welcomed into the lives of the youth, their families, the school, and the community. My people honored me by opening their homes and hearts to me, sharing their words and giving me their tears. An outsider wouldn't have been able to create the product I did. I was fluidly in the classroom, locker room, and on the bus with these kids. I stood in prayer with my young relations, and sang the Cheyenne Flag Song with the drum at the start of every game. The coach asked the players to circle up and listen to me share stories of college and travel. I encouraged the youth to want more for them-selves—not to *leave* the reservation but just to be a better person, and be the best at whatever it is they love to do. Formal education isn't for everybody; and as much as we need people to leave and learn, we also need people to stay and learn.

In the history of Lame Deer High School, which opened its doors in 1992 and maintains a 50 percent graduation rate, I am so far the only student to have gone to a four-year institution and graduate in four years, the only person to attend the Ivy League, and by far the only one to receive a master's degree. I know what I represent and I recognize my responsibility in this. For the first time ever, the word "master's" is floating around my reservation. I've heard young men say, "You're making a film about basketball for your master's? Man, I want to get a master's!"

Just the other day, I got a message from a young girl back home. "Ever since I can remember, you've been my role model, gradu-ating from Lame Deer and going to an Ivy League college. I want to be just like you, successful. You're beautiful in every way. There are like rays of sunshine that spring out of you every time I see you. You're spec-tacular. I love you." My heart soars. Words from the youth are the purest affirmation that I've done it the right way: I left the rez, but I've never left the rez; I am still there, and they are still with me.

We're taught to be humble about things so it always makes me a bit uncomfortable to speak this way, especially awkward having to write it. When I shared my uneasiness with an older lady friend of mine, she responded, "I know it never feels right tooting your own horn, but you, my girl, need to blow it loud for your relations!" People ask me, "How did you do it?" and it's always hard for me to answer that question. One step at a time, I guess. Creator has and continues to bless me as I journey in this life. I have been gifted with voice and the ability to craft words to create images. It's time for us to tell our own stories, and I will tell them for all those who share my experiences but cannot write them down this way.

Writing is my sanctuary, my freedom, but also my duty. As I fly back and forth between poverty and privilege, both states existing on and off the reservation, I realize I am a super-exposed, bicultured hybrid. With that, it is my responsibility to teach the world about the Northern Cheyenne people, and, likewise, it is my responsibility to teach my people about the world.

Mókéé'e náheševéhe. Natsistahe.

"You have a strong name," my aunt told me. "*Little Woman*. That was your grandmother's name. You should always let the people know who you are, in Cheyenne, when you speak."

I am of the Morning Star people; I dance with and for the Thunder Valley *tiospaye*. Though I come from the sky, my heart beats from deep within the hills. At the core of my identity is the land—it is who I am, and I am where I come from.

Case 5

LOOKING INTO
THE SUN

JACK CARPENTER

DOI: 10.4324/9781003165378-6

Jack Carpenter

In Jack's childhood, he and his friend fight, play, and explore. By middle school, these friendships fall away, and Jack sees himself (and is seen by others) as a nerd, someone who has difficulty understanding how friendships work and what is expected of him. He develops a few close friends in high school with whom he can laugh and have adventures, but in college, again, the few friends he makes drift away, and he does little to keep them. A period of depression, during which he cuts his wrists, is followed by the re-emergence of both male and female friendships and work toward a more conscious connection to others.

My first memory—my best memory—is of Jason and me charging down my front yard under a bright summer sun, armed with neon plastic baseball bats and wildly clipping the heads off of dandelions.

> "Defend Dandelion City!" Jason yelled.
> "Defend Dandelion City!" I called back, swinging wildly.

We ran across the open field, driven by a frenzy of energy. We slowly tired out, sat down on the ground, and figured out what to play next. And that's how it went, day after day, during summer vacation: just my best friend and me running through life as one big adventure.

With about fifteen other kids in the neighborhood and my brother Tony, who is a year and a half older than I, I was never at a loss for something to do. We roamed freely from yard to yard, into the woods, along the river, to the fields behind Mr. Davidson's house, and back home again. Time was measured by when we all had to be home for dinner. Neither I nor any of my friends had a particular identity: at any given hour I was a king, a spy, a police officer, a Ninja Turtle, or a ghost. I didn't even realize that there was or should be anything different about the two girls on our street—they joined in naturally with our large group of boys.

We filled the yards around Driver Lane with noise and running and games every evening during the school year and all day during vacations. As soon as we finished our morning cereal, my brother Tony and I rushed outside to knock on doors and find out who was around. When my brother wasn't around to fight, play, and explore, Jason and I were inseparable. Being kids together was great: Anyone could be anything, and at the start of each new game there was a sense of freshness, a feeling that anything could happen.

As I moved into middle school and high school, I dwelled on those memories in a way that I knew meant that stage of life was gone. What happened to those days? Everything seemed so open and free, so warm and happy. I have such good memories of being a little kid. I have mostly bad memories from then on.

When I was in fourth grade, my parents took me to the optometrist. I was supposed to be picking out a pair of glasses, but no one had glasses in fourth grade except Erica, and everyone thought she was a complete nerd. And now I was getting glasses. I knew what this meant for me.

"But Jack," the optometrist cooed, "you'll get to pick out your own pair of glasses. And there are lots of people who think glasses look really handsome."

"And," I sniffed, "and that's supposed to make me feel better?" I knew the optometrist was just trying to make me feel better, but I vaguely hated her for treating me like this. The world could be cruel, I knew, and I didn't want or need anyone to help me blind myself to that fact.

By the end of elementary school, my adult teeth started coming in with visible patches of orange on them. The dentists didn't really know why; they guessed it had something to do with having too much fluoride or being sick when I was a baby. I felt like the ground was sliding out from beneath my feet, that I was still a kid but the kids around me weren't. There was a way they looked at me, as if from a distance, and I learned that it meant they were judging me. I wasn't the same as everyone any more; I was becoming somehow different. Around girls I began to be nervous and couldn't think or talk straight. I still had a couple of friends to play cards and games with, but it didn't feel like being back with the kids on Driver Lane. There, everyone did everything together; here in school, some kids would play with you and some kids wouldn't. Before long, I realized that the number of kids who would play with me was getting smaller.

By sixth grade I didn't have many friends—really just one, another kid also named Jack, who also had glasses and liked reading. Most other kids either made fun of me or humored me, both of which were painful. Jack and I used to talk about time travel and outer space— his dad was an astronomer, so Jack knew about all kinds of interesting things. Jason and I saw each other less and less in school. We weren't in the same class anymore, and the teachers started putting me out in the hallway to do math problems on my own. Doing math became a minor addiction with undeniable social consequences that I tried to ignore.

Besides, Jason had grown—a lot. He looked good, and I felt a sense of awe when looking at him. One of the girls on Driver Lane had a crush on him now, and she was so nervous around him that she didn't spend time with us anymore. More and more, I looked at Jason like an older brother. He was bigger than me, he got along with other kids better, and I knew that he'd protect me from the other kids at school. Meanwhile, my actual older brother was having a much harder time fitting in—it began when he took an interest in music and the arts. But despite all the help I got from Jason and all the time we spent together, I started getting the sense that Jason and I were just friends out of habit.

The problem with me keeping friends was that I liked school. No one liked the kids who were good at school. I figured this out about three years too late. Before I realized it was happening, I was already labeled a nerd, a fact one of the neighborhood girls shared with me one day on our hour-long bus ride home: "Yes, Jack, duh, everyone thinks you're a nerd. You have glasses and you read books and do math all the time. I still think you're okay—I mean, you are a nerd, but I don't think it's that bad."

What? A nerd? What does that even mean? By the end of middle school, I knew very painfully what it meant. No one wanted to talk to me at school, and the other kids didn't even bother waiting for me to leave the room before making jokes about me. What had happened? I was so lost; things were hitting me too quickly. I had no friends. Even the other Jack stopped talking to me—he still looked kind of dorky, but people accepted him. And I had nowhere to go; my grade at school had only about eighty students, and everyone knew everyone's business and where everyone stood in some invisible hierarchy that remained elusive to me.

In middle school, new things kept happening that I didn't understand. On a bus ride home in seventh grade, Jason asked me if I wanted to go to a sleepover. He was inviting Jake and Mitch, too. Jake was in one of my classes, and I didn't know much about Mitch except that his parents were divorced. Jason and I used to do sleepovers back in second or third grade, but we hadn't done one in a while. The thought of being welcomed back into their circle was exhilarating.

During the whole sleepover, I felt like electricity was running through my veins. I got to eat potato chips and stay up late, but that was nothing—during a game of truth or dare, I made the very difficult decision to actually tell the truth about liking Stacy Pilamar.

"You like Stacy Pilamar!?!?"

"Yeeeahhh," I confirmed, tentatively, waiting for their response.
"*Everyone* likes Stacy Pilamar."

"I don't," said Jake. They started talking like a noisy crowd.

"Yeah, right, I bet you do. Everyone does, she's so hot," said Jason.

"Yeah, well, she's not as hot as Jessica."

"You think Jessica is hot?"

"Hot boobs at least."

"Jessica Barone, not Jessica Smith."

"Well, duh, not Jessica Smith. She looks like a cow."

"Yeah, I know."

What was going on? I had never heard anyone talk like this before. I'd never even told anyone that I liked Stacy Pilamar.

"Stacy Pilamar. Good choice," said Jake.

Mitch interrupted, "Still not as hot as Jessica."

"Do you think I have a chance with her?" I asked, figuring they'd probably know better.

Mitch laughed and then stifled it. Jason didn't say anything and looked at Jake.

"Well …" Jason started, "maybe. I mean, I don't know. I don't talk to Stacy Pilamar much."

"I bet she totally likes you," said Mitch.

"Really!?" I asked

"No," Jake said, shoving Mitch. "He's kidding."

"Wait, really?" I asked again.

Jason said, "Um … well, why don't you ask her to dance or something?"

Mitch laughed.

"What?!" I demanded.

"Nothing," said Jason. "Hey … come on, let's play Super Mario."

Later that night, Jake went to his backpack and pulled out a videotape.

"Check this out," he grinned.

"Aww, you brought it! Sweet!" laughed Mitch.

"What is it?" I asked.

"Porn, duh," said Jake.

I watched in absolute silence as I saw body parts and things being done that I had never even imagined. I was intrigued but also embarrassed, and felt like the other guys were violating some private moment by cheering at the screen and commenting on what was going on.

"You guys, Jason's parents are going to hear us and we're going to get in trouble," I warned nervously.

"No way, we're all the way down in the basement and they're asleep. Besides, watching porn without the sound on is lame."

Afterwards, Mitch and Jake made fun of me for being silent during the porn and for not wanting to go with them to set off Black Viper firecrackers behind the Davidsons' house.

That sleepover left me feeling completely stunned. On the one hand, I felt closer to these guys, and closer to Jason, than I had felt toward anyone in years. But I also felt like I was getting in over my head: I didn't understand why they said most of the things they said, and although the gossip and swearing and dirty talking was exciting, it also seemed strange and wrong. But these guys were cool and I needed them to like me.

I had the same problem at school. The guys made fun of me a lot, and most of the time I had no idea what I had done. Even the guys who felt vaguely like friends acted as if they would turn on me if I did the slightest thing wrong. Things were even worse with girls. At a school dance I finally did ask Stacy to dance. She said yes, but in her awkwardness and lack of eye contact, I knew she was just dancing with me out of pity. Sad and angry, I told myself I was going to change.

I figured if I wore clothes that were more like everyone else's I could pass for cool, or at least not be made fun of. I pushed my parents to let me get contact lenses, and the dentist was finally able to put shiny white caps on my teeth. It was my first year of high school, and I had been doing 300 sit-ups per day since the end of seventh grade. Jason told me I'd get stronger if I drank more milk, so I stopped drinking soda and started drinking about eight cups of milk every day. Bit by bit, I figured out how to get by, although I still didn't like or trust almost anyone around me. I needed a friend, someone who wouldn't hate me, and I needed a girl—at least one decent, respectable girl—to like me.

Meanwhile, the Driver Lane kids didn't hang out together anymore. One girl became popular—and later, a heroin addict. Tony spent all of his time practicing for band concerts and going to an Air Force training club. He'd show up at home only to grab a bite to eat and then dash out the door again. Jason was in different classes and could bench-press more than my body weight. His older brother spent all his time in the band room, and kids started joking that he was gay. The kid who lived behind me started hanging out with the "dirties" who smoked in the school bathroom. As for me, I started to read philosophy: *Zen and the Art of Motorcycle Maintenance* and *Siddhartha*, Alan Watts and Krishnamurti. I became obsessed with how to get past what I considered the shallowness of cool kids, ditsy girls, showing off, pointless assignments … everywhere I looked in the world I thought people were shallow and simple, and I hated it. Every once in a while, I'd look out across the fields where we all used to play, and they'd be silent. It was eerie.

Tony and I still had each other. We had always been close, and over time we grew out of our petty brotherly squabbling and developed a kind of pilot–copilot relationship in everything we did. He built things and I programmed the electronics for them; he was the driver and I was the gunner; he learned to juggle and I learned to hold him up on my shoulders while he juggled. We gave each other code names, and with a touch of pride and mischievousness we referred to ourselves as The —— Brothers. Yes, we were still close, but he just wasn't around much anymore.

Around this time, I was lucky to make a couple of friends. The first was Andy. I was invited to a sleepover for a bunch of kids who liked a card game that I was into, and Andy accidentally broke a door latch at the host's house. I noticed that he was upset and scared that he would be sued and unable to pay for the door. I didn't know him, but he seemed really upset, so I found a few tools and put the door latch back together. When I was done he asked if I wanted to play Super Smash Brothers, a video game, and he began teaching me the game that we would go on to play together for years. We also played cards and cracked jokes—what we called our Regulars. So started a friendship that lasts to this day.

The second boy was Scott. We had played on the same junior soccer team for a few years; we were both fullbacks. We'd talked a bit, but we started hanging out together when we found that we both liked playing some of the same trading card and video games. Finding these two friends had come at a good time, as my brother had an increasing interest in the Air Force training camps, and I wasn't his copilot anymore. Whenever I asked him to do something with me, he was suddenly too busy chatting online with girls or off to do something related to the Air Force.

Like me, my father finds interpersonal stuff stressful. His job often involves dealing with unpleasant issues in human resources. He once said his favorite job before he got promoted had been writing bus schedules because it was like solving logic puzzles all day. His tendencies became more apparent to me as I got older. One time during high school I slept over at my girlfriend's house for New Year's; my parents and I had a miscommunication and they didn't know that I was planning to do that. The next day, as my dad and I were running errands, he kind of stared out the windshield and began a torturously drawn-out speech that went something like, "You know, the things that you do … can have consequences … and if something should come of actions that you take, it can affect your life in the future, so you have to be careful about things that could jeopardize …" I cut him off there. "Are you talking about me and Kristen? We're not having sex, Dad, it's fine." He seemed relieved and the conversation was dropped. By that point, I didn't blame him as much for his behavior. He had told my brother and me more about how stressful his own childhood was, and had even told us that he had seen a social worker to talk about his difficulty interacting with people.

When I think about my life, I realize that my parents didn't have a clear or decisive impact on my life. I don't think they've ever cared if I was a scientist or a teacher or an investment banker. Instead, they provided some kind of silent guidance. Looking through my old toys later on, I realized that the majority of them were educational, like chemistry kits, a microscope, puzzles. I liked that lack of direction from my parents, as I felt like I could do whatever I wanted. I think it contributed to my disdain for following directions (I lasted two weeks in the Boy Scouts and a month in the Civil Air Patrol) and gave me a chance to develop an independent mind. So, in their way, my parents had a big influence on me. I picked up a lot from them—patience and evenhandedness from my mom, being hard-working (sometimes to a fault) and not complaining from my dad, and a desire to live simply from both of them. These are character traits that they slowly transmitted to me over time and by example, so while my parents are important to the person I have become, there aren't many clear moments for me to mention.

It is my friends who have had the most noticeable, moment-to-moment influence on my life, and on that front, things were starting to clear up somewhat by high school. My new friends picked on me a little, but it was usually harmless one-upmanship and joking. I had trouble getting used to that. Finally, one of my friends told me bluntly, "When someone makes fun of you, just chill out and go with it. It's just joking around; you shouldn't take it seriously." And we laughed. When I think back to high school, that's about all I remember: laughing so hard that my sides hurt. That's not because our jokes were clever—they probably wouldn't make sense to anyone else—but because we learned to make fun of the world around us, to laugh at the ridiculousness of other people, the profoundness of stupidity, and the arbitrariness of teachers and parents.

And, bit by bit, I found myself in serious conversations with my close friends. Scott and I would talk about our frustrations with girls, and

Andy and I began forays into "what does it all mean?" Discussing how I felt about things was tough: most of the time I had no idea whether I was sad or jealous or angry—even happiness was tricky. I didn't always trust myself to be too happy, fearing that if I thought I was happy, something very bad would likely happen to me.

I was strongly drawn to these new conversations. Andy and I would go for hours-long walks around the school or the park and talk about girls, philosophy, track and field, and frustrations about school. We spent hours outside school practicing discus throws while talking about our throwing form and about life. I was impressed at how down-to-earth Andy was. In matters of girls, friendships, and relationships, he offered sound advice and gave me some much-needed help understanding other people. He predicted, for example, that my first girlfriend would want to marry me ("Some girls are just like that with their first boyfriend; they think they've found The One"), and he was right on. This was weird, because Andy wasn't even in honors classes.

I felt better, more relaxed about life. Scott, Andy, and I spent all of our free time together doing something: playing ping-pong, video games, cards, Frisbee, pool. Even as we talked about our hopes, our fears, and girls, we were always doing something. I didn't think about that until one of my teachers mentioned the differences between how guys and girls talked, how guys would sit looking at something else, whereas girls would face each other. I thought this over a bit. The idea of looking Scott or Andy in the eyes as I told them about myself ... it would be overwhelmingly awkward. I didn't try it. I could talk to girls that way, but I couldn't talk to another guy that way.

But it turned out that I couldn't always avoid having to face my friends and talk. Bored one Saturday night with nowhere to go, I lounged around a dusty TV room with a few track teammates who I didn't hang out with much. We were looking for an adventure. Adventure, adventure, always looking for an adventure. Our collective desire to Do Something became more and more heightened with each break in the meager conversation, and each time we looked at our limited options. We lived in Millhaven, where there are three stores that all close before eight.

Someone suggested getting in the car and driving around: "Let's just go out and see what we find." Maybe we hoped that if we went out, something crazy and exciting would happen. By this point, however, I was 16 and more skeptical of that possibility; the older I got, the smaller town seemed.

As we were about to drive past Scott's house, one of the guys suggested we pull a prank on him. No one had any good ideas and besides, Scott's parents were not the sort to take a prank lightly—their house was furnished with the neatness of a museum gift shop. One of the guys bought a pack of cupcakes, so we settled for sticking two cupcakes to the windshield of Scott's van and drove away giggling. When Scott found out, he didn't talk to me for a week. I found this ridiculous, since we were in all of the same classes, did track together, and had about a 95 percent overlap in our group of friends. After a week, Scott approached me after track practice.

> "I expected more from you," he said, staring at me with a disappointed look.
> "It was a joke! Just some stupid prank," I protested.
> "I thought, here's a guy who's got my back, no matter what. And then he does something like this," Scott said, more upset than I expected.
> "Dude, it didn't mean anything, it was just a joke."
> Our conversation continued like this, reasonably, but on two completely different planes. Eventually I got the sense this wasn't working.
> "Look," I said, searching for a way to get through to him, "I don't consider this important. I see that you do, and for that I'm sorry. But you know that if anything really big happened, you know, like something serious, I'd have your back."

I really didn't know what I meant. I knew he wanted to hear this and that I did like having him as a friend, but I couldn't imagine what something "serious" would be. A breakup with a girlfriend, I guess, or maybe if someone tried to beat him up. Scott seemed relieved: "Thanks man." I thought to myself, "That was strange." Our friendship went back to normal.

Although we saw each other every day, I didn't understand Scott. We both ran track, did well in math, played the same video games, even liked the same girl a few times, and yet, I didn't understand so much of what he did. We spent a lot of our free time together, but he seemed to alternate between being very demanding and not caring about me. He didn't congratulate me when I got my SAT scores back. When I told him that I was voted track captain, he just stared straight ahead and was silent. And when I found out I was accepted early into Dartmouth College, he darted out of the classroom without saying a word. I thought he was a pretty weird guy sometimes. I mean, wasn't he the one always talking about the importance of friendship?

There wasn't much time left to figure it out. As college acceptance letters came in, I knew that soon we'd all be going our different ways. I would be going up north to study government, while Scott was going to be hours away studying engineering and Andy was headed to a local state school to study art. After all the hours we spent getting to know each other, I guess I should have been upset about leaving, about having to start over. But I wasn't upset, because even as our last summer vacation came to a close, I just couldn't imagine it happening. It just didn't seem real.

On the day of my high school graduation, I didn't ask anyone to sign my yearbook and I left early so that no one could take pictures with me. Being there felt awful.

College was interesting. Once we all got past the first few months of telling stories about the pranks we pulled in high school and the places we'd gone on vacation, I found out that the people there were interested in discussion, interested in thinking. This was a nice change of pace: I could bring up a book I read without being called a nerd. I could share my musings about how society worked without getting blank stares.

On the second day of school I had found the Ultimate Frisbee team, a mysteriously open-minded group of astounding athletes and good-natured partiers. By the second half of my first year, my large roving pack of freshmen, high on possibility, had been narrowed down to a small group of teammates sobered by familiarity. I split my free time between Jack and Kate. Jack was another young man who looked much like me, struggled endlessly over ideas of morality and relationships, and shared my name. Kate was a cute girl who seemed fun. Besides, ever since I started dating in high school, I hadn't gone more than a couple of weeks without a girlfriend, and I really wanted one again.

I dated Kate for a year, even though after the first month I knew we had nothing in common and couldn't stand being around her. Most of the time I didn't even want to get intimate with her. But whenever she wanted to break up—about twice a week—I would adamantly defend the idea that we could make our relationship work.

"We just don't have the 'spark' that it takes to have a good relationship," she'd say. "There's no such thing as spark. A relationship is just about getting along," I said, thinking her naïve. Then one day, like so many other days, she called and said she wanted to break up. Something must have suddenly changed in me, because I just said "okay" and was glad it was over.

Shortly after breaking up with Kate, I started flirting with Aldina. Aldina was like a drug for me. She was everything I wanted and kept me in enough delicious pain to keep me coming back for more. She read constantly, despised the fakeness she saw everywhere in the world, and swore viciously in unprovoked fits of rage. One hour we'd be lying on the college green, looking up at the night stars and asking ourselves about the point of living, and the next hour she would hit me and scream, "Get away from me, I'm no good; I'm just going to end up hurting you more!" Once I took her chicken soup when she was sick, and I couldn't read her expression—it was somewhere between thankful and sad. She was a challenge and a mystery, and I wanted to learn more, to share her pain.

I stopped trying to meet new people and held on tightly to a small, familiar circle of casual friends, all Ultimate Frisbee teammates. I indulged in the familiar, feeling warm and satisfied while lying down with five or six other girls and guys, having hot cocoa, and watching movies or playing Super Smash Brothers for hours and hours.

But something was wrong. I began intentionally misleading the people around me about my life. I rarely mentioned Aldina. I implied mysterious involvements, rarely looked people in the eye, and avoided giving straightforward answers to even the simplest questions.

"Where are you going?" Jack asked, catching me as I was leaving our room.

"I don't know. Nowhere, just doing stuff," I said.

"Are you going to see her again?" he asked, disapprovingly.

"I don't know, maybe," I said, flashing a grin. And maybe I was. And maybe I was just going to the dining hall.

I still managed to have some conversations with teammates, since I was often asked for advice. I shared with them the painfully idealistic thoughts in my head; looking back, I think people told me their problems because I was calm and listened, not because of the advice I gave. Jack and I were starting to grow apart, as he had begun seeing a new girlfriend and was becoming disenchanted with Ultimate Frisbee. I wonder if Jack knew that he was my only friend. As he drifted out of my life, I didn't fight to hold on to him.

I had a few confidants left—all girls. But they weren't quite friends. I couldn't hang out with them like I could with guys, getting comfortably lost in games. And there was always the chance that one of you would start liking the other. But they had such a powerfully attentive way of listening, and I was constantly amazed that I could get such sympathy and thoughtfulness from them, no matter what I said.

Around this time I started cutting my wrists. I don't know why. I didn't particularly want to die, although I always figured that it wouldn't matter if I did—after all, I'd be dead so I wouldn't care. That thought was oddly comforting and I indulged in it. I hid the cutting and didn't tell anyone about it, but on some level I was hoping someone would notice. I sometimes wore an armband, both as a way to cover it and a way to draw attention to it.

Cutting myself was an exciting secret. I could feel the imminent possibility of death, a liberating thrill. It was the final ace up my sleeve, and I liked the idea of always having an escape route. Besides—and I felt this without any sense of drama, emotion, or exaggeration—I just didn't see the point of staying alive.

Aldina had once asked me, in the midst of trying to sort out some Big Questions for herself, "Aren't you afraid that your life might just amount to nothing, that you'll just, I don't know … die and fade away into nothing, and no one will remember you?" Looking up at the crumbling ceiling, I considered the question briefly. "Actually, I think that's inevitable, and kind of a nice thought," I replied.

Telling my friends about the cutting was unimaginable. Eventually I did tell a couple of people, girls I was close to. Come to think of it, I've never told another guy about it. I wouldn't want them to try to help—that would be way too uncomfortable. If they ever found out I would say to them, "Never mind, whatever, that was a long time ago," and try to end the conversation as quickly as possible.

I never sought help, either from a professional or from friends; in fact, I didn't even think I had a problem. My world felt lonely and crazy, like a noisy bazaar where nothing really got done and most people were just looking to get what they could from you and leave. This feeling was sometimes relieved by moments of stunning natural beauty—like the time I hiked across a snow-covered farm near my house. As I stared blankly at the white expanse, I felt gripped by a force I can't quite explain. It felt like The World, the big world, was calling me back to its peaceful stream, and when I held a knife in my hands, I felt like maybe I could go join that peace. But those were the rare moments.

Returning home wasn't much relief. The pace of life in Millhaven now seemed painfully slow, and I didn't talk to my parents about my personal life. Andy was still around town—something about him seemed like he would never leave. My fingers danced over the familiar pattern of his phone number, and I wondered what it would be like to see him again. Finally, I drove up to his front door, just like always, and with big smiles we dove right into a rush of inside jokes and "remember when" moments. We sat in the car, blasted ska music—just like always—and I drove us off into the night.

It was like time in our friendship had never moved.

We drove through memories: by Turner's house on the corner, past the fields where we threw discus, through the little town, same as always. We settled into our Regulars: absurd humor, Super Smash Brothers, cards, tea. But half my mind was outside the room wondering, shouldn't things be different now? The inside jokes started to make me feel uncomfortable.

"And then Mr. Roberts would probably come by with just a grilled cheese sandwich!" Andy quipped.

I chuckled distractedly.

"It's just like that time when Donnie was like, 'Hey guys, we gonna throw discus today?'"

The situation was starting to wear on me. Shouldn't we have changed? Grown? So much had happened to me. Having the Regulars as a backdrop to all of this was at least some comfort.

As I drove Andy home, we decided to take a walk somewhere, just like we always did. I picked a hill near the orchard; we'd gone up there in the past to meditate. We silently made our way up the hill in a combination of reverence for the night and avoiding being caught. We got to the top, and looked out at the night scenery below us. There was a silence between us, periodically broken when one of us felt compelled to say something profound or funny. Mostly we just looked out and thought our thoughts.

I dropped Andy off without much more talk, and drove home wondering what would become of us. The familiarity was comfortable but it had started to seem shallow to me. Was that all we had? I looked back on all the time we spent throwing discus. What had it amounted to? And was I someday going to look back on my current life and friends the same way? I was leaving again, and I had no idea what things would be like next time I came back.

Little did I know I was headed off to the most miserable month of my life. Midway through my junior year, I took a trimester off from school to work in Shanghai with a friend, Kim. However, Kim hadn't actually been looking for a job and the trip turned into a mere journey abroad. I felt obliged to stay with her to look after her. I was miserable. Shanghai was much colder than expected, but since I considered the unproductive trip a waste of time and money, I refused to spend money on a winter jacket. Or on adequate food. Or on new shoes when mine became worn and uncomfortable. Or on museum tickets, tours, or activities of any other kind. Kim found me insufferable and depressing. "It's like you just can't let go of things," she said. When she told me this, I broke down and cried for several hours. It was true, and I knew it. I cried guiltily for all of my misery and all of the unhappiness I had brought her.

Those few hours of crying were a beautiful catharsis, and afterwards I felt resigned to letting go of my numerous philosophical disagreements with the trip. I smiled more and tried to make sure that Kim had a good time. That became very important to me. But underneath it all, I still couldn't let go of something. I saw how I had ruined our trip and felt pressed to change my life and my attitude in some way that I didn't quite understand.

In the spring after getting back from Shanghai, it was once again Ultimate Frisbee season. Things were looking better. I had a few more friends on the team and didn't feel quite so isolated when the team traveled to tournaments. I stopped hooking up with random girls at frat parties, which always left me feeling empty. I also started to get to know one of my teammates better, Mason.

Mason is tough to explain. He's the most brilliant person I've ever met and probably the most empathetic guy. He almost never slept and would do crazy things, like showing up at my apartment at random hours of the day wearing a pirate costume and carrying a boom box, a board game, and a bottle of vodka, and suggesting that we start a game of drinking Candy Land.

We started talking on and off, but I didn't think much of it. He was one of those guys everyone on campus recognized, and I figured that to him, I was just another face. But I found myself sitting on a couch with him more and more, talking about my Big Questions. We both stared out from the couch, as if peering into an abyss. I felt a kind of comfort in talking to him—he was good at listening attentively and then offering his thoughts softly, usually not by telling me something directly but by asking questions to get me to say more about my thoughts.

There was once, just once, when I shared my feelings about sex to him. I almost didn't say anything, and when I did I felt a naked discomfort. I continued awkwardly working my way through how to talk to him. When I finished telling him, Mason was smiling.

"What?" I said.

"No, nothing Socksy," he replied, calling me by my Frisbee team nickname.

I looked him over for a bit. "You've been grinning this whole time," I said. "What's up?"

"It's just … I'm so excited for you," he said.

After he left I tried to figure out why he was so happy. I think it was this: I was starting to open up, and he noticed.

While on the Frisbee team, I had long been critical of taking the game seriously. I tried hard and wanted to improve and become very good, but I felt that caring too much about it would mean more attachment and eventually more pain. I was silently critical of teammates who seemed too invested in winning.

That spring our team found itself making a fierce comeback in a game that would put us on track for nationals. I was on the defensive line with Mason, who was playing even better than usual. In the end, we did it—we came from behind and won. After the game, we were exhausted but happy and out of our minds cheering. At that moment we really came together as a team. Mason was crying, I think because he found it all so beautiful. When I saw him I felt like I'd been hit on the back of the head. What had I been doing? I felt like a little kid who'd been pouting, while Mason lived to put a smile on other people's faces—including mine, no matter how hard I resisted. I had to wake up.

In my senior year, I started going out of my way to welcome and mentor the new freshmen. And I really enjoyed it. I also was dating Summer, a thoughtful and quirky girl from another college whom I met playing Frisbee. We had so much in common and quickly became close. We'd go for long walks, sharing and laughing and getting to know each other. I think she's the first girl I've dated whom I really cared about, not as a girlfriend but as a person.

In the past, whenever I had a disagreement with a girlfriend, I'd think she was just crazy or needy and not thinking straight. I wasn't much interested in taking an open and honest look at her or at myself—I just thought I was right and wanted to prove it. Maybe I had been maturing without noticing it, and of course it helped that I actually liked Summer, so when she was upset I really felt bad too. That was new to me.

At any rate, things were looking up. I had fewer bouts of depression, although there were still some. I cut myself only rarely and it felt less intense when I did. I started having conversations with friends about ourselves, which was tough. It was still so much easier to talk about some shared interest like Frisbee or Super Smash Brothers, or to talk about our personal problems as abstract things, like, "I think there's too much pressure these days to be successful."

One conversation that sticks out was with one of my roommates. He was talking about what his plans were for after college, and I had the sense that he was upset. I instinctively wanted to pull back from the conversation, but at the time I was sitting in the passenger seat of his car and couldn't leave—at least he was driving and couldn't look me in the eyes. So he talked, staring straight ahead, and there was pain in what he said: pressure from his parents, feeling lost about his life, a loss of control in his relationship. It hurt me to listen to it, and I sat there squirming. In the end, though, we did talk. I asked him questions, threw in some assurance and advice, and in the end felt a lot closer to him. We had been roommates for three years but hadn't had an open conversation until then—just a few months before graduation.

Getting closer to my guy friends was a funny feeling. On the one hand, they were fun, interesting people I wanted to talk to and get to know better. On the other hand, talking to them about their pain and fears was for me like getting a shiatsu massage: I knew it'd probably feel good afterwards, but while it was going on I felt a pain deep in my core. I couldn't figure it out—despite all my introspection and meditation, this habit of avoiding closeness didn't make any sense to me. These were, after all, my best friends.

Everything seemed to come to a climax at the end of college. It was about a week before we all departed, and the seniors were lazing around in the indolent days between the end of finals and the start of the graduation ceremonies. Mason came bursting into my apartment ranting excitedly about "the coolest trail he'd ever seen" and how we "had to go." By that time, mainly through Mason's influence, I had learned to ease up a bit, to leave my comfort zone and try things even if I didn't immediately see the point. We talked about things on and off as we made our way to the trail, which led down to a small outlook over the river. We found a broken-down couch there, where we sat and continued talking, with the conversation drifting toward more personal territory. We looked at each other on and off; I was getting better at making eye contact with other guys when talking about serious things.

I don't remember exactly how he told me, but he ended up saying something about how he really liked me. He might have even used the word love—he was the kind of guy who could say that about other people. I don't know if I've met any other guy who could pull it off. I was blown away; it was the first the time another guy had said something like this to me. "Mason," I told him, "I have no idea what you see in me." "I know, Socks," he said. It's been two years since that conversation and I still don't get it.

That day Mason also talked about some things he was worried about in his life. Like everyone else, I respected Mason for being so outgoing and determined to help everyone feel welcome and have a good time. I thought he was invincible. But he told me then that he felt compelled to be like that because he was insecure about whether people liked him. I didn't know what to make of that, but I was at least somewhat comfortable hearing him out and I opened up about some things in my life too. I told him how I was crippled by a lack of meaning in my life, that sometimes I didn't feel any reason to live, and that I felt like a man living after the world had ended. I felt better after having said these things to him. It is a happy memory for me.

College graduation day was sad and awkward. I stuck around for pictures and to say a few goodbyes, but it hurt to hear everyone tell each other that they'd keep in touch, since I knew that a lot of them wouldn't. Sure, we were all friends while on the Frisbee field together or while playing Super Smash Brothers, but would any of it stick? Mason and Jack and everyone else—would I ever talk to them again?

I knew Summer would be staying in my life. The more we got to know each other the more we found that we liked to do together—cook, run, read, travel. I could talk to her about anything and be bluntly honest about parts of me that I was afraid of.

Feelings of depression were much rarer for me now. I was starting work as a teacher, a job that kept me on my toes and thinking more about my students than about myself. I had always heard that helping others was supposed to feel good, but I didn't grasp how true that was until I had the chance to experience it for myself as a teacher. I stopped cutting myself, not by making an active decision but by letting go and forgetting about it. Cutting had drifted into my life on some unremembered day with little conscious thought; years later it similarly faded away.

There was, however, one clear moment along the path to stopping: the suicide of my cousin. He was very young, just barely a teenager. The reasons aren't completely clear, but he seemed easily frustrated, often unhappy, and had recently gotten into fights with kids at school. What affected me about his death was that I saw myself in it—I kept telling myself that it could have been me. Seeing that, I realized that being alive was a kind of gift. Seeing him die and realizing that I could have died too made me feel like I had been brought back to life, that

I had both the dead man's gift of putting down his burdens and the living man's gift of life. I somehow felt as if I had died too, but that since I was in fact still alive, I could live peacefully on borrowed time.

In retrospect, I am not sure how to understand my cutting. Part of my uncertainty is that I never had anyone to talk it over with, to help me anchor this confusing situation with experience and an outside perspective. I also wasn't in tune with my feelings at that time. Maybe I was alone and sad. Maybe there was something therapeutic about the way cutting made me feel—like I had my own life in my hands. Sometimes I didn't feel like living, and sometimes I just felt like trying to make others notice me. How serious had I been about what I was doing and how much was I playing? There's no easy answer, and I don't worry about it anymore. I told very few people about it at the time, so no one asks me about it now. I still don't quite see it as a problem, but as some harsh terrain I had to cross and have no desire to tread back over.

The summer after graduation I moved back home. The next day, Andy joined me in my living room, where we played Super Smash Brothers, drank tea, and played cards. We talked about how weird it felt to graduate. He asked me about Frisbee. We got lost in another hour-long game of cards. I realized I'd never asked him about his art before. I made a mental note to do that sometime.

A little bit later I got an email from Andy: "If you want to hang out I've been working on this theory that we DON'T have to do it for eight hours. We can just watch a documentary or go to the park or something so the entire day isn't sacked."

I was sort of shocked when I received this. Did he feel like the day was "sacked" if he spent it hanging out with me? Or did he think that I didn't want to hang out with him and was trying to be polite? I realized then that I had no idea how he felt about our friendship—was he just seeing me out of habit or out of boredom, or did he actually enjoy doing things together?

I don't know what to do next. Andy and I joke around a lot, so it's hard to tell what he is really thinking sometimes. But in recent emails, things don't seem like jokes. For example, he casually dropped in a line about having panic attacks at three in the morning. I know that his parents are stressful for him, that he went to college to become an artist, and that he was laid off soon after getting his first job and can't find a new one. I want to help Andy, I want to say something, but I have no idea how to do it. I guess that's the way it's always been for me. I could never quite face my feelings around friends, couldn't quite share something about me that was real and raw. And although I'd like to open up with Andy, I'm afraid it'll be too painful to see how he's feeling all at once, to look at his feelings face first. It would be like looking into the sun. Did I ever mention that? That's what I think friendship between guys is like: the sun. You know it's there and if you pay attention you'll feel its warmth, but you can't look at it directly.

Case 6

A LATINIDAD
I CANNOT, WILL
NOT, HIDE

VIANA TURCIOS-COTTO

DOI: 10.4324/9781003165378-7

Viana Turcios-Cotto

Viana grew up in challenging circumstances in an impoverished New Jersey city, where she was raised by a passionate single mother who had journeyed from Honduras to the USA in search of a better life. Viana escapes the under-resourced educational system by receiving a full scholarship to an elite private high school, but is faced continually with the stigma of being an affirmative action student and is haunted by the fear that she is "not supposed to be there." At her Ivy League college, Viana becomes more confident in her abilities as a student, asserts her pride in her Latina identity, and finds a place within the school's tight-knit Hispanic community. As she gets involved with her 6-year-old brother's struggles at her old elementary school, Viana makes plans for a future in education and child psychology while recommitting herself to her heritage and family ties.

"Yeah, the thing that I like about SEEDS (Scholars Educators Excellence Dedication Success) is that it's based on economic status instead of on racial status," I say as Lisa and I walk to lunch. "They have cutoff points. Your family has to make no more than a set amount according to the number of people in your family. So we have white kids in the program too. I think colleges should do something more like that rather than just look at race."

"See, I still have problems with that," she replies. "If I were to have applied to SEEDS, I wouldn't have been accepted. See, my thing is—what about those like me who are in the middle class and can't get help because we make too much money, but aren't rich enough to go to boarding schools and stuff? … It's not fair that we don't get any help just because we have more money than you."

Frustrated, I say good-bye and walk away, pretending I am in a rush to get somewhere. I cannot help but feel that Lisa was upset that I was able to get into a program like SEEDS, and somewhat envious that I went to Phillips Exeter Academy. She thought it was unfair for people like me who "don't make as much money" to get help. Sometimes I feel like yelling, "*I'm poor!* It's not that we make slightly less money than your family, who own a house in the suburbs and can afford to take family vacations and buy all brand-name clothing and go tanning and get their hair done all the time. *I am poor!*"

Too often, I see the white middle and upper classes argue against affirmative action. I, too, disagree with the proposed action that is based on race; but I support programs that base aid on economic status. Many white people are poor as well and could use the kind of help I have received. I feel Lisa thinks that only a few people of color deserve to attend selective schools and the rest who go are granted free rides. Does she think I deserve to be there?

"You went to Exeter?" That is the shocked response of almost everyone, no matter whether white, black, or brown, once I reveal that I attended Phillips Exeter Academy. Yes, it is a prestigious, elite, majority-white school, but it, too, had to join the trend of diversifying its student population. Therefore, a little poor brown girl from a little poor city was the perfect answer for Exeter. I was the exact opposite of the stereotyped rich white male Exonian. However, I was not accepted into that school or into my Ivy League college just because I am "brown" or Latina, and this is something I have had to prove to myself and to many around me over the past seven years.

Growing up in poverty, survival was a challenge. The oldest daughter of a single mother, I helped her raise the three younger children since the two fathers did not. I worked hard in school because I knew that was what was expected of me. I was the typical overachiever who worries and stresses, which I do to this day. Somehow I have succeeded academically, but no matter where I am in the world, I am always reminded of the money troubles that my family faces.

What has gotten me here? Why have I made it all the way to college when so many others from similar backgrounds have not? Maybe it is my mother's strength or high expectations. Perhaps it is because I am the stereotypical overachieving oldest child. Could it be because of my teachers and their support? Could it be my determination and resilience? Maybe it is the poverty that I am fighting to get away from. Perhaps it is because I can project myself into the future and plan accordingly. Could it just be fate or luck? This is what I am trying to understand.

My first memory takes me back to when I was almost 4 years old. By that time my mother and father had split up. My mom, my younger sister, Isis, and I relocated from New York City to Paterson, New Jersey. My father had court-ordered visits and was allowed to take Isis and me to his apartment on weekends. One weekend, instead of returning us to my mother, my father abducted us to Honduras, my parents' native country. He moved us from concrete hut to concrete hut in the countryside of Honduras every two weeks. I am told we were in constant motion for six months during which 2-year-old Isis and I ate white rice every day with Honduran black beans in a bowl full of black bean water. While Isis always remained at home with our father, I was allowed to walk down to the *pulperia*, or market, across the street by myself, but Isis and I were never together without our father around.

Viana Turcios-Cotto

My memory of my rescue is that I am 4 years old when a woman with sunglasses and two men in suits walk into our dark, concrete hut. Running through the darkness with me in his arms, my father and I reach the backyard and he propels me over the concrete wall, in an attempt to hide me in another yard. The woman shrieks, "Danilo, what are you doing? Don't let her go!" My shirt lifts up and my belly and chest rub against the rough concrete wall. My toes desperately search for a solid surface to rest on but all I feel is cold water in the deep laundry sink full of water beneath me. A man runs to me, wraps his big hands around my tiny waist, and thrusts me back over the wall into my father's hands. "What the hell are you doing? Are you crazy? She would've drowned! Take her back!" he remonstrates. I am now back in my father's arms and we are in the living room. Isis is hiding, crouched behind the sofa chair my father and I are sitting in. I am perched on his lap, head buried into his chest and arms wrapped tightly around his waist. "Danilo, let her come to me! Let her go!" the woman demands. "I'm not holding her back!" My father lifts his arms to demonstrate my freedom.

The strange woman with sunglasses speaks directly to me, "Mamita [Sweetie], don't you see who it is? Don't you recognize me?" She pulls her sunglasses off. "Mami? Mami!" I scream. "Isis, it's Mami! It's OK!" Jumping off my father's lap, I dive into my mother's arms. A huge smile stretches across my face as I squeeze my mom with my skinny arms. Isis deserts her hiding spot and dashes to my mother to join the reunion. We go to a hotel room where we shower and put pretty dresses on. My mother has told me Isis and I ate with such hunger it seemed we had not eaten in months. The next time I saw my father was through court-ordered, supervised visits in the United States when I was 8 years old.

My father has been a big part of my life, although he has not been around for most of it. He never held a steady job because he would hardly ever go to work; when he did, he was usually late. Because of him, the man I marry will need to be ambitious and motivated, not just *seem* educated like my charming father. He must be a man who seems likely to be with me forever. I will not be rushing into any weddings! And I know that I, too, will be ambitious, motivated, and making my own living in case things do not work out as planned. I cannot be dependent on him because I will not allow myself to need welfare like my mother did when she left my father.

I have spent much time wondering why I am so resentful and unforgiving towards "that guy," as Isis and I have termed him. Is it because I blame him for our poverty? Is it because I feel I grew up fatherless? I think it is because he had nothing to complain about and yet he could not handle being a father. I am mad because of all the lies he told us. He had three beautiful, smart, good, loving daughters; spent four years gaining Isis's and my trust and love back; had a second chance when Jasmine, his third daughter, was born; and yet he chose to throw it away, chose not to fight for it, to give it all up. When I was 12, he took another trip to Honduras and never returned, losing his U.S. residency. Luckily for him, this means he does not have to worry about the 50,000-plus dollars in child support that he owes my mother.

I just thank God for giving my mother the strength to leave my father when she did, because I cannot even imagine what my life would have been like if we had stayed with him any longer. Although my mother has been human and thus not perfect, she has been my fuel, my inspiration to accomplish all my goals. I have never met a woman with my mother's relentlessness and strength, and I hope to emulate even half of it. At age 17, my mother left Honduras for Paterson where she had family. She and an aunt, Concha, hired a *coyote*, a man who helps people get across the border for a living. They trekked through northern Mexico and swam across the Rio Grande at the U.S. border. When I was 17, my challenge was to finish my fourth year at one of the world's wealthiest schools. Deportation and death were not real concerns.

My mother has four children and has raised all four alone. Although she is still with the father of the two youngest children, we do not all live together, not because we do not want to, but because of circumstances. Mario has his own business, a laundromat, in Brooklyn. He has provided financially for all of us, especially his own children, but my mother has raised all four without him living with us. "Mario, you need to sell the laundry and just move in with us," my mother asserts. "The day you want your children's love and affection they're going to give you a kick in the ass and they're not going to want to deal with you. They haven't had their father around like they should have." His living arrangement has been one of the few sources of arguments between my mother and stepfather.

Maybe if Mario had lived with us, I would not still be resentful towards my father because I would have had a replacement father. Mario has been involved with my mother since she left my father, but I did not truly feel that I loved him until the end of high school. In order to survive, my mother went on welfare and was able to go to school to learn English while welfare paid for Isis's and my private preschool and day care. My mother never had a steady job but always had odd jobs that ended quickly. For a while she cleaned apartments and worked in a department store. She then sewed in a clothing factory with her sister Lydia and many other immigrants, most of whom were illegal.

My mother continued to apply her knowledge of sewing by making dresses for her girls and sewing beautiful stuffed bunnies, which she sold for sixty dollars each. Sewing is my mother's education. She became a seamstress at the age of 15 because her parents could only afford to send one child to school. My mother dropped out so that her older brother could graduate from the military academy, *Escuela de las Americas* (the School of the Americas), an academy based in Central America but headquartered in Georgia. He was supposed to become a great general and be successful. Fortunately, he dropped out of the school, which produced heartless killing machines for Latin America. Although he did live as a wealthy businessman in Honduras, he is now an illegal immigrant in the United States, earning less than my mother. Unfortunately, my mother was never fully educated. She took adult classes to learn English, she cannot write grammatically correctly in either Spanish, her native language, or English, and she cannot get her General Education Development test (GED) because she does not remember algebra or geometry.

However, sewing and all her odd jobs were not enough for her to support the family. Mario did give my mother money, but he also did not make enough to support himself and all five of us. The real problem was that there was a six-year difference between the youngest of the first pair of children, Isis and me, and the second pair of children, Laura and Anthony (Tony). Isis was finally going to school when Tony, the youngest child, was born. That meant my mother had to stay at home until Laura and Tony could attend school because she could not afford a babysitter or day care. Therefore, my mother stayed on welfare, a system with security that also assured her 300 dollars a month in food stamps; WIC (Women, Infants & Children) vouchers, which gave us free food such as dairy products and baby formula; Medicaid, which covered medical expenses; and Section 8, which subsidized our housing.

Many people believe that those on such public assistance wish to live that way and enjoy the free money. I hated it. It still brings such pain and tears to think about being on this assistance for ten years. My mother did not find a job and get off assistance until I was 14 and on my way to Exeter. Welfare had a program that sent people to a vocational program for a few hours during the day and then into a part-time job in the afternoon. The proudest I had ever been of my mother was when she was placed in "Food and Nutrition" at a nearby hospital and was no longer in the welfare system. While preparing trays of food, taking them to patients, and then picking them up, she plodded throughout the hospital for hours each day. My mother's joy and relief at getting off welfare compensated for her tired feet and achy back. Tears filled my eyes at the thought of my mother having a job and us getting off welfare. I did not have to go to Exeter as a child on welfare. When people asked me, "What does your mom do?" I could proudly reply, "She works in a hospital." I did not care what she did; I told them honestly that she brought people food and worked in the cafeteria. What I cared about was that my mother had a job, finally.

In order for my mom to work, and since I was leaving for boarding school, Isis had to help around the house. Isis and I—well, mostly I—had been babysitting the younger kids for seven years. I was definitely nervous about my daydreamer sister watching over them, but it all worked out. My mom regularly worked twelve-hour shifts. A few times she did not get home until two in the morning, but it all paid off because she was given a full-time position with benefits. After five years of working at the hospital, my mom and a manager got into an argument, which resulted in her simultaneous quitting and firing. While she got her license for commercial driving, my mother collected unemployment checks. For a few months she drove a school bus, but was then hired by New Jersey Transit, the state's public transportation company. She is once again starting at the bottom, working part-time and fighting her way to a full-time position with benefits. This job seems to be the one she is going to keep because the hourly wage is in the teens, and once benefits kick in, everyone in the family, including Isis and me, will be covered.

Honestly, what keeps me going is knowing how much my mother was able to handle. With all the pressure she had to support us and keep us fed, clothed, and healthy, my mother never turned to inappropriate behaviors such as prostitution or drugs. She taught by example and she taught me to work hard and keep a positive attitude.

As much as I love my mother and as much as I consider us to be friends, there is one thing that we will never see eye to eye on: her racism. Although she says she is not racist, my mother holds racist views. Ironically, her family is dark-skinned. I am one of the lighter members of the family because of my father's fair complexion. I am the color of creamy peanut butter and my mother, like many of her siblings, is the color of cinnamon. My Aunt Lydia has pleaded with my mother to understand and accept that we do have black ancestry, but it is always to no avail. "No, Lydia, our grandmother was not black. She was a bit dark but we aren't black. That's it!" responds my mother firmly.

Two of the biggest arguments I have ever had with my mother centered on the clash of our views on race. The first happened the summer before my first year of high school. Isis and I had been contemplating how to raise the topic for weeks. That weekend we were in Brooklyn visiting Mario at his apartment. Knowing what I was about to say, I took a deep breath and we walked into the small, dimly lit kitchen. Mario, with his back resting against the wall, sat on one of the little chairs around the square table. My mother sat next to him at the round corner of the table. "Mario, we wanted to talk to you and Mami about something. Now, I know that sometimes you guys might just be joking and stuff, but Isis and I … well, we were just feeling that sometimes you guys sound racist. I just don't like how you guys say some stuff sometimes." I stood in front of my mother darting my eyes between their faces and the floor as I passed this judgment on them. "What?!? No, we're not racist! I mean, I understand what you're thinking, but we don't hate black people or anyone. Whatever, if you don't bother me I'm fine, ya know," Mario defended himself. My mother's response, which was in itself racist, was: "I tell you all the time how I played with the black kids in Honduras. We would jump rope and go to school together. We don't have anything against black people."

My mother and Mario sent us away, as we held our tongues and remained unconvinced by their replies. On the way back home to New Jersey at the end of the weekend, my mom secretly admitted, "You know, Mario might be a little racist because his uncle had a restaurant in Honduras and his uncle hated the blacks that went to the restaurant. So I think that attitude rubbed off on him a bit. But I did play with the black kids."

Three years later, after finishing my junior year of high school, I am watching some talk show like Ricki Lake, when my mom comes in and sees a black woman and a white man kissing and says, "Ugh, what a sight." My mother looks down at my brother, who is about 8 years old at the time, and says, "Papito [Sweetie], you know you can't marry a black girl, right? It wouldn't be good." She continues speaking, laughing deeply from her belly as she makes an inappropriate joke I cannot remember now. She added, "People should just stick to their own races." My brother looks up at me from his spot on the carpet. With furrowed brows he asks me, "That's not right, right Viana? What Mami said isn't right, right?" I looked at Tony as I shook my head and rolled my eyes in disapproval of my mother. "No Tony, Mami isn't right. You can marry a black girl if you want to. As long as you love a person it doesn't matter what color they are."

Hearing my comment to Anthony, my mother yells from the kitchen, "And don't think I don't know about the boy you went out with. I know that black friend of yours was your boyfriend, don't deny it!" "Yeah and … so?" I defiantly reply. I knew what her issue was but I had had enough. "So? So!" my mother echoes in astonishment as she returns to the bedroom and begins screaming angrily at me. "Everyone should be with their own race; blacks with blacks and whites with whites!" I get off the bed and scream back: "Yeah, except that you'd prefer I be with a homeless, dirty white guy! Just as long as he's not black, right Ma? Whatever, I'm never gonna think like you. Just accept that! We should all stick to our races except that all of us should be with white people."

As I beat the mattress with a plastic soda bottle, Isis runs into the room and pushes me away from our mother. Having been screaming so close to each other, we had one another's spit on our faces. Anthony crouched on the floor in a corner, wide-eyed, not believing what he was seeing. "But being with a white guy is different!" my mother asserts. Isis, tired of being caught in the middle, yells, "*Yah!* That's enough! Stop it, both of you! Look, poor Tony. You OK, Tony?"

If we were cartoons, my mother and I probably would have been bright red with steam coming out of our heads. She left the room and I wiped my face of the tears that had spilled out with my anger. I still had one last thought, and I was not going to hold my tongue because she was already mad and I wanted to piss her off even more: "And what you don't know is that I have had white boyfriends, and Hispanic boyfriends, and mixed boyfriends! I don't care whether they're brown, black, white, green, yellow, red, purple! As long as he treats me good and we like each other, I'm happy!" I proclaim myself the winner of this argument since I had the last word. After hearing about the ordeal, my Aunt Lydia confessed that the thought of me being with a black guy kept my mother from eating for two days. Since that day, my mom and I have not spoken about race and race relations.

In Paterson I went to school with other Latino children, but also with blacks, East Indians, whites, and a few Asians. Paterson is a racially mixed city with a mixed public school system. In high school I was surrounded by people from places like Saudi Arabia, Japan, China, France, Mexico, Colombia, as well as most of the United States. I was also exposed to students in homosexual and bisexual relationships. This diversity has continued in college and has shaped my open-mindedness.

In the seventh grade I and eight other Paterson students were accepted into the program that led to my argument with Lisa—New

Jersey SEEDS, which was for disadvantaged children with academic talent. It involved intensive summer sessions and Saturday classes during my eighth-grade year. I recall my excitement in telling the news to my seventh-grade homeroom teacher one Monday morning. "Mrs. Mitchell, I got in!" We were in the hallway, getting ready to go into class and start the day. When she heard my news, her eyebrows, cheeks, and lips all moved upward, as she let out an excited squeal. Mrs. Mitchell was a strong-looking woman with broad shoulders and must have been almost 6 feet tall. She grabbed me by the wrists, and began flinging me up into the air while she jumped around in circles, forcing me to jump with her. She laughed, and all the students looked confused about all the excitement. At the time, Mrs. Mitchell was the only one who really understood the implications of my acceptance into the SEEDS program.

That summer the nine of us, along with another fifty or so students from West New York, Jersey City, Passaic, and a few other cities in New Jersey, were bused to a private day school in Englewood, New Jersey. After a tough but fun summer, the group was reduced in size by half based on the quality of our work, each student's effort, and how well each student got along with others. Phase II, the worst of the three phases of SEEDS, was dark, cold, and way too early. Every Saturday morning I caught the bus at 6:30 for classes that began at eight and ended at three. I had my SEEDS homework, which I did every Friday night, along with my daily eighth-grade work. During this phase we learned algebra and prepared for high school English and the Secondary School Achievement Test (SSAT). We also applied to and interviewed with private secondary schools.

When I asked two classmates in Phase II why they stopped coming to the program, the male said he had to get a part-time job and help around the house, and the female said her parents did not want her to go away to school. They were both Latinos. Of the nine Paterson students that had started out, six were Latinos. I was the only Paterson Latino to make it through the whole program. Two boys did not accept the offers they were given by private schools because not enough financial aid was awarded and because of long bus trips. That means that out of nine students, only two of us attended a private high school. I was honestly just lucky with Exeter.

I showed up to my Phillips Exeter interview in blue jeans and a T-shirt because I was so unexcited about interviewing that I did not bother to change my clothes after school. Worried that her broken English would not be good enough for the interview, my mom seemed more nervous than I did. I went into the interview and honestly do not remember doing anything other than just relaxing and talking to the woman as if we were hanging out eating ice cream. I have no recollection because I truly did not care, and for once I was not worried. After the admissions officer spoke with my mother privately, both women reappeared, laughing so hard and being so moved by their talk that my mom was wiping tears off her cheeks. "What the heck just happened?" I thought. We said our farewells and went home.

After a few months, the admissions officer who had interviewed us called our house. She left me in shock when she told me I had been accepted to Exeter, and she left my mother crying tears of joy. She also informed us that we were getting a free train trip to visit the school. My mother called Mario and all my family members to tell them that I was going away to New Hampshire to attend private school. As soon as I arrived on campus I fell in love with the school. I was lucky: I later learned that my grades and SSAT scores were not necessarily Exeter level, but they were great for a student from Paterson. I also learned that the SEEDS staff had only asked me to interview to fill empty time slots because the Exeter admissions officer had been nice enough to make the long trip to New Jersey.

My acceptance into SEEDS was very different from the acceptance into Exeter, but both had similar goals. Each wanted to help out underprivileged, bright, hard-working students. However, SEEDS accepts students based on economic status. Basically, if you are a promising student and your family is near or below the poverty line, you are accepted into SEEDS. At Exeter, grades were definitely a factor; my SEEDS advisors had to vouch for me because of my C in algebra. But instead of taking only economic status into account, Exeter considers race.

Every April, when college acceptance letters were coming in, affirmative action became the most controversial topic on campus. "You don't have to worry, you're Latina. Everyone's looking for Latinos. It's easier for you to get into college. But I'm Asian so it's gonna be really hard for me because I have to be so much better than all the other Asians," commented a friend nonchalantly. During high school I heard this regularly. The problem with affirmative action is that, too often, those who do need that extra help do not get it. Instead of accepting poor blacks and Latinos into these elite schools, those who get in are usually well-off.

People who claim a Latino background often come from wealthy families that do not even acknowledge this heritage until it is time to "check the box" on an application. This fuels the idea that "you are only here because you're Latina." I have been very involved with clubs and extracurricular activities at school since my elementary years. However, in high school I did it in part because I enjoyed them, but also because I thought they were my main ticket into a good college. I also thought they would give me some value, importance, credibility at such a fancy school that I "wasn't supposed to be at."

I was accepted at an Ivy League college, but during my freshman fall trimester I thought that I was not capable of surviving and would have been better off at a non-Ivy League school. That term I earned a high C average. I did not believe in myself and started believing what people had said: that I was only accepted because I added color to my class, not because I am capable and smart. That winter I worked hard to see what some effort would get me. My average that term was 1.22 points higher than my fall average. I started believing.

My involvement with nonacademic activities is how I demonstrate my value to myself and others. I have not only mentored and done research but also volunteered at the local public schools and been a teacher's assistant for a college course. I recently won a national scholarship, was granted a prestigious summer internship, and was tapped into a senior society. This is how I show others and remind myself that I am capable of being at such a great institution. It is not just because I am Latina but because I can bring a different experience, intelligence, and drive to the table. I *am* worthy. I must never forget that.

At college, I am very aware that I am Latina. Although I am light-skinned, I am still darker than most of the students all year round, despite their artificial tanning. My hair is long, wavy, dark, and very thick: I "look Latina." My *Latinidad* is so apparent that I cannot hide it, nor do I wish to. When I walk down the paths here, I hold my head high and look straight ahead. I have to show that I am proud to be who I am, even though I am different from most.

During my first year I was more involved with the Latino community than I am today, in my junior year. I attended meetings of the student Latino organization and enjoyed going to the dinners and dances put on by the Latino fraternity and other groups. Although I am still friends with a few who are involved and am still friendly with most in the Latino community, I have drifted away from it. Nevertheless, I am still known by most of the community members and as a Latina on campus. A few weekends ago, when newly accepted high school seniors visited the campus, I stopped by the reception at the Latin American, Latino, and Caribbean Studies house. I did not recognize the female giving advice to the visiting Latino high school seniors in the living room, but I thought it was my own fault because I never hung out with the community.

I whispered into a male Dartmouth student's ear, "Yo, Mark, do you know who she is?"

"Not a clue!" he immediately whispered back. Then he added, "I've seen her around, but all of a sudden she wants to show up at something and hang out with the Latinos. You know after this weekend she'll disappear and we won't see her ever again."

The Latino community at my college is somewhat unforgiving if you do not make your Latinidad always known. What is funniest about Mark's comment is that he never hung out with the Latinos his freshman year. The statement he made about the female in question is how I felt about him when he all of a sudden decided to join the Latino fraternity, even though he had never made himself a part of the community. Knowing how hard it could sometimes be to accept the group and have the group accept you in return, Mark was still as unforgiving of the woman as I, who had accepted the group and was accepted from day one. Logically, ethically, I know it is not good to reject people like this woman, because it can be a hard community to break into. People have their personal reasons for not being involved, and sometimes it is just because they do not like the others or because they are afraid of being rejected. Instead of helping these people make a smooth transition into the community to make it stronger, we talk about them behind their backs and fulfill their suspicions. We might act like this because we are bitter towards those who "checked the box" just for admissions purposes. Claiming Latino-ness to better their chances of admission, they deny it once they are on campus. It is frustrating because my college boasts that 7 percent of its student body is Latino, when in reality only about a third to half of that percentage self-identify as Latino. The college believes we have made great strides and that diversity is at its peak, but in fact it is not.

My strong Latina identity is interesting to me because I have not always felt I embody the culture. At home I have always been the skinny one in the family. My aunts and uncles called me *flacucha* or *flaca*, skinny girl, while growing up. They called Isis *gordita*, little fat girl. After years of this, we accepted our roles—Isis has accepted that she is the chunky one and I have always tried to be the skinny one. Thinness is the thing that all admire and try to achieve in my family. Therefore, Isis has been harassed by family members like our Aunt Lydia, who would tell her to stop eating because she was too fat and would warn me whenever I looked like I was gaining weight.

Isis's chunkiness, though, provides a body that many Latinos admire, with curves that our culture has accepted and that are typically beautiful features. Many give Jennifer Lopez credit for showing off her body and making a curvy body acceptable, but they fail to realize that her shape is newly acceptable only in the white community. A voluptuous, curvaceous body is what Latinas have always desired and what Latinos have always been attracted to. On Spanish-language television, thin women show off their hips, round bottoms, and breasts that add to the curves.

Perhaps more significant to my family than Isis's body type is the challenge confronting Tony. My brother has been diagnosed with a learning disability in reading and as having both attention deficit hyperactivity disorder (ADHD) and oppositional defiant disorder (ODD). Having been told that he learned differently, he felt that it meant he had a "mental problem," as he puts it. He believed that he was innately dumber and less capable of succeeding in school. Therefore, he struggled to learn how to read, and when it was too hard he became frustrated, yelled at whoever was helping him, and walked away from the reading session. He eventually stopped trying because he was afraid of failing.

Having read Tony's individualized education plan (IEP), which informed teachers and parents of what the school was doing to attend to Tony's learning difficulties, I noticed that a few things stated in the doctor's report were not addressed in the IEP. Fortunately, I had taken a great course on special education in my freshman year of college. Taking the course to better understand my brother, I learned the laws and practices and the steps a parent could take if their child was not being adequately served. Sophomore year, in early September, I was at home when Tony's fifth-grade teacher called on three of the five days of his first week of school. I talked to the guidance counselor, school psychologist, and Tony's teacher on my mother's behalf. They were convinced that the school was not enough for him and that he needed to attend a special education school with kids at his intelligence level. Although Tony has many difficulties, he is a very bright boy, but because he has very little self-control, he is unable to put his intelligence to good use.

After hating his school at first, he has just finished his second year there, completing sixth grade. Now he is only a few months behind his reading level rather than two years behind, and he has become more confident that he is smart and capable of succeeding. Striving to do well, he has started stepping in the right direction to overcome some of his insecurities. Anthony has been my inspiration for my career choices.

Seeing the struggles that both my mom and brother have gone through with school makes me really angry and passionate about helping those who may be in similar situations. Although my first language, Spanish, is not as good as I would like it to be, I can still communicate effectively with Spanish-speaking parents. I hope to advocate for people who struggle with the laws or with the language and who are impeded from understanding their situation because of them. In my teacher certification courses, I am learning techniques that would include all children and even make a child who believed he was dumb feel adequate and capable. Much of my brother's low self-esteem comes from school, and I hope to boost children's self-perceptions while they are my students.

Although education is a great passion of mine, becoming a child psychologist is my goal. I believe that education and psychology are intermingled and that my passion for both is due to that belief. Speaking about his thoughts and feelings, Tony and I do not come to definite decisions and conclusions that "fix" the problem, but he always seems to feel better and at least listened to at the end of our conversations. I understand that it is easier for him to talk to me because I am his sister and he knows and trusts me, but I hope I can bring such comfort and relief to other children who just want someone to listen to them.

When I started my teacher education courses, I wondered how my mom felt about my becoming a teacher. People of color often choose professions such as business and engineering, fields other than education, that will bring them more money. I fully understand their choices and that sometimes they are influenced by parents, and although I do sometimes think I should just study business, it is not where my heart is. I decided to talk to my mother about my decision, in part to seek her approval but also just to inform her.

"Ma, now I don't know if I've talked to you about this but … how would you feel about me becoming a teacher? I mean, I still want to become a child psychologist but before that I'd like to teach. What do you think?" I asked apprehensively. "You know that I have always told you that I don't care what you become as long as you're somebody in life," she replied. "Graduate and be somebody; that's all I ask! You don't want to continue living this life. When you're a professional, you're not gonna have to worry about money anymore. That's what I want for all my children."

The most I can do to repay my mother for her sacrifices and all she has provided for us is to work hard to achieve my goal of becoming a professional. It will not only be a gift to her, but to me as well, for all of my hard work and strife. I understand more than most how important an education is to make your life happy and successful. As a rising senior at Dartmouth College, my family is still in Section 8 housing. No matter how much money we receive through assistance and from Mario, we are still just as broke and penniless as ever. My 40-year-old uneducated mother is currently earning close to fifteen dollars an hour. My 23-year-old boyfriend who has a master's degree is earning about thirty-three dollars an hour. Mami has a job; he has a career.

I am also proof of how important a supportive network is. I have had family and friends encouraging me and believing that I will succeed. In my senior year of high school, I met a freshman girl who is half black, half Dominican. She was a foster child with many blood and foster siblings. At the age of 12 she was raped, and at the trial her biological mother went against her, stating her daughter was never raped. The girl's boyfriend was in jail for selling drugs. This life is unimaginable to me, with hardships I wish on no one. Yet, she was accepted at a great boarding school. I promised her that I would return for her graduation. A few weeks ago, I kept my promise and returned to Exeter's 2004 graduation. My boyfriend thought I was crazy to return because of some silly promise I made. When I found Maria in line for the procession, she screamed out, "You came!" The people there to see her graduate consisted of three black female graduates, three teachers from her junior high school, her principal from junior high, and myself. We were her family, her friends, her support. She is off to Spelman College, a historically black female college, in the fall. She has thus far succeeded, and I know she will continue to do so.

I appreciate my life with all the ups, downs, and obstacles handed to me. I love all the people who are a part of it and am actually grateful for having had a humble upbringing. It has given me drive and has made me truly appreciate the little things. Many say this, but I get excited when a friend brings me a chocolate bar or when my mother makes my favorite meal, or when I see a chipmunk while I am walking around campus. However, I am exhausted. I am tired of struggling to survive at the elite schools I have been fortunate to attend. Seeing so many people in Gucci, Ralph Lauren, and Prada apparel does bother me and make me jealous. Yes, I wish I had Prada bags and Gucci shoes. But it also bothers me because it reminds me, makes me aware that even though my family is no longer on welfare, we are still at the poverty line. We still have to struggle every day and do not even come close to having the kind of wealth many of the people who surround me daily enjoy.

Because of my ethnicity, I have had to prove myself. On campuses where my Latino features have made me very visible, I felt that I had to step up and do as well or better than those around me. Luckily, I had many experiences in my younger years that made me strong enough for this challenge. I have family support and a reputation to uphold. I also have self-motivation and self-pressure that come from striving to be an exemplary oldest child. I know who I am and where I want to go. I will continue fighting to get there.

Follow-up

VIANA: FIVE YEARS LATER

DOI: 10.4324/9781003165378-8

Viana Turcios-Cotto

When I first read "A Latinidad I Cannot, Will Not, Hide" in its published version, I was uncomfortable at how exposed my life had become. In that essay, I changed people's names to protect their identity and wrote about my supposed hometown of Paterson, even though I grew up in Passaic, a neighboring city. Although rereading my chapter five years later made me think there was nothing too outrageous, I was still not comfortable with sharing the story with all of my friends and family. There were many events and information of others that I shared that they would not want to see in such public material. Therefore, by not letting them know about the story, they do not have to deal with that reality I lived and wrote about.

I think this feeling of wanting some cover or protection comes from my new work this past year. In the fall of last year, I began a doctoral program in clinical psychology at the University of Connecticut. One of the major aspects of clinical psychology that has become engrained in me is keeping confidentiality when others trust you with their personal information. This confidentiality feels broken in some of the stories written in my previous chapter. Nevertheless, I have another opportunity to add to current literature about young people of color and will do so, hopefully this time without breaking this sense of confidentiality of others.

My first chapter concluded at the end of my junior year of college. I am now gearing up for my fifth-year college reunion. Much has happened in the past six years, but economic status and race have continued to be important issues in my life. During my senior year at Dartmouth College, I woke up after a nap one evening with a terrible toothache. I tried to ignore it as the pain would lessen at times. Finally, I decided to make an appointment with a local dentist thinking that perhaps it was just a cavity. Since I did not have dental insurance, I knew all the costs would come out of my pocket as dental visits for the previous five years had. I ate all of my food on the left side of my mouth for two weeks as I waited for the appointment. Finally, the day had come only to find out that I needed a root canal as soon as possible. The dentist explained that it would cost about $2,000 for the entire procedure or he could pull out the molar for $100. Sitting in my car in the parking lot, I called my mother bursting into a rage of tears and heaving breath. There was nothing she could do to help me.

After talking to some friends, I decided to go to an advisor. We all figured that being a student on financial aid at such a wealthy school I would be able to get some help from some place. I explained my situation, crying again about the fear of losing my tooth, hoping that this man of color who also grew out of poverty would understand my plight. His response was, "Some of us just have bad teeth. My mother lost her first tooth in her early twenties, too. Sometimes, you know, it just happens." He offered to give me the $100 to pull the tooth. This was not a response I ever expected. It befuddled me that he could not understand the impact that losing a tooth would have on one's self-esteem, emotional health, and overall self-image. My middle-class friend Lisa felt I was over-exaggerating but as I told her, "You would never let someone pull your tooth and be OK with it if a root canal could save your tooth."

This is not a decision that most people at institutions like Dartmouth ever have to make because most have dental insurance or the cash to pay for such emergencies. I have family members with missing teeth because they could not afford dental care and they have expressed their embarrassment about this many times. My mother always made sure to bring us to the dentist as kids, using Medicaid to pay for our routine care and even the braces I wore for two years. When my mother began working at the hospital, she no longer received Medicaid, but also did not have dental insurance. I was an adolescent with a job and therefore paid for my own dental care out of pocket. My teeth were a sign of pride and still are. I often get compliments about how beautiful and white they look. They are one of the reasons I can smile proudly and speak confidently with others. Teeth are a symbol of one's status in society.

I decided to meet with another person, this time a female dean who was also of color. She could not believe the response I had received from the previous advisor stating, "If it ain't broke … I mean if the tooth is OK and it can be saved then there's no reason to pull it. I'm really sorry someone told you that." I never told her who I had spoken to previously, but felt validated by her statement. With emergency funds, this dean was able to find the money to pay for my root canal. In order to keep costs to a minimum, I went to the Tufts University School of Dental Medicine, driving down to Boston from New Hampshire two or three times within a month. I did the same with a dentist in Massachusetts for the crown. Surprising as it may sound to the previous advisor, I have not had problems with any of my teeth since.

During the year of earning my master's at the Harvard Graduate School of Education I worked various jobs, sometimes three at once, to stay afloat. That July I moved into a small but wonderful apartment with Robert, my partner, in Hartford. Although my mother was not terribly thrilled, as shown by the expression on her face, she agreed that it made sense. Robert, who is a Puerto Rican and Peruvian man, and I had been together for almost four years at that point, with three of them being long-distance. Moreover, legally I would not be allowed to live with my mother while she received subsidized housing, but I knew I would not be able to afford a place of my own. Therefore, moving in with Robert was accepted as a smart financial decision. My summer job only lasted for the month of July and I did not receive my first paycheck as a full-time elementary school teacher until the middle of September. Needless to say, I was strapped for money during August, especially when it came time to buy many of the necessary school supplies such as bulletin board materials. This period would have been virtually impossible to survive without Robert's help.

During orientation days and faculty meetings that first month, my principal always reminded us that we were privileged to be middle-class teachers while many of our students did not have the same fortune. I had to fight the urge to raise my hand and say, "Excuse me, I'm not middle class. I have a middle-class salary, technically, but I'm not quite there yet." Finally, in about November I started feeling less overwhelmed and more in control over my money situation. Since September, I had been saving money in a retirement fund as well as a savings account. I had also paid Robert back and started paying many credit cards down. Growing up, my mother taught me that a smart woman never told the man in her life how much money she really had. Although I disagreed with this thought, I did believe that a smart woman always had enough backing to live on her own if need be. The feeling and fear of having to depend on my significant other for survival was waning.

Robert and I are solidly middle class now, yet many members of our families struggle daily. Financially we are able to support ourselves so that we may live comfortable, stable lives. However, we do not have the means to provide for our other family members. Although it is not my job to do so, I still often feel guilty that I cannot give to my mother on a regular basis. She has told me that many of her acquaintances assume that my sister and I send her money consistently. This is expected, as it is the tradition that many Latin American families carry out, sending money back to their parents in their country of origin. I would love to be able to carry on this tradition and sometimes feel pressure to do so. But thousands of dollars in school loans and everyday expenses do not allow it, especially now that I am a graduate student again. It is still my hope that one day I will be able to help more financially.

Although money matters have always been a very salient aspect in my life, racial issues have not been far behind, especially since high school. As an adult, it has been interesting to see how often I am utterly shocked at what people still think and say. My time as an elementary school teacher consisted of three highly transformative years. The school at which I taught second and third grade was in the poorest neighborhood of its town in Connecticut. My first class was comprised of roughly equal numbers of White, Black, and Latino students with about 75% of the students being on free or reduced lunch. By my third year, there were two White students in my class of eighteen with about 85% on free or reduced lunch. Yet, I was one of only three teachers of color at the school, with a Puerto Rican man being hired at the same time that I was.

In order to improve teacher effectiveness, our faculty meetings centered around "Courageous Conversations." This was a book and curriculum of race-based topics meant to educate adults about the importance and difficulties of being a racial minority. The hope was that teachers would begin to understand the challenges faced by many members of the families in our school, whether it was the children or the parents. In turn, it was expected that teachers would be more understanding of certain situations and interact more sensitively and appropriately with parents and children. Perhaps this idea was too bold or the principal was too new and progressive, having been hired just months before me, but many of the teachers did not buy into this plan. They believed it was a waste of time and that they already treated everyone fairly. Albeit, all the teachers worked extraordinarily hard in the school, putting in more time, energy, and effort than one could ever ask. Nevertheless, they were still oblivious to the implications of certain conversations and interactions, using phrases such as, "I don't see race." After some time in educating oneself about race relations, one knows that not seeing race is (a) impossible and (b) dangerous. Seeing race does not mean you are racist; it means you are a human product of our human society. It is also necessary to see race in order to know that one's perspective and daily life might be very different because of their own race.

I quickly became an outspoken colleague at these faculty meetings, as it is in my nature and again, I was one of three teachers of color. At the start of my second year I joined the brand-new "Equity Team," which consisted of the teachers of color and White teachers from each grade level, as well as the principal. This team was responsible for furthering ourselves in our journey of racial awareness and developing the faculty meetings for the year. We spent hours every month or so working on these ideas. Yet, teachers would share with me their dislike of "Courageous Conversations" with sighs and "oh brothers," knowing I was of color, knowing I was on the committee.

During the first year of being a part of the team, several poignant events occurred in my personal life. One weekend at the beginning of the academic year, Robert and I went shopping for school supplies at Staples in the neighboring White, middle-class town of West Hartford. As we walked around with a cart full of notebooks, pencils, crayons, and such, a White woman approached us asking Robert for help with some supplies. He looked around and finally understood what was happening. He explained to the woman that he did not work there and was shopping too. She apologized and walked away. Although we were taken aback, we brushed it off blaming Robert's red collared shirt, which is the Staples uniform, and his youthful face for the mistake. A week later, we returned to the same Staples for more supplies. Again, a White woman approached Robert, interrupted our conversation, and asked for help with an item. Robert let her know he was not an employee. She walked away without apologizing. This time he was wearing a gray T-shirt with huge, red, block letters that read "PHILLIPS EXETER." We were unable to explain this interaction away.

Several months later, we went to Macy's to buy new luggage for a trip Robert was taking to England. He had been chosen by the National Education Association, the national teachers' union, to join a group of teachers in Grantham, England to learn more about the Magna Carta and its connections to the Declaration of Independence. Because of our frugal upbringing, we are both very careful shoppers. We looked at the different luggage and their prices for about thirty minutes. Finally, we went to the counter with the luggage we wanted. Before ringing us up, the older White man behind the register snidely remarked, "Oh, you're actually going to buy something." At that moment, I wanted to respond by leaving the piece of luggage there and saying, "We just changed our mind." Instead, I took a few steps away and let Robert take care of the transaction. The man might have made that statement because of how long we took to choose the bag or because most people just browse and do not actually buy much luggage. He might have also been bored or having a bad day. Maybe we looked too young to afford or to need the luggage. These are all thoughts that any young couple might have in response to such a comment. However, we also wondered if it was because of our race, something a young White couple would not have to think about.

I shared all of these events only with my principal, who is White, because I was afraid of the justifications and denial that would be proposed by the White teachers on the team. My principal anticipated my thoughts and feelings when she heard these stories, validating my reactions. Finally, one day at an Equity Team meeting I decided to share the Macy's luggage story with the other teachers there. The oldest teacher in the room responded with her own story about the day that she went car shopping with her teenage son who was dressed sloppily. To their dismay, they were unable to promptly get helped. She equated this experience with my own claiming, "Oh please, nowadays sales people are just rude to everyone. It's unbelievable how rude they can be. No one would help us." My original worry of justification and denial had realized itself but taught me that my intuitions and instincts are often feelings I should trust. I nodded my head in agreement with her but added that in my case we also wondered if race played a part in the event. My principal supported my point by explaining that the White teacher and her son did not have to factor race into their equation when thinking about their incident.

In these events, no one used derogatory terms or highly inappropriate behavior and therefore were not conspicuously racist. However, one cannot be naïve enough to believe that we are now living in a post-racial society. Many use the election of President Barack Obama as the prime example of the end of racism. While canvassing for the Clinton/Obama primary in February of 2008, several voters, both Latino and White, clearly stated that they would not vote for Obama simply because he was Black. After Obama's victory, the backlash and reactions demonstrated by so many Republicans and White Americans were incomparable to any previous elections. Moreover, those small, everyday events previously described can easily be seen as racial microaggressions, slowly chipping away at one's self-worth through acts of disregard towards others' feelings due to unconscious White superiority. Although perhaps everyone encounters rude people, one's own race as the reason behind that rudeness often only comes into question if the person experiencing that rudeness is of color. Most Whites do not have to wonder if another White person mistook them for a Staples employee because they themselves were White, or if they were spoken to rudely at Macy's by another White person because they themselves were White. However, for a person of color, racism, no matter how subtle, can always be a true explanation for the inconsiderate actions they have endured.

As a graduate student now, I continue to work on matters that impact people of color from urban areas. Psychology became an interest of mine in high school after an introductory course with an amazing teacher. Through several research and internship experiences in college and graduate school, I was able to meld the worlds of psychology and education together. These experiences, along with personal interactions as a teacher, helped me understand how children's and their family's mental health can hugely affect the family's ability to strive for educational attainment and financial stability.

Consistently, I dealt with many students who needed more mental health support than I was able to provide in my classroom. These students' difficulties often impacted the entire class because so much time would be spent on managing those students, rather than actually teaching the class. Moreover, because I taught at what was considered a "failing school" under the No Child Left Behind Act, any instructional time we did have was focused on test preparation. As time went on, it seemed that if I wanted to affect change in any community, teaching would be a slow-going method. Therefore, I decided to turn to a different career in which I was already interested. With a doctorate in clinical psychology, influencing policy decisions and creating greater changes for a larger group of people seemed more possible.

My hope is that my research will positively impact the lives of urban people by informing others about the cultural context of physical, emotional, and mental health, as well as educational experience. Moreover, through clinical practice I hope to be a pivotal component in supporting family systems by guiding families in ways to adjust their functioning. Potentially, this may have a much more far-reaching effect than as I might have as an elementary classroom teacher.

I have also joined the Working Families Party, a liberal political party in Connecticut originally founded in New York City. This party fights for economic and racial justice through political means. With campaigns and hard work promoting living wages, paid sick days, and higher taxes on the wealthy, they have slowly been making big changes in the state. After many door-knocking and phone-banking events for friends running for city council and then Senator Barack Obama, this fall Robert ran for a seat on the Board of Education. Officially, I was his treasurer but, naturally, I was his "right-hand woman." After months of what seemed to be never-ending work, many friends, family members, and the political team gathered at a local restaurant/bar to await the results of the election. Fourteen hours of poll-standing in the November cold were not enough to contain our excitement and celebration when we learned that Robert had been elected to one of the four seats. The most touching moment that night was when a member of the political team came to me and said, "Viana, it would be very easy to dismiss all of the work *you* put into this. You did an awesome job. Congratulations." So far, this experience has taught me that politicians' wives are some of the strongest people around. Too often they are not given the credit they deserve and instead are thought of as trophy wives. Fortunately, Robert comes to me for advice and my opinion. He often shares his thoughts and the events of board meetings. Although it drives me crazy at times, I appreciate him involving me in his political adventure.

At the moment, I am completely wrapped up in planning an affordable yet elegant event for our August wedding. It is a constant battle between my frugal brain and emotional brain, although frugality is winning this one as usual. It has been a group effort as many of my successes in life have been. With the help of our families, Robert and I should be able to start our lives as a married couple with little to no debt from the wedding. Having met a 21-year-old Robert when I was only 19 years old, we have been very fortunate that our development into adulthood brought us along the same path. Even though we have our disagreements, overall we strive for similar futures. As the years have continued to add up and time has rolled on, I have become happier and more confident. I greatly enjoy my life and hope for more of the same in the years to come.

Case 7

THE DEVILS WITHIN

RYAN GARCIA

DOI: 10.4324/9781003165378-9

Ryan Garcia

Born to Mexican-American parents in Southern California, Ryan experiences a harrowing childhood filled with violence between his parents, addiction, mental instability, and deep emotional unpredictability. At 14 years old, after his mother's sudden death, Ryan eventually finds solace, safety, and support in the home of his adoptive Latina aunt and her Anglo husband. Ryan's resilience brings him to a competitive college, where he relies on and celebrates the strong Latino heritage of his deeply challenged birth parents and the steadfast faith of his maternal grandmother.

On Saturday nights back home during my high school years, I would hear my name come on over the loudspeakers as I rushed for another touchdown. The announcer had a flair for putting an emphasis on the Mexican name that was so common in my neighborhood. "Gar-ci-a!" he would scream. Our team roster had a diverse mix of ethnicities including Filipinos, Anglos, and Latinos. I was fond of my teammates and the camaraderie that we shared, and the sports that I played gave me a platform to excel in high school. I enjoyed every minute of the excitement when I got the snap and took off running for the end zone or when I dove for that screaming line drive coming down the baseline. Growing up as a Latino in Southern California I was able to enjoy my adolescence and escape many of the prejudices that I had heard about from my grandparents and mother. Things had changed since they had come to the States, and I liked how everything had ended up. Many doors had opened that were not open to them in their youth. Although these advantages helped me in many ways, a downside existed. Being Latino created a duality of lives for me throughout my adolescence, and the hardships that I endured shaped me into who I am today.

As a small child, I viewed my lovely Mexican-born mother sustain blows from my father's bronze-colored hands. I have wondered about the impact of having a stereotypical abusive Latino male as my role model for relationships. The abuse that my Latina mother endured created a fear that I believe has made me gravitate toward relationships similar to that of my parents. I wonder, do I look for chaotic and unstable relationships in an attempt to replicate the one I viewed in my childhood? How did growing up in the midst of poverty in Southern California suburbia, the son of abusive, alcoholic, drug-abusing parents, form me into the man I have become? Have I managed to transcend the difficulties of my childhood and reach manhood unscarred? Did being adopted by new parents in my early adolescence undo some of the harmful effects of growing up in a chaotic family? After all I've experienced, how is it that

I am about to graduate from an Ivy League college and enter a prestigious job with a bright future ahead?

When I was nearly 5 years old and my sister Kelly was 2, my parents decided that their marriage had run its course. After several weeks of separation, my parents divorced. Looking back on the situation, I know that they made a good decision; neither one of my parents could have continued in the relationship without increasing conflict. I did not want my parents' divorce to occur, but it seemed the path of separation had been blazed by years of unhappiness.

At the age of 2, when I had a limited understanding of the world around me, I sensed that I wanted a father and a mother in my life. Yet, I did not want to grow up around and learn from the type of marriage my parents had. I have vivid memories of the growing tension of their failing marriage.

I was 4 and a half years old and tears streamed down my cheeks as I screamed at my father. My small feet seemed glued to my parents' bedspread as I stood, bouncing, on their bed, my hands and arms outstretched as I pleaded with them. My little sister crouched by my side and her eyes begged for my parents to stop fighting. All the while we both cried and yelled, "Daddy, please stop! I just want you guys to stop. Stop! Stop!" I must have repeated those words a thousand times. My body would not—rather could not—move to stop my father although he and my mother were only inches away from my grasp as they stood between the worn, brown dresser and the bed. The mirror on the dresser reflected the beads of sweat that gleamed on his forehead and the veins that seemed ready to explode in his tensed arms. My mother's mascara ran down her cheeks and her hair had become a tussled mess. She looked so small as my father dug his fingers into her shoulders. Instead of ceasing their argument, my father, with a fire in his eyes, knocked my mother to the ground with a forceful blow to the side of her head. The thud of her body slamming into the ground ended the noises that had been erupting from my sister and me. My father stepped over my mother and out of the room. My sister and I gasped in horror as we jumped off the bed to console my mother. Her arms embraced us and her eyes called after my father even though his angry fists had just clobbered her to the floor. She gingerly raised her bruised head as she begged, "Honey, please don't leave! I know that we can work this out. Sean, please don't leave me like this. Don't leave your kids like this. We can work this out. I am sorry. Please!" Her words broke into sobs as my father walked out the door. Her body crumpled to the floor and the three of us huddled on the ground in a pile of tears and sadness.

Ryan Garcia

So many factors had brought my parents to this point in their marriage. The constant fighting and unhappiness had stemmed from many things that I did not comprehend at the time—addictions, mental illness, and incompatibility. At the time, my sister and I were simply caught in the middle.

The addictions that added to the turmoil in my parents' relationship were brought to my attention during a harmless search for treasure. When I was about 8, I went into the bathroom to explore all the nooks and crannies for treasure. My vivid imagination created images of buccaneers, pirates, and swords protecting a mystical "X" that marked the spot of discovery and a booty of gold and jewels. I found a spoon. The spoon was just an ordinary soupspoon. Any young kid could find a misplaced soupspoon, but I found one hidden in a cupboard in the bathroom. "What the hell is this stuff on the spoon?" I thought to myself. Burnt, dark ashes hid the silver luster of the spoon's well. The bottom of the spoon had a multicolored hue that resembled oil mixing with water. I had not found any treasure, nor had I needed to fight off any pirates, but I had unlocked the door to one of my parents' hidden secrets.

While driving several months ago, in a moment of reminiscence, the time that I found the spoon crept into my consciousness. Sometimes elements of life are not understood until experience plays that cruel trick of stripping away the thin veil of naïveté. Thoughts of my childhood often slam into my head with the force of a bullet. Left in a state of confusion, I work to place the pieces of my jumbled memories into an aligned picture. The image of the spoon sprung up from a deep corner of my mind as I drove the car that day. I finally understood that the ashes that stuck to the spoon's silver tone had entered the veins of my family. My blood. My family had injected this fluid bliss into their blood, my psyche. The short high they reached forever scarred my cerebrum. A moment of pleasure; a lifetime of pain—this contradiction seems to be a common theme in the story of life. Small vials laced with white residue of private parties mushroomed around the house. The vials seemed to grow out of the cracks of the floor and suddenly blossom. Somehow my small hands found these little secrets. I hit the steering wheel so hard I thought I might have broken a finger. It's amazing how reality hits you as you mature. Scenes from the past, once gray and fuzzy, blend into a vivid interlude of clarity. My parents were drug addicts.

I recently saw a movie about drug use. I wanted to leave the theater when I saw the young girl cooking the heroin. A sledgehammer hit my chest and my heart fell onto the sticky theater floor. Tears swelled in my eyes from the pain. I am a man and I am not supposed to cry like a woman, I thought to myself. Trying to be the strong one that has a solid grip on reality has put great stress on me since my childhood. My grandparents and aunts and uncles understood what my parents exposed us to, yet they still expected both my sister and me not to fall into the temptations of drugs. I was supposed to set the example for my sister. Who was supposed to set the example for me?

I didn't want to be the father, husband, and son of the family. I wasn't ready for these responsibilities. "Mom, the kitchen is filthy and cockroaches are running all over the place. I guess I will just clean it; you go ahead and stay in bed," I said. Dirty pots, pans, and plates were stacked high in the sink. Moving a single item resulted in multitudes of cockroaches scurrying into the cracks on the walls and the disheveled drawers. I was about 7 years old at the time. Some days, I came in from playing outside with my friends and my mother was very attentive and helpful. Other days, she had not gotten out of bed for three days and did not even know if I was in the house or not. On these days, my mother was physically present, but her mind had led her into complete darkness. She became unaware of everything around her. When she slipped into this state of delirium, I had to care for my sister and me. I got used to making Campbell's soup. Food stamps and welfare did not allow for gourmet dinners, but I still had food in my stomach. I cooked, cleaned, and went to school. I had food, a roof over my head, and I was a straight-A student. Yet, my mom would not get out of bed. When her eyes would finally open, in a look of complete despair and surrender, my mother would say, "Listen to me, I don't want to live like this anymore, you two." Even though I knew she would not take her life, I hated it when my mother talked about suicide. I remember one incident clearly, when I was around 5 years old and my mother lost her temper. My parents had been arguing like they often did. This time my father screamed at my mother but his hands did not land any blows. His nostrils flared and spittle flew out of his mouth but he never raised a hand. He looked like a rabid dog ready to pounce. Luckily, he did not attack. He decided to slam the front door as he left rather than slam my mother against the wall like so many times before.

He barged out of the house and the wheels of his car left marks in the cement as he drove off. Everything happened so quickly that the door seemed to still be slamming as he drove off. Time froze during those abusive episodes. My father's car could be heard squealing around the corner. My mother could only plop down in a chair behind her. She crumpled into the corner like a pile of dirty clothes. Her bones seemed to melt within her body. Thick streams of mascara-stained tears rolled down her cheeks, she shook with quiet sobs, and her mouth quivered with pain and despair. She was lost. I could see her trying with all her might to keep her head from falling into her chest.

Her arms rose slowly and she reached out for the only support she could find—her children. Her actions begged for an eternal embrace—a permanent sanctuary. My mother said, "Kids, everything is going to be alright. Your dad and I will work things out. I will make sure that everything gets fixed. I do not want you kids to grow up in this kind of shit. You are good kids and don't deserve this!" Her voice shook with each sentence.

I asked her, "Why did Daddy leave?" To my dismay, her right hand suddenly flew into the left side of my face. My jaw dropped and a single tear ran down my cheek. "Why did you hit me, Mom? I didn't do anything," I said. She thought that I had blamed her for my father's departure. She had heard, "Why did you make Daddy leave?" I could only cry along with her, and she grabbed me and held me even closer than before. "I am sorry, I am sorry, I am sorry," she kept saying. My sister and I half stood, half sat while embracing our mother. We all wept.

Today, I wonder why my mother struck me; I was not hit often as a child, and I never received strikes to the face. I may have been spanked, but that did not even come in excess. The only explanation that I have is that my mother had transferred her anger toward my father into a blow to my face. The rage she felt needed to release itself somehow, and, as the nearest male, I fit the profile. I know that she could not find any alternative in her confused mind and I was the closest one, so she blamed me. I feel sorry for what my mother went through in those days. I forgive her for hitting me. It was out of her control—most things seemed to be out of her control in those days.

The devils that controlled my mother and kept her in bed all day wanted to crush the spirit of our house. I didn't understand why she was so tired.

She just kept crying. The sheets and blankets that enveloped her body became a refuge from the battle inside her mind. "Mom, are you okay?" She usually didn't answer me. One time, my grandmother tried to explain my mother's condition to me. "Your mother is a manic-depressive woman," said my grandmother. "She will be better when she starts taking her medication." I didn't know how the medicine was going to vanquish the devils that racked my mother's body with pain. How could pills get rid of a monster that lived inside her? Besides, my mother had a hard time remembering to take her Prozac, lithium, and Xanax. Either she refused to take them or she swallowed them down with big gulps of Bartle and Jaymes wine coolers. The names of the green, blue, and white pills had become common knowledge for me. I used to watch as she popped the handful of pills into her mouth. I knew that my mother needed to take these pills so she could take me to baseball practice. "I am going to be on the All-Star team this year. I need to make it to practice," I would say to myself. Looking back, it's funny to think that I was worried about making it to baseball practice. As my mother was going through a severe mental breakdown, I was worried about making the All-Star team. I realize now that I needed my times of ventilation from the stench of reality. I needed to run in the fresh air with other kids, to just be a kid.

I went to a private Catholic school in an upper-middle-class neighborhood from kindergarten through eighth grade. My classes consisted of mainly white students with a few splashes of brown and black. Even now, I believe that I am very much a product of the Catholic beliefs and practices that I imbibed in childhood. The colored rays of light that streamed through the stained-glass windows of my church are forever etched into my memory. Making the sign of the cross over my body has always been a daily ritual. My religion has become a comfort and support in my times of need. Like breathing, it is an automatic, subconscious activity.

I think of my grandmother, my mother's mother, when I think of religion. How she loves being a Catholic and going to Mass! The greatest honor of her life came when she received an award from the Pope. She glowed for weeks and still asks me if I have seen the award and all the pictures of the ceremony. I gaze at the award and the photos with a smile when she puts them in my hands.

If my grandmother had not always been around, I would not be where I am today. She knew when it was time to get us out of the house away from the devils of depression. "Come on kids, you are going to come over to my house for a little while." Those were the most beautiful words. "Mijo, are you hungry? I will fix you some albóndigas. That will warm you up." The magic of Grandma's food served as my escape from the constant bombardment of poverty, depression, and confusion. Looking back, I know that my grandmother's love and the faith she helped instill in me are two factors that saved me from ruin.

I was sitting in my grandparents' dimly lit dining room when the phone rang. I was about 13 years old. My mother had left for the supermarket to pick up items for dinner. She and I had been having a small argument prior to her departure—something to do with my homework. Nothing about the disagreement suggested that we would not apologize to each other soon after. I asked as she hurriedly left, "Mom, where are you going?" "The store," she responded. "See ya soon," I said in my sweetest voice. I had tried to apologize and tell her everything was all right by the tone of my voice. I had never really said the words "I am sorry," but I felt that things were settled from our argument. I vividly recall watching her walk out the front door of my grandparents' house—her wavy brown hair picking up as she stepped down onto the porch. She had lost weight then and looked very healthy. She always had to fight the weight but had finally gotten to a point that she looked fit, even vibrant.

In a little over an hour, the phone rang. I was still sitting at the dining room table doing my homework. An unfamiliar man's voice asked if I was Mary's son. "I am your father's boss. He received a call from the hospital and was told that your mother is in intensive care. He wanted me to inform you of the situation. Someone had found her unconscious in her car at the supermarket," said the unfamiliar voice. I thanked the man. As I hung up the phone, I yelled to my grandfather and sister, "Mom is in the hospital. We need to get over there right away."

My mother was not a stranger to the emergency room. A combination of severe asthma, chronic health problems, and self-inflicted wounds had given her plenty of opportunities to visit the E.R. Incidentally, the L.A. race riots of 1992 were in progress and many fires had erupted in the past few days. The smoke had turned the skies a dirtier color than usual. I wondered if the smoke had caused a severe asthma attack and she had not reacted quickly enough to take her medication. All these thoughts raced through my head as we drove to the hospital. Though the hospital was only several blocks away, the ride seemed to take an eternity. Every light signal would turn red as soon as we came near. My palms dampened with sweat as my nerves rose in anticipation of the worst. I gripped the door handle with white knuckles.

The hospital had become a familiar place to me because of my mother's frequent visits and because of my own asthma-related visits. As soon as my foot hit the hospital ground pavement, I took off running for the front desk. "Ryan, don't run, and calm down! Everything is going to be all right!" my grandfather yelled after me. I knew that everything was not okay from the tone of the man's voice on the phone. I reached the information desk and asked for my mother's room.

Multiple wires, tubes, and needles ran into her body. Small strands of her hair fell across her pale face. My mother always had a beautiful bronze tone to her skin, but something had stripped away her familiar glow. Her full lips looked chapped and dry. I reached for her hand

and felt her warm touch against my skin. As I touched her palm, the familiar smell of her skin seemed to float through the air. "Mommy, we are here. Please open your eyes if you can," I said as I stood over her. Her eyelids did not move. She remained completely still.

The physicians informed us that a man had found my mother slumped in her car. The doctors had done several tests upon her arrival and found that she had had an aneurysm. The aneurysm had burst in her brain and caused massive internal bleeding. "If she is to survive, then she will be heavily brain-damaged," said the doctor. "If my mother gets out of this alive," I thought to myself, "then she will be a human vegetable—not able to use her limbs, not able to communicate, not able to even process thoughts." At that point, I pictured my beautiful mother sitting in a wheelchair and drooling on herself, unable to touch me again with her tenderness. I fought off the thoughts of wishing for her death and prayed only for her to live. I told myself that I could handle having a brain-damaged mother.

It seemed like I didn't leave the hospital for two and a half days. The reception room became a familiar place as I slumped into one of the cushy chairs. Friends and family would come in with a half smile, half frown on their faces as they entered the room. I remember a constant urge to break down crying, but forcing myself to stop. After my many hours of waiting and hoping for the best, the doctor entered the waiting room. His blue hospital scrubs swished as he walked through the door. As his lips began to part, I knew what his next words would be. "I am sorry, but she has no brain activity. We have officially pronounced her brain-dead," the doctor said. As much as I did not want to hear those words, I knew they were coming. I had known as soon as the stranger's voice had asked me if I was Mary's son. Many times before, I had had premonitions of my mother's death, and now all my visions had become a reality. As I stood in the waiting room, digesting the news of my mother's death, I thought back on the years that I had dreamed of her death and why I had both dreaded and hoped for that day to come.

Pictures of my childhood slipped into my mind's eye. In one vision, when I was around 9 years old, my mother had started having a "mental episode" and was intent on drinking away the effects of her chemical imbalance. With a fifth of Smirnoff vodka in her hand, she kept taking long swigs. The bottle would hit her lips and she would follow it with some orange juice. This started at the house and continued as she drove my sister and me toward the mountains. We started going up this winding hill in the foothills of our local mountains. I could see the glazed look in my mother's eyes as she stared out the windshield. Her hands gripped the steering wheel tightly. The old brown Volvo swerved left to right as she clumsily adjusted the wheels in the tight turns of the mountain road. She was out of control and she knew it. I could tell that she was torn between having us with her and leaving us with family. Every minute on the windy road, I worried that my mother would steer us toward a dramatic ending—images of the brown Volvo flying off the road and cascading down the mountain's granite face kept passing through my head. She often talked of suicide and sometimes included us in her plans of starvation or some other means of death. I was afraid that this would be an occasion when my sister and I were included in the plans.

As large pines whizzed by the car, the steep ravine kept pulling my eyes to the side of the road as we neared its edge many times. Death seemed so near as the car's wheels slid off the pavement and kicked up the dirt of the road's shoulder. My mother's arms tensed as she veered us back onto the paved road. A quick yelp of fear broke the silence. My sister usually became quiet when my mother went into these states. She had learned that keeping quiet was the best thing that she could do. Her little scared eyes looked at me from the back seat and her small voice called to my mother to stop the car. The terrified tone in my sister's voice begged for the wild ride to end.

Tears welled up in my eyes. Tears streamed down my poor sister's face and her body shook. "Ryan, I want you to drive us down the hill. I can't do it anymore," begged my mother. "Mom, I can't drive the car. I don't even know how to drive. You can get us down the hill. You have to get us down the hill," I said and hoped. After pleading with my mother to stop the car, she finally pulled over and stopped. I climbed out of the front seat and into the back seat. My sister had decided to sit in the front; I lay down in the back seat and closed my eyes. As always, I had left my mother to her own devices and my sister with the burden of supporting her. My sister had always had the strength to be near my mother during these episodes. The strength she showed baffled me. When we finally reached the base of the hill, I opened my eyes and thanked God for our survival. My mother drove toward our house and I just hoped that we would make it home.

On the way, we stopped very near my father's house. My mother got out and crouched on the curb to urinate. She had simply pulled the car over, strolled from the driver's side, and used the car as a shield to the passing traffic. Thoughts pulsed through my head as she pulled her pants along her thighs. "Dad's house is only two blocks away from here. If we run, we can make it there before Mom even has time to catch us," I said to my sister. The frightened eyes of a beautiful young girl stared back at me with a look of apprehension. "We can't leave Mom like this all alone. She needs us to help her," my sister replied. "Screw that! I am makin' a run for it," I said. A trickling sound reached my ears, and my eyes moved toward the stream of liquid running over the curb's edge. Although the sun's light had long faded, I surveyed the area searching for some passerby that would see my mother pissing on the street. I knew that the opportunity had come for me to run.

My heart vigorously pumped blood into my legs. The dark, damp pavement flew by as I ran toward my father's house in search of an impossible solution. Tingles and shivers overtook my body as I ran in anticipation of capture from behind. I pictured my mother's hand reaching a distance of two blocks and clutching the top of my right shoulder. "Where the hell do you think that you are going?" she would have said. As my feet struck the concrete leading down my father's driveway, I knew that I had escaped a fretful episode.

When I reached my father's door, I breathed a sigh of relief. The brown wooden door was cool to the touch as my knuckles rapped a tune of despair. "Dad, are you in there?" I asked. "Yo, how is it going, mijito? What's up?" he replied. His eyes were reading my expression and his ears listened to my heavy breaths as my chest heaved and my eyes danced in confusion. "Dad, Mom is down the street and she is peeing on the curb. She is really drunk and she has been driving us all over the place. I don't know what to do. She stopped really close by so I decided to run over here," I said. His arm reached out toward my shoulder and I moved into his room. His familiar smell comforted me and his strong hand put me at ease. I knew that I had found a temporary refuge.

My mother's attempt to apprehend me was imminent and she would soon be knocking on the door for me. No longer than five minutes passed before my little sister came into the room crying. "Mom wants you to come out to the car and come home with us," she said. My mother, in a drunken stupor, followed close behind her. "Get your little ass in the car," she yelled in a burst of spittle. Strands of her hair fell in tangled masses over her eyes and her face was contorted from alcohol's poisonous power. The beauty of her face had melted away into a visage of my deepest fears—an intoxicated, lost soul.

My father lunged toward my mother. His angry hands forced her out of the room and toward the sloped driveway. Shutting the door behind him, he turned and told my sister and me, "Stay in here while I take care of your mother." Ugly, unforgettable sounds followed each push and shove as my father trounced my mother. The distinct clunk of a body hitting car metal rung out loud as my mother hit her head on the hood of my father's truck. Defeated by her ex-husband and betrayed by her children, my mother retreated in a battered state. My heart raced with satisfaction and self-hatred as I heard my father "take care" of my mother. My sister and I watched television for distraction from reality. Our role models, our confidants, our parents once again fell victim to abuse—both alcohol and physical.

In an attempt to assuage the situation, I reached for the phone on the wall. I heard my grandmother's voice through the line and I told her, "Grandma, Grandma. Mom is really drunk and can't drive the car anymore. We are at my dad's house and need you to pick us up. My dad says that she is okay but can't take us the way she is." "Okay, mijo, we will come and get you," my grandmother said.

Fifteen minutes passed as we anxiously waited for my grandparents to arrive. My sister, mother, and I climbed into the car and started driving down the hill toward our grandparents' house. My mother stunk of liquor and yelled at my grandparents: "You don't love me. My kids don't love me. Look what that bastard did to me. He hit me so hard. Look at my head. I have a fucking huge bump on my head. That bastard. Why did you go to him, Ryan? Why? Why did you do that to me?" My mother continued ranting about her condition as the car's wheels rolled us toward our destination. At a stoplight, she attempted to jump out of the car. My grandfather locked the doors, but my mother persisted on getting out of the car. "Let me out. I don't want to be with any of you. I don't want to be like this. I just want to die. Let me go," she yelled. With all of my strength, I grabbed her and held her against her seat. Sitting behind her in the back seat allowed me a quick hold on her arms as she reached for the passenger side door. "Stop it, Mom," I yelled, "Stop it. I am not going to let you go. Stop fighting against me. We are going home." My grandmother spoke to my mother in Spanish, "¡Mijita, cálmate!"

When we reached my grandparents' home, we all helped to get my mother into the house. Although she could walk, she stumbled and had a hard time staying on her feet. "I don't need your fuckin' help. I can do it on my own," she yelled. "Just get in the house, Mom. I don't want you to hurt yourself," I said. As I lay on my grandfather's bed watching television, my mother let out short gasps of pain from the back room. She called for my sister, "Kelly, come here honey. Mommy needs you." My sister has since recounted this scene to me. My mother had taken a large knife from the kitchen and cut open her stomach. Blood had splattered onto the bathroom floor and walls—red speckles of my mother's life had stained the whitewashed walls. In shock and horror, my sister helped my mother clean blood off the floor and walls of this horrible scene.

The night ended with my mother in the hospital. From that point on, I sensed that we would soon be back in the hospital to visit my mother in her last minutes of life. After this experience, I knew that my mother would die a young woman. I wanted this to happen because she was a danger to my sister and me.

I was 13 years old when I stood over my mother and watched her fade away. Tears streamed down my face and my heart ached. A unique and inexplicable pain gripped my chest. I looked at her sweet mouth and thought of the loving words and kisses that had surfaced from those full lips. She looked beautiful as she slipped into eternal sleep.

All those years of wishing for my mother's death had finally come true, and guilt streamed through my veins. Though my mother had been unpredictable and at times violent, I still had a deep love for her. In my fantasy of her death, losing her did not hurt as much as it did in reality. I already felt the loss of those moments of tender caresses and loving words as I held her clammy hand and sensed her spirit drift away. As I cried, though, a growing excitement arose in my heart. The desire for personal safety and happiness, for my sister and me, overwhelmed the feelings of love for my mother. The legal documents that gave my mother custody would now fall into my father's hands. In losing a mother, I would gain a father that I only hoped could provide the consistent love and safety that my mother had not.

Following a few days of tears shed, my sister and I moved from my grandparents' home to live with our father. We both brimmed with enthusiasm about the new living situation. During the years of our parents' divorce, the weekends that we had spent with our father were filled with hours of entertainment. Going to the theater, riding ponies, and watching television were typical activities when we were with our father. My sister and I perceived those fun-filled days to be a normal week at our father's home. Living with our father looked very promising after the heart-wrenching loss of our mother.

When I moved in with my father, he and I shared a bedroom. We even slept in the same bed. I liked sleeping together—the feel of his thick, muscular arm over my body gave me comfort. Being a manual laborer for most of his life and working out at the gym had kept his body in good shape. As I struggled with the loss of my mother, I would reach for his arm when I needed reassurance that he would care for me. Since my parents' divorce, I had not spent a lot of time with my father. The only men that I had interacted with were the fly-by-night men that

Ryan Garcia

my mother had brought into the house. I longed for a male that I could love and emulate, and now I finally had a consistent man in my life. With tenderness and care, my father would scratch my back and put me to sleep—his masculine, callused hands felt good against my skin. These reassuring caresses put me at ease and made the new living situation seem that much better. The masculine love that I had been missing for all those years was now supplied by the man I wanted it from the most—my father.

In the midst of my mother's death and the move to my father's home, I was at the cusp of my adolescence. A growing curiosity about the opposite sex had sprung within me. To my delight, my father had no problem talking to me about sex and showing me his full collection of Playboy magazines from the bottom of the bookshelf. All my questions concerning sex and women were always answered. He would tell me about "pussy" and "tits" all the time. "Take a look at this set of tits. She has a great pair," my dad would often say. The excitement of seeing the nude pictures and having my father treat me as an equal made me feel like a man.

I remember an occasion when my older cousin had come to stay with us for a short time. He and my father talked about the first time that they had had sex. "I remember how nervous I was the first time," said my dad. "I had gone down to Mexico with my cousin and I had sex with this prostitute. That was the first time for me. This fuckin' broad had droopy tits, but she really knew what she was doing. She had a lot of experience and it showed." I remember listening to the story in awe. My eyes were fixed on my father's lips as he spoke these words of wisdom. My father and cousin had lost their virginity at around 14 years old. Losing my virginity became a mental goal as I sat there listening to the two men's stories. I didn't want to be the only one that had not experienced sex. Having all this access to sexual material at the beginning of my adolescence changed my perception of sex. Although I had learned for years that it was a sin, I began looking at sex in a different light. I could not wait to slip myself into a girl's most secret part.

All these new thoughts raced through my head. My access to sexual knowledge seemed endless and my father's love seemed infinite. I often heard the words "I love you more than anything" spilling from his lips. Everything was perfect in our new house with our dad. My sister and I felt that we had finally reached a stable home with love and happiness. After only several weeks living with him, we would find out that every day would not be like the fun weekends. The daily duties of a parent would soon prove too difficult for my father. Lacking basic parental skills, my father began resenting me when I had questions about homework or school. "You are a smart kid," he said, "do your own damn homework." The added stress of raising children soon began to take its toll on him and he escaped his new existence through small bottles of tequila. The angry, alcoholic father that I had learned to fear during my parents' marriage reentered my life.

He often had the little plastic bottles by his side. When he felt the urge for a shot, he could simply sneak away and empty the bottle down his throat. Hearing the sounds of him heaving his guts into the commode became a common occurrence. Through his drunken fits of anger, my father's true existence became clearer to me. A man in his mid-forties who still lived with his parents in a converted garage—that was my dad. My grandmother, Dad's mother, continued to cook for him, wash his clothes, and not charge him high rent. All the things I had hated about him when he beat my mother started springing back into my mind. The love and tenderness that he showed began to dwindle and the lack of parental support he offered with school and sports started taking their toll. Like my mother, my father had his weaknesses and could not care for his children. I knew that my time had come to try to find a better life, and for good this time.

The summer following my mother's death, I had begun spending a lot of time with my aunt, the younger of my mother's two sisters. She even offered to take me to work in her office. The days I spent with her and my uncle, her husband, did not resemble anything I had ever experienced in either of my homes. The polite and caring manner in which they interacted with each other and their daughter seemed so different than my parents' relationship with each other, my sister, and me. The growing problems with my father only made their home seem that much more inviting. After a few weeks of worrying and thinking, I asked my aunt if I could live with her and her family.

Leaving my father's home proved emotionally difficult. I always seemed to be turning my back on one of my parents. First, I had left my mother for my father, and now I was leaving my father for another family. Even though these feelings of guilt rushed through my body, I knew that I could not live with another alcoholic parent.

Moving in with my new family became the best decision I had ever made. Worrying about being on time for school or having food to eat became things of the past. Consistent love and tenderness were offered in my new household and I knew that I had finally found my dream home. My sister had not joined me at first, but after several months of debate, I convinced her to move in with me. Finally, the two of us could live together in a stable, non-abusive household. The constant, steady love and attention that my "new parents" offered began stripping away the pain from my preadolescent years. The tense feeling of apprehension of another chaotic episode being around the corner finally left me. For the first time, I could focus my thoughts solely on school, sports, and my identity.

The four years I spent in high school differed immensely from my pre-teen years. Every morning, around seven, my adopted mother would open my door and say, "Rise and shine. It's time to get up for school." The sweet words became my alarm clock every morning. "Rise and shine" would ring through my ears for several minutes before my eyelids lifted and my eyes adjusted to the sunbeams streaming through the mini-blinds. Reaching into my drawer, I would always find clean clothes and underwear. Every weekend, my adopted mother would make sure that my clothes were washed for the next week. She would never allow the piles of dirty clothes that used to build up in my old room. She always made sure that I had clean clothes and a clean room. "Ryan, bring in your hamper and separate your clothes. I am going to start washing now," she would say. The prior lack of reliability and dependability in my life had been assuaged by my adopted mother's constant attention to the important details. Whenever I wanted something clean to wear, I had it. Whenever I was hungry, I was fed. I no longer worried about the simple procedures of life that had slipped by me on occasions during my childhood.

There were still a few aspects of my old life that I missed. Although I wanted the comfort of being a child under my new parents' wings, the jump from being treated as an adult to being treated as a child had come suddenly. I longed to talk like I had with my father about sex and women. Instead, I dealt with my sexuality and all the questions of my past on my own. Neither my sister nor I talked to each other or our adopted parents about our past. "Let your mother rest," my adopted mother would say. "She loved you very much, and that is all that matters. Your father loves you, too." I attempted to figure out who I had become because of all the things that had happened in my life, but my new parents did not wish to talk about it. Though they saved me from an impossible living condition, they did not help me overcome the internal questions I had. I struggled with my identity as a Latino male and the influences that growing up in a chaotic household had on me.

After high school, these questions would come into full blossom as I entered a new life at college. My successes in high school, both in sports and academics, ensured my access to a prominent college of my choice. After much searching and discussion with my adopted parents, I decided to head off for New Hampshire. The years I spent at the Ivy League institution allowed me to understand my ethnicity and openly speak with pride about my heritage. Through all the chaos of my childhood, I realize my mother had always instilled a deep pride for my heritage in me. "Never forget that you are Mexican-American, Ryan," she would say. "Don't let anyone take that away from you. That is who you are."

The years of my adolescence with my adopted parents had saved me from disaster, but they had also created new questions for me to answer. Living under the guidance of an Anglo father and a Latina mother gave me a new perspective on my culture. Although my Anglo father offered constant love, I could not speak to him about my questions of ethnicity. My adopted mother did not embrace her ethnicity as I did, so she did not offer advice on such topics. It finally dawned on me that I had to combine all the lessons I had learned through my life. My birth parents had both been unsteady and chaotic, yet they had instilled a pride for my heritage deep within me and given me the tools to succeed. My adopted parents had allowed those tools to blossom and ensured my success through their constant attention and love. Also, my grandmother's love and religion had served as beacons of light in my time of need. This collage of values and lessons would work as my guidance through life.

I have light-brown eyes, thick dark hair, nice full lips, and brown skin. My mother and father have passed these strong features on to me; yet I wonder how many of the internal demons that they contained have been passed to me as well. My slicked-back hair and my manner of dress resemble my father's sense of style, but I hope that I have overcome the negative images of women and relationships that he taught to me. The influence of having a father full of machismo and anger toward women has been a daily struggle, yet I know that I have overcome many of those evils. Likewise, the control I have over my existence does not resemble the turmoil that my mother lived in; I do not seek continual excitement as she did. Having a meaningful relationship with love and tenderness is more important to me than the excitement of conflict that my mother looked for in her relationships.

Born the son of Mexican-American parents, I am proud of my ethnicity, yet I strive to transcend the stereotypes of the Latino male. The turbulence that I lived through showed me the antithesis of my ideal life. My adopted parents' love, compassion, and dependability will serve as a guide to not replicate that environment for my children. All the influences of my life have shaped me into the man I have become; yet I am my own man now and dictate my destiny. I can finally take control. My entrance into a new chapter in my life will truly tell if I have succeeded in vanquishing all the devils that haunt my past and perhaps still dwell deep within me, but I feel secure that my own family and children will enjoy the stability and safety I sought as a child.

Case 8

IN MY WORLD, 1+1=3

YUKI KONDO-SHAH

DOI: 10.4324/9781003165378-10

Yuki Kondo-Shah

With a Bangladeshi father and a Japanese interpreter mother, Yuki is born in California, but moves for the next seven years of her life to Japan, where she lives happily and interacts with her mother's extended family. Fearing that Yuki's English speaking skills will not develop in this context, the family moves to Arizona where Yuki finds social life and teaching methods in the schools highly problematic. For her first couple of years on her return to the U.S., she felt like a foreigner—an anomaly. She longed to feel a sense of unity and conformity but her biracial background made this challenging. Yuki consistently struggled to define her identity, but it was not until after graduation from college when she became a college admissions officer that she understood herself well enough to claim "… neither my ethnicity nor any other person can define me. I reserve that right for myself." She looks back and considers the early struggles in her life that caused her confusion and pain "… also became the foundation of who I am." She claims she has been blessed by being a mixed-race person because "… [her] experience as a minority in America has made [her] more able to empathize with people's differences."

A Bangladeshi engineer and a Japanese interpreter marry and move to a Republican congressional district in the middle of the Arizona desert … Sounds like the opening line of a joke, right? Well, if this were a joke, then I'd be the punchline.

Whenever my parents and I walk together, be it on the busy sidewalks of London, in a chaotic market in Beijing, or along narrow pathways in Tokyo, the reaction from passing pedestrians is always the same. First, they scan my father, a lean man with dark skin, a mop of curly hair, and features that place him as coming from the Asian subcontinent. Next, they look over my mother's strong build, mochi skin, and straight black hair cropped close to her ears. She is clearly East Asian. Lastly, there is me, a mixture of my Japanese and Bangladeshi parents, looking a bit like both but not quite like the sum of the whole.

The passerby does his calculations—it takes but a couple of seconds—and then, relishing the joy of solving an arithmetic problem, he lights up in understanding, equation solved: a mixed-race child, the sum of two parts. Except that, unlike a math equation where $1+1=2$, mixed-race children don't come out equally. Half Japanese, half Bangladeshi, but not a whole anything. Add to that mixture a move to the United States at age 7, and the result is a whole lot of confusion. I'm 25 years old, and if you asked me to describe my racial identity—like one-quarter Bangladeshi, three-quarters Japanese—I couldn't do it. Where would my "American-ness" fit in?

People always have labels for others, neat little imaginary stickers that they attach to other people's foreheads to make it easier to understand where they fit in the world. Black, White, Asian, Hispanic, Old, Young, Rich, Poor, Immigrant, American, Foreigner. It's an easy task when individuals appear to fit into those neat categories, like items scanned at a supermarket, but it doesn't work with multiracial people, who are hard to place in the usual categories. You can scan and then rescan, but it's hard to come up with an appropriate label. Maybe the curious few will ask "Where are you from?" or "What are you?" But what happens when the labels people stick on you don't fit your self-identity?

I've worn lots of labels in my life. Some with pride, some with discomfort, some without knowing the label was applied to me. I lived in Japan until I was 7 (even though I was born in America … more on that later), when we moved to Arizona. When I was 18, I said good-bye to wide blue skies, Mars-like desert-scapes, and cacti. I traded in my T-shirts and shorts for puffy down jackets and long underwear to attend college in New Hampshire. Up to that time I had already worn lots of labels: *ha-fu*, the term for mixed-race Japanese people in Japan, and *gaijin*, which means "foreigner" in Japanese. Also new immigrant, Asian, biracial, Asian American.

This isn't a new story or an original narrative. Many people immigrate to the United States to start a new life and chase the American Dream, but my story was complicated in that my family didn't fit the usual labels. My father, an engineer by training, grew up as the oldest of eight children in a Muslim family in Bangladesh. He fought with his fellow countrymen for Bengali independence and took part in designing the national flag. He then worked as a civil engineer, designing buildings and bridges and developing infrastructure all over the Middle East and Southeast Asia. My mother was always an independent spirit. When she graduated from the Christian University in Japan, she looked around and found that all of her fellow classmates were married. Feeling restricted by the limited roles women enjoyed in Japanese society, she purchased a one-way ticket to the United States. After working briefly as a teaching assistant in California, she began her doctoral studies in cultural anthropology at Stanford University.

When my parents met on a train in Thailand almost thirty years ago, they probably never imagined the child they would have or the kind of world I would grow up in. Japan is a homogenous society, where 98 percent of the population is ethnically Japanese, and it's notorious for being a difficult place for foreigners to integrate into or gain citizenship. I recently read an article stating that 10 percent of marriages in Tokyo are international marriages—that is, between Japanese citizens and foreigners. That figure really took me by surprise. But walking around Tokyo in 2010, my mom and I did see many multicultural families with multiracial children—Japanese mothers with Brazilian fathers, a black mom with a Japanese dad. This was not common twenty years earlier. When I was born in 1984, citizenship laws in Japan discriminated against Japanese women, and only Japanese men could pass on their citizenship to their children. My pregnant mother realized that if I couldn't be a Japanese citizen, then I would be a Bangladeshi citizen through my dad. She felt that would not be ideal and made the decision to give birth to me in the United States. That's how a Japanese woman and a Bangladeshi man gave birth to an American citizen.

I was born in California but moved to Tokyo when I was 3 months old. My first memories are of spending time with my grandparents in Japan, playing with my peers in Japanese day care, and learning Japanese. We moved in next door to my mother's parents, so I was brought up with 100 percent Japanese influence. I attended Japanese day care, played with Japanese friends, and spoke only Japanese. Although I felt completely Japanese, my darker skin made me an outsider to my peers. I was called *kurokogepan*, or burnt black toast, because I did not look like the other children. Influenced by their parents, society, and the media, children learn at a young age how to categorize others. I wore the labels of "foreigner" and "outsider" but was too young to comprehend why. Since I didn't know myself as anything other than Japanese, I found those labels extremely hurtful. When I looked in the mirror, what I saw was a tan Japanese child, and I didn't understand why people would think of me as something different. Nevertheless, I had no trouble making friends and still keep in touch with friends in Japan. We played *mamagoto* (house) and *karuta* (cards), bathed at hot-spring resorts, and attended New Year ceremonies with my grandparents at the neighborhood Shinto shrine. It was a classic case of nurture over nature: I was Japanese and I didn't know anything else.

I spent most of my summers in rural Japan, camping in the mountains and playing with other biracial children at the international camp that my mom sent me to. The camp was in a small town of 30,000 nestled in the Japan Alps in the Nagano prefecture, near the location of the 1998 Winter Olympic Games. My mother, always wanting distance from the nearest neighbors, built a lone log cabin on the side of the mountain. For one school year I walked down the mountain path and through the rice paddies to attend school. The school rules did not permit parents to give students a ride back and forth from school, and you had to be beyond a certain distance from the school to have permission to ride your bike. Through summer thunderstorms and winter blizzards, students as young as six were instructed to walk to school in order to build strength and confidence. I loved going to school in the Japanese countryside, where we'd catch cicadas and observe morning glories for science projects and participate in Obon summer festivals to honor our ancestors.

In 1992 my mother decided it was time I learned English, since my father didn't speak any Japanese and I was unable to communicate with him. Although my mother was a professional interpreter, she grew tired of having to interpret between her family members. During a business trip to the Southwest, my parents decided that Arizona would be an ideal place to relocate the family. That was, by my childish standards, the end of my life as I knew it. I resented the move because I was taken away from my grandparents and friends, and I was horrified to find that I did not have the linguistic or cultural ability to fit in in America.

I was placed in English as a Second Language courses and "developmental first grade" at a public school in Arizona. My parents thought the "sink or swim" method was the best way for me to learn English, and so I was dropped without a life jacket into American waters. The majority of my ESL classmates were Mexican-American immigrants, and I felt that, with my skin color, most of my teachers and peers identified me as Mexican as well. Although I struggled to learn English, the Japanese education system had put me ahead in subjects like math and science, so by second grade I was able to join mainstream classrooms. At that point in my life I identified as strictly Japanese, and I missed Japan and resented my parents for the move to a new country where I did not have friends and couldn't understand the culture. My parents tell me that I would come home and ask questions like "Why do the American children raise their hands in class when they don't know the correct answer?" which reflected my confusion with a new education system. I had gotten used to the Confucian system in Japan, which emphasizes respect for elders, conforming to the group, and following directions. On Saturdays I attended a Japanese school in a neighboring city, where I could learn from government-approved Japanese textbooks and earn a middle school certificate—this symbolizing, at least to me, my Japanese-ness.

Yuki Kondo-Shah

My U.S. teachers would ask us for "personal reflection" and how we "interpreted" reading passages. This was quite different from the Japanese form of pedagogy I was used to. Teachers and parents would comment on how polite and respectful I was. My mother still laughs at the memory of other children's parents asking her how she raised such a polite, respectful, well-behaved child. Apparently, my politeness and good behavior made us stand out as foreigners. Teachers and parents who saw my mom picking me up from school would ask if I was adopted, as my mother and I looked so different that we didn't seem to belong together. This made me feel incredibly self-conscious.

I remember being teased for making grammatical mistakes and having a foreign accent, and I was embarrassed that I couldn't pronounce words the way my classmates did. It didn't help that friends who came over would comment that our house smelled like "curry" and that my parents spoke English with an accent. I spent the first couple of years in America feeling completely like a foreigner, counting the days until the summer break, when my mom would put me on a plane to visit my grandparents and friends in Japan. For me, going to Japan was going home to the country where I belonged and where I fit in. There I could tear off the labels of "foreigner" and "immigrant." Or so I thought.

As soon as I landed in Japan, the flight attendants looked at me and asked in broken English, "Where are you going?" I took great offense at this, as I was Japanese and should not have been treated as a foreigner! I would reply in fluent Japanese that I knew exactly where I was going. This was met every time with a surprised look and a condescending "Wow, your Japanese is really good for a foreigner." Of course, when this happens now, I smile and just keep moving on, but for an 8-year-old who was sensitive about where she belonged in the world, these comments compounded my sense of not belonging.

But the worst was yet to come. At get-togethers with my friends, I quickly learned that after a year abroad, I was hopelessly behind on the newest pop music, TV dramas, and youth culture. To my horror, I would sometimes forget phrases in Japanese, and words would flow out of my mouth in English. My friends would look puzzled, sigh under their breath, and envy my English language skills. As time went on, I found that I didn't fit into Japanese society anymore because I was "too American," but I didn't fit into American culture either because I was "too foreign." I had become someone without a home, and that was terribly isolating. The Japanese label I longed to stick on my forehead didn't match those being placed on me without my consent.

When I was a young child, my tan skin was a mark of difference, and I felt it was a curse. I felt anger toward my parents for depriving me of my country of origin, where I could feel a sense of unity and conformity. I felt that if I had just one background, life would be simpler, and I was obsessed with wanting a "pure" identity. I felt that if I were just American, then I wouldn't have problems. I see now that what I meant at that time was "If only I were white." As I came to understand my own racial identity through interactions with other groups, I wanted to learn the markers and culture of the most "successful" group. I longed to identify with the majority group wherever I was, but because of my physical characteristics, I didn't fit into either Japanese or American society. When I was in Japan, I felt an increasing culture gap, which made it easy for others to label me as a foreigner. In America, I attempted to learn the cultural cues that would help me succeed socially—a goal that would become very important to me during middle school and the early years of high school.

In seventh grade I switched to a private prep school. This school was academically competitive and provided me with an intellectual challenge, but the demographics were high income and almost all white. At first it was easy to make friends, but I had a hard time really connecting with my peers. Even though I was involved in student government, I found that the issues I cared about weren't necessarily what my peers considered important. In the beginning I tried to fit in by being overly materialistic and focusing on my exterior characteristics, and was frustrated that I did not meet Western standards of beauty. I also wasn't an ideal student, as I studied only topics I was already interested in. I did join the debate team, which became a perfect outlet for me to express myself. Debate opened my mind to philosophies that changed the way I looked at my classmates and what we studied in the classroom. Foucault's theories on normalization and Naomi Wolf's "beauty myth" challenged the way I perceived myself and my relationships with others. Traveling around the country to debate tournaments made me feel successful. I began to reorganize my priorities and became more interested in the pursuit of knowledge rather than consumerism or shallow relationships.

I have always been extremely close to my parents because there are only the three of us. During college, and even now that I am starting graduate school, I call my mother every day and tell her what's happening in my life. Some of my friends think it's overkill and wonder why I have so much to say to my parents. I am especially close to my mother, and maybe at first it was because she was my connection to Japan. My parents were stricter than the parents of my American friends, and they made sure that I followed the values I'd learned in Japan— politeness, respect for elders, and responsibility. Although I spent some of my childhood resenting that my parents were immigrants, I was also hyper-protective of them. For example, if a bank teller was impatient with my mother because of her accented English, I felt angry. During my senior year of high school, I was bullied by classmates who made prank calls to our house mocking my mother's accent, which really hurt.

When it came time to search for a college, I wanted a school that made diversity a priority. Coming from a high school that lacked diversity, I was looking for an environment where I could find role models and mentors. During my search I was in touch with the dean of Asian American students at the college I did ultimately attend, and was delighted to receive emails from the president of one of the student Asian American organizations. Once I arrived on campus, however, I changed my mind about participating in this organization, as I felt that joining it would put me in a narrow category, and it wasn't a label I was comfortable wearing. I felt that the numerous Asian American organizations didn't offer a community in which I could participate because they were very country-specific: the Chinese Cultural Society or the Korean Students Association, for example. I felt that the East Asian students would doubt my authenticity if I showed up at one of their meetings because I didn't look fully Chinese or Japanese; and, sadly, because my dad hadn't taught me about South Asian culture, I was afraid of being called out as a fake or a poser if I tried to associate with the South Asians. As a prospective student, I had admired the diversity of student organizations and felt it was wonderful that so many diversity clubs and organizations existed at the school, but at the end of the day, I didn't feel that as a biracial Asian American I could find a space where I fit in and felt at home.

For obvious reasons, I'm 100 percent supportive of interracial relationships. Since I am the product of an interracial relationship, it would be difficult not to be in one myself. Fortunately, I have my parents' full support in terms of whom I choose to date. My mother is generally more modern about dating than my father, and I frequently seek her advice about romantic relationships. My dad is more old-school; although he is already worried that I am too old not to be married, he thinks dating is unnecessary. Being in an interracial and intercultural relationship, however, my parents are very accepting of men from any background. Many of my friends' parents would frown upon their bringing home a partner from a different background, and it's a relief to know that the racial background of my partner will never be an issue with mine.

I have always been attracted to multiracial men. Whether they are Japanese and Caucasian, African American and Caucasian, Native American and Mexican, I find both their physical characteristics and their multicultural background incredibly alluring. When I was younger and didn't know many other people who were multiracial, my attraction stemmed from a nearly desperate need to connect with others who might have had experiences like mine. I would sometimes incorrectly impose on others the idea that because they were also mixed race, they would understand where I was coming from or that the relationship would somehow be easier. It was as if I believed a magical chain of common experiences connected all multiracial people. Clearly this was silly, but looking back on it now, I see that it was my way of trying to find relationships with people I thought were like me. I now recognize that just because a man and I are both multiracial, it doesn't necessarily mean that we have anything else in common.

I am especially flattered when multiracial men find me attractive. Asian American and Asian men generally do not pay attention to me. I can't really explain why, but it seems that I am simply not their target. That being said, it is difficult for me to admit, but my most serious relationships have all been with Caucasian men, and my most recent and most serious relationship is with a Caucasian man I met at Stanford. Nevertheless, I've always found myself frustrated by these men's lack of understanding about the minority experience in America. On the one hand, I think it is unfair to generalize that Caucasians can't understand the experiences of minorities, but on the other hand, I recall countless fights over a boyfriend's lack of understanding or lack of passion for the issues that I care about. I also am acutely aware of being the "different" one in a relationship and am wary of being in partnerships where my mixed background serves as fodder for an "interesting" conversation.

During my early experience working in Asian college admissions, I constantly feared being detected as a fraud; after all, I was not a real Asian because of my mixed background. I was afraid that my colleagues and, more important, the students and families I met in my work wouldn't be satisfied with my knowledge of Asian culture, history, and norms. I was supposed to represent Asia in the office and be the local expert on all things Asian, and I wondered if I was capable of this. So I faced my fear of being an incomplete Asian and started to learn more about the community. I began to study the history of various ethnic groups and pulled out National Geographic maps to test my geography.

Yuki Kondo-Shah

I found that I genuinely enjoyed this process and began to take real pride in identifying myself as an Asian American. While I spent most of my childhood being Japanese and my college years identifying as a mixed-race minority, I began my professional career as an Asian American. It was all part of a process of growing and feeling comfortable with my place in the world.

Growing up, I hadn't thought much about my Bangladeshi heritage. Because I grew up in Japan and America, I identified more with those cultures. I often questioned my father's lack of interest in teaching me his language and culture, particularly given his willingness to fight in the Bangladeshi war for independence. Why fight to protect your homeland's culture and language if not for your own children? I still feel a sense of "racial melancholia" when it comes to my Bangladeshi identity, and when I visit Bangladesh or interact with South Asians in the United States, I don't know the correct cultural gestures or things to say. I have tried to talk to my father about this, but he just jokes and says that it matters only that children speak their "mother tongue"—by which he means my mother's tongue. I'm always in trouble when friends ask me about Bangladesh, because to be honest, I don't know much about the place. While traveling with my family to Bangladesh in 2008, I was surrounded by people who looked like me and expected me to be able to communicate with them, but instead found me unable to utter a single word.

In my previous role as a college admissions officer, I read around 2,500 personal statements written by high school students who revealed their innermost thoughts in an attempt to gain a place in a highly selective school. Many of these essays were well crafted but lacking in creativity, but a few were so powerful and personal that I found myself haunted by the students' words for days. One such essay was written by a multiracial woman who told about her mixed-race background. She shared her most intimate thoughts about her identity—how she had reconciled her feelings about herself and the way the outside world perceived her. Perhaps her words spoke to me because I could empathize with her lack of confidence and identify with her predicament. We were trained as admissions professionals not to have personal bias or to be swayed by emotions, but her words struck a chord with me. She described an incident when a classmate mocked her background and she found herself upset and crying. After speaking with her mother, she realized that only she had the power to define who she was. She wrote: "I realized I had no right to be ashamed of who I was. I put my energy into mourning the cultures that were absent from my life instead of embracing the one that helped me become who I am. My other cultures are here. I see them every time I look in the mirror. But neither my ethnicity nor any other person can define me. I reserve that right for myself."

Her words were so powerful, and her level of understanding so mature and sophisticated for someone so young. I found myself wishing I had been able to think at that level at her age, and possibly have avoided much of the confusion I had faced. Looking back, however, I can see clearly that the period of my life that caused me confusion and pain also became the foundation for who I am. I have benefited from my international background and from being exposed to many countries and cultures when I was a young child. I have also been blessed by being a mixed-race person because my experience as a minority in America has made me more able to empathize with people's differences.

I recently began graduate school, and being in a new environment and meeting new people remind me of how my identity makes me stand out. Almost every day for the past two months I've gotten the comment "Your name sounds Japanese but you don't look Japanese." Nevertheless, for the first time in my adult life I have found a community of Japanese people who accept me and treat me like I am one of them. It's a very new feeling, and because I am polite and my mannerisms are Japanese, they sometimes jokingly say, "You're almost more Japanese than Japanese people!"

This new experience—being a graduate student, meeting new people who have new expectations about who they think I am, and getting oriented in a new environment—has brought up old memories of trying to fit in or carve out a space where I belong. I spent high school being acutely aware of being a minority but not knowing what to do about it. I spent college being proud of being a student of color and organizing communities around this shared experience, while also being fearful that I wasn't Asian enough to be accepted by other Asians. I spent my initial years as an admissions officer fearing that the community would not accept my credentials as an Asian American. But here at graduate school, I'm fully embracing my identity. I'm actually surprised by the ease with which I sign up for Asian American organizations that I would have shied away from as an undergrad. My definition of Asian American has become more sophisticated, and I know that there isn't just one common identity within this group. Most of all, I know that my experiences and my knowledge matter. I'm happy that my background and experiences give me access to many spaces and groups, and the acceptance I am now getting is the validation I've been seeking for so long from others and, most important, from myself.

Case 9

IN SEARCH OF
A *SANGAM*

ASHA GUPTA

DOI: 10.4324/9781003165378-11

Asha Gupta

Asha spent her childhood as her Indian immigrant parents' "perfect" daughter. During her adolescence she deals with the conflict of being "raised in one culture under the guidelines of an entirely different one" and tries to balance herself as both a "dutiful Indian and an independent American girl." Increasingly, her search for wholeness leads to clashes between herself and her parents. In college she embarks on relationships with people from varied backgrounds. On a trip with her mother to India, Asha comes to see her search for personal identity through the metaphor of a sangam *– an Indian word for "meetings of bodies, be they geographical, physical, spiritual, intellectual." Ultimately, she comes to see herself as a good Indian girl, "just not the one my parents have in mind."*

As the plane descended into Indira Gandhi International Airport in Delhi, India, the chattering of Hindi from my fellow passengers grew louder. I had been anticipating this moment for seven months. It was the fall term of my junior year in college, and I was going to India to research educational systems through a grant I received from my college's center for international understanding. It had been eight years since I traveled to India, and I knew that the trip would be a challenge for my identity as an Indian-American female. Would I be comfortable? Would I be able to relate to the people? Would I feel as lost in India as I did in America? I had decided not to force myself into a process of active soul-searching. Rather, I would open myself up to the culture and accept what naturally occurred.

The moment I walked out of the Delhi airport the hot midnight air enveloped me. I felt a distant and singular sense of familiarity. There was a mass of people waiting outside. Family members waving, pointing, yelling excited greetings. This is the way it is in India. I had forgotten. When loved ones travel, especially internationally, it is a huge family event. I scanned the crowd and my eyes landed on my *maasi* (aunt), then *naanaaji* (maternal grandfather), my *mausa* (uncle), and finally my 9-year-old cousin. They all rushed forward to give me a hug and welcome me home.

I felt like a foreigner for the first few weeks I was there. While I had memories of previous visits and had a connection to the country through my parents, I was detached from the daily goings-on, as if I was only an observer. As this "foreigner," I did not think much about the implications of the culture on my life. After all, I was there to observe schools as an American and my relatives viewed me as an American; that's what made me interesting to them.

Since starting college I had been neglecting my "Indian side" and it eventually became normal to go about my life without connecting to it. I did not participate in the events of the college's South Asian group because I felt they marginalized the culture by perpetuating stereotypes. Their "culture nights" tended to focus on superficial things that would easily entertain, though not necessarily educate: midriff-bearing fashion shows, dances from Bollywood films, brainless skits that mocked what they were supposedly celebrating. These were not the things I associated with being Indian. As it seemed there were no outlets to express that side of me, a sort of deactivation occurred. But once I was back in the country of my ancestors it was not long before I began to feel India in me. For better or worse, the land and people and sights and smells and tastes and sounds could no longer be compartmentalized in the back of my mind. The objective mindset of an observer/anthropologist was slowly and surely being replaced by the personal subjectivity of a participant. I remember thinking on several occasions, "This country is *me*. This is where I come from." It was overwhelming to feel a sense of place, a kind of responsibility to the land because it had become a part of me.

This does not mean that I love everything about India. On the contrary, there are many things that infuriate me about the way things work there. For example, it is rare for a woman to walk down a street without getting ogled by men who feel entitled to let their eyes and mouths wander wherever they want, embodying the power of the patriarchy. I experienced this everywhere I went. In a small town, a group of young men once followed me, trying to take my picture, as though an Indian girl in a tank top and sneakers was the most incredible thing they had ever seen. Also, corruption is apparent in everyday life, as bribery is a common method of getting things done. And, as expected, the level of poverty and division of classes were extremely difficult to come to terms with. A society structured upon such obvious and ancient hierarchy left me questioning my own biases; how could I judge something I didn't understand? But while I had to accept these things to a certain extent, I was accepting them in an entirely different context than before. I was personally offended by the negative things I saw and proud of the positive, as if I had something to do with it. Limbless beggar children and beautiful ancient temples struck a similar sense of ownership within me. My many emotions – fury, excitement, anger, confusion, and fondness – were heightened and transferred to a part of me that hadn't been tapped in years.

Asha Gupta

These sensibilities were intensified when my mother joined me about a month after I arrived in India. We traveled together quite a bit. She was hesitant at first, wanting to stay in Delhi with the family, but I insisted that we explore the country, as we both had seen little of it. We touched all sides of India, even venturing into Nepal, and these travels gave us a perspective on the culture and land that we had never before experienced. Every place we went was like a mini-country within India, each with its own language, food, dress, and lifestyle.

We traveled to two places known for their *sangams* (meetings of bodies, be they geographical, physical, spiritual, intellectual) – Allahabad and Kanya Kumari. Allahabad is the village that sits on the convergence of the rivers Ganga, Sarasvati, and Yamuna. It is considered sacred because of this *sangam*. Once every twelve years, millions of people travel to Allahabad for the *Kumbh Mela*, a Hindu bathing festival of rebirth. Kanya Kumari is the southernmost tip of India. The *sangam* here is again one of water: the Indian Ocean, Bay of Bengal, and Arabian Sea – three immense bodies coming together at a single point, creating a breadth and depth of endless blue waves. Breathing the air was intoxicating; all that water, all those different entities from different places that had seen different things coming together to create one being. I felt very connected to these *sangams.* The separate waters are akin to the mishmash of different origins I have felt within myself, never knowing where I fully belong, *if* I fully belong. Being in Allahabad and Kanya Kumari gave me some comfort with these issues, made me feel that my own distinct parts were as natural as the bodies of water themselves. My mother's presence personified these challenges of identity, and gave me a soothing sense of foundation.

Our travel experiences, combined with spending time with family members (some I'd never met prior to this trip) and being in the country of my heritage, gave me a new take on myself – who I was, where I came from, where I was going. While I did not feel that I could completely identify as an Indian or an American, I became more comfortable with both the distinctiveness and synthesis of these cultures within me. My mother expressed her personal struggle with immigrant identity when I asked about her own cultural identification on our journey back to America. She looked at me with confused eyes and said, "You know, Asha, after living in America for thirty years and going back to India this time, I realize that there are things about each place that I both identify with and don't. Truthfully, I feel kind of lost." That moment was one of the closest between us. Despite our disparate personalities and opinions, and the number of fights we'd had about our battling cultures, I will never forget how well we understood each other then.

That moment of understanding with my mother was particularly meaningful because my parents and I grew up very differently, so we rarely relate to each other's personal cultural experiences. Both of my parents are from India. My father was born in a section of India that is now in Pakistan. He is the eldest of five children from a religious Hindu family. His family was poor, and they experienced terrible hardship traveling to India from newly formed Pakistan during the 1947 Partition of India. They settled in Delhi, where my grandfather started a business that still operates today. My father had to play parent to his younger siblings for much of his youth, as his father was hard at work and his mother was preoccupied with health problems. Despite these hardships, he excelled academically, and in the early 1960s earned a scholarship to an American institute of technology, journeying across the world as the first of his family to come to America. My father later earned a Ph.D. at an Ivy League university. Following his schooling, he returned to Delhi to meet the women his family had selected for him as possible wives. One of these women was my mother, whose story is quite different.

My mother's family quickly grew prosperous after their own struggles during Partition. The eldest of four children, my mother grew up mainly in India, but also in other parts of the world, as her father worked for the United Nations. Her family was very close; my mother's mother was extremely loving and fulfilled her maternal duties above and beyond the expectations of a good Hindu. My mother also excelled in school and was one of the few women at her college in India to study chemistry. She also studied the hard sciences in America, until she returned to Delhi in 1970 to consider marriage.

My mother and father were introduced with the intention of marriage. They went out a couple of times and decided they were a suitable match. Six weeks after they met, they married and subsequently returned to America to start their lives together. Four years later, my sister was born. I came along six years after her. My mother did not pursue her love of the sciences after my sister was born, as she chose to devote her life to her family and home.

Upon setting foot inside our house there is no question that we are an Indian family. Many of our paintings are of traditional Indian scenes. Our living room is full of Indian furniture, painted wooden screens, and sculptures (one of Gandhi and one of Buddha). Small bronze figures of Indian gods and goddesses, a miniature replica of the Taj Mahal, and a large map of India add to the thematic décor, and the scent of *agarbathi* (incense) permeates the air. Most evenings, my mother can be found preparing dinner, usually spiced *daal* (lentils), *chawaal* (rice), *achaar* (Indian pickle), and some form of *sabzi* (vegetable).

My parents raised my sister and me very "Indian," and sought to integrate their host culture into their native cultural lifestyle. As a result, I grew up being proud of and interested in my heritage, no matter how frustrating it was trying to balance two cultures. As a child, I liked telling people that I came from India and spewing out random facts, such as, "Did you know the Taj Mahal is in India?" or "My aunt lives in India and she talks British!" and the eternally proud pronouncement, "I've *been* to India. I'm *from* there."

By grade school I had traveled to India quite a few times. The experiences I had of the heat, countless people, poverty, sounds of street merchants, itchy mosquito bites, spicy foods, and loving relatives only intensified my attachment to the culture. It also helped that one of my father's brothers lives near us with his family. My sister and I are close to these cousins, who are the same age as we are. As we grew older, we talked through a lot of cross-cultural issues we had with our parents, laughed at the family idiosyncrasies, and shared a rare mutual understanding that was not possible with our "American" friends.

Many Indian families in our area, including mine, used to go to a devout Hindu man's house every Sunday where his living room was transformed into a religious space. The floor was covered in white sheets, and we'd all sit cross-legged, shoes off, listening to his words. He would read aloud sacred texts and preach, and we would all sing *bhajans* (religious songs) while he played the harmonium. At the end of the service we would all stand and sing the traditional ending song, the *arthi*. During this song people would go to the front of the room one by one and hold up a plate with a lit *dhiya* (wick made of cotton dipped in butter) and edible and monetary offerings, moving their arms to make an *Om* shape with the flame. Afterward, we would all eat the *prasad*, the blessed food, which was usually *halwa*, a saccharine and oily sweet. I never questioned these religious customs, nor did I feel strange taking part in them. On the contrary, when remembering these times I feel a sense of safety and warmth. Everyone knew each other. I have grown up calling my parents' friends "Auntie" and "Uncle"; it is these sorts of traditions that have kept our Indian community close.

I was the quintessential "Daddy's little girl." My father is wonderful with children; they love him as much as he loves playing with them. He spoiled me and we had very happy times together – he made me laugh harder than anyone I knew. I always wanted him to put me to bed because he invented the best stories, came up with fun games, and created the greatest songs. I was a smart kid, which made my parents proud; there are few things more important to Indian immigrants than their children's education. I have no complaints about my childhood; my home life was worry-free and secure, and as the cute and precociously bright baby of the family, I could get whatever I wanted. I was happy.

Things started changing when I was in middle school. I transferred the idolatry I had for my parents to my big sister, who was in high school. I became her confidante, her partner in crime. I lied to my parents when she had boys over, and went to the "library" with her when she was actually going out with friends. I felt a bit guilty for lying, but by age 12 I related to my sister better than to my parents and our solidarity was in some ways necessary. I was beginning to like boys, listen to rock music, question religion, and realize that I did not always agree with my parents' values. All of this made them unhappy and apprehensive. My father and I were not getting along, and it seemed his temper was becoming our fifth family member. My mother's worry that I was straying from my academic focus became overbearing and I suspected that things would get much harder when my sister left for college.

Once I was the only child in the house, my parents and I started arguing more and more. I began to note the differences between the way my family and the families of my American friends worked. With the new choices and decisions that came with my age, it grew harder for me to feel normal, given my parents' reaction to the changes I was experiencing. For instance, they expected me to remain obedient and unquestioning, ignoring the fact that I was getting older and forming my own value system, which often conflicted with theirs (seemingly unavoidable when raised in one culture under the guidelines of an entirely different one). When I disagreed with them it was taken as a sign of disrespect. A typical response to my questioning was, "We are your parents. You do not question us. We know what is best." This upset me because I felt that I should be most comfortable expressing my views and standing up for my beliefs with my parents, which is, admittedly, a Western ideal. I was different from my sister, who usually internalized her discontent in order to prevent a conflict. This led my parents to believe that she had been more obedient than she actually was, which made my "disrespect" even more unexpected to them. They thought the issues with my sister had prepared them to have better experiences raising me, but I usually ended up speaking my mind, knowing it would likely escalate into hours of screaming, crying, and slamming doors.

The fights with my parents continued through high school. During that time I never could keep my mouth shut – I *had* to speak my mind and do some things I knew they disapproved of. I knew this would lead to more fighting, but I had a real problem with not being allowed to say what I thought to my own family. It was so hard to deal with the pressure I felt from them and from myself to achieve the über-identity of the perfect mixture of a dutiful Indian and an independent American girl. I was to excel at school, obey my parents, maintain their traditional values, repress any sexual desire or questioning, be home by ten at night on weekends, get into a good college, respect my heritage, participate in extracurricular activities, star in the school play, and so forth. It was confusing for me to maintain this identity and also experiment with things I felt were natural for my age, but which my parents most certainly did not. I did not want to fight with my parents, but I felt it was my right to express myself regardless of whether or not they agreed.

Despite the negative situation at home, I managed to accomplish a great deal in high school. I maintained high grades, participated in community service activities, was involved in drama, had good friends, and won awards. My parents and I agreed that these activities were important and expected. While I fulfilled these expectations, however, I never received the praise I wanted from them. I still wanted more than anything to please them, yet the only recognition I received was from other people. I just wanted my parents to tell me they were proud of me, without my having to ask, but they only told me what I was doing wrong and did not really understand why I needed to hear *from them* that they were proud of my accomplishments. This hurt and left me confused about what they wanted from me, and what I wanted from myself. How much did I have to fit into their mold for them to be happy with me? I could not be the perfect Indian daughter, having been raised in America. I had low self-esteem despite the positive qualities others thought I had, and was struggling hard to maintain some sort of control over my identity. This confusion and need for control manifested itself through a mild eating disorder and an omnipresent sense of unhappiness.

It appeared to others that we were a happy family. I never talked with my friends in detail about my situation at home; I did not want to air our dirty laundry, and I did not think anyone but my sister could understand. I felt that I had no control, and although I stuck to my beliefs, the two people who mattered most to me never accepted them.

As easy as it is to paint my sister and me as victims, we both know, despite our own resentment, that our parents cannot be demonized. They had reasons for being so angry and disappointed with us. I believe much of it has to do with their upbringing – just as my sister and I are confused about our identity as American-born children of immigrants, so too do our parents struggle with assimilation while trying to preserve their heritage. Their own parents' ideas about raising children in 1940s and 1950s India were the models my parents followed in America, where blind respect and obedience are far less easy to come by.

My sister is the only other person who understands the dynamics of our family and we depend on each other for advice and sympathy. Our connection is unbreakable. I could not have handled many of the issues I've had to deal with without my sister's support. She is my blood, my kin; she is a part of me. Whatever happens in my future, I need to be close to my sister, my *didi*. I would not feel complete without her.

While my family has had a profound effect on my identity, I have also been influenced by the relationships I've had. I fell in love for the first time during my freshman year of college. We were an interesting match. He was a moderate conservative from a close family, loved heavy metal music and girls who looked like Southern belles, and was extremely logical. Then there was me, the die-hard liberal from a dys-functional family. I hated heavy metal, dressed more like a hippie than a belle, and existed for emotion. But these differences were what made us interesting to each other. My boyfriend challenged me, and we made each other look at things from another perspective. Granted, we argued all the time, but we were learning so much and our love was new and exciting. We gave each other our virginity and our promises.

After some time, however, our differences got in the way of our happiness. I found myself becoming so dependent on him and feeling inadequate. He seemed to consider what I said unimportant and when we disagreed he would be condescending and arrogant – a definite change from when we first got together. I didn't like who I became around him; I was silencing myself trying to be the girl that he wanted me to be, and this was infuriating. He had no real interest in my family or my roots, and I drifted away from those things. I felt most fully "American" with him, because those were the ideals he held high. During our junior year, we spent six months apart while studying abroad (I was in India, then London) and we realized that we were no longer meant to be together. I knew that I needed to be with someone who could respect all parts of me, especially after I reconnected with my heritage in India.

Asha Gupta

In London, I got involved with a female student. It was my first experience with a woman I was truly interested in (this was more than typical experimentation), but I was quite relaxed about the situation. I have always thought it natural to be attracted to people of the same sex and I have many gay, bisexual, and queer friends, but I knew my parents and extended family would be horrified if they knew. I was in awe that this woman wanted to know things about me that my ex-boyfriend never seemed to care about, and I was inspired by her dynamic and radical personality. We continued to date for a short while after returning to school, and her influence on me made me more politically active and aware. We have since remained good friends. Our relationship made me more conscious of and comfortable with my attraction to women, though I am primarily attracted to men. I view my sexuality as a fluid and flexible thing, and do not label myself as this would only serve to constrict my sexual identity.

I was happier with my last boyfriend than I had ever been with anyone. We were together for a year, ending the relationship when I graduated from college and he was still a student. We shared many interests and beliefs and were deeply in love. He loved me for who I am, not who he wanted me to be. We shared all of ourselves with each other. I felt whole with him and comfortable in my skin. He was so giving, loving, and accepting, which made me more conscious of how I could be a better person. He raised the bar as to what I expect from a partner, particularly that he or she will bring out all parts of me with reciprocal pride and comfort.

Though these represent my most recent relationships, my romantic life really began at age 15, when a high-school senior started paying attention to me. He was smart, funny, charming, and caused me much heartache and teenage trauma. Other romances include a hippie I met at the beach, a bisexual actor ten years my senior, a heroin addict, a born-again Christian, an egomaniac with an Asian fetish, and a fun-loving goofball who had had a short stint in prison. These romantic partners and others I have experienced, though all very different, have one thing in common: they are all white.

I have never been involved with a person of color. Although I think this is merely a matter of circumstance, I know it is no accident that I have never been involved with an Indian man. I think this has to do with fear, the fear that an Indian man will want to impose on me the subservient role that Indian women have had for generations. Many Indian-American men I know see how their fathers are treated by their mothers and view that sort of relationship – being pampered, treated as masters, and feared – as the ideal. These men often have dated white girls throughout adolescence, but when it comes to marriage, they want an Indian girl, often one from India. Of course, these are generalizations and I know not all Indian men are the same, but my fear nevertheless prohibits me from objectively entertaining the idea of being with an Indian man.

Most of the men I know are white, and they tend to be more compatible with my personality than the Indian men I know. It has crossed my mind that I may be rejecting the idea of being with an Indian man to spite my parents or to transcend tradition, but I do not believe this is the case. I keep my romantic life hidden from my parents for the most part, so it is not something we discuss. Furthermore, I want to please them. Although I do many things that go against their beliefs, I have often wished that my values were in line with theirs. I would rather reach a level of understanding with them instead of doing things that make them angry.

I have thought about ending up with an Indian and I do see the benefits of such a situation. We would have a sense of understanding that I could not have with a partner from another culture. If we were to have children, it would be easier to have a common history. It is true that I have not actively sought out an Indian man, but I don't feel any need to at this point in my life. I admit that I should work on my bias against Indian men, but I believe that will happen by meeting more Indian men to whom I can relate – not typical "good Indian boys."

I am not the typical "good Indian girl." Feminism, activism, sex, and drugs have played a part in my life. If my parents knew they would be appalled. They could never imagine their Ivy League, highly motivated, work-driven daughter would even think about doing drugs. Neither of them has ever smoked or consumed alcohol – the result of an unbroken promise made to their parents and each other. They have reconciled the fact that I do drink occasionally, but it makes them uncomfortable.

The codes of my culture even travel with me to the bedroom. Sometimes while being sexually physical, my mind wanders to thoughts of my ancestors and certain family members. I think about how appalled they would be if they could see what I was doing and feel what I was feeling. It is an obsession with making my family proud and honoring my culture that is at the crux of my struggles with identity. This worry extends to almost every aspect of my life, but I nevertheless cannot deny myself the things that bring me joy. I am not promiscuous; I am young, curious, and safe. I am not an addict; I experiment lightly. I am more an artist than a scientist. I am a good Indian girl … just not the one my parents have in mind.

I began to achieve a greater sense of security with this cultural duality in my last year of college. My trip to India gave me a renewed outlook on my identity and how to stay connected to my Indian side, so I decided to involve myself in South Asian cultural activities at school. I joined three groups in one term. When I expressed my objections to the Asian culture nights and the stereotypes I felt they perpetuated, people listened and many agreed. Changes were made and an activist mentality began to influence the way these Asian groups thought about their culture.

I also wrote about my experiences and talked about my trip to India. For a comparative literature course, I wrote a lengthy prose and poetry piece about immigrant mothers, their daughters, sexuality, exoticism, and the balance of cultures. The work came naturally, as these were all issues I had thought about a great deal. I was extremely proud of this piece, and part of it was published in a student literary magazine. I read some of the pieces at an Asian drama group's production (which I helped organize) centered on the deconstruction of stereotypes of Asian women. I spoke to a group of freshmen at the college president's house about my trip to India, and also held a discussion about the trip and how it affected my life when I came back to campus.

All this action was driven by my newfound connection to my culture, my personal culture – what I had made of myself after serious thought and introspection, visiting the country of my ancestors, experiencing relationships with people who validated the whole of me, and really connecting to the different aspects of myself that make me who I am. I was able to relate who I was through the work I was doing and sharing with others. I feel strong now, and confident in my cultural ties to both America and India. My confidence has strengthened my relationship with my parents, and I think we are beginning to understand each other better. It is really all about sharing. As we learn more about each other's cultural contexts, the previously closed doors of communication open wider. And while it is still at times an uphill battle, I am eager to take on the challenge, and not just with my parents. I love expressing these issues and my thoughts rather than keeping them buried and unexplored. It is as though a well within me was tapped and a rush of different rivers flowed out together, shaping me, shaping others, creating a *sangam*, a meeting of bodies, identities, and cultures.

Part II

CHALLENGES

DOI: 10.4324/9781003165378-12

Theoretical Overview

Within the field of adolescent research there exists a debate over whether adolescence is typically a period of storm and stress, of alienation and separation, or a more harmonious evolution in which positive feelings about self and family are extended into the larger realms of peers and society. Each of these perspectives has merit and accounts for the different individual circumstances and coping styles of a complex period of human development. One point of agreement in this debate is that adolescence is a period of radical transformation of the physical and psychological self. Even under the best of circumstances, adolescents travel an exquisitely poignant journey through difficult developmental terrain. Finding one's way would be challenge enough, but when the ground is continually shifting with the ongoing physical, emotional, and cognitive growth of this period, the journey becomes full-time work for most adolescents. When the ordinary stresses of adolescence are overlaid with extraordinary additional stresses, there emerge important risk factors for healthy development. The cases in this section explore both the dangers and strategies for coping with these challenges.

Our notion of "challenges" implies obstacles or special difficulties that must be negotiated in addition to all the more "typical" preoccupations and developmental tasks of adolescence. Challenges are important both because of what they tell us about adolescent coping strategies in general, and because many adolescents face such circumstances at some point. If we add up all the adolescents who must deal with challenges such as physical disabilities; serious illness; divorce; the death of a parent, sibling, or close friend; physical or sexual abuse; mental illness; and so on, we can see that significant challenges, whether acute or chronic, represent, if not the norm, at least a sizable subsample of all adolescents. An autobiographical exploration of challenges also provides the reader a window into resilience. It allows us to learn which coping strategies, character traits, and social support appear to be most protective and even promotive of adolescent mental health.

Each of the nine cases included in this section represents a distinct challenge to healthy psychological growth at multiple developmental periods as recounted at college age: (1) the impact of a rape during the first weeks of college, (2) the struggle to find belonging as a Native American woman at an elite college, (3) the healing power of Lakota culture on a Native American army combat veteran, (4) the special challenges posed by a physical disability, (5) residual trauma from having a family member killed at the hands of police, (6) immigration and acculturation trauma of a Vietnamese refugee, (7) coping with learning disabilities, (8) coming out as gay during college, and (9) the impact of sexual abuse in the context of foster home placements and multiracial identity. Taken as a whole, these cases highlight both what is unique and universal, at least for Western culture; unique, in terms of specialized issues these problems raise for adolescent development; universal, in that the cases highlight the way in which the tasks of adolescence remain relatively constant even in the face of powerfully destabilizing events and extraordinary stressors. The overlay of preexisting emotional, social, or physical problems, combined with historic inequities and injustice, to the already daunting tasks of adolescence can further complicate the transition to adulthood. At the same time, and more hopefully, the evolving ability throughout adolescence to engage in abstract, analytical thought in combination with increasing emotional and physical autonomy and separation, and the ability to reconstruct one's social support system, can make it possible for the adolescent to overcome some of the more debilitating psychological effects of these issues.

Self-understanding is one of the more important aspects of emerging adolescent abilities for overcoming serious challenges. Prior to adolescence, childhood is characterized by the embeddedness of the child in his or her family and the profound tendency, whether for better or worse, to identify with important persons and norms within the family. The increasing importance of the peer world and the simultaneously evolving capacity to see parents as less powerful and more fallible are conducive to a loosening and diversification of earlier identifications. This evolving capacity for perspective can facilitate healing through important substitute relationships such as teachers, mentors, peers, families of friends, and others (Noam, Powers, Kilkenny, and Beedy, 1990). Such healing may be necessary when families have not been sufficiently nurturing, protective, or enhancing of self-esteem. While these relationships may also be important at earlier periods, the adolescent can increasingly see their *self* through the eyes of these important others. This fresh perspective allows the adolescent to take a more autonomous approach to creating a self of their own choosing. There has long been recognition that this emergent ability to gain self-knowledge and perspective through interaction with others—this "looking glass self" (Cooley, 1902; Mead, 1934)—helps explain why positive relationships can have such a restorative effect on the damage of earlier events. This "mirroring" becomes especially salient in peer and romantic relationships during this time (Sullivan, 1953; Erikson, 1968) as the adolescent learns to take a perspective on themself by means of gradually modifying the self he or she sees reflected in the eyes of peers.

Self-understanding has been shown to be an important "protective factor" (Beardslee, 1989) in ameliorating the risk to healthy psychological development from serious life stressors. Ideally, self-understanding should lead to action that transforms one's adaptation to circumstances, or even changes the circumstances themselves. It is only when insight leads to new and better means of coping with life's challenges that we can say the individual is rising to the challenge. Indeed, insight without action can reflect a profound sense of hopelessness. The cases presented here all reveal the adolescent biographers reacting to significant stress by first developing insight and then taking steps to make things better.

Multiple cases in this section of the book face challenges due to traumatic experiences in childhood and adolescence. These include sexual abuse, rape, war, historic trauma, parental death, parental abandonment, and more. Different forms of trauma can affect individuals in different ways based on factors related to the nature of the trauma (one time or ongoing), whether or not it is disclosed and addressed, and whether there are multiple and chronic forms of stress. In addition to this contextual aspect, individual coping mechanisms and traits can impact the long-term effects of the traumatic events.

An important field within developmental psychology is devoted to studying individuals who are resilient or seemingly invulnerable, or at least less vulnerable, to serious risks and stresses that have been shown to affect negatively the mental health and long-term adjustment of many children. This relatively new field represents a significant historic shift from studying almost exclusively those individuals who succumb to developmental risks to studying those who are equally exposed but who overcome the risk and remain healthy. Among the factors shown to place children at risk are serious mental illness of a parent, physical or sexual abuse, serious marital discord, poverty, emotionally unsupportive relationships with parents, foster home placement, and parental alcoholism (Rutter et al., 1975; Rutter, 1979; Werner, 1989). The impact of Adverse Childhood Experiences (ACES) (which include trauma, abuse, neglect, and more) have been found to have lifelong impacts on physical health and often lead to premature death (Felitti et al., 1998). The original ACES study found a correlation between the number of adverse experiences and the severity of impact on physical health in adulthood. Other studies that look at the psychological impact of risk factors on mental health find differing degrees of relative risk for each of these and other factors. Some findings indicate that when only a single risk factor was present, the probability that a child would suffer from a psychiatric disorder was no greater than for a child in a family without any of these risk factors. However, two risk factors produced a fourfold increase in the chances of a psychiatric disorder in the child; four risk factors produced a tenfold increase in risk. It would seem that most children can cope with a certain amount of stress stemming from these risks, but when overloaded with multiple stressors, they become exponentially more likely to succumb. Many children and adolescents, however, do not succumb even under such stress. Therein lies a hopeful avenue for understanding how some children are protected, or protect themselves, against the vicissitudes of serious stress. We might speculate that whatever these protective coping mechanisms are, they appear to promote good mental health in general and could therefore be helpful even in low-risk individuals.

Three of the most important protective factors to emerge from research are: (1) personality features, such as self-esteem, (2) family cohesion and lack of discord, and (3) external support systems that encourage and reinforce the child's efforts to cope (Garmezy, 1985; Masten and Garmezy, 1985). Protective factors are not fixed attributes; they are subject to development or reduction over time within the same individual, and those that may aid in coping at one time may not work at another. Thus, these factors should be seen as dynamic; the resilient individual is one who can adapt his or her coping strategies to changing situations. In this sense, protective factors should not be seen as fixed traits of the individual or circumstance, but rather as interpersonal and interactive. This is what Rutter (1987) refers to as protective *mechanisms* or *processes* that the individual may apply or modify as needed.

The cases here reveal a variety of risks and developmental vulnerabilities, as well as a number of protective coping mechanisms. These mechanisms are employed to secure important emotional needs, and with the dramatic emotional development during adolescence these needs themselves undergo transformation.

Beyond the protective factors related to individual characteristics, there are social, cultural, and community factors that can protect against the full impact of various risks related to trauma and social, economic, and community stressors. Some of the cases in this section discuss external support that intervened to buffer the effects of multiple adverse risks and experiences. These include mentors, strong identification with positive cultural norms, faith, mental health counseling, special educational support programs, family, and friends. This contextual, environmental aspect of protective factors is important because it can be strengthened through public policy that helps those who are not fortunate enough to be born with inherently resilient characteristics.

The impact of refugee trauma and the stresses of acculturation are described in the chapter "Seeking the Best of Both Worlds," wherein the adolescent tasks related to separation and individuation become especially poignant in the context of an immigrant family having fled a war-ravaged Vietnam. The traumatic experience of emigrating under such circumstance can understandably have profound effects on both the individual and the nature of family relationships. In addition to all the normal preoccupations of adolescence, and beyond the typical parent–child conflicts of the period, this author demonstrates how hard it can be for immigrant adolescents to integrate the best of both cultures if their family demands exclusive loyalty to the native culture. His strategy of alternating his behavior to whatever culture he finds himself in is often effective for immigrant adolescents (Oppedal, 2016) and is even associated with positive mental health (Rogler, Cortes, and Malgady, 1991). In this case, however, we can also see the tremendous emotional stress and developmental risk this form of adaptation can cause. At the same time, the case also illustrates how his increasing competence and validation in the larger culture gradually creates a new and respected role in his family as the intercultural go-between. By the time he writes his autobiography in college, he describes ways in which he has been able to influence his mother in rearing his two younger siblings so as to lessen some of the pain and acculturation conflict he experienced.

Sexual trauma and its aftermath is the subject of two cases in this section. In the chapter, "Is This My Life?", the author describes an acquaintance rape during the first few weeks of her freshman year at college, and traces its impact over time. The incidence of sexual assault among college women suggests that one in five experience unwanted sexual contact, while one study found that 12% of college women experience sexual assault during their first semester, leading to a clinically significant increase in depression and anxiety (Carey et al., 2018).

In the chapter "Multihued," the author describes having been sexually abused while in foster care. Research shows that early disclosure and parental and professional support predict improved outcomes. However, our author was not able to access that support and reports ongoing difficulty with intimacy and trust in romantic relationships (National Child Traumatic Stress Network, 2009).

The chapter "Holding My Breath" describes the many psychological challenges to coming out as gay for the first time as a student in college. The author recounts the isolation from friends and family, the false identity, the fear of being found out, and the inability to conceive of a fulfilling life. In this uplifting account, he found the courage to come out to family and friends after experiencing affirmation and support through his first romantic relationship with another man. It was the unexpected acceptance and support he received from his parents and straight fraternity brothers that made his self-acceptance and positive new identity possible. This interpersonal support provided the protective factors helping to establish a healthy gay identity, something frequently not available to many LGBTQ youth. Research shows that acceptance and support for LGBTQ youth from parents reduces depression, anxiety, and other mental health conditions compared with those without parental acceptance (D'Augelli, 2002).

The chapter "Figuring Out My Life" explores the challenges of living with learning disabilities. The author describes the frustration and shame she felt during high school at her inability to process information as quickly as others. When it was time for college, she wanted to avoid the stigma of learning disabilities and convinced herself that she no longer needed any learning support. Typically, only 24% of students inform their college of the learning disability, and 69% do not do so because they believe they no longer need the help, despite the fact that people don't normally outgrow learning disabilities (Horowitz, Rawe, and Whittaker, 2017). Fortunately, her college contacted all incoming freshmen in advance to inquire about any needed learning support, and while she was reluctant to accept the help, it turned out to make all the difference in her college success. Unfortunately, this type of outreach and offer of support is not available to many college students.

The chapter "Forever an Awkward Adolescent" illustrates how physical disabilities can also pose additional challenges along the adolescent pathway. This author's story illustrates the research findings that adolescents with physical disabilities typically have positive self-esteem, close friendships, and positive family relationships. However, the degree of intimacy in friendships tends to be less than peers without physical limitations, and they tend to participate in fewer social activities. The latter two may be causally related. Our author describes very similar experiences while also showing remarkable self-understanding in his attempt to adapt his physical abilities to the developmental tasks of adolescence. He repeatedly stresses his own responsibility for his adjustment and happiness, and the need to find some means of "fitting in" with his able-bodied peers lest they give up trying to relate to him and leave him to his " 'default' pigeonhole ... of a short, oddly postured disabled kid." And he writes repeatedly of having to create "a persona I could live with" by mirroring himself in the eyes of his peers. This search for identity by means of acceptance and validation by his peers is another important task of adolescence. Thus, he demonstrates the interaction of developmental tasks and protective factors, identity formation and self-understanding respectively, which together serve to compensate for the risks of isolation and dependence his physical disabilities represent. Thirteen years later and in his mid-thirties, he writes a follow-up chapter (included here) from the perspective of a successful executive in a disability advocacy organization. He writes about what has held true and consistent in his life, which life goals his disability has impeded, and what new challenges and opportunities for growth he anticipates in his future.

The nine cases in the Challenges section of this book reveal much about the opportunities of adolescence for growing stronger through challenge. Unfortunately, not all such challenges are met so successfully. These autobiographers do, however, represent the fortunate fact that most adolescents who face such circumstances do somehow find a path to productive lives. The following cases illustrate how such challenges can be met, and though the life stories could not be more different, their pathways to overcoming barriers have much in common.

References

Beardslee, W.R. (1989). The role of self-understanding in resilient individuals: The development of a perspective. *American Journal of Orthopsychiatry, 59*, 266–278. https://doi.org/10.1111/j.1939-0025.1989.tb01659.x.

Carey, K.B., Norris, A.L., Durney, S.E., Shepardson, R.L., & Carey, M.P. (2018). Mental health consequences of sexual assault among first-year college women. *Journal of American College Health, 66*(6), 480–486. https://doi.org/10.1080/07448 481.2018.1431915.

Cooley, C.H. (1902). *Human Nature and the Social Order.* New York: Scribners.

D'Augelli, A.R. (2002). Mental health problems among lesbian, gay, and bisexual youths ages 14 to 21. *Clinical Child Psychology and Psychiatry, 7*, 433–456. https://doi.org/10.1177/1359104502007003039.

Erikson, E.H. (1968). *Identity: Youth and Crisis.* New York: W.W. Norton & Company.

Felitti, V.J., Anda, R.F., Nordenberg, D., Williamson, D.F., Spitz, A.M., Edwards, V., Koss, M.P., & Marks, J.S. (1998). Relationship of childhood abuse and household dysfunction to many of the leading causes of death in adults. The Adverse Childhood Experiences (ACE) study. *American Journal of Preventive Medicine, 14*(4), 245–258. https://doi.org/10.1016/s0749-3797(98)00017-8.

Garmezy, N. (1985). Stress-resistant children: The search for protective factors. In J.E. Stevenson (Ed.), *Recent research in developmental psychopathology (Journal of Child Psychology and Psychiatry Book Suppl.)* (pp. 213–233). Michigan: Pergamon.

Horowitz, S.H., Rawe, J., & Whittaker, M.C. (2017). *The State of Learning Disabilities: Understanding the 1 in 5.* New York: National Center for Learning Disabilities.

Masten, A.S. & Garmezy, N. (1985). Risk, vulnerability, and protective factors in developmental psychopathology. In B.B. Lahey & A.E. Kazdin (Eds.), *Advances in Clinical Child Psychology (Vol. 8)* (pp. 1–52). New York: Plenum Press.

Mead, G.H. (1934). *Mind, Self, and Society.* Chicago: University of Chicago Press.

National Child Traumatic Stress Network Child Sexual Abuse Committee. (2009). *Caring for Kids: What Parents Need to Know about Sexual Abuse.* National Center for Child Traumatic Stress.

Noam, G.G., Powers, S., Kilkenny, R., & Beedy, J. (1990). The interpersonal self in life-span developmental perspective: Theory, measurement, and longitudinal case analyses. In *Life Span Development and Behavior* (pp. 59–104). New York: Routledge.

Oppedal, B. & Toppelberg, C.O. (2016). Acculturation development and the acquisition of culture competence. In D.L. Sam & J.W. Berry (Eds.), *The Cambridge Handbook of Acculturation Psychology* (pp. 71–92). Cambridge: Cambridge University Press. https://doi.org/10.1017/CBO9781316219218.006.

Rogler, L.H., Cortes, D.E., & Malgady, R.G. (1991). Acculturation and mental health status among Hispanics: Convergence and new directions for research. *American Psychologist*, *46*, 585–597. https://doi.org/10.1037/0003-066x.46.6.585.

Rutter, M. (1979). Protective factors in children's responses to stress and disadvantage. *Annals of the Academy of Medicine, Singapore*, *8*(3), 324–338.

Rutter, M. (1987). Psychosocial resilience and protective mechanisms. *American Journal of Orthopsychiatry*, *57*, 316–331. https://doi.org/10.1017/CBO9780511752872.013.

Rutter, M., Cox, A., Tupling, C., Berger, M., & Yule, W. (1975). Attainment and adjustment in two geographical areas I—the prevalence of psychiatric disorder. *British Journal of Psychiatry*, *126*, 493–509. https://doi.org/10.1192/bjp.126.6.493.

Sullivan, H.S. (1953). *The Interpersonal Theory of Psychiatry.* New York: W.W. Norton & Company.

Werner, E.E. (1989). High-risk children in young adulthood: A longitudinal study from birth to 32 years. *American Journal of Orthopsychiatry*, *59*, 72–81. https://doi.org/10.1111/j.1939-0025.1989.tb01636.x.

Case 10

IS THIS MY LIFE?

DOROTHY JOHNSON

DOI: 10.4324/9781003165378-13

Dorothy Johnson

In this case, Dorothy describes how her need to be "attractive and loveable" leads her through a series of romantic relationships. In high school, she has crushes on boys who, like her, are out of the mainstream—"loners and geeks" who she hopes will like her. In college she becomes sexually active and then has to deal with the impact of a sexual assault early in her college years. With James she feels safe and loved; when faced with the decision to break up, they choose to get engaged. Dorothy is happy with her pregnancy and the birth of her son, though her desire for approval brings her to yet another new relationship.

My hands were shaking fiercely as I clutched the plastic handle of the test strip. I was sure I had done it wrong—I think I got more urine on my hands than on the frustratingly small strip—but in less than the three minutes advertised, a placid blue plus sign appeared in the circular window. I repeated the test, but three minutes later I was still pregnant.

I was more exhilarated than scared—I can't even say I was especially surprised. But as I sat on the floor of that tiny bathroom, my heart heavy and empty at the same time, I felt full of life and yet horribly alone. I was in fact alone—all my flatmates had gone out, and I had taken the opportunity to learn if my suspicions were true. I had never had a late or missed period since I began menstruating at the age of 15—"Aunt Flo," like a disagreeable distant relative, usually arrived too soon and always overstayed her welcome. I called James almost immediately after dragging myself from the bathroom. I longed to have him hold me in his arms, to see his smile and receive a kiss of reassurance. I felt an invisible cord connecting me with James as I listened to the tinny ring, waiting for him to pick up the phone. During the contraceptive-free summer that led up to this moment, James and I had a running joke—every four weeks I would tell him, "I have good news and bad news. The good news is, I got my period. The bad news is, I got my period." Now I held my breath and prepared my words. When he picked up, I told him that I had good news and bad news: "The good news is, I didn't get my period. The bad news is, I didn't get my period." James was happy, but I could tell that the possibility of our having a baby was too much to comprehend via telephone.

I called home some hours later. I wanted to get my mom alone, but she was running out the door and couldn't talk for long, so after being passed briefly from mother to father to brother, I still had not relayed my big news. After, amid my sobs and the concerned questions of my flatmates—I had told them almost immediately about my predicament—I composed this email to my mother:

Mom,

Okay. Here goes. So … I didn't want to tell you this over email, but I couldn't get you alone on the phone just now, and it will take me a week to get up the courage again.

I took a pregnancy test today and it came out positive. I'm happy and excited (and, of course, scared). But more than anything, I'm scared that you won't be as happy about it as I am, or that "people" will think I'm throwing my life and education away. I should be much more worried than I am, but deep down I believe that this is what I am really here to do—be a mother. Writing, theater, Latin … everything else I've been studying (except Astro this summer) sort of seems like details in comparison. I know this does not sound like the kind of thing a mature, ready adult would say … I'm really struggling to explain how I feel.

To be fair, I had hoped this would happen a few years from now, after I'd gotten out of college—I don't think that being pregnant and in college is ideal … I talked to James earlier this evening—he is also very excited, and a little scared. He's been talking for months about how much he wants to be a father. He's going to try to find a job near Hanover/Boston so we can live together next year when I go back for my last two semesters (I'm still planning to take classes this winter, and will only need two terms after that).

I don't see this as "the end," only as an alternate route. But you're probably furious with me. I don't blame you—I just wish you wouldn't be. I hope you can be happy, at least, that I am happy. I'm sorry for not doing things the way you would have hoped they'd be done. Who knows what the next several months will bring? In the meantime, I'm just going to try to take care of myself. Lots of iron and calcium.

Love,
Dorothy
Your Happy Daughter

I did not receive my mother's reply until the next morning.

I'm speechless. Cameron is very sad. Dad is going to go through the roof and blame it on me. My feelings are, as you might expect, mixed. There's a lot to think about and to grieve before being happy. And there's a lot to be angry or disbelieving about before thinking that you can actually deal with this. I'm sure I will be happy and excited for you. And for James. And I will be helpful. Count on that. But count on my saying that I knew you needed to do other things before this.

Holy Shit (which may be a tiny bit better than just "shit") xxo m.

I suppose this was the best I could have hoped for. What upset me the most about this email was my mother saying that my brother Cameron was "very sad." I didn't expect my parents to be thrilled about this right out of the gate, but I hadn't thought about how my pregnancy would affect my relationship with my younger brother. The realization that becoming a mother would irreversibly distance me from him was, and still is, what affected me the most. My friendship with Cameron has been so pure, whereas my relationship with my parents has always been tainted by their expectations, so the loss of their esteem was easier to bear.

I was glad to be a continent away when I finally got my parents on the phone.

Their first reaction was distress over how to break the news to their own parents, and their second was to suggest that I wasn't ready to have a baby. My parents have a habit of reminding me when I've disappointed them of all of the help they've given me—help that is often unasked for and unneeded and is rarely worth the price of later reproach. When I talked to my father later that week, he suggested I get an abortion and "wait to have a baby." Thus, it is no surprise that I did not ask my parents for help.

Self-reliance is very important to me; it is the key to freedom. In one of my favorite photographs of myself, a 2-year-old girl marches down a long gravel driveway that is bordered by autumn-colored forest, her hand raised in the air. Fifteen feet behind follows her young, thin father. This image describes my feelings about and the reality of my childhood. I remember spending a great deal of time exploring on my own, although after looking at this photo I am sure that my parents were really just a few steps behind.

During high school I embraced what seemed to be my permanently iconoclastic state, and took my isolation as a sign that I was too wise to make friends with people my age. I worked at increasing the divide by wearing strange clothes—scarves, petticoats, Star Wars T-shirts—sometimes even cross-dressing and reading *Das Kapital* as I walked between classes. I developed a reputation as a sexually liberated pagan Marxist and loved the attention I received.

As you can imagine, this made it difficult to find a boyfriend, and I was desperate for one. I purposely cultivated crushes on boys I thought would be likely to date me—I would latch onto loners, geeks, and traditionally unattractive boys and hope they would take an interest in me. Each spring, with hormones raging, I would get close to achieving my goal, but I was usually clutching at shadows. I will catalogue my few conquests here.

Freshman year: I attracted a dangerously thin bipolar pianist, who on Tuesday would ask me to his junior prom, on Wednesday insist to his friends that we weren't dating, and on Thursday invite me to a movie. Our relationship ended with a phone call—he had thought I would "put out," and although I was secretly willing to, he probably expected me to make the first move.

Sophomore year: I dated a manic-depressive actor who had a girlfriend I didn't know about. I almost gave him my virginity. We were making out beneath a covered bridge, and had I not had my period I would have responded to his inquiring "Yes?" with my own whispered "Yes!" We broke up when I became too involved in trying to help him with his cocaine addiction, but he insisted for years afterward that he still loved me.

Junior year: I spent a year masturbating and writing a sci-fi romance novella about a man I could truly love, Xern, the futuristic bounty hunter.

Senior year: I chased after Nate, a boy who had once had a crush on me. We parked by the lake one winter night and he told me not to tell anyone we had kissed. He said he didn't want to date me and that we should stay friends, but he liked to hear me say how much I loved him and then tell me it could never be. He made me feel exhausted and used. I eventually changed my phone number and stopped speaking to him altogether.

I insisted to myself that I was better off single, that I was going to an Ivy League college and would find boys there who would be interested in me, and if I didn't I could still get pleasure out of reading and writing, and that as a feminist I shouldn't feel that my self-worth hinged upon having a boyfriend. But although I told myself this, I couldn't help but think I was deficient in some way, since my three best friends *always* had a real boyfriend whereas the boys I dated were ashamed of me. I was so desperate to seem and to be an adult, and in my mind having a romantic relationship was integral to adulthood.

It was unfortunate that I went to college with something to prove.

I wanted to prove to myself that I was attractive and loveable. I gave my virginity to the first guy who would have me. His name was John, and he was everything you could expect of a John—not a bad guy. I thought that because I was intellectually opposed to religious beliefs that sex is bad and virginity should be preserved as long as possible, being a sexually active woman was a sign of power and liberty.

Only a week after my first time having sex, my temple of sexual concepts crumbled. After two drinks at an excruciatingly dull party, I decided to go home and watch *Star Wars* and then go to bed. I was followed home by Amir, a friend of a friend, who said he had never seen *Star Wars*. I couldn't find a nice way to make him leave my room, to get off my bed, to take his hands off me. I kept repeating, "No, this isn't a good idea, this isn't a good idea," but the bond between my body and my mind was broken. I was too terrified to move.

Having been at college only two weeks, I decided to pretend it never happened—I didn't want rape to be what my college experience was about. This was a big mistake. Immediately after being assaulted, I tried to make the event insignificant by insisting to myself that my body was merely a chariot in which to transport my magnificent brain, and that what had happened to me didn't matter at all. Sex didn't mean anything at all. This is the mantra I would repeat to myself whenever I remembered that night, but it was impossible to shake my disappointment in myself. I had an image of myself as being strong, wild, brave, and I could not forgive my cowardice. I should have died fighting Amir off—I couldn't understand why I hadn't.

I spent two weeks in Europe at the end of fall term, touring through Austria, Switzerland, and Italy with the Handel Society of Dartmouth College. The Handel Society is a community choir of adults and students, and the weekly rehearsal was the only thing that remained constant throughout my four years at college. I joined the choir because I realized during orientation week that I would go nuts if I didn't spend some time with adults. The Handel Society tour was by far the best experience I had in my four years at Dartmouth, and when I returned from it I had almost completely forgotten the tragedy I had suffered only weeks before.

But my mother, who believes that happiness is impossible without absolute honesty, sensed that I was hiding things from her. She was horrified when I told her that I had lost my virginity. She said I shouldn't be so proud of myself and was furious at me for betraying all of the things she had taught me (I wasn't quite sure what those things were, as my parents and I had never had a sex talk). She said that if I couldn't handle being at college, then maybe I should stay home. In an effort to transform her anger into compassion, I told her I had been raped and that I was capable of handling my troubles. My mother, who is a minister, is the only person who can make me cry. She said that when you have sex with someone you give a piece of yourself to your partner, a piece you can never get back. That was exactly what I had tried to protect myself from—the feeling that I had given away parts of myself that I could not get back—and the greatest pain I had ever felt crashed upon me. Mom was sorry for me, but also angry that I had been drinking before being raped. She demanded that I promise her not to consume any more alcohol and not to have sex with anyone without telling her. I said I would not make these promises, though I did make a promise to myself.

When I returned for the winter term, I braided a piece of yarn and tied it around my hips as a reminder that I only wanted to have sex with people I really loved. It was humbling to think that I needed a physical reminder to preserve my ideals.

I remained celibate from January until May.

Sometime in the middle of that chaste period I met James. I was guarding instruments in the music department, a windowless basement labyrinth (hardly conducive to romance); he approached and started a conversation. I told him more than he would ever care to know about the Petrarch text I was translating, making no effort to flirt. I was sure this gangly, long-haired boy could only be interested in one thing, and I wasn't ready to get entangled. I continued to see James in the music department, where I worked and rehearsed for the Handel Society, but circumvented several offers to "hang out." Finally, I accepted his invitation after spending a day together at a theater festival—I had been impressed by his quietly comic performance and by his talent at the piano. He took me to see a local band, and I fell asleep with my head on his shoulder. When I woke, he kissed me gently. Everything about James was gentle. The first time he spent the night with me he encountered the chastity cord. When I explained its purpose, he was more understanding than I would have expected any man to be, and he was glad that I wanted to wait.

This experience meant a great deal to me—not only James's sweetness, but also that I had the courage to tell him I wanted to wait.

My relationship with James developed rapidly. About a month after we started sleeping together, he discovered I was not on birth control. Having sex was still relatively new to me, and when James didn't provide condoms, I didn't really know what to say. I was a little too head over heels to let practical things like protection get in the way of a romantic moment. Somehow, it didn't seem strange to me that after only a month of dating, James and I would be talking about what we would do if I became pregnant.

But I wasn't pregnant, and I did start taking birth control. In retrospect, it was kind of silly for me to start taking the pill that summer, since James and I spent less than a fortnight of it together. James was at Dartmouth over the summer and I was traveling the globe—and in between I flew to Hanover to visit James. I managed to visit him every three weeks, often enough to keep the relationship alive, but what really sustained it was the letters we wrote to each other. James had elegant handwriting, and his letters (and flowers, books, and other gifts) found me all over the world. It was unbelievably romantic.

During the following year—my sophomore, his senior year— my relationship with James continued to blossom and take root. We sang Handel's *Messiah* together in the Handel Society, and he was in the pit band for the theater department production of *Hair*, which I helped stage-manage. We were well occupied and almost exclusively in each other's company. We had separate dorm rooms, but we slept in the same bed almost every night. We had only a few "rough patches" during that year, the first when he realized I had given him herpes simplex (i.e., cold sores), and the second when I told him about my rape the previous year. James was very sympathetic—almost too sympathetic— and frustrated that a person who had hurt someone he loved so much could go unpunished.

James and I argued about what to do about it—I was still determined not to do anything. Then one day we saw an article in *The Dartmouth* saying that the guy who had raped me was currently spending an off term at Wellesley. The fact that *he* should be chosen to spend a term at Wellesley suddenly awakened me to the negligence of letting his crime remain a secret. How could I put a whole college of girls at risk?

Although James, my mother, and my own conscience had been unable to convince me to take action, my body eventually forced me to act. Since the assault, I had been having a reaction to cold water, aspartame, and caffeine. Every time I took a shower or drank a Coke I broke out in hives all over my arms and legs. I already had a bad habit of scratching itchy bites, so soon my limbs were covered in scars. I felt disgusting, and my mother made me feel even worse. James was the only person who didn't judge me, and his sympathy brought me closer to him. The doctors told me it was probably a stress reaction and that I shouldn't worry about it, but then I started having trouble breathing. Finally, on Christmas Day, more than a year after the incident, I ended up at the hospital with breathing trouble and I decided it was time to stop stressing my body and settle the score.

I resolved to call Amir on the phone—I still wasn't ready to pursue legal avenues. Shaking and full of tears, I told him that he had raped me and demanded that he apologize. He said, "I'm sorry you feel that way. Please don't cry. I hate it when girls cry." I didn't care that I hadn't gotten a real apology from him—what mattered was that I had made the call. I had been brave. I had taken back the piece of me that had been lost.

The following year I did give a statement to the police—I didn't think it was possible to sob as much as I did the afternoon I relived my rape. But there were no reliable witnesses and the case was dropped.

It may seem strange for me to weave back and forth between my flourishing relationship with James and the rather sad business of the violation of my body, but feelings about both were present in me for years. *Star Wars* was my favorite movie of all time, yet every time someone mentioned it I was filled with remorse, anger, self-disgust, self-pity, and ugliness. Oddly, of all the consequences of my rape, this is what hurts the most—that a film that once resonated with the nostalgia of my childhood was now an irreversible reminder of my failure to defend myself. James, on the other hand, praised me each day for my thoughtfulness, cleverness, beauty, and sweetness, and I learned to love myself again. You can see why I was loath to let James go.

I helped James find a summer job near Dartmouth so I could visit him while I was studying over the summer. He was working fourteen hours a day at a summer-stock theater, but two or three times a week I would drive to see one of the shows, bring James back to my apartment for the night, then return him to the playhouse and get back to Dartmouth for my 9 a.m. class. I shouldn't have been lonely—Cameron was staying with me, and we spent hours each day playing cribbage, eating nachos, and watching reruns of *The Office*—but I was. I was very lonely. As I walked home from class each day, I would hug myself and take deep breaths, dreaming of the next time I would see James. After more than a year of sharing a bed—in the months before his graduation we had actually shared a house, living out a domestic fantasy—it was excruciating to sleep alone. And although Cameron was great company, he could offer me little encouragement about my academic pursuits. I was beginning to feel that I was only a mediocre writer, a mediocre director, and in general a mediocre student. While feeling like the center of James's universe, I had failed to realize how short I was falling of my own expectations.

Dorothy Johnson

These alternating sensations of longing and failure, combined with feelings of despair at my own insignificance and the rainiest summer on record, created regular emotional breakdowns and consumption of pint after pint of sorbet.

I eventually realized that the reason for my hyper-emotive state was probably the pill. I decided that since James and I only saw each other a few times a week and I would soon be going to London, I might as well stop taking it. James was skeptical and disappointed. He said that if I stopped taking the pill we would have to go on the rhythm method, stop having sex, or just wing it and hope I didn't get pregnant. I asked about using condoms, but it seemed he would rather not have sex than use them—I don't blame him for this. We discussed what would happen if I became pregnant. I didn't think about the reality of what getting pregnant would actually mean. But I didn't have the "it can't happen to me" syndrome—as soon as I went off birth control I sensed that this was what I was in for.

I admit that I could see being pregnant fitting in nicely with my iconoclastic image of myself. I also admit that my positive attitude about the idea was partly influenced by the thought that if I got pregnant, James would have to stay with me. James was good with his piano students, and I felt that despite his not having known his own father, he would be a great father himself. I believed I would be a good mother—in fact, I might be better at mothering than at any other thing I could do with my life. I never once considered that having a baby would interfere with my finishing college. The more I thought about it, the more desperate I became to nurture and care for something. I would rub my hand along my stomach and imagine a baby growing inside. I imagined a little girl who looked just like me but with James's blue eyes sitting in my lap reading a book. I was certain that if I became pregnant I would be the happiest woman in the world.

But two months went by, and a week before James and I were to go our separate ways—he home to Kansas City, I to London to study theater—I still was not pregnant. James and I were beginning to see the clouds gathering in the distance, which put some strain on our relationship. He tried to break up with me, but I talked him out of it. Then when my twentieth birthday came around, he forgot it. I tried not to let this bother me, but I realized this was another bead on a string of missed opportunities for him to show tenderness or indulge me the way he had when we first started dating.

I cut my hair—a symbol of a new chapter in my life—and drove over to break up with James. I didn't want to, but I sensed that he wasn't as excited about our relationship as he used to be. But I really didn't want to lose James, and almost as soon as I started to speak my words became tearful whispers. We decided that instead of breaking up we would get engaged. It would be a two-year engagement, and if at the end of the two years we were still together and still loved each other, we would get married.

You may have noticed, dear reader, that James and I had a tendency to only see two roads at any intersection, when in fact we were "thru-hikers" who shouldn't have worried about the roads at all, but just which direction was north. Thus, we saw two roads: break up or get engaged. And since we still loved each other and the relationship was mostly working, we could not break up. I think the fact that this was the first significant relationship either of us had had, and that we both had relatively low self-esteem, contributed to our decision to stay together. In fact, I think that most of my major life decisions have stemmed from a desire not to end up like my parents, who fought constantly while I was a child (and still do). Some part of me wanted to protect myself from the unhappy relationship I knew was possible. And frankly, another part of me wanted to stick it to my parents—to show them that I could do what they were unable to do: find a loving partner at a young age and have a perfect marriage.

My mother was furious when she found out I had gotten engaged. She said it was too soon, and perhaps she was right—but then again, perhaps not.

When I realized I was pregnant, I almost didn't believe it. I had gotten my period on my birthday and left James only eight days after that. We had made love the day I left, which according to my cycle would have been a barely fertile day. However, if we hadn't gotten engaged we wouldn't have made love at all, and Luke, whom I now cherish above all else on earth, wouldn't have been conceived.

At this point in Luke's childhood, I am absolutely grateful that James and I decided to get engaged and make love on the 25th of August, although I was ambivalent about my pregnancy at first. We exchanged these emails shortly after my happy discovery:

> *Dearest James,*
>
> *I've been thinking of you all day—thinking of us, and our immediate future. I talked to my mom on the phone again, and she told me that my dad is still hoping I'll reconsider giving up the baby. Mom warned me that, whatever choice we make, it will be very difficult for us.*
>
> *I've assumed that you want to keep the baby without really asking you what you want. I realized that what both of us envisioned for our future has been shaken, and seeing the look on your face yesterday as*

we struggled to figure things out … I thought I should at least ask: Are you sorry that this happened? Would you rather it were easier?

I'm happy. I'm excited, for my sake, but my mom reminded me today that I was thinking only of myself, and I felt suddenly guilty for having let this happen to my family, but at the same time I think my parents should be able to suck it up and rejoice with me.

But I was in tears, afraid that this could make your ambitions impossible, or even just painfully difficult.

So please, tell me if you are having any worries or wishes. I am happy and excited for myself, and for you, and for us, but I want to make sure you get a chance to tell me how you feel, in case you feel trapped.

I love you. I think this baby will be wonderful and beautiful and bring joy. I think happily on your being a father, and my being a mother.

I love you. I'll talk to you soon!

Ardently Yours,
Dorothy

Dearest Dorothy,
Your mom is right that no matter what is decided, we will face challenges that will tax our energies and frustrate our ambitions. She is also right that supporting our pregnancy puts unexpected strain on people who never asked for it, namely your family.

The birth of a child prevents me from obtaining a long-term job or graduate program in Music right now. But, I feel that you and your family are feeling much more of the immediate impact. This pregnancy is contemporaneous with Cameron's applications to college, and so I can imagine Cameron feeling some of the younger-sibling want of resources. I am at a flexible time in my life, but Cameron and your parents are not. I feel guilty too, for passively relying on their resources without ever consulting them in the matter.

You too are not at a time when you have much time to spare. I must admit that I feel that nursing a baby while going to Dartmouth is unrealistic … If you go through with keeping the baby, you will have to keep your mind open to the workload being altogether too much. Of course, I do not want that to be true, and I offer my presence and support to ensure that we can make it together, but, it's possible that it's impossible to do both at the same time and do justice to what are both very worthy responsibilities. You know very well how little spare time a student at Dartmouth really has.

If we decide to give up the baby, then we both will have to agree that we have made a very costly and irresponsible mistake in not using birth control. That is what I will conclude, anyhow, that I have made an irresponsible and costly mistake, and have done you and your family wrong. I want to be able to admit it when I've made a mistake, and I'm prepared to do that.

At the same time, I have always been sincere in my attraction for fatherhood. Also I know that you very genuinely want to be a mother. What I have written above constitutes the facts of the situation as I see them, but the morality of the situation, i.e., what we should decide, depends on our aims. I can envision us as a small family together, happy and comfortable after the now inchoate struggles have passed. That vision requires that we put providing for the child first. I can envision you finishing your next two years of college with total freedom and us concentrating on our engagement and choice of apartments and kittens. That vision requires putting school first. My vision of putting both school/career and child first is somewhat less carefree. We would be risking doing both poorly. Trying to have everything risks everything.

The vision of you finishing school without (more) strain or worry, and of my being able to get an anchor into the world, makes me most happy. I do not feel trapped. If you decide to keep the baby, I will be there to help you and work for us, if it takes living and working in less than desirable circumstances, and find a way to be happy while doing so. After all, we'll have each other.

But again, the vision of you being able to finish school on schedule makes me happiest. We want to be able to enjoy having time with our baby. I imagine that if you have a child, you will want to be able to spend all day with it. Not only does it need that attention, but also I wouldn't want us to miss out on it.

What do you think?

Love,
James

James and I never seriously considered abortion an option, although we were both pro-choice. I went to a counseling center in London to find out what steps I needed to take—foods to eat and avoid, medical appointments, etc.—but it turned out to be an abortion counseling service, and once I told them I was planning to keep the baby, they wished me luck and showed me the door. I am still pro-choice, but the choice I made was to keep my baby. I knew I would be able to handle it, and at the time I saw it merely as living my life out of order—what would it matter if I were married and had a family before I finished college instead of after?

Although I said before that I was ambivalent, I was sure I wanted to keep the baby—I was too proud and excited not to. I was, however, uncommitted to the survival of the fetus. I recall with shame my hope that I would miscarry so I could regain my pre-pregnancy freedom but not have to suffer the guilt of ending the pregnancy myself. Throughout my first trimester I harbored these feelings of indifference toward the little life developing inside me. Granted, I was frustrated at being alone and in a foreign country, with bad food, bad weather, and medical bills draining my bank account. My body also shut down each day at 7 p.m., making it difficult for me to engage fully in my theater studies—but I didn't share these ugly hopes of mine with anybody. Frankly, part of me was still uncertain that I was designed for motherhood at all. My mother had told me at a young age that I "lacked sweetness," and I had told her more than once that I never wanted to become a mother if it would mean being like her.

But pride got the better of me. I have never liked being told that I can't do something—I was determined to rise to the occasion of motherhood, regardless of my doubts about my poor financial situation, possible "lack of sweetness," and inexperience with children. I also looked forward to finally reaching adulthood and earning my parents' respect. The summer before I started college, my father and I had a terrible argument, which ended in my screaming at him, "I never listen to you, Dad, because you treat me like a child!" He yelled back at me, "You *are* a child!" If I excelled at being a mother, it would prove that I had, indeed, grown up.

I remember the moment I fell completely in love with my baby. In the middle of the fourth month of my pregnancy, safe at home in Pennsylvania with James curled up behind me, I felt the first kick. James felt it too—our baby was suddenly more than a little fish visible only on an ultrasound. Our baby had a personality, revealed by his active feet. I curled my limbs around my belly, as if by doing so I could bring myself closer and completely embrace the little life inside me. From that moment on, I counted down the days until I would be able to meet my little boy.

The joy I felt in anticipating my son's arrival shielded me from the reactions of the Dartmouth community. I could tell that people looked at my huge belly and wondered how *I* could possibly be a Dartmouth student—I still encounter the same reaction when I push the stroller around campus. It's like wearing a scarlet letter, though the letter is so badly stitched that no one quite knows what it stands for. Some people see a "D" for "dumb"—the stereotype that girls who get pregnant while in school didn't care enough about their education to use birth control. Some people see an "S" for "slut"—as though a woman gets pregnant by having multiple partners. Some people see a "W" for "waste"—why would someone want to throw away their education by having a baby in her junior year? I am not dumb or a slut; I graduated cum laude with high honors and am on my way to graduate school.

But to return to my story, just as people now see baby Luke and refuse to believe I'm still a student, people refused to believe I was pregnant until I was in my third trimester—I guess they thought I was just fat or had a really impressive beer gut. Although I was due to deliver on May 21st, I took classes in the spring semester. Each classroom presented problems related to my increasingly round body, usually an insufficient gap between desk and chair or the number of stairs I had to climb to get there. I had "daymares" of suddenly going into labor in the middle of a lecture about labor unions in the 1930s, of Professor Nelson serving as midwife as I screamed so loudly that everyone in Hanover could hear me. And all the while I was feeling my little boy's active feet.

In Professor Luxon's class we discussed the perception of the sexes during Milton's era: Men were rational, strong, Godly, bright, and all about the brain; women were emotional, weak, Earthly, dark, and all about the body. On May 25th, when my water finally broke after I printed out my final papers, you can imagine how emotional, weak, and concerned with my body I was.

The six-word story of my childbirth experience: Stabbing pain. Epidural. Nap. Beautiful boy.

That was on Memorial Day. I went to class the following Monday, my episiotomy still healing, the loose folds of my post-pregnancy belly delicately tucked into jeans I had been unable to wear for months, my breasts huge and heavy with milk.

I have observed an interesting behavior among Dartmouth girls. They often stop me while I'm pushing the stroller, lean over my smiling boy—Luke is *such* a flirt—and sigh, "Oh, I want one!" I know they say this to display their appreciation for my son's friendly demeanor, but it bothers me. It is as if they are saying that they wish they could have a baby, but because they are planning to go to graduate school or have an internship lined up or are otherwise driven and hard-working, they can't have one now. I think this attitude is what makes people frown on having children young. My ambition has not waned since I embraced motherhood, although I have tempered my obsessive desire for fame with my appreciation for stability.

I have never been happier to be a woman than I was when I was pregnant, never happier to be human than I am now, as a mother. Luke is the first person in my life I haven't had to impress. I'm sure every Dartmouth student wishes they had someone who loved them as much as Luke and I love each other. I love my little boy and he loves me, body and soul, unconditionally, and no stereotypes or shocked looks could possibly diminish that joy.

But things don't always turn out as we plan. As I write this, I sit in my ready-to-rent-clean apartment, most of my furniture gone, ready to move back home with my parents. I am planning to pursue a PhD in English Literature. I applied for programs within driving distance of my parents with the thought that James would be coming with me and my parents could help out. But James is not coming with me. We got to the end of our two-year engagement and decided that we should end our relationship—it was not easy getting to that point.

For the first five months after Luke was born, I experienced an unparalleled degree of domestic bliss. James taught a few piano lessons every day, and then we would spend the rest of the day together, playing games and watching movies as we interacted with Luke. I started classes in the fall and James spent the mornings with Luke.

We were sleeping in separate bedrooms by the time Luke was five months old. My parents have slept in separate bedrooms as long as I can remember. Until we stopped sleeping in the same bed, I never realized how important sex was in my relationship with James. Today I still wonder whether this was why, five months after Luke was born, James told me out of the blue that he no longer loved me. Something about our relationship, which I thought had been resurrected after our doubts the previous summer, had gone askew, and James was able to tell me serenely that he no longer loved me, that he didn't find me physically attractive, and that he wanted to have the option of seeing other people someday. I was horrified. I felt like someone had replaced all of my internal organs with dead fish. James seemed dispassionate and diplomatically apologetic about the new state of affairs, which made things worse. Things had been going so well! I was living out my domestic fantasy, sending out applications to graduate school so I could support James and Luke, and I was on the track to finish my BA on time—and suddenly James dropped this bomb on me.

I did not deal with this crisis in the way a responsible mother and dutiful fiancée should. Instead, I allowed myself to fall head over heels in love with someone else—someone who happened to be much older than me, and married. This man said more than once that it was "not a fair fight" between him and James because James was young and suddenly unromantic whereas he, the "other man," had the advantage of not having to argue with me about whose turn it was to do the dishes. For four months I carried on the affair without James's knowledge, but as my lover and I became more careless about where we were seen, we eventually got caught. My parents already caught me writing some very sensual emails—my relationship with this older man relied heavily on love letters that were twice as passionate as the ones James and I wrote to each other. I was forced to spill the whole truth, and I clung proudly to my love for this older man despite my parents' disgust and insistence that I give him up. My mother considered my affair a betrayal of her trust and accused me of being selfish. She even said I possibly harbored secret desires for my father and was projecting them onto this older man. But I didn't go looking for older men; I happened to fall in love with this particular man despite his age and not because of it, and I have been happy with him for reasons that have nothing to do with either of my parents—although the reason I allowed myself to cheat on James does.

When James told me he did not love me, he said he just wasn't as romantic as I wanted him to be and that he would never be able to live up to my expectations. I could see he was right, and my determination not to end up in a loveless relationship (like my parents) allowed me to cheat on him. Pressure from my family to marry James both before and after Luke was born also contributed to my weakness, especially because my parents had bent to the same pressure when they found out I was on the way. Once James told me he did not love me, I considered my relationship with him over.

My parents never said "I love you" to each other. They never kissed. They fought every day and talked about each other behind their backs. I spent my entire childhood wishing they would get a divorce. I suppose this is why I jumped ship at the first sign of trouble—I was determined not to get tied up in a loveless relationship that would drag on forever.

I had always believed that cheating was wrong—that a woman should at least dump one man before moving onto the next—but things with James were complicated. I couldn't break up with him because we had Luke and I needed his help, because we shared an apartment I couldn't afford on my own, and because I held out hope that James's unromantic attitude was due to lack of sleep or a passing mood. I continued to fall more in love with this other man as James continued

Dorothy Johnson

to fall farther out of love with me. James and I had rather ugly fights about who would be the primary caregiver if we lived apart. Even during these fights I didn't tell James about the other man because picturing the future without him was still too scary.

James is gone for now. I say "gone," although James is still planning to be part of Luke's life. And I say "for now" because I still hold out hope that he will return. I usually enjoy analyzing myself and trying to figure out my motivations and desires, but my head aches when I try to understand how I can be in love with someone older than my parents and yet still wish to have a normal suburban family with James. I've given up trying to understand the way my brain works. All I know is that I love James (like a brother or a friend) and that I would love him more if he came back to me, and that I also love this older man, who loves me the way I need to be loved, but who inspires hatred in my parents and whom I cannot marry.

I have spent the last two weeks without James. I see my lover twice a day, but I spend most of the day playing with Luke. It is an echo of last summer, except with fewer naps. I enjoy motherhood as much when it is tiring and tedious as when it is exciting.

But I've discovered that I have an almost insatiable craving for approval. Luke can't give me this. James refused to. My lover can—because he too needs to be loved and approved of. My parents praise me, as does my brother occasionally, but somehow this still isn't enough. I am ashamed for wanting more than my fair share and for not being able to transcend this hunger for affection. I am lucky that mother-hood came upon me because Luke is the only being I haven't felt the need to impress, and we can bestow endless affection on each other without keeping score.

Case 11

I WALK IN BEAUTY

DAVINA RUTH BEGAYE TWO BEARS

DOI: 10.4324/9781003165378-14

Davina Ruth Begaye Two Bears

Growing up on a Navajo reservation in Arizona, Davina experiences in her own family the dysfunction, depression, alcoholism and low expectations that are the legacy of centuries of oppressive and paternalistic federal policies toward Native Americans. She attends a combination of schools on and off the reservation, and while she is in the top 10 percent of her high school class, she is accepted to Dartmouth College where her college testing service makes sure to inform her that she is in the bottom 10 percent of incoming freshmen. What begins as elation to being accepted to an Ivy League college becomes a long period of deep homesickness and feelings of inferiority in the face of the overwhelmingly white and privileged educational preparation of her classmates as evidenced in their willingness to venture their opinions in class on any subject. She becomes depressed, withdrawn, and virtually mute. She eventually finds her voice and regains confidence when she engages with Native American students at Dartmouth where she feels at home and cared for through culturally affirming activities and friendships.

Sleet pelted down from a steel-gray sky. It was a cold Thanksgiving Day in Winslow, Arizona on November 28, 1968. Anita looked out her window from her bed at the Indian Hospital. The naked branches of the trees rattled in the wind, but Anita was happy. She thought again about the birth of her first child, and curled protectively around her newborn daughter. At the first sight of her baby in the delivery room, Anita had cried, "Oh, look at my shiny baby!"

The name "Shiny" has stuck with me, but my real name is Davina. Like my mother twenty-six years ago, I face the ultimate challenge of childbirth and parenthood. My husband and I are happily expecting our first child this year. A family of my own is something that I've always wanted—a family free of alcohol abuse, poverty, and divorce. Our baby will be born in Wisconsin, my husband's traditional native homeland. He is Wisconsin Winnebago, or Ho-Chunk. I am Navajo, or Diné. After we graduated from Dartmouth, we traveled across the country to Arizona, where we lived and worked for four years. I was able to enjoy being with my immediate family after being away from them while back east attending college. Now it is my husband's time to enjoy his family after eight years of being away from home.

While in Arizona, my husband and I had the unique and gratifying opportunity of working for the Navajo National Archaeology Department. The contract archaeology we were exposed to instilled in us valuable, practical knowledge concerning cultural resource management. My experience with the Navajo Nation will always be precious to me, because it gave me the opportunity to work for my people and to learn to speak more of my language, and because it introduced me to the beauty of the land that makes up the Navajo reservation.

Now we are applying our education and experience to the Ho-Chunk Nation, as they begin to develop and grow in this area. It is my husband's turn to work for his people, and to learn from them.

Our interest in cultural resource management took root while we were both students at Dartmouth. I perceive cultural resource management as a way to maintain and preserve a group's language, culture, and traditions—a challenge facing many Native American tribes today. My interest in this area was greatly encouraged at Dartmouth and through Dartmouth's Native American Program, Native American studies department, and anthropology department, where I learned more than I could imagine about Native American culture, history, and current affairs.

Whoever thought that I would attend college back east? Not me, although I am the daughter of college-educated parents. My real dad and mother met in 1966 at Northern Arizona University, where I am currently finishing up a master's degree in anthropology. My mother graduated after eleven years of hard work; my dad never finished.

As a college student and in general, mother did not trust any man. Although she befriended many of her male suitors, she was not interested in having a "boyfriend." Then she met my dad. He was different, and intrigued her with his intelligence, sophistication, sarcasm, and in-depth knowledge of life in the Navajo world and in the white world. He was unlike any other person she had ever met.

For the first part of my life, we lived, or tried to live, as a family—a mother, father, and four daughters, of whom I am the oldest. My father was never home like a parent should be. I remember tramping through deep snow when I was 3 in search of Dad in the seedy bars of downtown Flagstaff. It was common for him to leave us to fend for ourselves with no money for rent, food, school supplies, whatever. Who knows what he did on his excursions? My mother rarely followed him to his "drinking get-togethers." The times he did make it home, he was often drunk out of his mind. His stays with the family varied from a few days to a few months, then he'd disappear again—no note, no warning, nothing. Often, he would get a job, then take the paycheck, leaving us penniless. The whole process repeated itself again and again like a broken record. But my sisters and I were always happy to see him. I loved it when we were all together as a family.

My dad had many friends who believed in his potential—professors, co-workers, etc. Time after time they tried to support him with job opportunities, academic extensions, and numerous second chances, because they saw him as an inquisitive and intelligent person. But he would always let them down by quitting and then drinking.

I ask my mom questions about him often, because my dad is no longer living. He passed away in a drinking and driving accident in 1985. He was never happy on this earth. The predicament of Native Americans—primarily their loss of land, language, culture, and traditions—plagued him, driving him to liquor, despair, and finally to his untimely death. To my mother, he often patiently remarked, "You are so innocent. You just don't understand." She, faced with the reality of raising four girls and the trials and tribulations of his alcoholism, found his remarks infuriating and of no practical use or help. Neither my mother nor her four daughters could rescue or change him.

However, I learned from my dad in many ways. First, he influenced me not to be what he was—an alcoholic. I'm sure that I'm not the only Indian person who experienced this life while growing up. Many children go through the same, or worse. Native Americans have the highest rate of alcoholism of any ethnic group in this country. My father's life showed me that alcohol means you can never live happily or accomplish your goals. He could not hold a job, finish school, support his family's basic needs, or even try to live life in a good way. He tried, but was not successful. Second, and more positively, my dad instilled in me a love for books and reading. My mother tells me that he began reading to my sisters and me when we were very young. I remember him reading books like *The Secret Garden* and *The Wizard of Oz* for our bedtime stories. Despite my dad's faults, I cannot stop loving him, and he will always be my dad. But, unlike my dad, I will not let myself get swallowed into a black hole of depression and drink myself to death.

My mother's example of perseverance was our saving grace and my standard to follow. Instead of giving up on her education, she went from class to class, semester to semester, and year to year. It was to our advantage that she stayed at NAU; otherwise, we would have had no place to live. She worked odd jobs and kept us clothed, well fed, well mannered, loved, and happy. What more could a child ask for? We didn't care that our clothes were all secondhand or from the church donation box, because deep down we knew that our mom would always be there for us. Children need love, care, and support from their parents. My mom was all of that to us. She was the person who came to all of our school functions; she made sweets for our bake sales; she helped us with our homework or found someone to help us; she cooked dinner every night and made sure we went to school every day. My dad's drinking was always a problem, but she did not let it get her down, just as she doesn't let any bad news or crisis get the best of her even today. In my eyes, my mother always comes out on top with her kindness, generosity, and grace intact. She is the backbone of who I am today; if it weren't for her, how could I have survived? I remember one time, however, that my mother did briefly let go.

My teeth were chattering, I was so cold—but kept watch and tried to look calm. Cars were easily seen from the huge sledding hill that we six girls huddled on. Sledding was fun for the first hour; my two cousins, three sisters, and I screamed and laughed at the top of our lungs as we raced down the hill dipping crazily and sometimes crashing into snow. Our "sleds" were plastic garbage bags, but we didn't care— we were going down that hill fast. But that was an hour or so ago, when our jeans were still dry and we were warmed by the activity. Now we were pressed close together for warmth under our plastic bags against a tall ponderosa pine tree. All of us were soaking wet. Our socks for mittens weren't working anymore. We were freezing. I felt embarrassed as warmly dressed white people passed us in their stylish snow suits, boots, mittens, hats, and scarves, asking if we were okay, or where our parents were. If they had really wanted to help, they could have taken off their snow suits and given them to us.

One by one the cars went by, none of them my mother's blue Dodge Colt. As I listened to the girls whimper and cry, I thought of my mom's behavior over the past couple of weeks. Every now and then I uttered a comforting phrase: "She'll be here soon, don't worry. The laundry should be done soon," but even I began to wonder if she had left us for good. I would never have thought this before, but it was as if she was changing into a different person. At night, I crouched next to the heater, which was connected to the living room, and listened to my aunt and mother as they partied with men I did not know. I had never been so mad or scared in my life. I hated what my mom was doing. She began smoking and drinking and, worst of all, she was doing it in our own living room! Yeah, Dad drinks, but not Mom, too! It was a nightmare coming to life. It felt like the world was being turned upside down and inside out. I felt myself begin to panic, because I realized my mom was giving up, just like my dad. Her eyes were different; she seemed like she was in a daze. My mind raced as I thought about my sisters and me. Who is going to take care of us now if both Mom and Dad drink? How are we going to live? Are we going to wander from family to family looking for care? How could my mother do this? Why do people have to drink? Finally, I saw the Dodge, and I watched it as it inched its way up the hill, making sure it was really my mom. Yes, it was her. I yelled, "Mom's coming!" We all ran toward the entrance of the park, and straight for the car. I looked in the back and saw the laundry was neatly folded in plastic bags. I felt so relieved that she had done what she had said she was going to do, and that she had come back for us. We were all smiling again, and crying tears of joy, as we surrounded her. "Mom, Mom, it was so cold!" "We were freezing!" "I'm tired!" "I'm hungry!" She began to cry, too, and hugged and kissed us all.

She told me later that that day brought her back to reality. We shocked her out of her depression when she saw us there frozen and looking like a bunch of drowned rats. At that point she realized that her purpose in life was her children, and that she could not give in to despair just because she felt like it. We were depending on her, and she couldn't let us down. And she didn't. After that day, she stopped acting "weird" and became "normal" again. At least that is how I thought of her, and I knew that it was a miracle. I think to myself, would I be where I am, or who I am, if she had failed to change that day? Or would I, too, be a drunk, giving up on life, because of the example set by both of my parents? I know that all of my strength is a result of my mother's love, care, respect, and encouragement. I am who I am because she chose not to give up. Many parents do.

Unfortunately, my mom and dad divorced in 1978. It was for a simple reason—my mother did not want us girls to grow up hating and disrespecting my dad. She thought that while we were still very young, we should still love, care for, and have some respect for him, and she did not want us to lose that. Otherwise, she said, she could have gone on living the way we had. It was this same year that she also met my stepdad, a nuclear scientist, who lived in my home community on the Navajo reservation. He had befriended a very powerful Navajo medicine man, and was living out this dying man's last request. The medicine man wanted the Navajo children of my home community to stay at home. He was tired of seeing young Navajo children bused out to boarding schools, where they would forget their Navajo teachings and be away from their loved ones. It was his dream to build a school in our home community that would not only teach the regular subjects, but more important, teach the culture and language of the Navajo. He asked my future stepdad to do this, and it was being done. My mother's home community on the reservation was having a dinner in his honor, and in a shade house, among all my mother's relatives, he and my mother fell in love.

I guess I was prejudiced, because I could not believe that my mother would replace my father with a disgusting, rude white man—and that's what I thought of him. I'll be the first to admit that I could not stand anything about him. I was the oldest and therefore knew my real dad the longest, so of course I would react this way. Before I knew what was happening, my mother and stepdad were married, and we moved to my home community of Bird Springs and began attending Little Singer School—the result of the medicine man's dream. It was and is a spectacular accomplishment—a school composed of two geometric domes facing east, powered by wind generators and heated by solar panels from the sun. Everyone in the community pitched in and worked together to build this dream, and my sisters and I were lucky to be part of the first class.

It is ironic that it took a white man to bring my mom and us girls back to our "roots." We had lived on the reservation before, but that was in Tuba City, my dad's home community. Thus, it was my stepdad who was responsible for a very precious time in my life. In Bird Springs, we lived with our maternal relatives, which is a Navajo custom, for the first time. It was during this time that my sisters and I learned to read and write in Navajo, listened to Navajo being spoken all the time, and discovered more about what it is to be Navajo. Although my real dad was fluent in Navajo and knew the culture, he did not pass that knowledge on to us. My mother did the best that she could, but she is not fluent in Navajo, although she understands it. She knows the values Navajo women hold, and that is what she passed on to my sisters and me. We were so happy during this time. I thought of my dad often, but we never saw him. He knew where we were, and we got mail from him once in a while, but he never came to visit.

Life with my stepdad, although difficult at times, was a learning experience in and of itself. He accumulated hundreds of books for our growing library, and my sisters and I always had plenty to read. My mother encouraged us as well by making sure that we visited the library in Winslow, Arizona. My stepdad was also into every electronic gadget imaginable, and worked to acquire the latest innovations in computer software and hardware. He was self-sufficient and pursued several business ventures during this time. Good came out of each one, even though they failed financially. We were always with my mom and stepdad on their business trips, and traveled to places we never thought we'd ever get to on our own. I'll admit that life with my stepdad was always interesting and a constant wonder. Although I found him extremely annoying most of the time, what he gave to my mom, my sisters, and me can never be measured or appreciated enough.

Thus, I learned from and was influenced by all three of my parents—my dad, mom, and stepdad. However, at a very young age, I knew that I wanted to excel academically. Why do poorly in school, when you can just as easily do well? Why not try your best and challenge yourself to do better each time in everything, mental and physical? If you fail in one area, you may succeed gloriously in others. As I reached junior high and high school, I was further motivated to do well academically because of the negative stereotypes that I encountered. Many people believe that all Indians do is live off the government in a drunken stupor. This mentality was unfortunately passed on to their children— my classmates. I always wanted to be a good student and to challenge myself; I was always trying new and different things. I do not like to sit back and let opportunities pass me by. I may be scared to death, intimidated, and embarrassed, but I know that I can do it, and that it will be good for me. "It" can be anything. I may not win or succeed all the time, but at least I've challenged myself to do something different and new, and I've learned and matured because of the experience. Of course, to do this, or even to think this way, you need a solid foundation and someone who believes in you. For me, it was and is my mother and family, and now my husband.

I was always a good student, and by junior high knew that I wanted to graduate in the top 10 percent of my high school class. As a high school student, I purposely took the hardest courses offered, because I knew that it would be good for me in the long run. By my senior year I was ready to go to college at any one of the three big universities in Arizona, where I had been accepted and offered scholarships. One day, however, my high school counselor called me out of class to meet Colleen Larimore, then the Dartmouth Native American admissions recruiter. I was one of two students who my counselor thought should meet Colleen, and I remember sitting in a deserted classroom watching a video on Dartmouth. I had heard of Dartmouth before in passing, and I knew that some Navajo guy was rumored to have gone back east for his college education. I thought it was interesting that a Native woman was all the way out in Winslow recruiting Native American students for a college in New Hampshire, and that is the reason I followed through the somewhat intimidating application process. I toiled over the essay, rewriting it several times. I chose to write about the phrase "no pain, no gain" as my personal quote. At the Flagstaff mall, my mom and stepdad ate lunch with me as I sealed the envelope to my application. We made a special trip from the reservation that day to mail my Dartmouth application by the deadline. A couple of months later, Colleen called me at home and asked if I would like to visit the college for free. I couldn't believe it! Of course, I said yes—this was a big deal for me and my family. My first airplane trip ever was my visit to Dartmouth.

Leaving Flagstaff was scary, and I cried a little when I saw my family waving at me through the airport window. The little plane I was in bounced amid the fluffy white clouds; the turbulence was bad. "Are we going to crash?" I thought to myself. It reminded me of driving on the dirt roads on the reservation, with all the bumps and dips making my stomach tickle. I smiled in delight and uneasiness.

My trip to Hanover began with paranoia. I was convinced that I would get mugged and lose my ticket. So I patted it every so often in my purse to reassure myself that it was still there, safe and sound. But once in Boston, I relaxed. The people talked funny, and the air smelled like fish, but I was feeling great. I made a friend, a Mohawk student who was also participating in the admissions office fly-in program. Talking with him made the four-hour layover in Boston go quickly. While I wasn't looking, he swiped my ticket, and I never knew it until he asked me where it was. In a panic, I searched my purse frantically, and then saw him staring at me, clearly amused. "You took it! Give it back!" I shouted in relief. I felt like an imbecile, that it took no more than friendly conversation with a guy to put me off my guard.

At last we took off for Hanover. We landed in a small airport, similar in size to Flagstaff's. Right away I spotted two Indian students there to meet us. One guy was light-skinned and tall, with wavy hair and a pointy nose. The other student looked Navajo. They were laughing and snickering at something funny, and welcomed us coolly. They continued to entertain themselves with inside jokes and humor, ignoring me, as we loaded our luggage into their car and sped into the pitch-black night.

Navajo was being spoken to me out of that blackness, and it shocked me so that I didn't hear what was said at first. I blurted out, "I don't speak Navajo." I thought to myself, of all places, why the hell does this have to happen to me here in New Hampshire, 2,000 miles away from home? It is highly embarrassing for me to admit that I can't understand Navajo to another Navajo who speaks it. But the students carried on with their jokes and snickering, oblivious to my embarrassment. "This is going well," I thought to myself. "What a great first impression I must be making—a Native student who can't even speak her own language. They probably think that I prefer not to speak my own language, or that I prefer not to be recognized as a Native woman." I agonized about what they were thinking about me as we drove on and then dropped off my friend.

Suddenly, the Navajo guy asked if I wanted to stop off at the Native American House, because he needed to find out where my host lived. I acquiesced. Instantly, visions of Indian students madly studying, crouched over their books and calculators, frowning in deep thought, danced through my head. I imagined them in well-lit rooms, where book-shelves lined every wall. At the Native American House we descended a rickety staircase into the basement, and my vision shattered. No books? No studying? Several students lounged around a glowing TV, each cas-ually gripping a bottle of beer. Cigarette smoke filled the air. I tried to compose myself, as I was offered a smoke and a beer. It was like a cold bucket of water had been thrown on me, and, in shock, I managed to decline their offers.

For someone who attended study hall at the BIA (Bureau of Indian Affairs) dormitory every night, and never "partied," it is not surprising that my first encounter with college life shocked me. I though that every person would be studying their brains out, especially since this was an Ivy League school and a weeknight. Was I actually that naïve? Some students do, and others don't. My first "reality check" of many during my stay at Dartmouth occurred that night at the Native American House. My host during my stay at Dartmouth was a Navajo woman from Shiprock, New Mexico. It surprised me that other Navajos were actually this far away from home and succeeding. She and her friends and roommate took me around campus and entertained me during my trip. I visited a Native American studies class with her. Only four students were present, and they were engaged in a class discussion of the film *Broken Rainbow*, which documents reloca-tion on the Navajo and Hopi reservations and the strip-mining for coal. Never in all of my high school education had we talked of similar subjects or current Native American issues. I was impressed and dumbstruck with this spectacular experience and discovery.

Most of the NADs (Native Americans at Dartmouth) were happy to meet me, and their enthusiasm to show me a good time was contagious. To me, the Native American students were the most sophisticated, intelligent, and outgoing Indian people I had ever met. The whole of Dartmouth radiated a seductive power. I could sense the seriousness, tradition, and prominence of this institution, as well as the pride the students held in it. I experienced a kind of intellec-tual ecstasy—I could feel that the whole campus was there to edu-cate and that the students were there to learn. I knew by the end of my trip that I belonged at Dartmouth, among students who were like me. I felt motivated to learn, face new experiences and challenges, and meet new people, in order to broaden my horizons and open my mind.

Back at my high school in Winslow, Arizona, I wore my newly purchased Dartmouth sweatshirt with pride. A classmate asked if I would like to be interviewed about my acceptance to Dartmouth on the local radio station. I agreed, and my parents heard me in Bird Springs. I remember wondering if anyone cared or knew where or what Dartmouth was. But it was a great feeling to know that I was on my way there. I could feel it in my bones that I was going, even before I received my acceptance letter. I think of it all as a dream come true, especially since I only applied to "see what would happen."

When I returned to campus as a first-year student, I was tested like never before. I think an omen arrived in the mail before I went to Dartmouth—it was a message printed on my achievement test scores: "Based on your performance on this exam, you will represent the bottom 10 percent of the student body at the college of your choice [Dartmouth]." For someone who graduated in the top 10 percent of her high school class, this was alarming news. What a way to build a student's confidence! I wonder if they actually thought they were doing me a favor with that little bit of information. To this day, I curse the standardized testing company that sent me that letter, because their message became lodged in the back of my mind—a constant reminder of just where I stood. At least that's what I thought.

During "Freshmen Week" incoming students get a head start on life at Dartmouth and take placement tests. It was during this time that our Undergraduate Advisor (UGA) group held its first meeting. I had just finished moving into Woodward, an all-female dorm. The UGA group was designed to help freshwomen/men during their first year at college. Most of the women in my dorm belonged to my group.

We decided to meet outside, and shuffled onto the front lawn, scattered with bright red and yellow leaves. As we sat in a circle, I promptly began to freeze my ass off on the damp grass. The sun was out, but it was a chilly fall day.

Our UGA, a sophomore, smiled sweetly and began to explain a name game to us. As I looked at all the unfamiliar faces, I felt afraid, intimidated, alone, and different. I was, of course, the only Navajo or Native American person in our group. A pang of homesickness stole into my heart. Our UGA finished her instructions and we began.

The rules were to put an adjective in front of our name that described us and began with the first letter of our name. The object of the game was to introduce ourselves in a way that would help us to remember everyone's name. "Musical Melody" said a proud African American woman. A friendly voice chirped, "Amiable Amy," and everyone

---

smiled in agreement. I couldn't think of an adjective to describe me that began with D. I racked my brain for an adjective, anything! But it was useless. "Oh, why do I have to be here? I don't belong with all these confident women. Why can't I do this simple thing?" I remember thinking. My palms were sweating, my nose was running, and my teeth began to chatter. I looked at all their faces, so fresh, so clean and confident. It was finally my turn. I still couldn't think of an adjective. In agony, I uttered "Dumb Davina." "Nooo!" they all protested. Amiable Amy interjected, "Why not *Divine* Davina?" I shot her a smile of gratitude, but I was horrified and embarrassed. How could I have said that and been serious? Talk about low self-esteem.

My first term at Dartmouth went well academically. I received an A, a B, and a C. But I was lonely, even though I was friends with several women in my UGA group. It was hard for me to relate to them, because I felt they did not know who I was as a Native American, and where I was coming from. They also didn't understand my insecurities. How could they, when they believed so strongly in themselves?

I look back at my first year at Dartmouth, and realize that I made it hard on myself. I took it all too seriously, but how could I have known then what I know now? It took me years to be able to think of myself in a positive light. My mother always told me, "You are no better than anybody else. Nobody is better than you." Unfortunately, at Dartmouth her gentle words were lost in my self-pity.

Going home for Christmas almost convinced me to stay home. I was so happy with my family, but I didn't want to think of myself as a quitter, nor did I want anyone else to think of me that way. I came back to an even more depressing winter term. My chemistry course overwhelmed me and I flunked it.

Chemistry was torture, and I could not keep up no matter how hard I tried. A subject that I aced in high school and actually liked did me in that term, and made me feel like a loser. What went wrong? It was just too much information too fast. I was depressed, and my heart was not really in the subject. Finally, I accepted my predicament. I'm not science material, and that's that.

Why did I do so horribly? My note-taking skills were my downfall. They were poor at best. The crux of my problem was trying to distinguish the important facts that I needed to write down from the useless verbiage quickly. By the time I got to writing things down, I'd already have forgotten what the professor had just said. In this way, valuable information slipped through my fingers. Not only were my note-taking skills poor, but so was my ability to participate in class discussion. At

Dartmouth, one was expected to follow everything that was being said, think fast, take notes, ask questions, and finally deliver eloquent opinions, answers, and arguments. It was beyond my limited experience and self-confidence to do so. "*Say something!*" I screamed mentally, but it was useless. Fear paralyzed me in class. Outside of class I'd talk, but not in class amid the stares of my peers. My freshman English professor and I would have conversations in her office lasting two or three hours, but in her class, when faced with all my peers, I became mute. Once, Michael Dorris, my Native American studies professor, asked me outside of class why I did not speak up in his freshman seminar on American Indian policy. I was tongue-tied. Incredibly, I felt that if I spoke up in class, I would be perceived as stupid. It did not help matters that the discussions there utterly lost me most of the time during my first couple of years at Dartmouth.

On one occasion I did speak up—in an education course, "Educational Issues in Contemporary Society." It was a tough course with tons of reading. Participating in the weekly seminar was a significant part of the grade. I never talked to anyone in class. But the professor was always nice to me, saying "Hi" whenever we ran into each other. That day was just like all the other days of the past few weeks. Seated around the oblong table were about fifteen students, the professor, and a teaching assistant. The professor did not lead the discussions; he was there as a participant just like us students, and we determined the content of the seminar. I came in, sat down, and my classmates began to express themselves, taking turns at center stage. I looked from one student to another and wondered how they made it look so easy, wishing that I could, too.

On this day I sat next to my professor, and as usual was lost. The words, ideas, arguments, and opinions whirled around me like a tornado in which I was mercilessly tossed. Too many unfamiliar words, analogies, and thoughts were being expressed for my brain to comprehend, edit, sort, pile, delete, save, etc. But this was nothing new—all of my classes at Dartmouth were confusing to me and extremely difficult.

Out of the blue, as I sat there lost in thought, my professor turned his kind face toward me and asked, "Davina, why don't you ever say anything?" His question was totally unexpected, but not malicious. Rather, it was asked in a respectful tone that invited an answer. Everyone stared me down; they wanted to know, too. I was caught off guard, but thought to myself: this is my chance to explain why I am the way I am. I began hesitantly, frightened out of my wits, but determined to let these people know who I was and where I was coming from.

Davina Ruth Begaye Two Bears

"Well, I have a hard time here at Dartmouth. I went to school in Arizona. That's where I am from. I went to school in Tuba City, Flagstaff, Bird Springs, and Winslow, Arizona. So I've gone to school both on and off the Navajo reservation. The schools on the reservation aren't that good. But in Flagstaff, I used to be a good student. Bird Springs, which is my home community, is where I learned about Navajo culture in sixth and seventh grade. I got behind though, because the school didn't have up-to-date books. I mean we were using books from the 1950s. I really liked it though, because I learned how to sing and dance in Navajo and they taught us how to read and write the Navajo language. I learned the correct way to introduce myself in Navajo, so even though I got behind and had to catch up in the eighth grade, it was the best time of my life, and I learned a lot about my language and traditions. Then when I went to eighth grade and high school in Winslow, I had to stay in the BIA dorm away from my family, because the bus didn't come out that far. So the dorm was for all the Navajo and Hopi students who lived too far away on the reservation. Winslow was a good school, but I don't think I was prepared for an Ivy League school like Dartmouth. I mean it's so hard being here so far away from home. I used to be in the top 10 percent of my class—now I'm at the bottom of the barrel! Do you know how that makes me feel?"

I couldn't help myself and began to sob. My words were rushing out like they had been bottled up inside for too long.

"It's awful. I feel like I can't do anything here and that the students are so much smarter than me. It seems like everyone knows so much more than me. All of you, it's so easy for you to sit there and talk. It's hard for me to do that. I envy you. I feel like I'm always lost. I hardly ever understand what you guys are talking about. It's that bad. My note-taking skills aren't that good either and it causes me a lot of problems in class, makes me get behind. I mean we never had to take notes like this at Winslow. And it's hard for me to participate in class discussion. I mean at Winslow we had to, but not like this. My teacher would put a check by our name after we asked one question. We didn't sit around a table and talk like we do in here. We didn't have to really get into a subject. We didn't even have to write essays. I only wrote one term paper in my junior and senior year. My English teacher would always tell us how much writing we'd have to do in college, but he never made us write! I'm barely hanging on, but here I sit and that's why I don't participate in class discussion."

I finished my tirade. It was quiet. Nobody said a word. Then my professor leaned over and jokingly admitted, "Don't feel too bad, Davina.

I don't understand what they're talking about half the time either." We all smiled, and it was as if a great weight had been lifted off my shoulders. I'm so glad he prompted me to speak that day, and his comment helped me to put it all in perspective. Not everything a Dartmouth student says is profound. It was in this class that I received a citation, which distinguishes a student's work. My professor wrote, "Courage is a sadly lacking quality in the educational world we've created. Davina dared to take steps on behalf of her own growth (and ultimately for her fellows) in an area where she could reasonably expect to be tripped by an insensitive and dominating culture. It was a privilege to accompany her." For Education 20, I received a grade of a D with an academic citation, simultaneously one of the worst and best grade reports a student can receive. "Only I would receive such an absurd grade," I thought to myself in exasperation, but I was proud despite the D. After that day in class, my self-confidence went up a notch. In my junior and senior years at Dartmouth I began to participate in class little by little. By the time I hit graduate school, you couldn't get me to shut up.

During my first year at Dartmouth, I did not find much comfort with fellow Native American students. Why was I so lonely? Isn't that what the purpose of the Native American Program was—to make students like me feel at home? Wasn't I having fun attending NAD functions and parties? To be honest, I participated, yet I did not feel accepted or comfortable among the other NAD students. It was partly due to my lack of self-confidence. Besides, it was apparent that they already had established friends and, except for a few of them, did not seem too concerned about the welfare of new students. I was an outsider, not yet a team player. Although I often talked to Bruce Duthu, the director of the Native American Program, I still felt at a loss around the students.

Finally, spring term arrived after a long, dark, cold winter, and I made a new friend. This time it was different, because with Cheryl I felt at ease. She was a fellow Indian woman. We could relate to one another, and she at least had some idea of where I was coming from. However, it was the Dartmouth Pow Wow that really began my initiation into becoming a full-fledged NAD.

The night before the Pow Wow was a balmy one. As Cheryl and I sat on the marble steps of Dartmouth Hall, we alternately criticized and laughed about Dartmouth life. She lit up a cigarette with a practiced hand and offered me one. I accepted and tried to be cool like her but my lungs refused to cooperate, and I coughed out the smoke. She chuckled at my pitiful attempts, but I didn't mind. I was smoking with a friend and was finally happy. At length, we got up and headed toward the Native American House, or "The House," as it's fondly called. We entered the front door. The House was quiet and peaceful as I stepped into the study room. On my left, grocery bags full of food lay haphazardly abandoned and ignored. Where was everybody? We were supposed to be dicing up tomatoes, onions, and cheese, shredding lettuce, and most important, making fry bread dough. I knew that it would take a lot of work to do this for our Indian taco booth and Pow Wow, so I rolled up my sleeves and began on the tomatoes. At length, a few more NADs trickled in. "Look at Davina, she's so motivated. Oh, I better get up and help; you're making me feel guilty," Bill teased. After everything was chopped, diced, and shredded, we called it quits. But the next morning, I went straight back to The House, worrying about the fry bread dough. We needed to make enough to feed several hundred people, and that would take time. I began to mix the appropriate amounts of flour, baking powder, salt and warm water, kneading the dough to the right consistency. Cheryl came down from her room upstairs at The House and joined me. After we'd been there a while, Richard, a Navajo guy, came to help. I was secretly happy that I'd beaten him to the job. Navajos are supposed to rise early and he was late. Did I catch a look of embarrassment on his face? He lined a trash can with a garbage bag and we poured in our dough, Cheryl's Winnebago dough mixed with my Navajo dough.

After the dough was made, we rushed to the Pow Wow grounds at Storr's Pond—a grassy camping area about a mile from campus. Already a line had formed and customers were waiting patiently for their authentic Indian food. We lit our butane stove, put on the cast-iron frying pans and loaded them with chunks of white lard. The day steamed, and so did we, all day long. I didn't get to see much of the Pow Wow, as the line to our popular Indian taco stand was never-ending. I slaved away, and in the process, relaxed in the familiarity of making fry bread. A fellow NAD would pass me a nice, cold Coke every so often to quench my thirst. We flapped dough with our hands, joked, laughed, and sweated as each golden round of fry bread was snatched from us for the next hungry customer. By the end of the day, I was covered from head to toe in flour, my back and shoulders were tight, and my feet hurt, but I was at peace and happy. I sensed a feeling of camaraderie with the NADs for the first time. The day ended; I got a back rub from a NAD medical student, and it was time for the '49.

The "host drum" group and their family brought cases of beer and began to sing Kiowa '49 songs of romance and pretty Indian girls. We gathered in the picnic area and built a huge bonfire. I drank a beer, my first since coming to Dartmouth, then bravely tried a wine cooler. I visited with the family of the host drum, and we laughed loudly together under the twinkling stars. Soon the singing coaxed us into a round dance. The wine coolers took my shyness away, and my feet stepped in time to the rhythm of the drumbeat and the words of the song.

After a couple of hours my eyes and body drooped with fatigue from all the hard work, the drinks, and now the dancing. I wanted to take a hot shower, wash off the smell of grease and smoke, and sleep. A NAD asked if I'd like a ride back to my dorm, and as I was leaving, several people thanked me for my hard work. After eight months at Dartmouth, I finally felt like I belonged and was part of the Dartmouth Native American family. Never underestimate the power of fry bread.

It's amazing how much my life changed after that day at the Pow Wow. Now I couldn't wait to attend all the NAD functions, visit with the other NADs, and enjoy my time at Dartmouth. I wondered if everyone had to prove themselves to the NADs like I did. Did I prove myself? Or did I just become relaxed enough to finally have a good time? Maybe it was both.

Friction did exist in NAD, as people always complained about NAD being too much of a clique, shunning those who were not "full bloods" (full-blooded Indians). I know who I am, a Diné, even though some idiot will always say, "You don't look like an Indian." Well, excuse me for not wearing war paint, buckskin, and feathers. How someone can be ignorant and arrogant enough to know what an Indian "looks like" is beyond me. I've suffered through too damn much not to be an Indian. But I also know and understand the beauty of being Navajo—the strong matrilineal and clan ties; the lessons in my grandmother's strict admonitions; the taste of broiled mutton freshly slaughtered; the feel of dirt in my hair; and the love and wisdom of my mother. How I've lived is Navajo, even if I don't speak and understand my own language fully. How can anyone quantify what part is Navajo and what part is not? I just am. I think some people question what part of them is Indian and what part is not, and that's not healthy.

My sole problem at Dartmouth was that I did not possess self-confidence. I often looked down on myself, thinking that I wasn't good enough, smart enough, sophisticated or rich enough—whatever—to be a part of the Dartmouth family, my UG group, or a part of NAD. That was always my problem. It took time for me to rise above my self-defeating attitude.

My sophomore year was so totally unlike my freshman year that it's comic. We had a huge and awesome class of incoming Native

American freshmen and freshwomen, or '91s, as they're referred to (by the numerals of their year of graduation). All of a sudden, enthusiastic young NADs were popping up everywhere, thirsting for friendships and a good time. I promptly began befriending them and having the time of my life. Aside from the friends I had made in my UGA group, the NADs were about the only people I hung out with. Why try to make friends with people who don't seem to be interested in you? Why make that effort? I'm not sure why it works out that way, but it did in my case. I can honestly say that I never really got close to a white person, other than my roommate. Why is there such a boundary between groups? Was it just me, or was it everybody? I remember getting drunk a couple of times at frat parties, and having long conversations with white people, but then I would never talk to them again, and they weren't my friends.

In the fall of my junior year, I changed my major from visual studies to anthropology. Professor Deborah Nichols became my mentor. I enjoyed her courses on the prehistory of North America. Ever since I can remember, I wanted to go back in time to see what life was like before Columbus. Also, I loved learning about other Indian tribes. Before I came to Dartmouth, I thought that all the Indians east of the Mississippi were extinct—killed off or removed by the United States government. My eyes were opened at Dartmouth. Dartmouth gave me a strong and true sense of Indian pride. Where else could I have taken classes specifically focusing on Indian life, history, literature, and culture; met and listened to Indian tribal chairpersons, scholars, performers, and artists, as well as traditional elders? The principal chief of the Cherokee Nation, Wilma Mankiller, Dartmouth's own Michael Dorris and Louise Erdrich '76, the Lakota educator Albert Whitehat, and members of the American Indian Dance theater were just a few of the people who spoke and/or performed at Dartmouth through the Native American Program, Native American Studies Department, and NAD. Dartmouth's commitment to Native people inspired me to finish my education and to develop and nurture my own growing desire to work for my people or people of other tribes.

Professor Nichols encouraged me to look into the field of archaeology. But after a summer at the field school at Wupatki National Monument in Arizona, I decided that I was uncomfortable excavating the places where Indians once lived and had died—anyway, it goes against Navajo religion and teachings. As Professor Nichols did not want me to lose my interest, she presented other options in the field of anthropology. She pointed out that I could help Indians get the remains of their deceased ancestors back, as well as their sacred and ceremonial objects, which were being held in museums all over the country, or I could work on repatriation and reburial issues. Through research for a term paper, I learned more about these issues, and was instantly converted. Anthropology need not be the field most Indians love to hate. Instead of being an anthropologist who takes away from Indian people, I will be an anthropologist who gives back—through work with repatriation and reburial, or in other ways.

My interest prompted me to apply for the senior internship at Dartmouth's Hood Museum of Art. It was an intimidating prospect, but I decided to go for it anyway. I was accepted as one of only two senior interns. It was a glorious experience. I was able to handle the Hood's collections of Native American material objects as I helped transfer them from Webster Hall to a new storage annex at the Hood. I had the privilege of co-curating a major exhibit on Native North American basketry, which entailed conducting research on each and every basket in the collection.

The Native American Program was the reason I chose Dartmouth, and it was the reason I stayed. When I speak of the Native American Program, I am also including the Native Americans at Dartmouth student organization and the Native American studies department. NAP was the basis upon which I received my education. NAP ensures that Native youth who were raised in remote areas on Indian reservations, often living in poverty, and not able to receive the best education that money can buy, are given a chance to excel at an institution such as Dartmouth. Many Native students attend Dartmouth because they know that with such an education they will be better equipped to serve their home communities or other Native communities. I am such a person.

NAP ensures that Native students are taken care of. They are not forgotten or ignored. It is hard enough getting through college, but it is even harder when you are 2,000-plus miles away from home and you hardly have contact with any other Native people, aside from students. Although I may have felt ignored by other Native students at first, that was partly my fault, as I did not reach out.

Although Dartmouth strives to keep all of its students, some do not make it. My inner strength is my family, as I mentioned, and my beliefs. I believe that we should leave the past behind us—grow from it, learn from it—but go on with your life and do the best that you can. Why not try to make life better for yourself and others? Why waste our time hurting ourselves or others? Just live your life in a good way, the way you want to live it, and be happy. Enjoy it while it lasts.

Davina Ruth Begaye Two Bears

I've always felt that way. I guess that's why I try to do well in everything I do. I'm not saying that I am better than anyone else. I'm just saying, do what you want to do in beauty. My people have a saying that we use in a prayer: "Walk in beauty." I just realized that's what I always try to do: live in a beautiful way.

Case 12

AN UNPREDICTABLE JOURNEY

JOHN AROUND HIM

DOI: 10.4324/9781003165378-15

John Around Him

This is the story of a young man brought up as Lakota on the Pine Ridge Reservation in South Dakota. Like so many of his Native peers he must battle the many systemic inequities and dysfunctions that lie in his path to the future he dreams of. He experiences profound loss and chronic stress that make it difficult for him to believe in himself and see a way forward. His identity and belief in himself suffer. He decides that joining the Army offers a means to college after enlistment, but he must first endure the further traumas of war in Iraq. Harrowing combat experiences make clear the psychic price he must pay for a college education if and when he returns home alive. Through his perseverance, strong Lakota identity, and help from some mentors along the way, he pushes through these multiple challenges and builds the life he thought was not possible.

One night our job was to guard a factory. White concrete walls with guard towers surrounded the building, which manufactured parts for Iraqi military vehicles. The factory, a tall, steel-frame, metal structure, stood partially demolished with its walls blackened from air bombings early in the Iraq war. The rest of the compound was littered with vehicle parts. Our mission was to provide security and prevent looting. Whatever civil order existed in Iraq before the invasion had now vanished. Locals, looking to sell just about anything to feed their families, commonly took to looting. Two 65-ton steel, sand-colored tanks, call signs Bravo-33 and Bravo-34, provided us with both protection and shelter. During the war, tanks doubled as killing machines and living quarters—eating, bathing, and sleeping were done on the tank. Each consisted of a four-man crew: a loader, a driver, a gunner, and a tank commander.

Since this particular factory was notorious for being attacked, we were always on high alert. A highway lay between the factory and a large village, with a dense community of houses that allowed the insurgents to fire quickly and blend in to their surroundings. This was the nature of urban warfare. Ambush, sniper fire, mortar fire—we prepared for the worst. Fear was constant. A gate on the south end of the factory provided the only way in or out. To prevent an onslaught, we positioned a tank in the gate. One soldier stood guard near the tank and another one in a tower along the wall approximately 50 yards away to provide support. Everyone took up shifts throughout the night, rotating through the two guard positions.

I remember it was dawn as my shift came to a close, and the sky was coated a rose-pink hue. The air was crisp. The rest of the crew was sleeping in a small guard building near the gate, most likely a previous security checkpoint for the factory. This was home during the guard missions. I proceeded to wake Specialist Russo for his shift. A medium-built White man from Chicago, Russo was honest and hard-working. I had a lot of respect for him, and we were good friends both in war and on the home front. That morning, we talked for a little bit, mostly about four-wheeling, American food, and family. Later, my body fatigued, and I staggered toward my cot to lie down. I untied my bootlaces, which were tightly bound, and the relief to my feet was instantly gratifying. Aside from boots and Kevlar helmets, which were optional, we slept in full gear: socks, undershirt, DCU (desert camouflage uniform), and armor vest. Most of us wore our helmets to bed because, in this environment, chances of surviving a hit were slim.

I always did a quick weapons check before sleeping. It was routine, like brushing your teeth. My dirt-covered rifle, locked and loaded, stood upright against my cot. I felt for my pistol, attached to a holster on my thigh. For me, there was something strange and bone-chilling about the routine weapons check. It added to the constant fear of attack, but it was also a reminder of the possibility of death. My life depended on how fast I could reach my weapon. Weapons check done, I closed my eyes for what seemed like a few minutes. Then suddenly, "Boom!!!" An orange light pierced my translucent eyelids. My immediate thought was, "What the hell was that!" Simultaneously with the explosion, I heard Specialist Russo shriek, a cry horrifying and unnatural. His cry made me cringe, like nails on a chalkboard.

My ears were ringing. The inside of our sleeping quarters was shrouded in dust as I fumbled out of my cot. An object, lodged in the wall of the building, was burning red and sparking, orange embers falling to the floor. The object illuminated the dust in the room, encompassing everything in an eerie red glow. For a minute I thought I was dead. It all happened so fast; still deafened by the explosion, we all jumped to our feet, grabbed our weapons, and shot out the door of the guard building. We instantly began surveying the perimeter in front of the factory. Breathless and angry, I scanned the perimeter too. We were ready to kill anything with a weapon. Nothing! Some of the other guys attended to Specialist Russo. He was hit with shrapnel, but his injuries did not appear to be life-threatening. This was good news. Assessing the damage, we found the explosion was from an RPG (rocket-propelled grenade). Russo had been standing on the right side of the tank when the RPG hit the left side of the tank, exploding on the commander's hatch. The stem of the RPG, the propulsion piece, was catapulted into the wall of our sleeping quarters. By all accounts, Specialist Russo was very lucky. If he had been standing a few feet closer to the front of the tank he would have absorbed most of the explosion.

Upon returning to the safety of our base camp later that day, the tank crew sighed with relief, some joking to ease the trauma of the RPG incident. "That was fucking close!" someone said. "Specialist Grady, if you die can I have your snack food?" pleaded another. Guys would facetiously joke about laying claim to a soldier's possessions if he or she were to die. After the wisecracks died down, everyone retreated to their bunks either to write letters home or rummage through care packages.

Standing alone near the tank I began to feel nauseous and had difficulty breathing. My legs felt weak. That was a close call, maybe too close. I was shocked to my very core. It is difficult to describe the feeling, but my existence was suddenly put into perspective, and I felt myself *change* in that moment. It was my first real experience with combat. It was dark out and as soon as I was alone, I kneeled next to the tank and could feel the tears trickling down my cheeks. I tried to act tough and "John Wayne" it, but it was no use. I could not hold back. A sense of submission began to overtake my body. I thought it was only a matter of time before my own death. I was amazed and sad at how easily life could be taken away. Crying near the tank, memories of family, friends, and home began to flood my mind. My dreams of going to college and making my dad proud—all of it seemed to be slipping away. I did not want the guys to see that I was so emotional. I did not want to discourage anyone. I nevertheless knew what I was fighting for at that point. I was fighting to go home.

It is remarkable how the chaos and violence of war brought into focus my deep affection for home, a feeling that from then on impelled me to stay alive during the war. Rooted in every Lakota family is this profound affection for home. Home is bigger than me or you, bigger than money or power. Home is not just a domicile, but an expression that is reflected upon regularly, almost like a prayer, and it would go something like this: always put your home and everything in it—family and Lakota culture—before yourself.

Growing up in my home on the reservation was a time of great happiness and emotional contentment. I lived with my parents, John and Linda Around Him, my two sisters, Amaris and Clovia, two brothers, Milton and Samuel, and various relatives from broken homes whom we often cared for. Our home is located in the backcountry near Kyle, South Dakota, a small rural community on the Pine Ridge Indian Reservation. Our little, light blue, government house is nestled in a small canyon, a kind of oasis among the bare hills and rolling prairie, and accessible only by dirt road. A stream runs nearby and pine trees line the tops of the canyon cliffs; I fondly remember hearing the sweeping sounds of a cool breeze brushing over the treetops, the relaxing murmur of the streams, the hum of the grasshoppers in the meadow, and the sweet smell of ash trees. My dad and I often went on hikes near the stream to open beaver dams. I spent many summers sitting on the porch of that light blue house, watching the dust from the dirt road do a little pirouette. The land is rich in chokecherry, wild plum, and crabapple trees. The family often picked chokecherries for my mother who used them to make *wojapi*, a type of pudding and one of the traditional foods of the Lakota people—my people.

My mother was a slender woman with dark brown skin and long black hair. She was very pretty and growing up we had a loving relationship. She read bedtime stories to me—my favorites were the *Care Bear* books. Although she only reached the eighth grade, my mother was quite literate. She was a fantastic cook as well—the intoxicating smell of her sweet oven bread often filled the house, which was always stocked with food and coffee in case any guests were to stop by. To be a Lakota meant sharing your home with others, a principle my mother personified.

My father, too, enjoyed making people happy, especially his children. When we did a good job, whether in school or doing the chores, my father would praise us. He believed in education and made that known to his children. He also took on a lot of responsibility in the community—helping Native American inmates find a spiritual path, fighting to revive the Lakota language, and conducting Lakota prayer services for families. I admired his optimism, selflessness, and devotion toward seeing improvement in the lives of others in the community. We occasionally made trips together to Martin, South Dakota—a small farm community located off the reservation—to buy house and lawn supplies. During our trips to town we would listen to old Lakota ceremonial songs on the stereo, and my father would tell me about the old ways.

My father was a singer and song keeper. He sang for many traditional Lakota medicine men from the Pine Ridge Reservation who have since passed away. He often regaled us with the songs he sang during ceremonies held by Dawson Has No Horse and Joe Eagle Elk, medicine men not known to the outside world, but highly revered on the reservation for their connection to an ancient past, a connection that the U.S. government tried to deny the Lakota people by outlawing many traditional customs for most of the twentieth century.

In the 1980s, my family and I often attended Lakota *yuwipi* ceremonies, a type of prayer service conducted by local medicine men. Yuwipi ceremonies were often held in a basement and conducted in the dark. I especially enjoyed the time right before the ceremony started, when all the people would gather in the basement and sit on blankets that lined the cold floor. Shaking hands with the elders was important, my father said. Originally a social custom of the West, shaking hands on the reservation has come to symbolize one of the four sacred values of Lakota culture—respect. So, before the ceremony started my family and I walked around the room as if in some kind of procession, greeting and shaking hands with everyone. Then I would sit with my mother and watch as others greeted each other. The smell of prairie sage, bitterroot, and flat cedar filled the basement creating a very sanctified environment. The medicine man would address the people and instruct the singers on what songs to sing. The drums cracked like thunder and the floor of the basement seemed to shift beneath us. This powerful experience often moved me. Most importantly, ceremony connected us all.

Those days of quiet rituals of family and community life were forever altered just eight days before my 11th birthday. I was home with my mother, up late watching TV while she was doing some chores around the house. I can distinctly recall the house smelling like ashes and kerosene, which came from the woodstove. I remember walking down the hallway and for a split second seeing my mother in her bedroom. I bid her "good night" and was off to bed. She was preparing to take a bath after a hard day's work of cooking and washing clothes. Exhausted, I fell asleep fast, but the time between falling asleep and the ensuing chaos seemed short.

"Jon Jon, wake up, there is something wrong with Mom!" urged my sister, Clovia. Needless to say I was startled and quickly sat up in bed. My room was dark, but I could see a light coming from the hallway and set out to investigate. At once, I heard a commotion. I walked into the hallway and into my parents' bedroom. Blinded from the bright lights in the room, it took time for my eyes to adjust. As the room came into focus I saw the family circling the bed where my mother lay motionless.

Apparently, my mother was in the bathtub when they found her. I saw my father kneeling next to the bed, nudging my mother and calling her name. "Linda!" he pressed. His austere expression characterized his approach to any challenging situation. Meanwhile, my brothers, sisters, and I stood behind him, our aunts surrounding us, watching, as my father tried repeatedly to wake my mother. The fear in the room was palpable.

While waiting for the ambulance, I too began to panic. My body, my emotions, and all my thoughts were suspended. I will never forget the moment when they called me over to the bed where my mother lay. I did not understand why I was summoned to stand next to her; everything was happening so fast. My aunts encouraged me to try and wake my mother. I walked over to the bed, my body trembling. "Call Mom's name," Clovia urged. My aunts, brothers, and sisters said the same: "Call her name!" The pressure was unimaginable. I stood next to my mother's motionless body, calling her name. "Mom." No answer. The room was silent. I tried again, this time with more force: "Mom, wake up!" My voice shaking, I was frustrated and angry. "Mom, wake up!!" It was no use. She would not wake up, and soon after the ambulance arrived.

I remember feeling relieved when the ambulance came. Two tall men, reservation paramedics, put my mother on a stretcher and carried her out of the bedroom, down the narrow hall, and out the front door. A cold chill moved through the house as they carried her from our home. I remember the sky was clear that night, and the stars were out. The air was cold and crisp. They put my mother in the old white ambulance, its red lights flashing, as they drove her to a nearby hospital off the reservation. My father and a few others followed the ambulance. I stayed home telling myself that the hospital will fix her and I did not need to worry. Besides, I had school the next day. I remember feeling anxious, but expecting to see my mother in the morning. Hours passed before my sister woke me again.

"Jon Jon, get up," she said in a subdued voice. Finally, the anticipation was over; I was going to see my mother. I climbed out from under my sheets to my parents' bedroom. The house still felt cold and damp. My father sat whimpering on the bed where my mother had been lying just hours before, his elbows on his knees and his face in his hands. Everyone was quiet. My father could not control himself, and his cries became louder until they filled the house. I put one arm around my father's neck and I, too, began to sob. None of us slept that night. We just sat there in my parents' bedroom—confused.

It was not until later in life that I began to understand the impact that my mother's death had on my family. Growing up we were loved, protected, appreciated, and had stability. I could not have asked for a better upbringing. After my mother's death, our home life changed dramatically. The family now lacked stability in an environment that was already prone to family dysfunction, and we were forced to take care of ourselves. We had to cook our own meals, wash our own clothes, and clean our own rooms, things my mother did for us. I often cooked for my little brother, nephews, nieces, and my father. I constantly took on house chores like sweeping, mopping, and washing the dishes. My father would often say, "Jon Jon, you can't depend on anyone. You have to take care of yourself." My father's lesson on independence, I think, was borne from his watching, like a powerless spectator, this dysfunction move into our once stable home.

Black mold had spread through our house. The light blue carpet that came standard with the home was chock-full of dirt and discolored. Clouds of dust would engulf the hallway in the wake of children running through the house, likely the cause of several cases of pneumonia. Eventually, the decision was made to remove the carpet and we walked on un-tiled floors for some time before my father could afford to fix it. I also remember that a male relative, his wife, and children were living in a tent on the lawn outside our home. There was a wobbly table outside the tent, on which they had placed an electric pan used for cooking. There were also a few canned goods and bowls that sat on the wobbly table. I could not imagine the hurt and shame they felt after being reduced to living in a camping tent. Like some families on the reservation, we lived under these conditions for some time.

When my mother was alive, we faced hardships, but managed to keep our home in balance. Her death left us in a haze. We were absent any instructions to understand or take action against the unfavorable changes that were happening in our home. On occasion I would ask myself—are Lakota people supposed to live in disrepair? History books, news outlets, and research articles are always highlighting the latest calamities of Lakota people—high rates of violence, dilapidated homes, poor health, etc. After centuries of resilience in the face of challenges, it is easy to see how one additional tragedy in the lives of so many Lakota families could be enough to drive them to surrender to the low expectations imposed on our reservation. It is a virulent cycle of marginalization and disempowerment. Having the power to control one's destiny, for some Lakota families, seems like a fairytale entirely removed from the realities they experience every day.

Growing up I held onto the belief that the power to defeat dysfunction, which plagued the reservation, rested in education. Education as power was difficult to believe in when the very schools that were tasked with providing that education were crippled by dysfunction too. The truth is I was far from academically prepared for any opportunities after graduation. In fact, a majority of students in our area perform under grade level when it comes to reading, writing, and math. Most reservation schools have not been able to reach a level of function that will allow for greater academic outcomes and opportunities for students. When I graduated, I walked across the stage with approximately seventy students and roughly five entered college directly after high school. That is less than 8 percent!

With a lack of proper preparation, students progress through school with low expectations. In this environment, it is hard to believe you are destined for the best schools or the best jobs. Why? The reason is because there is a pervasive notion that it is OK to settle for less—community college or dead-end jobs. Many Lakota students in this context do not even entertain the idea of applying to or attending a quality college. Faced with limited job options, so many students also become dependent on assistance from the U.S. government. Most depressing is seeing students slip into a life of violence, drugs, alcohol, and poverty. To avoid the hardships, I felt I had no choice but to enlist in the Army, face the perils of combat, and later solve the puzzle that is applying to college. Like me, students from my reservation oftentimes do not take the direct route to college that is so common for many non-Native students in this country. Without a quality education it is significantly more difficult to find one's way through life. As a young man, I felt I was "lost" to this cycle of dysfunction.

This sense of being "lost" also had an effect on my sense of identity. I was proud to grow up on the reservation. I identified myself with one thing and one thing only—Lakota. I lived and breathed the Lakota culture and way of life. I was given a Lakota name—*Ozuye Cikala* (Little Warrior), went to ceremonies, and sang with my father at various sun dances throughout the reservation. I attended an all-Indian, tribally run school. These, I thought, solidified my identity as Lakota. So, as a young man, to have my identity questioned was difficult.

I felt that the foundation on which my identity rested could give way at any moment. Students would insinuate that rather than being Lakota, I was of more Hispanic or Middle Eastern ancestry—no doubt due to my thick black eyebrows and dark wavy hair. These were heavy blows to my sense of who I was, so I had to be tough to counteract the insults. Like so many other kids on the reservation who feel uncertain about who they are, I began to carry a lot of anger as a defense mechanism. I started to wear angry facial expressions like a mask, so that my anger was apparent to everyone around me. The mask let the other kids know, before they had a chance to make fun of me or hurt me, that there would be consequences. Unfortunately, a side effect of maintaining this outward appearance would come in the form of anxiety.

I became anxious in just about any setting—in the classroom, hanging out with friends, and sometimes around my own family. With a dysfunctional home life, the challenging social and academic maze of high school, and my increasingly repressed feelings, exhaustion began to set in. The idea of furthering my education was losing strength. I was willing to settle for the low expectation set for people from the reservation—a low-paying job, little education, and dependence on the government.

Identity, I feel, is something that not all families talk about on my reservation. There are many positives—culture, community, and love. Fears and insecurities, however, get brushed under the rug. The reality is that teasing and indirect comments about identity are common, but positive and direct discussions about forming a strong self-identity often do not occur, due perhaps to a lack of education on the subject. So, not only did I live with this sense of not having any direction in life, but I also felt that I somehow did not belong. Is it not clear how some students from the reservation are sent adrift in this sea of dysfunction? In this tempest of uncertainty, I was reaching a breaking point. Then, I was given the much-needed push to keep the idea of furthering my education alive.

Giles Morris was a young, energetic, jovial, White man from Boston, Massachusetts. He was also my high school English teacher. Reservation schools often rely on outsiders, usually young White people from the East who will stay two or three years, tops, or the castoffs from the surrounding school systems, which makes the quality of education inconsistent. Giles, however, was able to bring into focus my fondness for reading. He was the first teacher, that I can remember, who required his students to read an entire novel. In fact, it was the first time I read Shakespeare and *The Great Gatsby*, literature considered critical in most schools. One day, Giles introduced the class to *The Catcher in the Rye* by J.D. Salinger. I will never forget this book as I immediately related to the main character, Holden Caulfield. I could not put the book down and read it every chance I got. Despite all our apparent dissimilarities, I, like Holden's character, was displeased with my school and the way my life was unfolding. Like me, Holden was dealing with the loss of someone very dear to his heart, a loss that disturbed the normal function of his family, life, and identity. Holden not only affirmed for me that life is full of hardship, but that holding on to those hardships can make life's journey much more difficult. I needed to somehow *let go* of all the pain I was carrying. I needed to further my education. My only option at the time, as I mentioned (and this is true for many students on my reservation), was to join the military.

I made the trip to MEPS (Military Entrance Processing Station) in Sioux Falls, SD during my senior year in high school and signed up to join the Army. I did my eighteen-week basic training at Fort Knox, Kentucky. A year later I was deployed during the initial invasion of the War in Iraq. We spent a week or so near the Kuwait/Iraq border. There were a few fights during the invasion, but it was not until we got to Baghdad that the level of combat increased. In addition to providing security for key locations such as municipal buildings and factories, we also conducted routine security checkpoints throughout the city. War, at times, seemed like an impassable hurdle in my journey to attain an education, but there were familiar hurdles that I continued to negotiate.

To a certain extent, a soldier expects to find himself imperiled from enemy fire, but facing bombardment on my identity is quite a different thing. It happened during our convoy, thousands of military vehicles inching toward the capital city of Baghdad. The sky was a clear blue, and the day was dusty and hot. Our convoy drew to a halt near a small Iraqi town, so we decided to dismount our tanks, get some fresh air, and stretch our legs. It was common for some Iraqi locals to approach our tank, mostly men dressed in traditional Iraqi robes. We were wary at times because you never knew where the enemy was coming from, but these encounters were mostly cordial. One of the Iraqi men looked to me and casually said, "Are you Kuwaiti?" My tank crew had a good chuckle. My tank commander caught his breath and said, "No, he's Indian! Red Indian? You know, feathers?" While I recognized his attempt to remedy the confusion, and forgiving his stereotypical depiction of Native people, the question was yet another glancing blow to how I identified myself. Why couldn't I just be a Lakota warrior or an American warrior? Serving during wartime was seen as a huge honor in Lakota country, an honor connected to the history and traditions borne from the countless deeds carried out by Lakota warriors of the olden days. Yet, how am I supposed to live up to this honor when my identity as a Lakota warrior was put into question? What I began to realize was that issues with identity do not fade over time and, instead, they become heavy burdens to carry unless you choose to deal with it.

I had no intention of staying in the military after my enlistment was up, so five months following my tour in Iraq I was honorably discharged. I became a counselor's aid at a drug and alcohol treatment center back on my reservation. Providing a service to my community through working with troubled youths was rewarding. It was during this time that my own life started to take a turn for the better. I had the good fortune to meet my future wife, Deana Wagner, a member of the Cherokee Nation of Oklahoma. She graduated from Brown University and joined Teach For America as a member in the inaugural South Dakota corps. She was placed as a high school Science teacher at my former school. When I first met Deana I was afraid to reveal my world to her, a world that had been so full of dysfunction, but she was completely understanding and non-judgmental. She also has a passion for helping Native people. Most importantly, she accepted me for who I am and where I come from. She is everything I could ask for in a friend and companion. It was the start of a strong and beautiful relationship.

Overall, the two years I spent on the reservation after my military service were positive, because I was thankful to be surrounded by family and friends once again. My relationship with my father evolved and seemed renewed. While I was growing up, we never spoke of anything too deep or personal, but now, as veterans of war, we had something in common. We often talked about war. We would talk about the psychology of the mind during wartime and how fellow soldiers often would resort to brutal tactics. He confessed to me the few times he came close to death. My father was, in fact, wounded during Vietnam and awarded the Purple Heart. We also talked about his time growing up and his struggle with alcoholism. He talked about a time when he would receive his paycheck, leave some money with our mom and my brother Milton (who was an only child at the time), then proceed to the nearest bar and spend the rest of it on booze. It was a dark chapter in his life, but he eventually stopped drinking for the sake of his family. He wanted to provide a better life for his children and did so by turning to a life of Lakota culture. Singing was my father's calling, and it helped to set him on a positive path. We found room in our relationship to talk about our feelings, which was long overdue. It was healing to see this side of my father because it showed that he, too, felt lost in terms of his place in the world. We began to talk about the difficulties we experienced around the time of my mother's death, an ordeal that prevented us from having an ideal father–son relationship. I cherish the conversations we had and the time we spent together after I left the military. I think the conversations with my father gave me the courage to continue examining my own identity, this at a time when a secret about who I was suddenly emerged.

One afternoon when I was 24 years old and working on some client files at the treatment center, I received a phone call from a woman I did not know:

"Hello, son," she said.

"Who is this?" I asked.

"This is your mom," she replied.

I was not sure why, but in that moment I was quickly boiling with anger inside. My anxiety kicked in and my heart rate began to race. There was nothing left to do but react.

"You're not my mother!!" I said and I slammed the phone down.

I was furious! Who does this woman think she is? I knew my mother was Linda Around Him. I sat in the office of the treatment center for a few hours, trying to gather my thoughts and composure. I was shocked by the mysterious woman's statement as well as my very emotional reaction. Why was I so emotional? The truth is there had been nagging incidents in the past that had unsettled me.

I remember a hearing at the tribal offices in Pine Ridge where a man motioned his hand toward me and said, "OK, so the child's name is John Little Hawk?" My father quickly responded, "Little Hawk? No! His name is John Around Him." I turned to my sister feeling confused and anxious. She shook her head in disagreement and reassured me that I am an Around Him. On another occasion a relative walked up to me and said, "My mom says Linda is not your real mom." I remember these incidents vividly, and in each case my siblings were quick to reassure me that we shared the same parents. Growing up I was never treated differently from my brothers and sisters, and so I never doubted who my biological parents were. Nevertheless, the strange incidents piled up over time and the doubt gradually increased. After the call from the anonymous woman claiming to be my mother, I finally decided to confront my father and family about it.

One evening soon after the unsettling call, I beckoned my family into the house for a meeting. My father often brought us together whenever there were any issues in the family, but never would we meet at the request of any of us kids. My father, my sister Clovia, and my little brother Samuel sat around our dining room table in our small, light blue house. I was very nervous and could feel my palms getting sweaty. I sat next to my father and told him that a woman had called claiming to be my mother. My father appeared uneasy and shifted a few times in his chair. I finally mustered enough courage to ask: "Dad, was I adopted?" His head dropped immediately and he began rubbing the back of his neck, concentrating on what he wanted to say. His lips gathered and contracted. Then he said:

"Well son … yes … you were adopted."

His voice was a bit shaky. He paused for a moment. I noticed I was shaking too and couldn't swallow. My father pressed on:

"When you were a baby your mother left you at the hospital. She was having a hard time with alcohol and drugs. The nurse at the hospital knew who I was, she knew I was related to your biological mother, so she called and told me what happened. So, Linda and I went to the hospital. Linda picked you up. She said in Lakota, 'Let's take him home.' That night we brought you home with us."

The words "Let's take him home" resonated with me on a deep and profound level. My deep affection for "home" was cultivated from the dawn of my existence. It was an emotional moment for everyone in the room. Inside, I felt a sense of relief at hearing the truth. The revelation of my adoption began to shed more light on who I was, and I felt like I could begin to bring some closure to this gray area in my life. I tried gathering my thoughts, and spoke through tear-filled eyes:

"Well, Dad, thank-you for telling me. I don't want you guys to worry. I am not mad. This does not change anything. You will always be my dad. Linda will always be my mother. Milton, Amaris, Clovia, and Samuel will always be my brothers and sisters. You raised me and brought me into your home and I thank you for that."

I hugged my dad, turned, and embraced my brother and sister as well. I have since come to find out that many of my relatives and family members knew about my adoption and that they collectively tried to keep it a secret. My aunt says they feared I might rebel if I knew about the adoption, which is understandable. Would I have rebelled or run away like some adolescents dealing with adoption or divorce do? I do not know. What I have learned, however, is that life is not only a journey of discovering your identity, but also one of confronting the difficult question—are you willing to accept your identity, imperfect as it may seem? Wrestling with this question is a step toward reaching some semblance of peace with who you are.

A friend who was a counselor at the alcohol and drug treatment center helped me put things into perspective. The counselor said, "John, these things are difficult. Just know that your dad (John Around Him) probably saved your life." These were powerful words at the time.

Indeed, who knows where I would be had John and Linda not walked into the hospital that day. This part of me, the adoption, would no longer be a source of insecurity, but a reminder of how lucky I was. From what I am told, my biological mother still struggles to this day with some of the challenges that made her give me up for adoption. I discovered that I have several other sisters and brothers who have been raised by other relatives. Some of these siblings I have met and others I have not. I have also discovered that we share Mexican ancestry through my biological mother, confirming early suspicions of my having mixed ancestry, the truth of which was comforting. My father, John, always told me that a part of being Lakota is having the ability to forgive. I decided that I would no longer hold onto to my feelings of anger and resentment, which spawned from my troubles with identity. Instead, I would forgive myself by accepting my adoption and my mixed heritage. I also think that I am willing to take steps toward forgiving my biological mother. Talking about it here has been an act of forgiveness in itself and a step toward achieving peace.

After two years of working on the reservation, a fire inside of me was stoked and I was driven more than ever to pursue higher education. Deana was accepted to the Harvard School of Public Health to pursue a Master of Science degree. Around this time my father, whom I had come to respect and love with all my heart, and who also believed in education, lost his life in a battle with cancer. I followed Deana to Massachusetts and enrolled in Boston's Bunker Hill Community College (BHCC) in hope of finding better opportunities. My experience living in Boston, which included working in a pastry shop and attending community college, opened my eyes to the challenges of inner-city life. Many of my classmates were minorities. Several were from countries in Africa and Asia, and all lived in low-income neighborhoods with inadequate public education. Growing up, it was easy to think that life was less troubled for those off the reservation. As my horizons have expanded, I have come to realize that poor education does not discriminate. Even though these students often held multiple jobs, had families to care for, and made long commutes, they still came to school.

At BHCC I met Wick Sloane, an adjunct English professor who taught Expository Writing and was to become my mentor and friend. I came to learn that Professor Sloane is a staunch advocate for students from disadvantaged communities and writes about equity issues for people who are enrolled at two-year institutions, who often have fewer opportunities open to them than students at four-year colleges and universities. He would track down students who disappeared from school to find out the reasons why, and to offer his help. Professor Sloane believed in me and thought I belonged in a four-year college. He too understood the tendency among impoverished students to settle for less, so he encouraged me to apply to Dartmouth because of its excellence. With some college preparation and a below-average high school record, it took me some time to believe I could succeed at Dartmouth. Rather than play down my chances, for once I dared to believe that I was destined for the best. So, I applied for admission to Dartmouth in winter of 2008. When I later received an envelope from Dartmouth in the mail, with so much of my future hanging in the balance, I remember feeling almost paralyzed before opening it. The letter read: "We are pleased to inform you that you have been accepted ..." I could not believe what I was reading. After the feelings of hopelessness I experienced living on the reservation, the memories of dodging bullets during war, finally, I felt I was given a break. It was truly an amazing moment.

I was excited about meeting new people and continuing my pursuit of higher education, but my transition to Dartmouth was far from easy. Dartmouth was yet another mirror forcing me to reflect on my identity, which was still a work in progress. Academically, I did great my freshman year. Still, as a much older (I matriculated when I was 26 years old), Iraq War veteran, Native American, undergraduate student, I struggled to find my place within the Dartmouth community. I began to feel isolated and searched for a place to "fit in." The following year I promised myself I would make an effort to build relationships within the Native American and greater Dartmouth communities to prevent further isolation. What started as a plan to build relationships turned into one of the most tumultuous years of my Dartmouth career. I found myself losing sight of my priorities and responsibilities that I had set for myself at the outset. I began dedicating less time to doing homework and going to class, and not surprisingly, my grades began to decline and passing my exams became a desperate battle. I had a growing and familiar sense of self-doubt and nervousness. A pattern of academic and social difficulty, similar to what I had experienced in high school, began to develop. I could feel myself reverting to those old methods of repressing my feelings. This time I was ready to tackle my issues head on and I decided that I would no longer hide from them. So, I sought help.

Through counseling I was able to slow down and take a closer look at myself. I was too worried about trying to "fit in" at Dartmouth—fitting in was something I have dealt with my whole life. In the process, I sacrificed my own values and goals. First, I was officially diagnosed as having suffered from anxiety, depression, and low self-esteem. This was another revelation shedding light on the shadows of my identity. There was a sense of relief in having the ability to name the problems I dealt with on a day-to-day basis. In high school, and somewhat at Dartmouth, my psyche translated these problems into the belief that I was defective and a failure. I thought I could never compete with the best at institutions like Dartmouth because my anxiety was a barrier. I could never be a person capable of making change. I was broken. Due to my anxiety I had head tremors and sweaty palms while speaking in front of my classmates, and the disorder fed into further negative thoughts that I would be perceived as a fool or idiot by my peers. Second, in this cloud of self-doubt, I was forgetting why I came to Dartmouth in the first place—to help my community fight dysfunction. I began to realize that it was my own insecurities that prevented me from taking a firm hold of my identity and my goals. Counseling helped me see this and get back on track with my coursework while putting some of the pieces of my life together. Learning about my anxiety and ways to cope was liberating because I had hid from it for too long. Slowly but steadily, I gained confidence in my abilities and chances of success at Dartmouth College, and I did so with decreasing anxiety and a growing internal sense of peace. Counseling certainly helped me perform to my potential during the latter part of my undergraduate experience.

My Dartmouth experience was great and I don't regret any second of it. I will never forget walking across the stage with my diploma while my wife and her uncle, my sisters and little brother, my uncle through Lakota adoption—Albert White Hat—and his wife, and several others who have supported me along my journey looked on in the audience. During the NAD (Native Americans at Dartmouth) graduation reception, I took the opportunity to thank those who have helped me along the way, especially my late father—John Around Him Sr. My dad wanted an education for me more than anything in the world. I think he was frustrated at how difficult it was for Lakota students to get a good education. He was tired of watching students suffer from the realities of poverty, drugs and alcohol, and dysfunction on my reservation. Receiving my degree was my way of saying, "Dad, I did it. Thank-you for making me who I am today. I will continue your mission of helping our people." Looking back, even though my father and I did not directly discuss identity, he showed me that I was not alone in trying to make sense of who I am. Perhaps, finding our identity is a constant and evolving journey that we all take.

I am thankful that my father *showed* me the Lakota way of life. It is the Lakota way of life that I eventually intend to support using what I have learned at Dartmouth through bringing new institutions to the reservation, such as schools systems that have shown elsewhere that they can produce successful college-bound students. It is my hope then that students in these schools will someday, like me, return to the reservation and help rebuild and heal our community. I also want to establish a program to preserve the Lakota culture and language by bringing more focus on language education and preservation. I intend to work to ensure that both the state and federal government recognize the serious problem of severely inadequate education systems on the reservation, and commit them to join us in improving educational opportunities for Native youth.

The trauma of my year in Iraq has loosened its hold and I am now able to look back on the richness of my early life as well as its extraordinary challenges with acceptance and a quiet mind. I am beginning to understand that growing up I was a kid who lived his entire life filled with anxiety and low self-esteem. My life on the reservation, my war experience in Iraq, and my time at an Ivy League college have made for an unpredictable journey, but one that has provided me with loving relationships and strengthened me for what lies ahead. I have overcome a lot, and in the process, I have learned to accept who I am and to truly just be myself. Finding one's identity is not always easy, but it is a journey worth taking. I will bring with me on my journey a simple axiom for living that my father taught me: "a person who cares and who takes an interest in the success of others will make a difference."

Case 13

FOREVER AN AWKWARD ADOLESCENT

DAVID KENNEDY

DOI: 10.4324/9781003165378-16

David Kennedy

This is the story of a young man born with serious physical disabilities. David describes the tension between his parents over how high their expectations for his autonomy should be. His father's "legendary penchant for interfering" results in his doing everything for him, whereas his mother, having "less patience with incompetence," expects him to learn to do for himself. College becomes a new opportunity for forming close female friendships and for academic achievements, but these are tainted by doubts over whether he is held to the same standards as his peers. And he asks, "What is to become of my sexuality?" and envisions "a 35-year-old with the sexuality of a 14-year-old, and the prospect does not please me." As he plans to begin graduate school for a career in media, he will not accept society's narrow expectation that he should practice his profession as a representative of the disabled because he says, "I do not think of myself as a disabled person."

My first clear memory is from nursery school. When I was 3 years old my parents sent me to a small nursery school for three or four hours about twice a week. It was in the basement of a local church, and I distinctly remember being carried down a long corridor past beautifully colored stained-glass windows. Someone was carrying me and pointed out the colored shapes that were on the opposite wall as the sun shone through the windows.

I should note that at this point I had not yet learned to walk. I still think of it as "learning" to walk, but this is not quite accurate. Because I was born with physical disabilities, the first three to five years of my life were interspersed with multiple operations, where the doctors tried to stretch my hamstrings surgically. After each of these operations I was put in a plaster cast—at one point, both legs up to the waist. It was all in an effort to unclub my feet so that I might someday be able to walk. Everyone was very excited when I finally did, spontaneously, while waiting with my father in a doctor's waiting room. My parents and all their good friends were in tears, I guess, because the professionals had been about evenly divided on whether I'd ever walk at all. I don't remember this important occasion, however, which is one of my peculiar tricks of memory—I never seem to understand the full implications of various "remarkable" events in my life.

I don't have a lot of clear early memories of my parents. I always took them for granted, at least until I began to figure out ways that I might lose them. Like when I began to realize that their marriage wasn't that great. They really should have divorced twenty-five years ago. Except then, they wouldn't have had me! Even so, they are very unsuited to each other, and their arguments and periodic leavings and returnings were a bit of a cloud in my childhood.

I am sometimes embarrassed and worried about how little their sour relationship has seemed to affect me. I have had moments of tears and fear during particularly bad patches but, by and large, I have never had those self-blaming feelings that everyone says kids have when their parents have problems. I think it is a testament to my parents that despite their trials, life at our house always had a sense of security and permanence. I don't know if they did it on purpose; more likely, it was their conservative view of how one conducted one's life that did it. Breakfast was always there. Dinner was always at 6:30. Everything was predictable. At the time, I came to envy my friends' younger, more adventurous parents (they went to movies—we never did), but now I think that it was better for me to have parents who took refuge in routine. I never really worried that I wouldn't be taken care of, that I wouldn't be loved.

I entered adolescence (and eighth grade) at about the time we made a cross-country move. Thinking back on that period, I am certain that the move was good for me. For one thing, my best friend had moved away the year before, at a time when our relationship was becoming difficult. We first became friends, at age 5, because we shared a disdain for the crowd. We weren't joiners. For me, this trait was determined by my disabilities; I had had to learn how to entertain myself. The fun I had was sedentary: matchbox cars, model planes, books about WWII fliers, and TV—which spent a great deal of time catering to the imaginations of would-be fighter pilots and space travelers. My friend also liked these things, but more by choice. After a while, we reinforced our reclusive tendencies, and as we grew older we grew farther and farther apart from our peers who were either getting into sports or getting into trouble.

Predictably, as puberty struck, my friend and I began to reevaluate (separately) where we stood. I suspect that my friend began to see that others his age were having a lot of physical fun, horsing around in ways that seemed impossible, or at least improbable, for me. Suddenly going over to each other's houses to play with Lego no longer sufficed to sustain our friendship. I, too, began to identify with other peers, people who also stood out, but who seemed to have made the transition from Lego to a kind of makeshift intellectualism. When a group of us began reading *The Lord of the Rings*, my best friend did not join in. Soon after this, he moved away.

For my family, our move across country was very traumatic, though they tried to act as though it was an adventure. My main concern was whether I would be able to survive in the new public school I would be entering. Having spent all my grade school years at an "experimental education" school on a college campus in my hometown, I was not used to a structured school environment. The realm of real schools was a mysterious and sinister one in the lore of this "campus school," and I'm afraid I bought into the horror stories of academic rigor and regimentation, which passed for information on public schools among my 12-year-old schoolmates. I think that entering middle school in the new town, far from any familiar people or places, was the best way for me to get into regular schooling—kind of like being thrown into a pool as a way of learning to swim. As it turned out, it was all right. I gained confidence in my academic abilities by having my intelligence confirmed for the first time by grades. The teachers there were every bit as human as in my other school, and the kids were far more numerous, so I could hide in anonymity. At least, that is what I thought. Actually, because of my disabilities I was almost instantly known, or known of, by everyone in the school. I was also treated with uniform kindness and curiosity from the first day, but even then I wondered, as I do now, how much of that kindness was actually pity for me because of my disability.

Since I have been physically disabled all of my life, I have managed to cope with the purely practical problems arising from this with a minimum of fuss on my part; I felt no loss, because I had no feelings of "normality" to compare with. One of my physical problems is that I am short, about 4 feet, 2 inches tall. Until I began growing whiskers on my face and driving a car, I was constantly mistaken by strangers as being a little kid. It's a hell of a pain for a 16-year-old boy to be handed a kiddie's menu every time he enters a restaurant. It is even worse when mere coherent speech is greeted with awe. If explaining to the old lady in church that I am taking five classes in high school provokes an assumption that I must be terribly smart, how am I supposed to know whether I really am or if everyone is just impressed that I don't drool on myself? I have high standards for myself, perhaps not as high as many straight-A college students, but I am always impressed when I witness, say, good writing and intelligent conversation in others and I aspire to such standards of intelligence. During my teen years it was a constant nagging irritation that everyone around me had what I felt were extremely low expectations. I never knew where I stood.

Almost everybody treats me well, whether or not they really know me. In fact, I gained a reputation among some of my high school peers for being really smart, even though plenty of students within my range of ability (such as those with whom I went through an Honors

English program) had better grades and study habits than I did. After a while, I began to realize that people were predisposed to treating disabled people with extra kindness. Perhaps, I thought, my "smart kid" reputation, which I considered to be disproportionate to my actual abilities, was part of this extra kindness. Supporting this notion was my observation that many people who had known me for a long time, even some members of my extended family, tended to express admiration for my accomplishments with an enthusiasm far beyond what I considered to be appropriate. I was able to gauge this by comparing my parents' response with that of my brother and certain close friends, all of whom had gotten used to the fact that, indeed, I had learned to walk and talk and go to school like any normal kid, and hence, responded in a more subdued fashion to what were, after all, fairly minor accomplishments on my part.

My desire to do well academically did not, oddly enough, compel me to become an especially studious student. My parents never really put the pressure on me to get straight As, and when I came home with report cards that were mixed As and Bs, they seemed to feel these were fairly wonderful. Either they were too old to understand grade inflation, or they were falling into the same trap I already explained—being glad that I was still alive and walking and apparently intelligent. I tend to think that it was a little of both, which means that I have been guilty, on occasion, of taking advantage of the very tendency that I despise. I have often allowed myself to rest easy in others' low expectations. This is something that I continue to fight in myself. Still, it was terribly important to me that I never got less than a B. I constructed a sort of artificial line of performance, below which I told myself my parents would be disappointed. For some reason, I was never too concerned about what my teachers or my friends thought of my grades; I looked solely to my parents for approval on that score.

If, as I surmised, people's expressed admiration of me was exaggerated by the issue of my disabilities, then how could I be sure exactly how much of that praise and admiration had been earned and how much was phony or misplaced? Naturally, as I moved through adolescence, I cared more and more about where I stood in the grand scheme of things. Since the whole business of looks and sex appeal was entirely outside my league, my only arenas for competition and comparison were in academics and in "being likable." I tended to look to everyone I met for approval, and conversation was my weapon. At first, I was just naturally inclined to have an odd sense of humor, and to express both this humor and my interest in history and politics in conversations with adults and with as many interested friends as I could find. Around my senior year in high school, I began to sense that being able to carry on a conversation about a wide range of topics was not just fun but an asset, too.

I have long thought that one of the real handicaps of having congenital disabilities is that one often grows up isolated from all the trivial things that adolescents banter about: music, girls, cars, clothes, films, TV, and magazines—the whole range of popular culture is a special language that the adult world too easily dismisses as unimportant. But for the teenager cut off from this language, relating to peers who are already leery of him or her because of a disability is doubly difficult. The goodwill most people have to "give it a try" with the disabled teen may be there at the beginning, but unless the teen is able to "run with the ball" and "fit in" at least by speaking the same language as his or her peers, the goodwill quickly turns to embarrassment, and then the disabled teen will be ignored. If it were up to me, people who counsel disabled kids and their parents would stress the importance, often denigrated in "normal" kids, of "fitting in."

In retrospect, I think that a lot of what I was doing in high school was constructing a character, a persona, I could live with. Most adolescents do this, but for me, it was doubly important because the character I had, my "default" pigeonhole in the eyes of others, was that of a short, oddly postured, disabled kid. I wasn't sure at the time, and I'm still not positive, just what kind of persona I want to have. This has made constructing myself an ad hoc process. For the most part, however, I think I have been able to impress others enough with images other than disability. When I get scared, though, when I think about it too much, I wonder if it's all my imagination. Does everybody still think of me as a disability, and not as a person? I don't know. I'll never really know for sure, because I am always suspicious of others' response to me. I guess that I function from day to day on a veneer of faith; I survive with happiness and pride by assuming that other people see me as I see myself.

My parents are two people whose reactions to me I have trusted. From my mother I get a cartload of political convictions, or perhaps prejudices, because at times I think that her convictions are as much prejudice as they are considered opinions. I count among the greatest gifts of my college years the ability to critique and analyze my own political and social beliefs. By and large, I inherit from Mom a respect for what good can be done by government, along with a profound and unquenchable skepticism that prevents me from ever being satisfied with what government or any other authority is doing. I realize, because I have seen it in my mother, that this is a frustrating way to approach the world. Always having to "bitch, bitch, bitch," not because it's right or good or a citizen's responsibility but because I can't contain myself, is a burden—especially in a society that frowns upon excess in expressing one's views.

Having lived for the most part away from my mother for four years, I have found that I still care deeply about what she thinks of my actions. I don't think I could ever pursue a career, for instance, that violated her standards of morality. This cancels out a lot of possibilities, but fortunately, I have no desire to become a stockbroker. Nevertheless, as I pursue graduate studies in mass media and popular culture, I find myself wondering about how she would feel about my being an advertising copywriter, or a television producer or network reporter. I tend to think that as long as I stay true to my own standards, I will not run afoul of hers, but sometimes I am not sure, and that worries me.

One of the peculiar dynamics of my relations with my parents has been growing up in an atmosphere thick with a history of Dad's legendary penchant for interfering. When I was much younger this didn't bother me, because I sought the security he provided. He was always the provider, the caretaker. In fact, he even helped dress me in the mornings right up till I entered high school. He was always looking for ways to make my life easier. Of course, the problem with this is that it retarded the development of my self-sufficiency. Mom was dead set against this. It wasn't that Mom was uncaring, it is just that she had less patience with incompetence.

In the long run, she was right; it was more help to me to force me into doing things myself than to smooth out any remotely rough areas of day-to-day life. As I got older, Mom became increasingly adamant that Dad was now an abnormally doting parent. She felt that perhaps it was more selfishness on his part—his need to feel needed and in charge—than a true concern for my welfare, which kept him so involved in my physical challenges. Eventually, she began to suggest to me that I ought to resent his "interference" as much as she did. In a way, this was good, because it finally caused me to increase and jealously guard my self-sufficiency. At first for Mom's benefit, but eventually for my own, I began to oppose my father's instinctive moves toward helping me dress, get in and out of cars, put on jackets, and so on. He knew that it all was for the best, and I no longer saw him as my guardian for life. Instead, I began to see him as a friend, a father, and sometimes a pain!

Our relationship has since changed for the better. We now have more arguments than we used to, but they are adult-type arguments.

And on the whole, we share a mutual interest in each other's lives. I am sure that he harbors more than a little "controlling interest" in my life, but if he does, he at least is honest enough to admit it, and often interrupts himself mid-sentence, chuckling at his own tendency to criticize and worry the joy out of new adventures.

Other people, too, have influenced me in less vital, but no less enduring ways. I think that I first got a taste of the joys of discussing politics from the high school librarian. He was a balding, middle-aged man with a bit of a paunch, and a wonderfully dry sense of humor. A fan of George McGovern, he introduced me to the blessings of "Norwegian charisma" while we both watched Walter Mondale stumble through the 1984 campaign. I would come in after lunch and wander over to his office, where we would swap political stories we had heard or read about.

Here was a man, as well educated and articulate as my parents, and with similar political stripes, who actually enjoyed watching the "march of folly" that politics provides. It was a liberation for me. There were very few of my peers with whom I could talk about politics, either because they didn't care or because my views were hopelessly out of sync with theirs. For two years, then, I was able to spend at least an hour of every day just yakking away about anything that popped into my head. In fact, from testing my wings with him, I was finally able to spar with my parents on political topics.

I suspect that this kind of jabbering contributed as much as anything else to my interest in editorial journalism. When I approached the journalism advisor about taking the journalism class (thereby becoming a member of the paper staff), I remember that I had a goal in mind of writing a column. My work in his English class impressed him, so he helped me convince the editor that I should have my own column. In retrospect, I am sure that part of his admiration of me was that damnable tendency I mentioned earlier—to see any accomplishments by a disabled person as a miracle—but I guess I didn't really mind it that much if, in the end, I received recognition purely on my own merits.

I am sure that is one reason why I loved writing that column and the one I wrote for four years in college. In college, I began my column before very many people knew who I was. Consequently, when I got favorable comments from strangers, it was all the more special to me. For the first time in my life, I could be sure that I had earned every bit of the praise I got. I am a person who has never been short of expressions of approval from others, but anonymous praise is like gold to me. This is why I look forward to continuing writing of this nature and then, hopefully, as a career.

There is one incident from my adolescence that has had perhaps the greatest impact on my outlook. During the long drive from the West Coast to what would be my college in the East, I became seriously ill. At this point, the most severe aspect of my disability stemmed from the effects of severe scoliosis on my lung functions. As I grew, my spine curved even more; the more it curved, the more it applied pressure on my lungs. Hence, my breathing capacity was getting progressively smaller. While a spinal fusion operation at age 10 prevented this from becoming fatal, as it turned out, the procedure left enough room for worsening to make it nearly so.

Knowing that the high altitude we would have to endure on the drive east would make me uncomfortable, my doctors prescribed an oxygen tank that I could use whenever I got too tired by the lack of oxygen. Unfortunately, this did not solve the physical problem of actual breathing, and the result was a potentially deadly spiral; the more oxygen I breathed in, the less my brain was induced to stimulate breathing—the less I breathed, the less I was able to expel carbon dioxide. By the time I had reached my destination I was unable to sleep, because I would stop breathing and wake up.

At one point, I was told that I would never recover fully from this malady—as, in fact, I have not—and that I had about five years to live. The only alternative was to surgically install a permanent tracheostomy so that, in addition to using extra oxygen at night, I could have the help of a respirator in breathing. We waited a few weeks in the vain hope that somehow I would spontaneously pull out of this hole, and during this time I continued to prepare for my first day of classes, which was less than two weeks away.

Most of the people around me, my mother and father in particular, saw my entering college as a fantasy. After all, I did look pretty bad, and I could barely cross a room on foot, much less walk to class. Only my older brother seemed to think that they were all overreacting. For all of my life he had lived with the constant and recurrent threat that I would die, that I would never walk, that I could never do thus and such. Every time I had taken a turn for the worse he had been told that "you'd better come and see him; it could be the last time." Every time I had "proved them wrong," as he put it to me. While he was particularly worried with this incident, he still felt that as long as I was certain I would start college on time, there was hope.

To hear him tell it, I am some kind of brave hero for having kept my faith in my ability to recover. From my point of view, it wasn't bravery or faith. I never really realized how serious my condition was. All along, my mind refused to accept the gravity of the situation. Instead, I whiled away these "sick" hours thinking about how I'd decorate my dorm room, and what classes I would take. Finally, it got bad enough that it was decided to do the tracheostomy. Within a week I was going to my first class. To me it seemed natural. It was what I'd planned all along. I was feeling much better; the oxygen with the respirator at night left me quite healthy during the day, and I was doing what I wanted to do.

In a number of ways, this incident is typical of my outlook as I have grown up. First, it shows how I have generally dealt with adversity: I ignore it. I refuse to accept it. I do not think of myself as a disabled person. While this has helped me thus far, it may not continue to do so. Out there in the nonacademic "real" world, disabled people, like any minority group, have to organize and vocally assert their rights. I have always shied away from doing this. For one thing, my relatively privileged family background has to a large extent smoothed my path. I have not had to advocate strongly for myself because money and my father's position as a doctor have advocated for me. Besides that, though, I simply do not want to be labeled. I take no particular "pride" in being disabled, even though I have as much reason to do so as any disabled person. It all comes back to that nagging problem—how can I earn praise and self-esteem without having my disability in the equation?

But as I inch toward a career, perhaps in journalism, certainly in some kind of media, I am finding that I will have to fight society's tendency to view me primarily in terms of my disability. In my chosen field, there is a tendency to pigeonhole people. Blacks report on race issues. Women report on feminism. I don't really want to be a writer or producer of columns or programs about disability. I understand that people see me as a useful tool—articulate, intelligent, and poised disabled people are hard to come by because so many of them have social disabilities that come with their physical problems. Some would say that it is my duty to serve society in the most natural way possible to me, to become an advocate for disabled people. While I accept the logic and morality of this, I simply don't want that!

In addition to calling my attention to this desire in me to be seen in my own terms, my near-death episode also made me more aware than I had ever been before of how important my relationship with my brother is. He was 14 when I was born, and I am pretty sure that he got short shrift because of the all-consuming problems of my infancy. Although he may harbor some resentment toward me, he also has a devotion to me that I always find surprising. Most importantly, he has supported and challenged me consistently throughout my life—from the time he set out to teach me to get up after falling down, to the times he questioned my opinions and forced me to take steps toward independence and maturity that I was unwilling to take. While others let me grow up somewhat spoiled and lazy, he insisted that there was no reason why I couldn't do dishes or cook dinners. During my years at college, the longest time I have ever lived near him, my brother has had a major role in helping me grow up.

By far the richest time in my life has been my four years in college. The intellectual benefits have been enormous, not so much in the amount of stuff I have learned, but in the atmosphere. My college and I were peculiar matches. Traditionally a very athletic campus, it nevertheless fits my personality in that its students have tended to opt for a kind of athleticism that emphasizes the enjoyment of the sport over outright achievement. I, too, get most of my enjoyment out of activities that have no intrinsic value, no tabulation of results.

Socially, college would have been a waste for me had it not been for my fraternity. It is a cliché that fraternity members learn as well as party in the frat, but it really is true in my case. My fraternity was atypical; a coeducational fraternity for non-joiners. Because some of the members had the courage to invite me to rush in the spring of my freshman year, I was able to live for two full years in a house with eighteen men and women who considered themselves a true family. We cooked together, studied together, and fought with each other over how to take care of our family and the structure that housed it. Because I lived with these people, they had plenty of time to get to know me.

Far from shutting me up in a closed community, my fraternity experience gave me the confidence to branch out and become better acquainted with others on campus. When people met me, I was identified with my newspaper column and with my fraternity. Thus, I was more than just a disabled student; I had other identities to start me off. I used them as a launching pad from which to make other people understand who I was in a deeper way.

Before writing this meditation on my adolescence, I was asked, among other things, "What makes you want to get up in the morning?" I think that my first answer would be, "Whatever it is I have to do on that particular day." This illustrates an important tendency of mine. All my life I have done what's been put in front of me to do. Kids go to school, so I went to school. After that, in my family, you go to college, so I went to college. After college, you either get a job or continue your education, so I will attend graduate school. I pay my bills. I do my reading. I grade papers. I cope. I get along. At the same time, however, I am motivated by a need for approval from others.

Some aspects of adolescence are harder to cope with than others. I often wonder what is to become of my sexuality—I cannot envision (except in erotic dreams) a time when a woman would find me attractive enough to spark a long-term love relationship. I have read of other people far more disabled than I am who have found both love and sex with compatible, willing partners. Yet, a paraplegic is, if immobile, still normal in appearance. I am not. I am short, my back curves severely, and because of my rapid metabolism and restricted abdominal cavity, I am skinny to the point of being emaciated. I have had many female friends, but what could possibly provoke them to see me and be sexually attracted to me?

I have tried on two occasions to move closer to two different female friends. In both cases, this consisted of my acting as comforter and patient listener in time of crisis or stress. On both occasions, they appreciated it and the friendships deepened. But in both cases, I suspect, they had no idea that I had any other motive than a friend's concern. And in each instance, I felt like a beast, because I knew that I had ulterior motives. I know something of the dangers of a male–female relationship based on the weak and emotionally distressed woman and the strong "I'll take care of you" man, and I have no desire to become a "co-dependent"— with or without sex.

I look at the future of my sexuality and I see a 35-year-old with the sexuality of a 14-year-old. In this area, I am likely to be forever an awkward adolescent—and the prospect does not please me. At the same time, I hope that the sense of humor, the curiosity, and the weightlessness of carefree adolescence can be preserved to some extent. I look around me and see many people in both journalism and cultural studies who seem to have retained these characteristics. Perhaps I can, too. I hope, finally, that I do not ever really grow up.

In sum, I have come a long way. Because of me and those who have supported me, I have accomplished many things and done a lot of growing up. I am still an adolescent, though. Only an adolescent has the audacity to hope for what I hope for, which is—everything.

Follow-up

DAVID: THIRTEEN YEARS LATER

DOI: 10.4324/9781003165378-17

David Kennedy

Everyone likes to think of themselves as unique. Nobody likes to admit that they are subject to "textbook" psychology—the courses of their lives determined by recognized trends and phases. Reading what I wrote thirteen years ago, I am struck by how typical I was and how predictable the changes in my life—and lack of changes—since then have been. My disabilities and life history may make me seem different to others, but I know just how common my life experiences have been. This doesn't bother me; in a way, it's even comforting.

In some ways, thirteen years ago, I was at the tail end of adolescence. I had graduated from college and was halfway through graduate school, so I had lived on my own for almost five years. I had distinct interests and a good idea of where my talent lay, and had a coherent worldview. I knew (or thought I knew) who I was, what kind of person I was.

Looking back, I realize that I was actually in the deep end of adolescence, and that I'm only now really leaving that period behind me. I was still very dependent on my parents, not physically, but emotionally and philosophically. I had little "real-world" work experience, and no real leadership experience. I had no sexual experience at all, at least none that involved other people. I had no strong, deep relationships with anyone, platonic or otherwise. I was like what has been called a "functional alcoholic," a person with a definite drinking problem, but one that doesn't interfere with most everyday life activities.

Yet I was a mess. Parts of me were fully developed, but others woefully underdeveloped. I didn't realize it, in fact, because my deficits didn't prevent me from living a seemingly normal life. I was happy and was either unaware of my problems or, because they hadn't caused anything bad to happen, figured they weren't anything to worry about. Remember my tendency to ignore my medical problems, and therefore be able to survive them? I think that the same held true for my emotional and developmental problems: I felt okay. People seemed to think I was okay, so, I thought, "if it ain't broke, don't fix it."

Before I get into these deeper, more troubling matters, I need to make a list of the ways I have changed in thirteen years:

1. Thirteen years ago, I thought of myself as a political radical, or at least a lefty dissenter. Today, I am still left of center, but in other ways I am quite conservative, and think maybe I always have been. Growing up during the Reagan administration, I assumed that authority was always wrong, possibly corrupt, definitely stupid. I figured that I'd carry this attitude through all of my life, like my

parents, who were never satisfied no matter who was running the country. During the Clinton administration, however, I discovered how restful it could be to sit back and be comfortable with the group in charge. I still enjoyed analyzing and sometimes disagreeing with the finer points of policy, but I quickly got used to feeling that, basically, people in government at all levels were good, smart people who thought mostly like I did about things. If they did stupid things or advocated policies I didn't like, the difference was more like that between Catholics and Episcopalians than between Hindus and Muslims. Lively debate was still possible, but I felt that those in authority and I were heading in the same direction. It was during this time, too, that I began to feel that a lot of what was wrong in the world was due to faulty systems, not faulty people. That's an idea that has played a major part in my professional life, but more about that later.

2. Thirteen years ago, I had rarely, if ever, experienced open hostility or competition from my peers. An Ivy League education is supposed to be "competitive." In my experience it was difficult, but not competitive in the personal sense. Nobody wanted me to fail so that they could prosper. Also, if people disliked me, they kept it to themselves for the most part. I don't know whether this was because my disability made them feel that it would be inappropriate to oppose me, or because I hadn't yet tried any activities that brought me into real conflict with people. The result is that I was totally unprepared emotionally for open interpersonal conflict. Also, I lacked even the most basic skills for competition and conflict—skills that most 8-year-olds acquire after their first few Little League games. I've come some distance since then, but I still avoid conflict, even when it is necessary, and several times I have missed the signs of serious interpersonal conflict until it was too late.

3. My parents separated, my father found another love in his life, and my mother died of cancer. These events had their impact, but that impact has been gradual. Even my mother's illness and death had less impact on me as they occurred than her absence has had in the six years since. I have missed her support and guidance greatly. At the same time, I have been able to make my own way in my hometown in a way that I couldn't have if she were still here. I feel bad saying so, but I know that my mother would understand. She was always the one who wanted more than anyone for me to be my own person. Meanwhile, my relationship with my father has improved in some ways and deteriorated in others. We now

relate to each other as adults, and Dad has expressed pride in my accomplishments.

4. After graduate school, I settled in my hometown. I did so because there was a job available, my mother also lived there, and the attractiveness of familiar territory led me home. I still live there, and probably will for some years to come. While I often think about an alternative career, I have no strong desires to leave my home just for the sake of starting over in a new town.

5. The most significant change in me over the past thirteen years has been the complete turnaround in my attitude toward my disability and toward working in the disability services field. The job offered to me in 1991 was a position at a new nonprofit organization in my hometown, an organization serving people with disabilities, that was governed and staffed primarily by people with disabilities. I had never heard before of such an organization. Philosophically, it rejected most of the negatives I had come to associate with dis-abilities: pity, charity, narrow group self-interest, paternalism, and segregation. Instead, this organization was a practical service and advocacy offshoot of the disability rights movement—another thing I knew nothing about even though I had lived with a disability all of my life. I started off doing publicity work for the organization, which wasn't so far from what I thought my career path in writing and media would be. I figured I would spend a year or two gaining work experience, while attempting to do some writing for our local newspaper. I never did write for the paper, not counting letters to the editor and editorials on behalf of the organization for which I worked. One reason was that I didn't have the energy and motiv-ation to pursue journalism while holding down a full-time job. The other reason was that, in the disability rights movement, I found an approach to disability that fits my personality and a mission I am uniquely qualified to serve.

The disability rights movement fits my personality in that it approaches individuals' problems by seeing systemic problems that are at their root. My organization not only helps individuals with disabilities deal with their specific concerns, we also identify ways in which the structures, policies, and practices of ordinary society make life more difficult for people with disabilities. For instance, we typically help an individual with disabilities deal with architectural barriers in a workplace, but we also work to remove such barriers wherever we find them. The disability rights movement has its roots in 1960s activism and political engagement. In other words, it views disability in the same way I view pretty much everything.

Most important, we work in this field not because we feel sorry for people with disabilities, but because we *are* people with disabilities, and because it is just. Previously, I avoided association with any kind of "disability community" because the only ways I'd seen such associations was in the context of charity, and that disgusted me. It also prevented me from truly seeing how my disability gives me a kinship and solidarity with others who have a disability. In a way, I denied myself an important source of support and pride. By working within the field as I do, I have reclaimed my membership in an exciting and vibrant community, rather than joined a sad and depressing begging crew.

The most important qualification for working in the disability rights movement is having a disability. I also bring a superior education and an analytical mind to the movement. I find that I am able to conceptualize disability issues in the abstract, while also emotionally connecting with them. There are many who can do one or the other, but relatively few who can do both. This transforms my choice to work in the field from a mere preference or convenience into a sort of mission. It also led to my taking on local leadership in the movement. I am now the executive director of the organization I joined in 1991.

One thing that hasn't changed in me is my wish to do something with my life that is both personally satisfying and useful. Finding and joining the disability rights movement has been the single most positive development in my life over the last thirteen years.

Although I would have learned more about my strengths and weaknesses no matter what I'd done after graduate school, the fact is that the work I have chosen has brought both my strengths and weaknesses into much sharper focus. I have already mentioned the strengths I have discovered. However, the weaknesses I have discovered may be more important in the long run.

In my original reflection, I wrote about not being sure where I stood in other people's eyes because I felt that they might be taking my disability into account when assessing my personality or performance. I implied that I didn't want or like unearned praise and admiration. I have since discovered that, even though I don't agree with it intellectually, I have become used to people "cutting me some slack," most likely because of my disability. I believe this caused me to be too dependent on being liked, which has led to some of the more serious problems I have had in my working life.

David Kennedy

When the executive director's position opened up, I applied for it. As I've said, I was probably the logical choice, based on my resume, life experience, and ability to understand disability issues. However, in retrospect, I see that I was really not prepared for leadership and supervision. I had no previous experience of either and understood them only in the simplest terms. There were one or two people in the organization who, I think, knew this better than I did, and once I became director they made it known in subtle ways that they didn't have much confidence in my abilities. Of course, this was a shock to me. It was the first time I had ever experienced real opposition—not to an idea or opinion, but to my actual abilities and personality. A vicious circle developed in which I was afraid to confront this opposition, which confirmed my weakness and encouraged bad behavior on the part of employees, which I failed to deal with because of my fear of being disliked and creating conflict, and on and on.

Finally, after several years of alternating bad times and good times, I have begun to get a handle on leadership. The biggest hurdle was finding out that if someone doesn't like me or is angry with me, the world doesn't end. My life doesn't collapse. At one point, I even discovered that two of my employees were complaining to the Board of Directors about my "inconsistency." I can't blame them, because, as I've said, I tended to let people get away with things I shouldn't have. This meant that less contentious employees often got better treatment than hard workers. Unfortunately, it took staff plotting and Board intervention to get me to face up to this and other related problems.

Gradually, though, I have changed the way I do my work and the way I relate to people, including those at work. I am more willing to confront people when needed. I procrastinate less. I have learned how to accommodate individuals' needs and strengths, while also holding them to a fair standard of performance.

The best thing about this experience, however, is that it has made me stronger. I always understood the idea that adversity makes you stronger, but never really believed it to be true. I had survived a lot of physical and medical adversity, and didn't see myself as being especially strong. Now that I have experienced the much more difficult forms of adversity found in the workplace and between people, I realize what adversity really is—and that I can survive it. As I said before, the world didn't end just because I screwed up, and this has given me the confidence I need to change myself in ways that will actually improve my performance. So, I guess you could say that I had to fail in order to learn how to succeed.

With all of this going on, it's a good thing that I am usually able to put it all aside and enjoy my free time at home. I still don't feel completely comfortable saying that I like to watch television, but it happens to be true. I don't apologize for it, but I'm certainly aware of the image it presents: a lonely guy letting his mind rot by watching the "idiot box" every night. For me, though, television is not a passive medium. I've always "read" TV. That is, I process it the way serious readers read books. Maybe a better comparison would be to say that I watch TV the way Roger Ebert watched movies. Even the worst shows say something and I'm interested in what TV shows say. It is both a relaxation and intellectual exercise.

Music is one of the few things that instantly reaches me emotionally. It is also one of the areas of my life where I don't mind saying I'm still an adolescent. If anything, I prefer today's music to the music I grew up with. My tastes are fairly broad. I like any genre of music if it is performed with passion and animated with ideas. The ideas don't have to be intellectually sophisticated or even admirable, but if I feel that something genuine is being communicated, then the quality of the musicianship or the sophistication of the composition isn't important to me. Music may be the only form of expression that I enjoy on a completely gut level.

My other spare time obsession is my website and "blog." I taught myself some of the basics of website design and, using blog software, created my own site on the Internet, which I add to several times a week. The blog has turned into the diary I always told myself I should keep, but never did. It's almost three years old now, and looking through the archives I'm amazed at how much I have written in small, unconnected nuggets, peppered with Web links to news stories, books, music, and other strange things I'm thinking or reading about. I don't get very personal with the blog, which probably makes it less interesting. I guess it's an indication that I am still too shy to share much of my inner self with the world, even though I'm pretty sure only a handful of people ever visit my site. Still, it's fun, and it will be easy to switch to more personal observations and thoughts if I ever resolve to do so.

I often spend hours working to make a single page on my site look the way I want it, but have to force myself to do the more difficult tasks. I know the professional work I do is more important than playing with my website. It helps real people live better lives. It improves my community. It's something I can do that most other people can't. My current work also has the advantage of being the status quo: As difficult as the road ahead may be, at least it's a familiar road. In addition, the idea of doing something for a living that I do for pleasure is very attractive to me.

Lately, I've been thinking about picking up my old idea of writing for the local paper. Since I like to watch TV and to write short pieces (as in my blog), I'd like to try to write a television review column. One of the benefits of living in a small city is that it may not be that difficult to achieve. I wouldn't do it for the money or recognition, but as a way to find out if I can combine my two greatest pleasures into something like a job. I like what I'm doing now, but part of me is restless to try something new, something different, something less safe.

I wish I could say that I've solved all of the "intimacy" issues hinted at and referred to directly in my original essay. While I don't feel that I am still an "awkward adolescent," in regard to sexuality and deep interpersonal relationships, I haven't made much progress. Sometimes I feel that I missed out on a window of opportunity—a time when other life concerns were relatively minor, and allowed space to pursue relationships. As a professional, and a single adult among adults with families and careers, I find few opportunities to explore relationships I should have explored when I was younger. I just don't have the time, and neither do most of my peers. Add to that the same old barriers, most of them in my mind, having to do with my disabilities, and I find myself still alone.

For the moment, I'm at peace with that. I have good friends—some of them co-workers, others people I have met through other associations, and still others people I have maintained contact with since college. There are people I can share my ideas and feelings with. It's of little importance to me that I'm not married, that I don't have kids. I miss the intimacy and strong devotion that these bring to my peers. However, I also know peers who, like me, have built their lives of other elements. In fact, I have lived as I do for so long now that I find it hard to imagine any other kind of life. That in itself may be the greatest barrier to forming deeper relationships. Cut through all the noble-sounding words, and it all boils down to what sounds like a sitcom cliché: I'm "afraid of commitment." Whatever. I'm certainly not going to go on some great self-conscious quest for love, connection, commitment. I can't think of any endeavor so dismal and boring. Either another cycle of my life will come about when new opportunities arise, or it won't. I'm keeping my eyes and ears open, but I'm not "holding my breath" for it, as the saying goes.

I'm finally finishing up this adolescence thing. It was delayed. Thirteen years ago, I was just beginning it when I thought I was finishing it. There are still more things to learn, more experiences I haven't had. It's possible that parts of me will always be 19 or 20 years old. I think I can live with that, and happily. On the other hand, I thought thirteen years ago that I knew what my life was going to be like, and have since been surprised in many ways. Thirteen years from now, will I be satisfied with my life? I don't know. But I'm pretty sure that whatever happens, I'll be a better person then than now, just as I think I am a better person now than I was thirteen years ago.

Case 14

QUEST FOR
PEACE

DEIRDRE HARRIS

DOI: 10.4324/9781003165378-18

Deirdre Harris

Deirdre's story explores the dark, lonely world of suppressed emotion. Following the death of her mentally ill father at the hands of brutal and overreactive police officers, Deirdre lost faith in her country and in the institutions designed to help and protect its citizens. Consistent with her family's pattern of silence, she suppressed all anger and frustration. Although she excelled in school and found some reprieve in writing poetry, Deirdre's success became a source of ridicule among her siblings, who tried to deny her black identity because of her intelligence. As difficulty after difficulty stacked up: living through the daily trials of poverty, multiple deaths of close friends and teachers, being molested by a stranger, struggling to acknowledge her emerging sexual attraction toward women, and the final straw—the Rodney King beating and acquittal—Deirdre's façade of the "smiling" perfect girl begins to crumble, and she starts the slow, painful process of coming to terms with emotions and thoughts long suppressed. This essay was written in her senior year.

My father was murdered while I was at my Houston, Texas elementary school. I was sitting quietly at my desk working on a class assignment when my teacher informed me that I needed to go home immediately. As I walked the three short blocks to my house, I thought about how good it felt to be outside instead of in that third-grade classroom. I was about halfway home when a weird feeling came over me. Why did I have to go home? Who had sent for me? What was so important that I had to miss school? My parents always said that unless we were dying, we had to go to school. Education was everything. So why was I sent home? Had something happened? I started to worry.

When I walked through the front door of my house, a wave of sickness coursed through my 9-year-old body. Something was not right. Something bad had happened. I could feel it in the air. Although I knew they were there, I didn't really see my brothers and sisters standing in the living room.

My eyes focused immediately on my mother, who was standing in the kitchen. She was the only person I could see. I watched as her skin drained of its natural color, and her beautiful face took on a look of utter despair and terror. Her body trembled as she doubled over, fell to her knees, and cried out, "He's dead, he's dead!" over and over again. I knew who she was talking about at once. I don't know how I knew, but I did. The "he" whom she was crying about, the "he" who was dead, was my father.

My mother lay on the kitchen floor for what seemed like ten minutes with tears streaming down her face and her voice trembling, now barely above a whisper, "They shot him, they shot him. He's dead, he's dead."

At that moment I could not grasp exactly what she meant. My whole body was overwhelmed with sadness, fear, and disbelief. There were so many questions. What happened to Daddy? Where was he? Who shot him? Why? I didn't cry. I didn't scream. I didn't say a word. I was in absolute shock. Nothing was real.

I went to my mother and put my arms around her. She wouldn't stop crying. She couldn't pick herself up from the kitchen floor. She had no strength, no power. What was going on? I was confused. I had never seen her like this before. What did it mean that Daddy was dead? I had never known anyone who had died before. What did it mean?

> *If you wanna get to heav'n lemme tell you how, juss keep yo' han' on de gospel plow. Keep yo' han' on de plow. Hold on, hold on.*
> —"Hold On," an African American Spiritual

A few months before my father was killed, his doctor told him that he no longer needed his medication or shock treatments. My father believed his doctor, whom he had been seeing for years. "Besides," he told my mother, "I have been taking this medication for half of my life to treat my schizophrenia. Now I am finally able to be normal." But soon after he stopped taking his medication his behavior became strange. He was no longer the calm and gentle person I've been told he had once been. My sole memory of him is how strange he was acting. He paced back and forth and repeatedly checked all of the windows and doors of the house. Later, he talked to himself and heard voices. His behavior frightened me. What was happening to him? Why was he so fidgety and nervous?

My brothers and sisters and I didn't know that he was sick. We noticed that he was changing, but we couldn't understand why. We were not told that he had an illness. My mother pleaded with him for months to take his medicine again. He refused. She pleaded with the doctor to reexamine him and to make him take his medication again. The doctor refused. He thought that the shock treatments and the medication were no longer necessary. Why not? Didn't he believe that my mother was telling him the truth about the pacing, the nervousness, and the voices? Although she knew that it could have been prevented, she had no other choice but to begin seeking both a restraining order for our safety and the institutionalization of my father for his own safety.

Deirdre Harris

My stepfather is the man whom I refer to as my "dad," as he is the only father I've ever known. (My biological father and mother divorced when I was a baby.) My stepdad was a self-employed watch repairman. He was a gentle man who used to bathe me and my siblings when we were young and volunteered for our Little League teams, but he didn't talk much. As a child, I used to sit on his lap and play with him, and he'd ask me questions about how I was doing and how I was feeling. I can't remember the last time I ever saw my dad alive. In fact, I don't remember anything about him. My mother recently told me about how I interacted with him because I have blocked all but one memory. I have no recollection of his face, his voice, or his touch. I refused to remember all that I had shared with him—including his love.

On that morning, January 3, 1979, while people were still saying "Happy New Year" to anyone who would listen, my dad got his gun and drove to his mother's house. The newspapers wrote that neighbors called the police about a man shooting into the air and at parked cars. When the police arrived, no one was outside. My father, the man who had been shooting, was already inside the house. His mother was not home. My father was there alone. The first two officers on the scene tried to get him to open the front door or talk to them. He refused to respond. They called for backup. Carloads of police came and surrounded the house.

They tried coaxing him out using a bullhorn, but he wouldn't budge. They threw tear gas through a couple of windows, and the house caught on fire. My father came running out of the burning house and right into the hands of a great number of policemen. As he ran out, unarmed, they shot him repeatedly, even after he was lying on the ground, unmoving. Witnesses' accounts in the newspaper described his limp body dancing on the ground from the impact of the bullets that ripped through him. Their accounts stated that it was "like watching an assassination." The police shot dozens of bullets into my father, an unarmed, mentally ill, black man.

I was not directly told any of this in great detail. I caught snatches of it here and there, mainly through the TV news, newspapers, grown-ups' whispers, and the interviews my mother gave on our living room couch to hungry reporters night after night.

They would not leave us alone because two officers had been wounded; one died a few days later. There were conflicting accounts about what happened. The official police report stated that they had no choice but to open fire because my father was armed and shooting at them as he ran out of the house. Witnesses to the shooting declared that he was unarmed as he ran out of the burning house. This clear discrepancy was just cause for a year-long FBI investigation, which revealed that the police report was a cover-up for the officers' mistake of getting trigger-happy on a defenseless black man. The firefighters' official report showed evidence that the gun that supposedly killed the officer was found charred, on the coffee table in the living room of the burned-down house. My father could not have shot anyone, much less killed someone. As it turned out, one officer had mistakenly shot and killed another officer while trying to shoot my father. The surviving officer injured himself when his gun backfired.

That was the year that I learned what "expendable" meant and to whom the term applied. I could no longer live in a world that saw me, and people who looked like me, as expendable. I could no longer say the Pledge of Allegiance at the beginning of each school day. How could I allow the words "liberty and justice for all" to cross my lips, knowing that they were untrue? Knowing that my dad did not get liberty or justice? Would the white police officers have paid more attention to what was or was not in his hands if my father had been white and not black? I would simply stand there with my hand over my heart and say nothing. I performed my own silent protest. My country had betrayed me.

I felt very alone and frightened. Which one of us would be killed next? Who would protect the rest of us from doctors who did not care to give us an accurate diagnosis? Who would protect the rest of us from brutes with badges and guns? Who? No one could protect us. It was horrifying to think that no one would come to our rescue, no one would get punished, and no one would care. In fact, the first question would be, "What did you do this time to bring it on yourself?"

My mind searched for a way out of this reality. My self-defense mechanism must have kicked in at that point because somehow I began to distance myself from my emotions. I struggled daily to keep my thoughts and emotions under control. In my all-out effort to protect myself from painful emotions, I had to suppress *all* emotions. I paid a price, however, because this protective measure stripped me of my passions as well as my anguish.

Throughout my schooling, my teachers never noticed that I wasn't saying the pledge to the flag. This oversight, I believe, was because I always did what was expected of me. I never got out of line. I was a "teacher's pet," a class clown, and an athlete. On the first day of school each year, my teachers were usually pleased to know that

Deirdre Harris

I was a Johnson kid because we all did well. I strove to be accepted by my classmates and had a smile for everyone all of the time. My father's murder did not phase me. I simply blocked it out of my mind. I never thought about him.

It wasn't too difficult not to think about him or how he died because my family never talked about him. After his funeral, his murder was a taboo subject. In the midst of our denial, however, the police department would call to frighten my mother into not pressing charges against them. They knew that they were wrong and they did not want to be taken to court. The FBI investigation showed clear evidence of police brutality with malicious intent. My mother, a newly widowed black woman with eight children and only a high school diploma, was scared to death for our safety. She did not want to risk losing anyone else. Her white lawyer convinced her that if she settled out of court she would get monetary retribution, but if she didn't settle, she would get nothing because "blacks did not win cases against the city" in Texas. So, she settled out of court. A couple of officers were fired, and we received a few thousand dollars. The settlement was able to pay for most of the funeral expenses and all of the lawyer's fees. To me, no amount of money could replace a human life, especially the life of my father.

I didn't witness any anger in my mother, and because she didn't display any anger, I didn't either. I followed her lead because I didn't know how I was supposed to react to this whole thing, other than to try my best to forget that it had ever happened. She said, "Being who we are and where we are has its consequences. That's how things are right now. We have to accept that and go on." Our extended family was nearby, also in Houston. Furthermore, we didn't have the funds to move anywhere else and we needed the support of our friends and family.

We restructured our lives after my father's murder. It took two years to reach a settlement, during which time my mother was preoccupied with finding a way to feed us. She had eight mouths to feed, in addition to her own, and she didn't have a job that could support us all. Mom was a very religious young woman who believed that "God would make a way somehow" and that "if you lived right, talked right, and prayed right, then heaven belonged to you." For a while we had food and clothes, and most of our bills were being paid. The bank miraculously allowed a one-year grace period for the house notes, which kept a roof over our heads. But we had less and less food, and funds were always low or even nonexistent. We could no longer afford to take piano lessons, or play on Little League teams. We could no longer take ballet lessons or drama classes. All of these things stopped abruptly. We understood that we had no money, so we didn't complain.

However, we couldn't understand why we didn't have food to eat. At one time or another, we each complained to our frustrated and overwhelmed mother that we were hungry. I'm sure that she hated to see us go to bed hungry, to wake up hungry, and to send us to school hungry. How could we learn when our minds were drawn to our stomachs and our hunger pangs? We were also constantly growing, but we couldn't afford to buy clothes. My relatives and people from the church and community gave us their old clothes to wear. We had to take the public bus everywhere or walk because our car had burned along with our grandmother's house. My mother eventually had to go on public assistance until she could acquire enough skills to get a job that paid well enough to feed us and put clothes on our backs. I hated the stigma of food stamps and school lunch cards. Being poor is "sinful" in this society, and I learned to be ashamed of our poverty, although I knew that what had happened to us was not our fault. Our sense of humor sharpened; we had to laugh to keep from crying, because our existence was so dismal.

I started constantly misplacing things and forgetting what I was saying in the middle of sentences because I had difficulty dealing with the present. I lost the ability or the will to concentrate. I was always so spaced out that I acquired the new nickname "the absent-minded professor" at home. Upon my father's death, my books, my writing, and my mother became my world. It was difficult being black and female and having a creative relationship with words while growing up in Houston. My verbal expression was indicative of my different way of thinking, and it set me apart from my siblings. I am the sixth child out of eight. I have four older brothers, one older sister, and a younger sister and brother. I felt misunderstood by them because of their teasing. My use of language caused me to stick out. Like most Texans I used words and phrases like "y'all" and "fixin' to," but I didn't have the drawl or the dialect of most Southern black people. Being an avid reader gave me a different vocabulary, and it also sharpened my thought processes. The combined effect of people, culture, and the shaping of language fascinated me. I read books about how people in various cultures lived and I took notice of how language shaped their interaction, their environment, and each other. I became fascinated with the possibilities of what could be, which helped to ameliorate my pain.

Something spiritual stirred inside of me when I expressed myself on paper. I used writing to take me away from everything. This desire to write down what was on my mind was an inexplicable, yet exceedingly powerful force. In sports I could only express myself within the boundaries of the game. Usually that was enough, as I could release a lot of frustration in a non-self-destructive way. But writing was an experience without restrictions. I wrote poetry about race relations, the oppression of females, religion, violence, and longings. I felt free of these things when I wrote about them, lessening the power of their hold on me. I felt like a healer and a creator. I felt important without feeling judged or alienated. I felt complete, lacking nothing. I spent as much time writing and reading as I possibly could. Only on rare occasions did I share my poetry. I learned very early in my life to fear sharing such deep emotions and thoughts with anyone.

I never thought to assign value to my way of thinking because it came naturally to me. Other people, however, valued my thinking process. They never let me forget that I was different. "You don't talk like us," they would say. "You soun' like a white girl." I wanted to forget that I was different because it made other people uncomfortable, which made interactions between us difficult. This made me uncomfortable with myself.

Like most people, my siblings often mistook my different way of thinking for me wanting to be something or someone other than who and what I was. "Why she talk propa' like white people? She muss wanna be white," they agreed among themselves, unable to understand or make sense of my unique behavior. This was not a compliment. They believed, as did I, that white people were greedy and violent. Nevertheless, because I would not conceal my intelligence, they would exclaim, "You're an Ono!" with great conviction.

Ever since I could speak, my brothers and sisters insulted me, and this continued throughout high school. I could not understand how the way I spoke indicated to them what I "muss wanna be." Still, my self-expression became unacceptable to me because it was unacceptable to others. I began to believe that I could not accept myself until other black people accepted me. New doubts augmented the loss of self-worth I had experienced upon my father's murder.

In my effort to be accepted, I found myself making constant readjustments so that I would not stand out. I didn't want to be considered different. My siblings taught me that to be singled out intellectually among other black people meant automatic rejection. If I were rejected by my black sisters and brothers, then I had nowhere left to turn for comfort or protection. Their negative reactions taught me to be silent or to suffer consequences. By the time I reached adolescence, I had become silent, reactionary, defensive, and eager to be accepted. When I met other black people I would wait for them to speak before I opened my mouth. This allowed me to judge the way that they expressed themselves so that I could have some idea of how they would regard me after hearing me speak.

The only person who constantly supported me through life and didn't think me a "freak" was my mother. A teacher's aide, she took an active interest in the education of all her children. Beaming, she would introduce me to people as "the smart one," which, although it saddened me somewhat, always made me feel that she was on my side. It seemed to make her happy to tell people that I was smart, so I dealt with the consequences. One consequence was that it made me very aware that I was different from my siblings. Throughout my childhood, strangers would exclaim, "This one here is going to college." I felt like a curiosity, somehow alienated, as if I were more desirable, yet less understood than my siblings. My mother's acknowledgment of my intellect seemed to give them permission to tease me, to dislike me, and to question my "blackness." They had bought into white stereotypes of black people—that we must all be alike, and that we could not excel intellectually, only athletically. My siblings had other gifts such as visual artistry, athletics, and technical knowledge, but I was the first one to go to a four-year college. I felt all the pressure was on me to succeed on behalf of my family.

I had conflicts sharing a bed with my two sisters, and the only other place available was with my mother in her king-sized bed. So I shared a bed with my mother from grade school until I left for college. That shift in sleeping arrangements shaped the dynamics of my relationship with my two sisters until high school. Pam, who is two years younger than me, became very close to my older sister, Cynthia. They shared laughter, clothing, and secrets. They made fun of me while I looked on, feeling left out, lonely, and betrayed. They were friends. It was them against me. I escaped into my books and writing even more. It wasn't until Pam and I attended the same high school that we became friends.

The new sleeping arrangements also influenced my relationship with my mother. After Mom became a widow, I tried, in my little kid kind of way, to make sure that she was okay. At night I'd occasionally hear her crying herself to sleep and I would ask her why she was crying. She really missed Dad. I didn't have tears of my own to shed. I was not an orphan because I still had Mom. She, on the other hand, had lost everything that our society said gave her worth—her husband. At that point I swore to never allow myself to become dependent on anyone or anything other than myself.

Though I continued to do well in school, I was struggling to hide my anxiety. I lived with the fear that someone else in my family was going to be killed. I didn't feel safe anywhere but I didn't show this fear. I put on smiles for everyone. Through the years, my mom and I became each other's confidant, but I couldn't share these thoughts with her. I knew better than to break the family taboo of talking about our father's murder.

Beginning in third grade, each year I was bussed to one school or another to be in special programs for "gifted" students where most kids were white, a handful were Mexican American, and only a few were African American or Asian American. I had become very conscious of race and of people noticing me. I spent a lot of time with Constance, whom I met when I first switched schools in fourth grade. She mostly kept to herself at school, but after school Constance hung out at the YWCA located directly across the street from her house. It didn't cost anything to attend, so I went with her. The two of us became insep-arable. We shared secrets, and I slept over at her house sometimes. She loved to read as much as I did, so we exchanged library books. We remained best friends throughout junior high school, where we were placed in the same honors classes.

The summer before I started high school, when I was 14 years old, I was molested by a stranger in my home. The house was being renovated that summer. One day the plumber and I were the only people in the house. He asked me to go back to the unfinished bathroom with him to show me what kind of pipe I needed to tell my mother to get. I had no reason not to believe him, yet as soon as we got to the bath-room I felt uneasy. The bathroom was very small, and he was standing much too close to me. Even more disturbing was the fact that he was standing between me and the door. He shut it behind him. When I turned around to ask what he was talking about, he pounced on me. He pushed me up against the wall and began groping me. I tried to fight him off but he was so big. His hands were all over me. My heart was beating fast. I had to get out of there. I tried talking him into letting me go. He wasn't listening. I tried to hit him, but he just grabbed my hands and pinned me hard against the wall and made me touch him. I panicked even more. Sweat was pouring down his white face and his hot breath was all over me; I almost got sick. Finally, after much struggling, groping, screaming, and fast talking, he let me go. I ran into my sisters' bedroom. There was no lock on the door, so I put furniture up against it. I curled up on the bed in a fetal position and tried to block out what had just happened.

The only thing that my mother had to say about sex was that it was to be saved for marriage, and I thought that it would upset my mom too much to tell her that I was molested. I didn't want to make her feel bad. I tried to protect her and I felt as if I were to blame. The reaction to my father's murder taught me that denial and silence were how to handle traumatic events in my life. I was becoming accustomed to suffering alone in silence. Constance was the only person that I felt I could tell. The next day I biked over to Constance's house and told her what had transpired. I was very upset and crying and I wanted to forget. But I could not forget. Instead, I stuck the memory in that section of my brain where I put things I couldn't handle. I was getting better at denying traumatic events. While my house was being completed, I spent time at Constance's; I didn't feel safe in my own home anymore.

Apparently, molestation was becoming an important issue in this country at that time. I read articles and books and watched a TV movie called *Something About Amelia* about a girl who was sexually abused by her father. I learned that it wasn't my fault. My body belonged to me. Still, I couldn't help but feel responsible in some way. I told myself I shouldn't have been there, but then reminded myself that I was in my own home and I had every right to be there. I was supposed to be safe at home. After the incident, I wanted to be invisible.

My grandmother died about a month later. I wasn't sure how much more I could take. I wanted to scream "NO!" at the top of my lungs to let out the pain that I was feeling. I didn't want males looking at me. I started wearing really oversized T-shirts and baggy jeans and shorts. I kept to myself. I felt trapped in a body that no longer belonged to me. I felt trapped in a life that I didn't want.

When school started I dove into my schoolwork and tried to keep my chin up. It was difficult having guys close to me, and I became very suspicious of them. I didn't want to be touched by anyone, but at the same time I needed to be comforted. I couldn't bring myself to tell my mother about what had happened, but I needed her reassurance that everything was going to be okay. I would sit on her lap and hug her. She would call me her "big baby" and roll her eyes but I didn't care as long as she held me. I forced myself to smile and pretend that every-thing was okay. I tried to project outward the security I craved inside. I longed to feel calm, but my stomach was always in knots and I never felt the same as before I was molested. I always felt on edge but tried hard not to show it.

My days were filled with church activities, school, reading books that I borrowed from the library, and hanging out with Constance at the YWCA. I listened to my brothers' and sisters' conflicts with Mom, but I told myself that I didn't have any. I denied the fact that I was sexually assaulted. I was the perfect daughter who never gave Mom any trouble nor had any problems. I did what I thought she expected of me. I did well in school, did not show any interest in boys, and put God first. I convinced myself that I also wanted these things for myself. Constance, though, was getting out of control. Her grandparents, who had raised her and her younger sister, both died within six months of each other and a few months before we started high school. Her mother moved into the house with Constance and her sister. Constance and her mom fought a lot. She needed things that I was incapable of giving her because I, too, was struggling. On weekends spent with her cousin, she was introduced to drugs. Before long she was skipping school and shooting up. I kept asking her why she was doing this to herself, but she didn't know why. I stopped asking her why, but I warned her about HIV transmission through sharing needles. We grew apart.

> Sister, you've been on my mind. Oh sister, we're two of a kind.
> So sister, I'm keepin' my eyes on you.
> —"Miss Celie's Blues," *The Color Purple*

At the same time that Constance and I were growing apart, Trisha and I were growing closer. Trisha intimidated me, but she was so appealing that I could not resist trying to know her and spend time with her. She had a radiant energy about her that was captivating. She and I both ranked first in our class the first semester of our freshman year. We were recommended by our math and science teachers for a special program for minority students. She didn't want to go, but I did.

The program at a New England boarding school lasted for six weeks each summer in high school. It opened up a whole new world for me. For the first time in my life, I was interacting with black students who were smart like me. It amazed me that they were not afraid to show their intelligence. For the first time in my life, I felt okay about being young, gifted, and black. The classes were surprisingly challenging. In the public schools back home I was usually bored, but there I constantly learned new things. I didn't feel compelled to stifle my enthusiasm for learning. I was, however, disturbed by the great discrepancy between my public school education and my private school education, which was so much better than what I got in public school. It upset me that I had to get a full scholarship to attend a school far away from home to get a challenging education. Most inner-city kids could not afford to wait on such "thoughtfulness" because most times it did not come.

Back in public school, my sophomore year, I decided that I was wasting my time at the Medical Professions High School. I wanted to own a bookstore and sell books by and about black people. I also couldn't stand to watch Constance slowly killing herself and not be able to do anything about it. I also knew I didn't want to be a doctor. After my father's misdiagnosis, I grew to mistrust doctors. So, I transferred to the Finance Professions High School, also known as FPHS. Before I left, I explained to Constance that I was not abandoning her. My mother asked why I wasn't spending as much time with Constance, so I told her she was doing drugs. There was nothing left to say. We were both familiar with how drugs were invading and devastating our own community and even our own home. Two of my older brothers' drug of choice was alcohol. In a drunken rage one night, one of them put his head through a wall, yelling that he wished he were dead. I thought to myself that he wasn't the only one who wished to be dead.

The magnet program at the new school had dedicated teachers. My favorite teacher, Jim Trails, took time out of classes when he saw that something was bothering us. I felt comfortable talking to him. However, the atmosphere there was so depressing. The feeling of poverty and hopelessness hung in the air. Many teenage mothers attended the regular, non-magnet high school because free child care was provided for the students' children. I felt other people's pain like it was my own.

I missed Trisha a lot also. We kept in touch by phone, but I wanted to see her. I called her two nights before Christmas when she said that she would be home, but strangely, no one answered. The next morning someone called very early, but I didn't answer the phone. A couple of minutes later Cynthia came in and woke me up with shocking news: Trisha had been killed in a car accident the night before. She was driving her parents' car home from her church's youth group meeting when she lost control. Her brother was seriously injured, but he had survived. I went numb.

That Christmas break, I felt ready to die. My heart felt so heavy. I marveled at the peace that I would surely have if I were dead. That's all I thought about for months. I didn't know how much more I could take without breaking down. Fortunately, Panu, who would become my good friend, transferred to FPHS the next semester, so I didn't feel so alone. In fact, because I was a counselor's assistant, it was my duty to show her around the campus. When I walked into the counselor's office, our eyes met and smiles lit up our faces that whispered, "Where have you been?"

My attraction to females began to surface a little because of Panu, but I still wasn't ready to acknowledge my attraction. She shared her poetry with me. She was first-generation American, and her parents were strict. Half an hour on the phone in the evenings was her limit, so we wrote letters to each other almost daily and exchanged them at school the next day. Panu invited me to her home often for dinner and to spend the night. We slept together in her full-size bed, but we made sure not to touch each other at all. Her parents got to know me very well through our in-depth conversations about India's culture and languages. Her father and I had many debates about the value placed on male and female children in Pakistani culture. Occasionally Panu's parents would lend her the car to go to a movie or to the mall on the weekend, but only if I were going because they trusted me.

I think that there was a mutual attraction between us. She and another friend would praise my body parts when the three of us were alone. Panu would feel my behind as we walked down the hall or up the stairwell. I was definitely attracted to her, but I couldn't bring myself to return her touch. We never talked about what her "love pats" were about.

By the time I was 16 or 17 years old, I disagreed with church teachings which were prejudiced against people who were different. The minister, whom I looked up to, said that homosexuality was wrong and that women should submit to men. I wanted no part of that, but I went to church anyway because it was expected of me and I didn't want to disappoint my mom. I also had become dependent on gospel music as a source of strength. I learned to take what was good from the sermons and leave the rest at the church.

The summer before my senior year, I went to the last session of summer boarding school. It was great to return and see my old friends again. I had become good friends with a girl from New York City named Lisa, and that summer we were roommates. One day, I got surprising news from one of my public high school friends. She sent a newspaper clipping that said people with HIV shouldn't be allowed to teach, and there was a feature story on Jim Trails. My favorite teacher had died. Once again, I suppressed my feelings and threw myself into my work.

That summer, our class visited colleges in New England. Lisa and I both decided that we wanted to go to the same New England college. I liked the campus and the students and the administrators that

I met on our visit, but mostly I liked the foreign study and language programs. I agonized over how I'd be received in this predominantly white college environment. I decided to apply because it was my right to go wherever I was accepted.

> *They said I wouldn't make it. They said I wouldn't be here today. They said I'd never amount to anything. But I'm glad to say that I'm on my way, and I'm growing more and more each day. Though I've been talked about and I've been criticized I've had to wipe so many tears from my eyes. But I'm still holding on to his hand.*
>
> —"I'm Still Holding On," a gospel song

Lisa and I were both accepted to the same New England college and we were roommates as freshmen. Our friendship didn't last the year. Lisa spent a lot of time in the room with her boyfriend. I studied best in my room and had problems concentrating because she and her boyfriend were so loud. She would try to be more considerate, but it never lasted. Her boyfriend, Chris, had moved in by the middle of fall term. Lisa got upset with me for locking our personal bathroom door while I showered. Between clenched teeth she said, "Deirdre, you need to keep the bathroom door unlocked. Chris had to go down four flights of stairs to use the public bathroom." I couldn't make her understand my need to feel safe. She didn't know about my molestation and my fear. By the end of freshman year we weren't even speaking.

In addition to attending classes, I joined the school's gospel choir, worked, and did some community service. Although I didn't attend church services regularly, gospel music and other African American music helped me through many days. Music reminded me that my ancestors, who suffered through the Middle Passage and were enslaved, had paved the way for me to be where I was and to make the choices I made. In meditation, I drew upon their strength.

I also became close to Eddie, a guy from my home city. We clicked immediately. We felt incredibly comfortable with each other. We spent a lot of time together and became best friends. He was having a hard time at college. He was gay, black, and, like me, had little or no financial support from home. When he confided in me about his sexuality, we became even closer. Part of me felt that I could open up to him even more because his gay identity made me feel safe with him. I didn't think that he would want to get close to me sexually. I grew up believing in society's assumption of heterosexuality; I naturally assumed that I was heterosexual although I hadn't even dated yet.

Deirdre Harris

Freshman winter, Eddie decided that he had to leave college. I panicked. I felt as if I was going to die if he left me. After a while and after much analyzing, I told him that my dad had died when I was younger and that I never got to say good-bye. I told him about projecting my unresolved feelings for my dad onto him. He understood, but he had to leave anyway. After Eddie left, I had no support whatsoever. I tried to explain to my mom why I wasn't happy, but she couldn't understand. She pushed me into staying. "Oh, you're tough, you can stick it out," she said. So I stuck it out.

This particular college was not good for my self-esteem. I stopped writing poetry my freshman year. Most other African Americans acted as if they were from higher economic classes than me, and they mainly seemed to be concerned with which elite black Greek house to join. Whites could not relate to what I felt at all. They couldn't seem to grasp that two or more drastically different realities could exist simultaneously. They were resistant to and doubtful of the validity of my thoughts, feelings, and reality. I believe their mistrust was due mainly to ignorance and fear, rather than hate.

College, for the most part, was a debilitating experience to endure rather than an empowering experience to embrace. Gradually, my spirit broke. I could not force myself to smile any longer. Many of my classmates' spirits seemed broken too. That is why Eddie left. What does this college do to us that breaks our spirit? For my part, I felt stifled, suffocated, and lacking a support system.

Although Eddie left, he and I remained close. I saw him during breaks from school. By sophomore year, I found myself falling in love with him, but I was confused because I thought that I was attracted to women. I just wasn't sure of anything. Eddie was sure, though, and he said that he must be bisexual because he had fallen in love with me. I told him that I liked him a lot but that I thought that I was attracted to women. He quickly yelled, "NO, you can't be!" He was the first person I told. It took me two years before I could voice that again. I dated only men throughout the rest of college. In fact, while I was on exchange at a university in California, I got engaged to Dan, a guy I loved dearly, but I was not "in love" with him.

We who believe in freedom cannot rest. When will the killing of black men, black mothers' sons be as important as the killing of white men, white mothers' sons? We who believe in freedom cannot rest until it comes.

—"Ella's Song," Sweet Honey in the Rock

Up until the first week of May of my senior year in college, I never talked about my father to anyone except Eddie. It was much easier to push this loss out of my mind and to concentrate on achieving. I was pleasing my mother and preparing myself for independence. When the video of the Rodney King beating came out, I was not surprised. I was horrified, but not surprised. I wasn't that naive. Police brutality was nothing new to me. Still, I did not know how to react to it. Occasionally, I'd think that maybe this time would be different. Maybe, just maybe, our lives would be valued and something would be done. The video was proof to the rest of America what we've always known in the black community—that black people are second-class citizens, not protected under the law, nor by the law's enforcers. In my gut, I knew that the people responsible for King's beating would get around the law somehow. They always did, and I had to acknowledge that fact.

Although the television stations played the King videotape as if it were going out of style, it wasn't until the verdict was announced that I was able to feel any emotion and begin to mourn the loss of my father. My fiancé, Dan, called and told me the news. My heart sank. Although I expected the acquittal, I really didn't want to accept it. My mind groped for any hope at all I had for humanity. I hung up in total shock. I just went to bed and tried to think about something else.

I awoke the next morning, and the reality of the previous night's telephone conversation hit me. The acquittal of the LAPD officers represented yet another bullet through the heart of my father, to whom justice had also been denied. All hope for humanity left me. I tried to get out of bed, but my legs could not hold me up. I fell onto the floor next to my bed and tears came streaming out. I had no control over myself. My whole body was in convulsions. I think that I passed out at some point, but I don't recall. I remember raising my head from the floor and thinking that Daddy was dead and that we were getting beaten and killed in the name of the law. Daddy was dead, and I didn't get to tell him that I loved him. I didn't get a chance to say good-bye. A knot formed in my throat, in my chest, and in my stomach. I was terrified. I felt like a helpless little kid who was confused and couldn't find her way. I didn't know what to do with my anger, but I knew that I had a right to it. I had a right to express that anger too.

I was afraid of my emotions, but most of all, I was afraid of my anger. Expression of anger is unacceptable even when it is legit-imate. This perception is especially true for women. Our society has no acceptable way of expressing anger. Therefore, black people's anger in this country has been left invalidated, which causes it to accumulate, to create a climate of hostility. I knew that most white people would not understand this concept. That would be acknowledging too much. They refuse to accept this concept because they continue to flourish financially from social conditions like the legacy of slavery and the "good ole boy" network.

My mother's comfort and happiness has always been a priority over my own. How could I express my anger without alienating myself from her and other people? I was determined not to be a part of the disappointment or chaos following the King verdict. This determination came at a great emotional and psychological price to me. It may have also had a physical price. My senior fall I found a hard lump in my right breast while performing my monthly breast self-examination. Upon discovering this intruder, I wondered where my rage had gone. If the rage didn't leave my body, then where did it go?

I went to class that morning, but I couldn't understand what people were saying. The professor mentioned the King verdict at the beginning of class, and afterward I went up to her and asked if she could make any sense of it. She could not. I found myself blurting out that my father had been unjustly murdered by police officers when I was 9 years old. She and the other students who were standing nearby didn't know what to say. How is someone supposed to react to something like that? I felt so alone and confused as I went back to my room and tried to make sense of my existence. I couldn't think straight at all. I was in a daze.

All alone in my room, I cried for the loss of my father. All that I could do was cry. I cried for my inability to change the state of the world. I felt helpless and hopeless, and for the first time in my life I was able to admit those things to myself. I felt that whatever I could possibly do was never going to be enough. Why was I in college if I couldn't change things? I tried to get involved in the rallies and other things that were going on, but I was not really there. I had no strength.

On Monday morning, I called a counselor that I had been seeing over at the student infirmary about my sexuality and about why the time I spent with my fiancé was harder than the time we spent apart. I told her that I couldn't recall the last time that I had eaten or had a good night's rest. She strongly recommended that I stay in the infirmary so that I could rest and start eating again. I was there for a week and was medicated for my depression. I phoned my fiancé and told him where I was. After much debate, I phoned my mom and told her where I was and why I was there. I could hear her disappointment. She couldn't quite understand why I was allowing myself to think about my father. She wanted to protect me from this pain, but I told her that it was already too late. I finally found enough courage to allow myself to think about him and how he died. I asked her to send me some of the newspaper articles about his murder that she kept in the file cabinet in her bedroom closet. She refused.

I got angry at her, but I didn't tell her so. She answered a few questions that I had about the murder, but she urged me not to let my mind get caught up in that pain but to keep on going. I should be concerned with my studies and forget about this mess because "God will take care of it," she said. I told her that God has given us the ability to take care of it ourselves. She was trying to protect herself from her own doubt, fear, pain, and loss. I didn't tell any of my friends where I was. I felt that no one knew exactly what I was going through and so they couldn't possibly help me, other than by giving me time and space to get through this.

Upon the suggestion of my counselor, I began to write poetry again. I felt so much better while I wrote poetry. I allowed myself to connect with the pain and sorrow that comes with grief and mourning. I didn't fight it any more. I let it all out. I wrote a letter to my dad. I wrote a letter to the Houston Police Department. But mostly I wrote poetry. One poem in particular, entitled "Discomforting Thoughts," helped me to get all of my feelings out in a coherent way.

> *When Daddy was murdered*
> *my universe was no longer together.*
> *I was no longer together.*
> *There was only chaos, fear*
> *and loneliness within me,*
> *and in the world around me.*
>
> *I constructed a high wall around me*
> *to shield myself from everyone.*
> *Everyone who had expectations of me*
> *and from others who did not*
> *yet know my name.*
> *I could not let anyone know*
> *that I knew that the world was not*
> *perfect. That I was not perfect.*
>
> *"Everything's fine,"*
> *said the 9-year-old smile*
> *that I politely pasted onto my face.*

Deirdre Harris

*I had to put on an innocent smile for
everyone.*

*Only rarely could I smile for myself.
Others needed the reassurance
more than I.
Besides, what was there to smile
about?
How could I let them down
without letting myself down?
Either way I was dying.
A part of me is dying every day.
Who could I talk to about
my fears, my frustrations, my failures?
Oh, and I do fear, I get frustrated, and
I do fail.*

*Why does it seem as if I am not
allowed to fail? I am human, right?
Why do I have such different thoughts
from my peers?
We do not speak the same language.
Not inherently, for I always speak
in terms for others to understand.
In the process, I lost a part of me.
I lost the meaning of my words,
and what I really meant.*

*Why am I so different,
and feel things so differently?
I appreciate my differences
—my uniqueness makes me special.
But it also makes me lonely.
It places unfair burdens on me.
On the outside I put on a front that
I've learned to hide behind.
It's called being polite, being a clown,
and being the intellect.
Doing the expected thing.
Always answering "fine" and "okay"
when I am not fine, and when I am not
okay.*

I hide the tears behind the laughter.
But how can I honestly cry
for having lost someone that I refuse
to remember ever having? Daddy.
The word seems so alien to me,
even coming from my own lips.
That's a word that the other kids used.
They were so certain that they'd get a
response from their calls to their
daddies.
What is it like to have a father, a
daddy?

Why don't I know what it's like to be
protected from hate and igno-
rance?
Why can't I let others know that I
hurt?
Why can't I admit to myself that I
have pain?
Why is everyone else's comfort
such a priority over my own?

I don't want to let momma down.
She works hard to make sure that I'm
okay.
She loves me and supports me,
so how can I tell her that there are
things
that I need that she can't possibly
offer?
Things that she does not understand?

Mom, I'm separate from you.
We are two different people.
You can't always speak for me.
I have to do that for myself now.
I know that I have to be strong.
That's one of the many things
that you've taught me.
But do I have to be strong all of the
time?

When do I get to be me?
A person with vulnerabilities and
dreams.
Maybe I'm not as strong or sure as I
let on.
I'm not yours or anyone else's Super-
woman.
In fact, I despise the term!
I am tired.

Although writing poetry helped me to gather my thoughts, it was not enough. I still felt so much rage. Still, I was able to sleep and eat more and was released from the infirmary.

I happened to be taking a self-defense class for women at that time, and a couple of male volunteers came in to simulate physical attacks. They wore protective gear, so when it was my turn I went off on them. While I was fighting them off, I thought of them as police officers like the ones who killed my dad, the ones who beat my brothers, and the ones who beat Rodney King. I also thought of them as the plumber. I had so much rage inside that I vented onto them. While I was beating them, the other women in the class cheered me on and afterward they applauded me. I simply did everything that we were taught to do, but I felt bad getting praised for beating people up. I have felt so beaten down that I had trouble beating others, even defending my own life. Who had taught me that my life was less valuable than my attackers' lives were? Why did I believe that bullshit? After I finished with the men, they took off their face masks and sat out for a while. One of them had a bruised eye. I felt that I should apologize for hurting them, but I couldn't. I had to protect myself. They knew what they were getting into when they took on the job. I did ask them if they were okay. I told them that I felt bad, but they had these cheesy grins on their faces and said, "No, no, you were great!" If I was so great, then why did I feel so bad?

Reality was beginning to set in again. I was getting concerned about my classes. My professors knew that I would be in the infirmary for a few days, but I had to catch up on my work if I expected to graduate the next month as planned. I had three midterm exams to make up, in addition to papers. I had been doing very well in my classes until I went into the infirmary, but when I took my exams I couldn't concentrate. A week or two after I completed my exams, I finally felt like myself again. I resorted to blocking out my feelings and concentrated on my schoolwork. My key motivation was the fact that upon the completion of my coursework, I could get out of there. I could leave this college and its discontents behind me and begin to nurture my broken spirit in a healthy environment of my choice. The sooner done, the better. I finished with grades ranging from B+ to A-.

I am still struggling with my anger, but I've come to realize that emotions can be controlled. At least I know that I won't hurt anyone by allowing myself to be angry. I feel as if I can finally be myself and not have to live up to people's expectations. I'm living for me now, not for my mom or anyone else. I've learned that I cannot be held accountable for other people's feelings, especially my mother's. I am going to have a talk with her face-to-face and tell her how I feel. It's okay to be angry, even at those people we love the most. It's okay to remember someone who is dead. I feel as if I can finally say good-bye to my father.

Case 15

SEEKING THE BEST OF BOTH WORLDS

PHUOC LE

DOI: 10.4324/9781003165378-19

Phuoc Le

This is the story of a harrowing emigration from Vietnam to the United States as part of the "boat people" crisis after the war. The author describes his struggle to be both a good son to his very traditional mother and to find a means to belong and succeed in the culture to which his family fled. As he enters adolescence, he begins to feel that his mother's many troubles and unbending ways are harming both him and his siblings. When he discovers that his stepfather is abusing his younger brother and that his mother will not intercede, he experiences a turmoil of shame, guilt, and powerlessness. His mother's insistence on traditional childrearing forces him to live a double life as an increasingly "Americanized" teenager on the outside while playing the role of dutiful son at home in spite of numbing sadness and overwhelming rage toward his mother. Eventually, it is his success in the world outside his family that allows him to gain his mother's respect and thereby influence how she raises his younger siblings.

"*Con không biết ma. đã trò qua bao nhiêu là nỗi khổ để đem con qua nước Mỹ nay*—You don't know how much I went through to bring you to this country," my mother said in a soft voice as she lay staring at the ceiling. A continuous stream of tears flowed from the outer corner of her eye down into her pillow. At times like this, I would sit next to my mother on our torn carpet while she recounted the tragedies that had happened to her in her previous life of misery, the life she left behind in Vietnam. My older sister Chau, on the other hand, could never stand to listen to our mother's repetitions. She would usually brush her teeth and go to bed or go to our other bedroom, close the door, and delve into the imaginary world of her romance novels. I remember praying at the start of the episodes that I wouldn't end up crying myself (because my mother instilled in me her belief that "*nam nhi đại trượng phu đỗ máu không rơi lệ*—real heroes never show tears even if they are bleeding to death") as these painful stories entered my mind. However, no gods or spirits answered my prayers, and after each occurrence I would feel low and unmanly because I had let tears fall even though I wasn't bleeding to death.

"*Dạ mạ*—Yes, Mom (respectfully)," I said. In Vietnamese a child must always acknowledge his or her parent with a polite "*Dạ*" (pronounced "ya"). It matters not that the parent did not ask the child a question; any less respectful response could very well lead to a beating! I learned this lesson soon after I learned how to talk (being polite was much better than being hit).

"When I was your age living in my village, I never had a full meal to eat," my mother continued. "Most days we would only be given one small bowl of rice and a dab of fish paste for flavor. I wasn't as lucky as you are today. I could never eat meat every day like you can." As far as I can remember, my mother would, without exception, start her stories by establishing that her youth was utterly miserable compared to my life of luxury. To this day I still am not sure whether by stating this she merely wanted me to feel grateful that I had enough food to eat or whether she was actually pitying herself as she realized the vast contrast between her childhood and mine.

"I was cruelly beaten daily by your grandmother and often for no good reason. She had fourteen children, but I was the only one who ever got punished. I don't know why. She'd beat me if I didn't fetch enough firewood for cooking. Or if I didn't cut up enough food to feed the pigs. Or if I stopped fanning her during those scorching summer days because my hands felt like jello." As my mother went on, at this point in her talk I would have a difficult time understanding her because her nose was plugged up from crying so much. Sometimes I tried to pay closer attention so that I could catch everything she said; other times I would not bother since I more or less knew by heart all that she wanted to say.

"The worst period in my life was after I married your father. I had just given birth to your sister when your father disappeared without a trace. I tracked him down finally in Hanoi. I found that he was living with his first wife, a woman that he never told me about. I was more than shocked that the man I loved and trusted lied to me."

After hearing my mother describe my father's deceit, I simultaneously felt resentment, sympathy, guilt, vengefulness, incredible sadness, and, oddly, joy. I resented and even hated my father for ruining my mother's life. The anger I felt inside was so overwhelming that I would often tremble while gasping for air. Sometimes I sat there and wished that he were standing right in front of me so that I could pick him up by the throat and slam him against the wall as hard as I could. I'd scream at him, "You damn asshole! How could you treat your wife like that? Don't you have a conscience? Is this the model that you want your children to follow? I am ashamed to be your son! But don't worry, I won't turn out to be like you, you piece of shit!" At the same time, I felt sympathy for the incredible pain that my mother must have endured since that episode. She did not do anything wrong; her only mistake was falling in love with a lying womanizer. Yet mixed with my negative emotions was a slight ripple of joy. I felt happy to see that my mother was courageous enough to take her children and leave him behind in his poverty-stricken home. I was shamelessly content that he still had to live in filth with his first wife while our family, although poor compared to others in America, had enough to eat every day.

Throughout my early childhood, occurrences like the one above were commonplace. Almost anything could provoke my mother into telling those stories: seeing happy couples walking together in the park, seeing my sister and me not doing our chores, watching television shows that depicted any aspect of Vietnam, and especially having her children do badly in school (i.e., not getting straight As). Those nights I would cry myself to sleep thinking of how much I should hate my father and how much I should love and respect my mother. I racked my brain wondering how my father could have consciously treated my mother with such inhumanity. "How could he? How could he?" I hollered silently to myself over and over. "There must be some reason for what he did. My mother must be leaving a lot of details out. I should not listen only to her side of the story." I convinced myself that I could not make final judgments about him until I heard what he had to say. Thus, for years I wondered what his story was.

My first memories are of escaping Vietnam and landing in Hong Kong on the way to our final destination, America. I only remember random scenes of our journey; the rest of what happened my mother has filled in through our conversations over the years. Thus, I have a fairly detailed knowledge of what happened in those few days that drastically altered our lives.

In the spring of 1981, my mother, then fairly wealthy thanks to a prospering business, decided that she wanted to give her two children educational opportunities that her country could not offer. I was only 4 years old and my sister just 6 when one ordinary night my mother told us to say good-bye forever to our homeland …

A blinding flash of light snatched me from my restful sleep. Five seconds later the inevitable boom of thunder crashed on our little boat and sent everyone into a state of panic. When I peered out at the darkness, I saw rushing at us some of the largest waves I'd ever seen.

"Mạ, con sợ qúa—Mommy, I'm so scared," I cried. However, the raindrops on my face camouflaged my tears, and the roaring thunder drowned my attempts to communicate with my mother. I finally caught her attention by pulling on her sleeve as hard as I could.

"Con đừng sợ nhe—Don't be afraid, son," my mother comforted. "It's just a little storm. It'll be over real soon." She covered us with a plastic bag, and we huddled so close that I could feel her heart pounding against my cheek.

"*Chị Hong, Chị Hong*—Sister Hong, Sister Hong," my uncle Oanh approached us from out of nowhere and said in a disconcerting tone, "there's too much weight on this end of the boat. We need more people to move to the bow. If we don't do it fast, the waves'll flip us right over."

"What do you want us to do?" my mother answered calmly.

"You put Phuoc on your back and I'll put Chau on mine. Then we'll slowly walk up there."

"Okay, okay," my mother approved. I did not realize what was happening. All I knew was that I wanted to cling to my mother for dear life. "Phuoc," she spoke directly into my ear because at any other distance the thunder would drown out her voice, "we're moving to the front of the boat. I'm gonna give you a piggyback ride, so you grab on as tight as you can, okay?"

"*Dạ*," I acknowledged and quickly climbed onto her back while the storm blanketed my body with what felt like a thousand pebbles every second. Without thinking, I immediately locked my arms around my mother's neck and grabbed each of my wrists with the opposite hand. Just as instinctively, I wrapped my legs around her waist and also bolted them in place. As we began inching toward our destination just a few meters away, my awareness of the surroundings increased tenfold compared to when I was sitting with my mother. I saw every wave as it crashed on the boat's side, I anticipated the direction of impending thunder, and I felt the blowing raindrops on my skin as if they were needles piercing all parts of my body. Another acute awareness was of my body's position in space. Because I did not budge, it seemed as though I became an extension of my mother's body. When she lifted her left foot to take another step, I felt the entire left half of my frame move accordingly.

"*Gần tới rồi con à*—We're almost there, son," my mother said, "don't worry." When I looked up, I saw the bow just a few steps away. However, I did not feel as though I could breathe a sigh of relief because a few steps is still a few steps. I kept my tight lock around my mother's neck and waist. It turned out that this choice saved my life, because just then a huge wave slammed into the side of our boat with such force that it threw her off her feet and sent us plunging into the freezing water of the South China Sea. I do not recall feeling scared. When I was under water, instinct made me hold onto my mother as tightly as I could, shut my eyes to avoid the stinging seawater, and close my mouth so that no saltwater entered my system. I do not know why I didn't panic.

I just didn't. Fortunately, the two of us avoided staying in the water long enough for hypothermia to set in. My uncle, who was following closely behind us with my sister, dived in after us when he saw us fall.

Following our dramatic rescue, the heavens blessed us with sunshine and peaceful waters. The gods also bestowed another miracle on us. Several days after our departure, just when we had almost depleted all of our food supply, we came across a cargo ship headed in the same direction we wished to go: Hong Kong. A year later in April 1982, my mother realized her dreams of raising us in a land where more opportunities and fewer obstacles lay before us. What my mother did not realize was that she herself would become the major obstacle in her children's future.

Throughout my early adolescence, I wished I had a better, more understanding mother. To this day I still believe that most of my "growing pains" could have been alleviated or missed entirely if my mother had also experienced these same "pains" when she was an adolescent. She did not know how best to assist me through my tough times, because she had no understanding of the cultural and social pressures facing teens growing up in America. She was often insensitive and apathetic when I came to her with an adolescent issue such as schoolmates making fun of me.

Puberty started rather simply for me in the sixth grade; there was no big event that announced its arrival. I remember exactly when I knew that I had entered this period of change. One evening while I was showering, I noticed that I had started growing pubic hair. At first I felt confused. "What's this stuff?" I asked myself. Thinking that it was just dirt or something, I tried rubbing it off. After a few unsuccessful attempts, I realized, "Oh, yeah, this is what my sex education class last year taught us. I'm supposed to start this business at my age. Don't worry about it. It's just puberty." I thought about telling my mother to make sure it was just puberty, but after some thought I decided against the idea because these topics were not spoken of in our household. Subjects such as sex, love, human genitalia, and rape were taboo in my family because they were supposedly "impure" things to talk about. We were not to adulterate our minds and hearts by bringing them up in conversation. Consequently, many issues that "normal" families in America talk about were never brought up in our household. This lack of discussion forced me to learn about them from other sources, such as television.

At first, I did not think that puberty was going to be the time of tremendous psychological change that the sex education videos at school had depicted. I felt like the same little kid I was before, going to class in the morning, coming home to do homework and watch television in the afternoon, talking to my mother before going to bed, and then repeating this same monotonous routine. The only other difference was that my voice started cracking when I spoke, but that did not bother me because I understood that was a natural part of human development.

Although I was only aware of my physical changes, I was also changing mentally. I remember my sudden self-consciousness, low self-esteem, newfound interest in girls, and awareness of my lack of peer relationships, all of which started in junior high. Now when I look back, it seems that my experience was nothing out of the ordinary for children of that age. Yet my life then had an additional *extraordinary* factor. The conditions under which I interacted with others my own age were, culturally, American conditions, while at home I confronted a Vietnamese cultural environment. On the one hand, my mother did not understand American culture and disapproved of the American beliefs (such as gender and racial equality, free speech in the family, etc.) that I had adopted. On the other hand, the children at school who were not Vietnamese did not accept the culturally Vietnamese side of me, probably because they saw it as strange and not "normal." (Back then it was a dream of mine just to be normal like everyone else.) I shall illustrate my point with a few examples.

Before the sixth grade, I never thought about how physically different I looked. I knew that I was Vietnamese, but I never felt that I was an outsider in school because of my skin color. When I began adolescence, however, I became acutely aware of my bodily characteristics. In grade school I was your stereotypical skinny, short, brainy Asian kid with a bowl haircut. When kids made fun of me by calling me "chink" or "nerd," I usually never paid any attention to them. This was true until the day I received a disciplinary referral and was sent home. During music class, a Caucasian classmate of mine, Eugene, was getting upset because Mr. Marmastein told him he was out of tune. The entire class giggled as Eugene squeaked the words to "Yankee Doodle Went to Town." I, being a wise guy, said loudly, "No more, Eugene, please!" With a frustrated look, Eugene quickly turned to me and yelped, "Shut up, you damn *chink*!" The old me would have just laughed it off without giving it a second thought, but that day a rush of anger swept through me, and I wanted to beat him up right there on the spot. The only thing that restrained me from doing so was my music teacher. I did not want to disrespect him by disrupting the class; I decided to wait until later.

When recess time came and we were all let out to the grass field to play kickball, I only had one thing on my mind. As soon as I caught sight of Eugene, I ran over and tackled him onto the ground with all the might that my 80-pound body could conjure up. We wrestled around on the grass throwing blind punches at each other until the recess supervisor pulled us apart and gave us both referrals. The principal sent me home because I was the one who started the fight. Eugene's words somehow triggered a highly reactive area inside me, an area that told me that I was not the same as everyone else, and this made me feel inferior. At the same time, though, the fight made me proud and confident because this time, unlike previous times, I had stood up for myself when others thought I would be weak and passive. However, my raised spirits received a powerful blow from my mother's reaction.

"What? You got in a fight because he said you were Asian? *Sau con ngu qúa vậy*—Why are you so stupid, son?" my mother said, as if she didn't believe that "chink" was a derogatory word. Maybe if I told her again, she would understand.

"But, Mom. That word is racist! He wasn't just saying that I was *Asian*," I repeated, "he had a different meaning."

"Who cares what he meant," she replied. "It's just a word. Those White people are all racist anyway. Next time he says that to you, just ignore him." Ignore him? *What*? How could I do that when Eugene insulted me? And how could my mother say that *all* Caucasians are racist? Didn't the fact that she uttered those words brand *her* a racist? "And they're bigger than you, you know. I don't want you to get hurt again. We're smaller than they are, so we just have to act our size. So next time he makes fun of you, just turn your head and laugh." I did not know how else to persuade her. My mother did not seem to understand that in America, equality is cherished and prejudice is not tolerated. Wasn't that why she decided to risk her life and the lives of her children to come here in the first place? My mother's words directly conflicted with what my teachers had taught me in school all these years. How could I reconcile this? I could not believe what she said nor do as she ordered, because the morals I had acquired in school were too strong. This incident posed yet another problem for me—when should I listen to my mother and when should I not? In the past, she had always taught me how to be a good person, including the dos and don'ts of life and the difference between right and wrong. It was simple—Mother was always right no matter what. Thus, I always listened and took her words to heart. Now that I recognized a flaw in her beliefs, I did not know what to do or who to go to.

Another example of my mother's lack of empathy was how she laughed at me when I told her that other kids made fun of my name. For as long as I can remember, almost everyone I have met has mispronounced my name at least twice before getting it right. It was such an embarrassing scene whenever I met anyone new that it made me wish I did not have to meet new people at all. The worst part of it was the name-calling I endured all my life. Through elementary school and beyond high school, my name was the subject of a laundry list of teasings. It may be difficult for others to understand how my name can be so damaging to me psychologically. However, it was not as if I had a name like "Jaime," which everyone pronounced "Himee." People can easily turn my name into vulgar words if they want to (and I believed that everyone around me wanted to). Here are a few of those hurtful teasings: "Fok," "Foo-ok," "Pook," "Fuck," "Phuoc you!," "What the Phuoc!," "MotherPhuocer." In my high school junior yearbook there is a picture of me playing volleyball (I was on the team). Underneath it the subheading reads, "Phuoc 'U' Nguyen spikes one!" Those kids did not realize that every time they poked fun at me I wanted to crawl into a cave and not come out until everyone was mature enough to accept my name.

The only person who understood my agony was my sister because she too has an uncommon name, but hers had less potential to be the butt of everyone's jokes than mine. On occasion when she and I went somewhere together, we would temporarily change our names to make the experience a lot more pleasant for ourselves. For instance, when I was a sophomore in high school and Chau was a junior, she wanted me to accompany her to a meeting of students interested in applying to college. She was sure that no one we knew would be there, so we decided to become "normal" for the evening. When the hosts asked us to write our names on those "Hello, my name is …" stickers, we picked random "American" names. As it turned out, we both found it easier to meet people when we weren't feeling self-conscious.

Whenever I told my mother about people making fun of my name, she would usually laugh and say, "Fuck? Ha, ha … isn't that a bad word? Ha, ha … That's kinda funny." At times like those I thought my mother was the most insensitive and uncaring person in the world. How could she sit there and laugh at her son when he had just told her that everyone in school was already laughing at him? Did she think that it would make me feel better if she laughed as well? Of course, I did not voice those questions. Thinking about it now, I believe that my mother's concept of emotional pain was completely different from mine. The physical pain and agony she endured for most of her life in Vietnam was probably ten times more intolerable than mine. That's probably why she couldn't understand the emotional pain I felt when kids made fun of me.

My mother also hindered my healthy adolescent development by refusing to let me associate with girls. I recall one incident in junior high when a seventh-grade girl wrote me a letter. Minh, a Vietnamese girl who played in the orchestra with me, sent me the first "I like you" letter I ever received; in it she expressed her admiration for me because I was smart and musically talented. Frankly, I did not have the slightest inkling what to think of the situation. No one had ever taught me how to initiate intimate relationships. The guy friends I had at school were all uncool "nerds" like myself who did not have any experience with girls either. I did not even consider asking them for help. I never had an older male role model to turn to with questions; the only older men I was in contact with were my uncles, and they were unlikely candidates because they did not grow up in America.

Asking for my mother's advice about girls would be tantamount to suicide. She always forbade my sister and me to date or see any members of the opposite sex until we were college graduates. One may think that she was just joking—no parent can be that strict, right?—but believe me, she wasn't joking. She strictly enforced her commands with severe actions. For instance, one day after school when I was waiting for my mother, one of my female acquaintances came up to chat with me. We were talking about how Mrs. Sloboda's world history test was too difficult. But when my mother drove up and saw us standing there together, she thought the subject of our conversation was something less than innocent. She immediately rolled down her window and screamed at the girl, "*Ây, đồ con quỷ sứ kia, mày làm chi với con tao rứa*—Hey, demon, what are you doing with my son?" My friend asked me whether my mother was yelling at her; I told her that she was just telling me to get in the car (this was one of the perks of having a mom who does not speak English). When I stepped into the car, my mother started chastising me for talking to the girl. She did not listen to my explanation and warned me that if she ever saw that scene again, I'd end up in an orphanage. That was the last time I stood next to girls after school.

There I was holding my first love letter in my hand, but I had absolutely no idea what to do with it. I did not understand my role as the male figure: Was I supposed to ask her out first or wait until she made the first move? Should I talk to her just as a friend or try to flirt with her? My mind was filled with confusion at the time. The only places I could think of to turn to for direction were Hong Kong mini-soap operas. These translated productions were usually set in ancient China, where a gentleman was one who followed the Confucian code of conduct and women were innocent and supportive. Honestly, I learned more about relationships from watching those shows than from any other source. They taught me that real men were brave, polite, chivalrous, confident, and independent, while women were caring, sensitive, nurturing, and passive. Of course, I am much wiser now, but back then I embraced these ideals. However, even though I knew from those movies how I *should* have acted toward Minh—who I thought was pretty and intelligent—I did not put that knowledge into practice. Instead of initiating any type of conversation, I tried to avoid her. Whenever she walked up to me to talk, I would turn around and walk the other way. Finally, after realizing that I seemed repulsed by her, Minh gave up on me and started seeing someone else. Later I felt like such an idiot for letting her go. "Why didn't I go for it?" I asked myself repeatedly. "Am I not a guy? She liked me! She really did, and I just let her go." I thought that I did not possess the qualities that a "real" man had, those qualities that the Hong Kong mini-soap operas presented to me. It was not until my last years in high school that I realized what "manly" qualities actually were. It was also then that my self-esteem gradually rose to a level where I was confident enough to look people in the face when I was talking to them. These changes came slowly and originated from an incident that was a milestone in my life. This incident served as the beginning of my long and successful struggle to break free from my mother's emotional influence.

The changes took place shortly after my mother allowed her ex-husband, my stepfather, back into our family. A few months following his return, I learned with horror what kind of man he really was. My half-brother Tai, a vibrant 14-year-old, told me that his father liked to pinch and bite him just for fun; he also liked to fondle Tai's genitals for prolonged stretches of time.

Something like this was not easy to accept or deal with, especially for a 14-year-old. I trembled at the realization that this beast of a man, this perverse monster, sexually abused his own son, my innocent brother. And all of this occurred right beneath our unwitting noses for weeks on end. "This cannot continue," I resolved. "I *will* not allow him to hurt my brother any longer!" Never in my life had I been more sure of what the right thing to do was. Although I knew that this could potentially hurt everyone else in my family, particularly my mother, I did not falter for a moment. I was willing to destroy my mother's happiness to protect Tai.

My method of expressing my frustration was to slam doors. Every time I saw my stepfather touching Tai's genitals, I would walk to my room and slam the door behind me. Our home only had two bedrooms, so Tai's father definitely heard and understood my signal. He understood all right, but he did not change, and the abuse persisted. However, my stubborn-headedness kept me from giving up. I wanted to reach a standoff, a sudden-death situation. That day came about two weeks after my initial resolution to fight. Thoughts of me being courageous or honorable never entered my mind; everything I did was by gut instinct.

It was a windy Saturday afternoon, and everyone was at home except for Chau, who was at work. My mother and stepfather were talking in their room while Tai and I played *Civilization* on my computer. All of a sudden Tai's father summoned him to their room. The inevitable happened, and again a rush of rage crashed into my body. I breathed hard as my heartbeat shot up like a bottle rocket. Shoving my chair behind me, I stepped out into the living room and looked into their room as I walked by. The scene did not differ from the ones I had witnessed over the past few weeks. After standing in the living room for a moment, I went to my room taking loud, heavy steps along the way and, upon reaching my destination, slammed my door with as much force as I could conjure up. I did it! My mother had to say *something*. I wanted to confront him that very moment; I wished that deep inside me there was a courage that would manifest itself now by giving Tai's father the hardest punch on the jaw. I waited for them to come in.

"Phuoc, what the hell are you doing!" my mother screamed as she raced over to my room and gave me a slap on the left side of my cheek. I still vividly remember the physical and emotional pain I felt the instant her hand landed on my face. "He's his father, and he can do whatever he wants with him. It's not like he's killing him or anything; he's just playing. And besides, it's none of your business! Now if you don't want to live here anymore, then I can always put you into an orphanage!" I knew then that my mother cared more about her own selfish needs than about the welfare of her younger son. My respect for her started fading behind a curtain of disappointment. What could I do? Everyone around me could not see what I saw, and after trying fruitlessly to expose the truth to them, this was what I received. Fear and alarm overwhelmed me at that moment, and I did not, could not, fight any longer. I had already drained myself of all the fortitude I possessed, and no matter how deep I searched, my well of courage was dry. At that time, fear—the emotion I detested most and the emotion I constantly encountered—took control of my mind. I didn't want to end up in an orphanage, a ward of the state. I didn't want her to put me in a foster home. No. No. I couldn't let that happen. "It was the wind, Mom," I responded innocently. "The wind slammed the door." And that was that. I was tired. I didn't want to feel any more emotions. I just wanted to lie in bed and pretend that none of it had happened.

I had never been more disappointed with my mother in my life; the time she ignored my pleas for new shoes, the time she made fun of my name, could not begin to compare with this. I wished she was not my mother. I wished that I had never been born into this backward family.

Two months later my mother kicked her ex-husband out. Apparently, he emptied her bank account with his gambling habits. While he had been staying with us, he constantly took her money to play cards at the local casino. Eventually, my mother had no money left to pay the bills. This time his leaving was for good, she said. His departure left me with a feeling of relief for my brother because it released him from constant victimization. Yet I knew that what he went through might leave lasting psychological effects.

The problems between my mother and myself did not spontaneously disappear when my stepfather left. I remember not feeling anything at all for her; it was as if my stepfather had taken with him all of my emotions about my mother and left only a void. I did not speak with her for half a year following his separation from us. I constantly asked myself how my mother, whom I regarded so highly—a woman who had risked and sacrificed everything for the sake of her children— could ignore the obvious abuse of her child by her husband. This inner questioning led to my emotional isolation from her. Withdrawing from my mother's world allowed me to step back and reevaluate from a different perspective my perceptions of her and myself. With the help of this new vantage point, I painted a new picture of myself and my relationship with my mother.

"*Thúa mạ con đi học*—(Respectfully) Mother, I am going to school." "*Thúa mạ. con đi học về*—(Respectfully) Mother, I am home from school." These eleven words, which tradition forced me to utter every day, were the only words I remember saying to my mother during those silent six months. How did I do it? What did I feel? What did I use to replace my relationship with my mother?

My first few weeks of silence I attribute to hatred. I loathed being in my mother's presence. When we were together in the same room, I never looked at her face or even positioned my body toward hers. At the dinner table, I swallowed my food without tasting it as fast as I could to shorten the torture of sitting near her. When we had company over and she asked me to come out and greet them, I stayed only long enough for them to see my fake smile before returning to my room. I did not think she deserved to be a mother, thus I did not treat her like one. I regarded her like a distant relative—with respect, but with no warmth or emotion. At night when my mother slept with Tai in her arms, so much anger welled up inside me that one time I released my rage by biting on a pillow with all my strength. "How could she go on like nothing happened?" I asked myself. "How could she not feel guilty?" Those nights I stayed up until two or three in the morning feeling sorry for my brother, furious at my mother, and disappointed in myself. I did not talk to anyone about my problems. Chau had isolated herself from the rest of our family, so she and I did not communicate, and I did not feel close enough to any of my friends at school to share with them my inner emotions. I also felt too ashamed to tell anyone about the unhappy circumstances in my family. Consequently, I existed for weeks like a walking balloon full of negative emotions just waiting to burst when I could no longer contain them. But I did not burst. I needed to appear strong, stolid (like the heroes in the Hong Kong movies). I needed to show my mother and myself that I did not depend on her for my emotions. The way I subdued these feelings is similar to what happens when a chemist immerses a helium-filled balloon into a vat of liquid nitrogen. Like the helium in the balloon, my emotions underwent a condensation into a colder, less active state.

For the remaining months of my silence, hatred and anger no longer played a large role in my reluctance to communicate with my mother. I figured, "Why should I torture myself with all these bad feelings? They don't do any good. I can't go on living so miserably." Convinced that emotions only hurt rather than benefited me, I gradually suppressed them. Soon I replaced those gut-wrenching feelings of guilt, sadness, and animosity with apathy and insensitivity. I no longer felt uncomfortable sitting next to my mother, because I had no feelings for her. Although I still remembered the events that occurred several weeks prior, it ceased to cause pain and anguish. My indifference made it easier for me to sleep at night, increased my ability to concentrate in school, and lifted the midnight clouds that hovered over me. In retrospect, I can understand the attraction of this defense mechanism; it was an easy escape from emotional pain and dependence on my mother. The side effect of my remedy, however, was that I lost the ability to feel other types of emotions as well, such as sympathy, sadness, and joy.

I felt like a machine. When I watched inspirational movies, I did not have warm, fuzzy sensations. When I was elected president of the sophomore class, my only reaction was, "Good, this'll look good on my college applications." When my friend Vu made a full recovery after undergoing chemotherapy for lymphatic cancer, I never felt ecstatic, just relieved for him. Now I realize the price of indifference, and I have been trying hard to gain back—with little success—my ability to feel deep emotions.

In the months following my isolation from my mother, I found numerous ways to convince myself that she had absolutely no influence on me and that I had completely and irreversibly broken away from her. I guess this was the rebellious stage of my adolescence. However, I did not rebel in the typical demonstrative fashion, like screaming "I hate you" to my mom or getting drunk. Instead, I rebelled in a passive way so that only *I* knew I rebelled, while everyone, including her, still thought I was the perfect son. One of my defiance strategies was to achieve top grades in my classes without putting in any effort. I cheated in almost every subject. After school, when my mother asked me if I had any homework, I always replied, "No, Mom, I'm already done." She never asked me to show her my completed work because she could not read a word of it. I also started lying a lot to my mother. One time I told her that my friends and I went to the library to study, but actually we drove to San Francisco and spent the day playing volleyball on the beach. I cannot count all the times that I lied to her and she never found out the truth. I felt much satisfaction knowing that I had some control over her; it raised my self-confidence and esteem and felt like sweet revenge for her dominance over me when I was younger. I simply wanted to believe that my mother had no part in my success in both academics and life. Yet I allowed her to continue assuming that I was the model son and that without her I would have been nothing. I figured she deserved at least that much because of the sacrifices she made in bringing me to America and raising me in a strange land.

What did I use to replace my mother's absence from my life? Certainly not other relationships! I found it difficult to make close friendships in high school for several reasons: my school environment, my inability to share feelings (mostly because I had no emotions), and the fact that I thought close friends were unessential for my well-being. The school I attended had the lowest SAT score averages in the country. Fifty percent of the student body was Black, while about 90 percent of the faculty was White; the remaining students consisted mainly of Hispanics and Asians, with a few token White students. Almost everyone came from poor households; I once read an article about our school that revealed that over 70 percent of the students' families depended on welfare as their sole source of income. I witnessed gang fights almost every week, mostly between Black gangs—the Bloods versus the Crips. But sometimes I also saw some action from the smaller Asian gangs like the Oriental Boyz. The extraordinarily high incidence of violence and drug abuse in my school forced the government to establish a gun- and drug-free zone around the school and the nearby housing complexes. Fortunately, I participated in the school's magnet program, called the Academy of Math, Science, and Engineering, that better prepared me for college. I limited the group of friends I hung out with mainly to other Vietnamese students from the Academy, and I stayed away from most of the Black students because I was afraid of being associated with any of the gangs. My friends and I had lunch together, copied home-work from one another, and joined the same clubs. However, outside of school we did not go out on a regular basis or call each other to have heart-to-heart conversations. Even when my friends did call me, we never discussed my family problems or feelings, probably because I didn't want to admit that I had any troubles at home. I also never developed strong companionships in high school because I did not feel that I needed them to make me content. I felt satisfied that I had friends to turn to when I wanted to copy homework from someone; other than that, I had no burning desire to have best friends.

Relationships with girls also did not fill the void left by my mother's absence. In my high school years a number of girls wrote me love letters, asked me out to proms, or tried to get to know me, but not once did I take the initiative to pursue a relationship with any of them. Sure, I went to their proms, but I only did it because I did not want to turn them down. It wasn't that I didn't find women attractive or that I didn't want a steady relationship; rather, I think that the combination of my mother's strict rules and a lack of male role models contributed to my nonaggressive behavior. As I stated before, my mother adamantly forbade me to have girlfriends, and although I wanted to establish my independence from her, I still needed to abide by her rules because I was living under her roof. The other reason I wasn't able to tell girls that I liked them was because I didn't know how. No one ever taught me the correct procedures for getting to know women, and what I saw on TV seemed too straightforward for my tastes. My closest male friend in high school, Vu, never had any experience with girls either. Thus, even if I wanted to go out with someone, I did not know how to approach her and ask.

I do not believe anything replaced my relationship with my mother. Her dominant presence simply disappeared as a result of my ability to suppress my emotions. How she felt no longer dictated how I felt. When she cried, I no longer cried; when she laughed, I no longer laughed with her; and when she told her disturbing childhood stories, they no longer affected me emotionally. It may seem heartless, but that was how I felt. I did not need anyone to take her place; what I *did* need, however, was to fill up the free time I had now that I wasn't spending it with my mother. I kept myself busy in high school by joining numerous clubs, volunteering at nursing homes and hospitals, playing on the tennis team, participating in math and science competitions, working, attending Vietnamese school on the weekends, and enrolling in night courses at the closest community college. I occupied my days with so many activities that on a typical day, I would not return home until eight or nine in the evening, and by that time my mother would be in bed.

In other ways, I came to understand my mother at a deeper level. In junior year I had a history class in which we learned about ancient China; we discussed Confucius's philosophy and how his ideals still permeate East Asian culture. One of the most important aspects of Confucian theory is its emphasis on role-playing in the family and in society. I remember writing a report on Confucian influence on contemporary Vietnamese society and realizing that my family performed the parts that he outlined centuries ago. Observing my family as a source for my essay, I learned that Confucius dictated our use of verbal and physical affection.

To this day I cannot say "I love you" to my mother, older sister, or younger brother. The only person whom I *do* verbally acknowledge my love for is Carol, my 4-year-old half-sister. It may seem strange, but Carol is also the only one that I hug, kiss, or show any other form of affection to. The same is true for my mother, Chau, and Tai—from an outsider's perspective it may seem as though all of us love only Carol. I also hear Chau verbalizing her love for Vinh, her fiancé, and it seems perfectly natural. What would be completely *unnatural* and unprecedented is if she said "I love you" to me, my mother, or my brother.

During elementary school my mother nurtured and cared for me as if I had just learned how to walk. One of the ways she made me state that I loved her was by asking, "Phuoc, where do you put your love for me?" My rehearsed answer was, "Mom, I put my love for you on my head!" (She considers the head the most important part of the body, so putting my love there meant that it was the most important love.) We kissed and hugged one another all the time and without reservation. By the time I started junior high school, however, we suddenly, yet intuitively, stopped being physically affectionate. Even though I missed

Phuoc Le

my mother's touch, especially when I witnessed her affection for Carol, I knew that its cessation was appropriate for my age. Thinking back, the start of my adolescence and newfound need to break away from the nest, particularly when kids at school filled my head with the notion that kissing your mom was "sissy" and "gay," influenced the shift in our relationship. A change in my mother's attitude also contributed; she no longer asked me where I put my love for her. Instead, she asked Tai, who was 2 at the time, this question, which I thought she had reserved just for me. It was as if the game had age limits, and I had already passed them. My mother now expected me to show my love for her by obeying her and bringing home the As. Accordingly, she showed her love by feeding and clothing me.

"*Con không cha nhú nhà không nóc*—Children without a father are like houses without rooftops." My mother never failed to remind me of this Vietnamese proverb whenever she wanted to show off how she had disproved the old saying. She was correct in her claim, because we never grew up with a father, yet our house definitely has a "rooftop." My mother played the roles of breadwinner and caring mother at the same time. She disciplined us while bandaging our wounds, taught us how to ride a bike and then cleaned our scrapes and bruises, encouraged us to succeed in the real world while wishing we would never leave her side. In December of my last year before entering college, I unwittingly replaced my mother as the rooftop and the foundation of my home.

The news jumped at me out of the blue. "I'm going to Vietnam next month to visit Grandpa and Grandma," was all my mother said. "I'll leave some money for you while I'm gone. I'll be there for a month." She never discussed with me the possibility that I did not want to take care of 1-year-old Carol and 8-year-old Tai for an entire month, especially December, when I had so many things to do in my senior year. She never taught me how to cook dinner, potty train Carol, comfort her when she cried, and keep the house clean all in one day. Yet I never raised a single objection to her vacation plans. The only thing I recall telling her while we said good-bye at the airport was, "Have a safe trip, Mom. Don't let anyone con you over there, okay? Let me know when you want me to pick you up." For the next thirty-one days I enrolled in a crash course in parenting in which the teacher and student were one—me.

The most difficult part of the day came after Tai got home from school. During those few hours before bedtime, I ran around my two-bedroom home like a madman in nerve-racking attempts to prevent my hyperactive sister from hurting herself while also trying to complete multiple tasks. Within a two-hour stretch, I made dinner, did the laundry, mopped the floors, took out the garbage, changed Carol's diaper when I forgot to remind her about the mini-toilet, helped Tai with his fractions and long division, answered phone calls from friends seeking advice on how to fill out college applications, and played with Carol to keep her from wrecking the floors I had just mopped!

Every night I longed for nine o'clock to come around so that I could put the two children to sleep and actually attend to my own affairs. This was the time during my senior year when the college application deadlines loomed. In addition to completing seven or eight college applications, I worked on finishing nearly a dozen scholarship applications, all of which kept me up late every night. Luckily, I did not have trouble finding a topic for my personal essays; it was easy to write about my experiences performing the duties of a parent and how much I learned from them. This topic proved productive; the following spring I was accepted to a prestigious college and also won a full scholarship to the school of my choice.

Looking back on that month, I recognize now the richness of my experience and just how much it contributed to me as a person. During that time I learned what qualities an ideal man and woman should possess. My firsthand knowledge replaced my archaic notions of men as chivalrous protectors of passive, caring women. Another new concept I developed was that there weren't any obvious differences between the required traits of a man and a woman. I no longer divided the genders and designated specific attributes each should acquire. It was as if I took my culture's gender role assignments and synthesized them into one person, and that was who I became. Whether it was hugging Carol to sleep when she cried in the middle of the night, explaining fractions to Tai, cooking, cleaning, or fixing the door handle, I did not feel as though I switched roles when I performed them. I never thought to myself, "No, I can't do this because I'm a man. That's not what I'm supposed to do. But, since Mom's not here, I *have* to do the woman's work." Those thoughts didn't cross my mind. What I did think, however, was, "Of course I'll do this. I'll do it because I love my sister and brother. No other reason."

Ever since my sister went away to college, my role and responsibility in my family has changed dramatically. I have much more say in household affairs than before. Now whenever I am at home I take care of all the bills and paperwork that my mother has accumulated over the months while I was in college. If there is a decision to be made, I usually make it and then tell my mother why I did so. I think she finally realized that I was old enough to make the right choices for our family. Along with my added responsibility, the weight of my word has increased markedly since high school. Again, I think my mother takes my opinion more seriously because I am old enough now to play the role of an influential person in our family. Knowing that what I say has a more profound influence on her than ever before, I have not wasted an opportunity to help my little brother and sister. Whenever I have a chance, I persuade her to change her ways toward Tai and little Carol so that they can have a smoother childhood than I did. By this I mean that I encourage her to allow them to make friends within and outside of the Vietnamese ethnicity, let Tai talk to girls his age because he can benefit from them and vice versa, and most importantly discipline them with words instead of whips. I believe my words have not gone unheard, especially those dealing with punishment, because since I started college I cannot recall ever hearing about her spanking Tai or Carol.

My years in college have allowed me to develop a new, more equal relationship with my mother. I think the time I spent at school 3,000 miles away has made us both appreciate and respect one another (although she would never admit that she respects or appreciates me). She now sees me as an independent individual, and I see her as both a mother and a friend. I know that she takes much pride in seeing me succeed in my academic life, but even though I want to make her proud of me and hope that she gains the proper admiration she deserves from those in Vietnam, I do not base my goals and aspirations on pleasing her. If in the process of attaining my goals I also make her happy, then I will have lived up to both my American and Vietnamese ideals—doing things for myself and doing things to show respect for my parents. I praise my mother when I see the improvements in the way she is raising Tai and Carol compared to her raising of Chau and me. I think she knows that she cannot apply every aspect of Vietnamese culture to children she is raising in America. When I go home for vacations, I still function as the man in the house, the person who takes care of the bills, fixes doorknobs, and attends the parent–teacher conferences. At the same time, I am also the only male figure for my brother, which puts pressure on me to be the best role model I can be. I play these roles willingly and with satisfaction.

As for my search for the culture that suits me best, I have come to the decision that neither Vietnamese nor American culture alone can fulfill my needs. Thus, I chose to pick out the best aspects of each culture and synthesize them into one. For instance, while I believe in the American ideal that every person is equal, I also disapprove of children not treating their elders with respect and proper manners. I do not consider myself Americanized or Vietnamized; rather, I'm enjoying the best of both worlds.

What are the issues that I am still struggling with? As I enter my senior year, I'm still trying to inflate the emotional balloon that I've suppressed for so long. Recently, my girlfriend, Jennifer, has been helping me recover my ability to feel strong emotions again. Last month she and I cried together, something I haven't done since my sophomore year in high school! However, I find it much more difficult to bring back the emotions than to tuck them away, and so far I haven't made much progress.

From the academic success my sister and I have earned, it may seem that our family is living out the American dream. We escaped from a war-scarred country that offered us few opportunities and arrived in a land we knew nothing about. My mother worked hard all her life to provide her children with a home that was conducive to learning. She created such an atmosphere by using the whip, along with guilt-provoking stories to encourage us to learn. Now that two of her children are excelling in their respective postsecondary institutions, my mother feels that she has done an admirable job of raising us. However, her feelings of pride come at a high cost to the relationships in our family. Maybe she did not know any other way to raise us than by using her native culture's means. She did not realize that most families who bring up successful children do not use the switch as their tool of support. I believe that practicing Confucian ideals in the family will lead to decreased communication and ultimately to feelings of isolation similar to those that Chau and I felt and are still experiencing. Fortunately, after seeing her family structure crumble because of her, my mother realized that her rearing methods needed improvement. She knows now that her children will inevitably become "Americanized" to some degree. Accordingly, she now allows Tai and Carol more freedom; hopefully, they will also live up to her ideals. I can sense that the relationships in my family are becoming more intimate. We all can hug and kiss each other now, and I am optimistic that in the near future my mother and I will be able to say "I love you" to one another.

Case 16

FIGURING OUT MY LIFE

ALISON MAY

DOI: 10.4324/9781003165378-20

Alison May

Despite undiagnosed learning disabilities in childhood, the 21-year-old, upper-middle-class, white author of this essay describes a highly successful school career. Alison's success, which masks a vulnerable sense of self-esteem, is attributable in large part to hard work and explicit compensations for what was diagnosed as visual and auditory dyslexia prior to her freshman year at college. A strong work ethic and intelligence are not, however, sufficient to earn Alison the grades she strives for and believes she merits. Despondent about her failure and the "unfairness of the world," she seeks advice and encouragement from the college's LD services coordinator, who is herself learning-disabled. Supported by family and friends, and with a new sense of assurance, Alison commits herself to a future career as a clinical psychologist who will relieve the emotional toll learning disabilities exact on others.

It was the summer of 1993, just after I had graduated high school third in my class of 237. During this final year of high school, I was accepted at a college in New England, and my classmates had voted me "Most Intelligent" and "Most Likely to Succeed." Although honored, I felt misunderstood by my classmates, and I entered the summer before my freshman year of college feeling alone, scared, and confused.

Although I had become close to a lot of my classmates, I felt that I had not established any true friendships because I had hidden who I really was. Nobody knew how much I had struggled to make the grade. Nobody knew how many times I had thought luck was the only thing I had going for me. And nobody knew how scared I was of being found out to be as incompetent as I thought I was. I tried to take comfort in what was to come—a new life away from home—but I wasn't sure I could be as successful in college as I had been in high school. In college, I feared I'd be the one who'd let everyone in her hometown down. I knew hard work and motivation had been a part of my prior success, and that I would continue my work ethic in college, but what if it wasn't enough to succeed? I had had to work so hard in order to understand even simple things, so I thought I couldn't possibly be intelligent. How could I rely on a trait I didn't have to get me through college? "Oh well," I thought, "I can't keep up this charade forever." I tried to resign myself to an empty peace by thinking, "It's out of my control."

Among the many letters I received from the college that summer was one from Mary Fox, the Student Disabilities Coordinator. It asked, "Do you have, or have you ever had, any learning disabilities?" That one question began a new chapter in my life. I hadn't been prepared for such a question, but I quickly armed myself against this absurd inquiry. Sure, many of my elementary school teachers had wanted to put me in special education classes because I had more difficulty understanding than my classmates. One of the child psychologists I saw even diagnosed me as mentally retarded! But I defensively answered that though I had apparently had some undiagnosed learning disabilities early on, I was fine now, and I did not want anybody "nagging me." I was threatened by the implications of this question, fearing that anything I achieved at college would be invalidated if I were offered special treatment. In the letter I received in response from Mary, she promised not to "nag" me; she only asked if we had documentation of any of the learning disabilities.

Mom decided to talk with Mary. She explained that it was my older sister Jennifer's kindergarten teacher, Mrs. Lin, who had first made Mom aware that I might be having problems understanding. Mrs. Lin had observed my habit of repeating slightly incorrectly the things Mom said to me. For example, Mom once asked me to get my brush, but I looked baffled and asked, "my braid?" Mom thought I was playing word games, but Mrs. Lin suggested that I could be suffering from a learning disability. Little was known at the time about learning disabilities, and they were diagnosed only in children who were severely affected.

Though perplexed, Mom acted on Mrs. Lin's suggestion. She began to analyze our conversations and noted that the problem practically disappeared when she made sure my full attention was focused on her, when she made tactile cues (when asking me to get my brush, she would pretend to brush my hair with her hand), and/or when she had me repeat back to her what she had said.

Once in Mrs. Lin's kindergarten class, however, I was still having obvious difficulty understanding what she said to me. When she noticed my anxiety and helplessness, she would gently ask if I understood. But I often felt so overwhelmed that all I could do was hide behind a charming, bewildered smile, or go to the corner and lie down on my mat. I learned helplessness at a very young age.

Mrs. Lin recommended that I be tested for learning disabilities. Unfortunately, the psychologists who tested me had no idea what my problem was. One said I was just being stubborn or disobedient, but Mom and Dad understood the great need for harmony in our family, so they immediately knew his findings must be wrong. Other psychologists thought I was deaf, or too disabled to read, so my parents finally gave up on having me tested. They decided to rely instead on a more reliable psychologist's advice (my great uncle's), who told them not to worry, saying, "She's so bright that she will grow out of, or compensate for, her learning difficulties."

But now, thirteen years later, Mom and Mary decided it would be wise to have me tested again. So, I found myself on my way to Dr. Milton's office. During that long car ride I recalled my school-age experiences of hearing teachers talk and feeling as if they were speaking in a foreign language. I seldom understood my assignments, and what was worse was that I didn't *know* I didn't understand, so I couldn't ask for help. Instead, I developed a hypersensitivity to the cues of those around me, and observing my classmates and the reactions of my teachers, I was usually able to piece together my assignments.

I still remembered the pain I suffered over one assignment I couldn't piece together, though it was twelve years earlier. Mrs. Escher was glancing at the exercises my class had just completed as we lined up for recess. When she got to mine, her face clouded over with anger, and she ripped me from the line of boisterous kids, who suddenly became very quiet. "What is *this*?" she demanded. I hadn't understood the assignment in the first place, so how could I understand the question she was asking now? She took my inability to understand as a sign of defiance, and bellowed at me, enraged, "You will stay in for recess and do this assignment correctly!" As my classmates filed out of the room to recess, I sat crying at my desk, wondering why I was isolated from everyone in my class. I felt not only the pain of my failure to understand, but also that I was a bad person for not understanding. Carrying all this emotional baggage into Dr. Milton's office, I kept thinking, "They couldn't find an excuse for my stupidity all those years ago, so why should they now?"

The testing was intensive. During several visits, I took a variety of tests, including the Wechsler Adult Intelligent Scale and the Woodcock-Johnson Psycho-Educational Battery: Tests of Achievement and Cognitive Ability. The tests were fairly straightforward, though certain ones really gave me a hard time. I couldn't hear the stopwatch ticking, but I knew I was taking quite a bit of time to complete some of the tests. At one point, when struggling with a motor-skills exercise, I said flat out, "I know it's wrong, but I don't know how to correct it." Although I felt a little embarrassed by the fact that Dr. Milton had probably seen some 7-year-olds sail through this activity, I had been prepared for my difficulty by low scores in prior motor-skills tests. Though I would've loved to ace this test, Mom had long ago helped me to understand that we all have different gifts.

Some of the tasks I found to be easy actually indicated a learning disability. For example, on a simple word-matching task, I scored perfectly when not looking at Dr. Milton, but when I looked at him, I answered incorrectly three times. This made sense to me: I had always listened without looking at someone when trying hard to understand what they were saying. It hadn't struck me up to then that this behavior might be unusual.

Throughout the testing, I was preoccupied by the fear that I was going to let everyone down. When I was little, I felt I had disappointed my parents when I didn't pick up on things as fast as other kids my age. I remember many times sitting in class concentrating hard on what my teachers were saying, but still often being unable to understand their questions while my classmates' hands waved wildly in the air. Some of my most vivid memories of such failures occurred as recently as my senior year in high school. In those uncomfortable moments, I became the kid who didn't want to be called on. It was especially frustrating because I had done my work, I had been paying attention, and I had been taking notes like a madwoman. I just needed more time than everyone else to process ideas.

My parents never in any way fostered my feelings that I was a disappointment. On the contrary, they made it obvious how bright they thought I was, and often said, "We feel like the most blessed parents in the world." Still, my insecurity seemed to go hand in hand with my learning difficulties, and I struggled to fulfill what I perceived to be my parents' expectations for me. I thought they expected this latest round of testing to verify that I had some learning disability—and perhaps would confirm that my difficulties had not been due to their neglect. I desperately wanted to absolve them of any concerns over their parenting. They had been wonderful parents—I was the faulty one!

When the testing was over, I was prepared to disappoint everyone—again. And now there was one more person I valued who I expected to let down—Dr. Milton. When my parents and I met with him to discuss the test results, I sat with the same pleasant smile that I had always hidden behind, feeling inadequate and only half listening as Dr. Milton explained my test results. We all understood that I often had trouble calculating the higher levels of abstraction between objects. For example, I had stated the major relationship between table and chair as "they are both necessary to eat dinner." When Mom and Dad commented that they would have said "both are pieces of furniture," or "both have four legs," I responded with a look that said "I never would've thought of that!" We all enjoyed a big laugh because our family relishes creative, innovative responses to things. When Dr. Milton finished talking, Mom asked, "Is this anything like dyslexia?" Dr. Milton confirmed that I did, indeed, have visual and auditory dyslexia. I practically yelled, "I did it? I got what we came for?" I was thrilled; I hadn't let anybody down.

I left the testing feeling the same as always. I didn't believe attaching the words "visual and auditory dyslexia" to me would change my life, though I did recognize that they affected my parents. Mom seemed transformed by what she had just learned. She could hardly talk about our visit without getting teary-eyed. I guess finding out that your 18-year-old is visually processing as an 8-year-old and auditorily processing at an even lower level would make any parent wonder what emotional price her child had been paying. Still, I felt I had fulfilled my part of the bargain, and that these so-called learning disabilities were in my past. I did not realize then that they would not only affect my future, but also serve as a new vantage point from which I would have to reinterpret my entire past. I was oblivious to the heart-wrenching feelings of inadequacy, inferiority, and alienation that would come later.

The rest of the summer and my freshman fall at college were times of discovery for me. I explored which of my behaviors, thought processes, slips of the tongue, etc. were due to my learning disabilities, and which were just normal mistakes. My family members became my test subjects, and they were eager to help me in my quest. They were also appropriate test subjects because we had established long before that each of us had very different ways of thinking. Having already laid this groundwork, we began to determine how I, the visually and auditorily dyslexic, processed differently from everyone else in the family. A few major differences emerged immediately. For example, Mom recalled a time when she had asked me to get something from the bottom, left drawer of the secretary. I stood there for about three seconds, appearing as if I hadn't heard a thing, but then I whipped down the stairs to the living room and came back with what Mom had asked for. Mom laughed with joy and wonder at the realization that she had seen me thinking in those few seconds. "Doesn't everybody do that?" I asked. It became clear to me that no, everybody does not do that. In fact, having great difficulty understanding and following sequences of instructions, even simple ones, had been one of the earliest signs of my disabilities.

Moreover, I realized that in all my auditory understanding of verbal material, there is an element of hesitation. When people speak to me, about half the time I must repeat to myself (often several times) what they have said before I can understand it. This repetition can help keep what has been said to me fresher in what seems to be my deficient memory, and, more importantly, acts to fill in the holes in my auditory processing. I have become skilled and efficient at using phonological and contextual cues from the conversation to fill in the gaps, little by little, each time I repeat the sentence to myself. Ninety-nine percent of the time, this process enables me to offer an appropriate response in a socially acceptable amount of time, so that the other person doesn't suspect that I am having difficulty understanding them.

That 1 percent of the time that my compensation process doesn't work, however, has caused some confusion to those I'm speaking with. This occurs most often when I'm preoccupied with another activity. For example, filling up the car at a gas station, my boy-friend Mark was going inside to pay, and he stopped to ask me, "Do you want anything when I go in?" Here's what happened inside my head: I heard, "Do you want anything," but I knew he had said more than that. I had grasped the approximate length of the sentence, and even the general syllable structure, but that wasn't enough. I quickly thought back to the last time we went into a gas station together and remembered that there had been "Slim Jims" on the counter. Mark had picked one up and had done a hysterical impersonation of the professional wrestler in their advertisements. I therefore concluded that his question had been, "Do you want anything, like a Slim Jim?" so I answered, "You know I don't like Slim Jims." (Note that the sentence I came up with had the same number of syllables as, and practically rhymed with, Mark's question.) Needless to say, Mark was confused. I have no name for these mental events I experience, but they present a wonderful oppor-tunity for me and those close to me to enjoy a good laugh, and to appre-ciate how even learning-disabled minds work so extraordinarily, if at times incorrectly.

My auditory glitches weren't always so funny, and I find humor in them now only because it is so obvious how far I have come since my major breakthrough at age 7. Before I was 7, I had felt comfortable con-versing with any adult, yet when it came to understanding directions, I felt everyone was suddenly talking in a different language. This made me feel lost, scared, and helpless all the time. I never knew what was going on, while all the other kids seemed to know. I was also scared of being left behind, and of making those I looked up to unhappy with me. I felt the world around me was putting pressure on me to act, yet I did not know what it wanted from me. I was like a message decoder who never got a break: As soon as I broke one code, the next would be waiting on my desk.

Somehow, I survived until my big breakthrough at age 7, when I began to understand that I wasn't understanding. This realization allowed me to ask others to repeat and clarify their directions, spoken

Alison May

or written. Suddenly, I could do the assignments that had seemed so confusing and was spared my futile attempts to do the work without understanding it. Nonetheless, my low self-esteem reminds me that I am still paying a price for all those years of not understanding.

Though my auditory processes for language were disrupted, my ability to perceive music was intact from the beginning. Mom and Dad were astounded when, at less than a year old, I could finish the tune of "You Are My Sunshine" after my music box had stopped. Hoping that the structure of the Suzuki method would help me learn sequences and patterns, Mom got me started on the violin at age 2. In fourth grade, I switched over to the cello, and in fifth grade, picked up the flute. I now play the cello only sporadically, and my family is amazed that I maintain my skill as if I had just played yesterday. Still, there seem to be some glitches in my playing. For example, I play notes in the bass clef while thinking of the names of the notes in treble clef, essentially playing one note while thinking of another. Apparently, I rely upon the position, rather than the name, of the note to read music.

I began to understand more about the effects of my learning disabilities when I got to college. I was shocked that Dr. Milton had recommended that I receive a waiver of the language requirement because I might have difficulty with the "Rassias method," which emphasizes speed and oral communication. After all, I had always been one of the top students in my French and Latin high school classes. I decided to give French a try, and was placed in French 2, which was mostly a review for me. I had some difficulty with the drills, during which my instructor fired rapid questions in French and demanded an immediate response. If I thought about what the instructor had said, that is, attempted to translate it into English, I became completely confused and responded incorrectly. But, if I blurted out the first French sentence that came to mind, I was almost always right. The drill instructor was impressed with my performance, and said he never would have guessed that I was dyslexic.

A lot of the non-dyslexic people to whom I've described my difficulties with reading have noted that they, too, have some of the same problems, though my difficulties seem more extreme. For example, one common problem I have is that I "read" a whole passage and realize that I haven't understood or remembered a single word. I commonly forget the beginning of a long sentence by the time I reach the end and have to read it three or four times to grasp the whole thing. This forces me to read very slowly.

I agree with those psychologists who believe that word retrieval is the basis for dyslexics' difficulty with reading. In other words, though I have a vocabulary in the ninety-ninth percentile, I hesitate each time I look at a word. The word is not backwards or scrambled (a common myth about all dyslexics), but I have a lag between seeing and recognizing familiar words in the context of a sentence. Sometimes, reading out loud helps to eliminate some of the difficulties, but because of my auditory dyslexia, the benefits are often minimal. No matter what strategies I try, reading is laborious and physically exhausting. Yet despite my hardships, I love to read: With each word I understand, I feel I reaffirm my parents' faith in me, and prove wrong all the doctors and psychologists who gave up on me.

Another area in which dyslexia affects me is in writing. I don't write letters backwards, but when I write by hand, I have to pay close attention to the formation of each letter. At the same time, I must think about spelling. It is as if my memory has not properly encoded what each letter looks like, so each time I try to write one, I have to wrack my brain for a template. My motor functions hamper me even more, which makes writing very involved and exhausting for me, not to mention extremely slow!

Adding comprehension to writing creates a whole new problem. When I am listening to a lecture, it is impossible for me to both take and understand my notes. Because I can't always rely on my auditory processes, I really need to have notes. Moreover, to get the gist of a lecture without repeatedly hearing or studying it, I have to write the notes down verbatim. Since I can't write very quickly, however, I'm at a stalemate. Luckily, my advisors recommended that I use a laptop computer for note-taking, and my laptop has been my savior. Typing seemed to compensate for my encoding difficulties because letters were no longer letters, but positions on a keyboard. I use my laptop to take notes mainly in lecture-based classes. Even so, I still do not do as well in pure lecture classes as in those that bring in discussion or use other media such as video clips. My repeated difficulties in lecture-based classes make me feel unwelcome in college, as if I don't belong. I've often cried to Mom and Dad that I shouldn't be in college, that college is an institution made for learning, not learning disabilities.

The limitations of the help my laptop can give me is revealed in paper-writing. Although typing helps me produce papers that are far better than I could handwrite, I still have trouble with structure and organization. Of course, it helps that I can cut and paste paragraphs

Alison May

in different places, but if I have no idea *where* to paste them, these functions are of only limited value. It's frustrating to know that all the elements are in my paper, but that poor organization and difficulty with sentence structure might obscure the quality of my product. Equally upsetting is my tendency to lose trains of thought: Often I have the perfect sentence and then suddenly lose it.

Like my writing, my speech is hampered by structural, organizational, and what I call memory difficulties. I have to concentrate very hard on what I say. When I don't, I tend to transpose letters and words. I often start speaking before I've had time to think through what I want to say. I will start the sentence, realize that it is not the best way to express what I'm thinking, then start it again, maybe even a few times, before I actually finish. This makes me sound like somebody trying to get out of a punishment: "She was … we were … it wasn't my … all right, I hit her first!" I also often switch sounds or words—for example, "Could you get me some poilet taper?"

I often don't realize that I've made such verbal slips until the person with me chuckles about them. Although I once would have been mortified to make such mistakes, I take them in stride now. It would be debilitating to handle them any other way! Still, I'd be fooling myself to say my verbal slips and organizational difficulties don't inhibit me. I have always preferred small groups of close friends and avoid large groups where the additional noise and confusion make it impossible for me to concentrate. Besides, parties are full of people who don't know me, and they might think I'm dumb, not learning-disabled. I believe it is this distinction that gets every learning-disabled person out of bed in the morning.

My verbal organizational difficulties affect me most when arguing or debating, which may be why I have always had an innate need for harmony. Besides having to think hard about what I'm saying, the stress of knowing that someone is angry with me is overwhelming. In addition, the interruptions that typically occur during arguments completely destroy my train of thought. When arguing with my boyfriend, for example, I quite literally can't keep up. I am still trying to respond to his first sentence as he argues on. And I can't share in the emotional aspect of the argument because I am so busy trying to analyze and remember what I want to say. Oh, I do cry when I argue, but I never know whether I am crying because of the emotions the argument has aroused or because I feel mentally incapable of arguing. I think crying is my grown-up way of exhibiting learned helplessness, although if there were a mat to lie down on when I felt lost, I probably still would.

I hear many people say they wish they could be kids again, to return to a time of less responsibility, with time to go out and play, and to be carefree—or so I've been told. When I look back at my life, I don't ever remember feeling like a kid, and I certainly don't remember the blissful harmony that everyone else seems to. What happened to my childhood? I'll tell you what happened: I was forced to grow up more quickly than other kids in order to make it in this world. At a young age, I learned that I had to figure out my world, and myself, or be left behind. I became highly introspective, always trying to figure out how to make myself learn at a rate commensurate with my classmates. By the third grade, I blended in pretty well academically, but I never felt that I did socially. I felt distant and detached from everyone else my age, and a lot older. Aware that school was easier for my classmates, I spent a lot of time worrying that not only school but life in general would be more difficult for me. While my friends were wondering whether to invite boys to their parties, I was understanding what my dad was going through as he battled depression.

I was also physically more adult than my classmates. I was tied for the tallest in my second-grade class, was chubby, asthmatic, and early to develop. I remember feeling envious of the smaller girls, but I didn't start thinking about fairness until third grade. Once I did, my world became even more bleak. How could others be cuter, smarter, and more athletic, while I was only bigger, dumber, and slower? Nevertheless, I never had trouble making friends because I was always kind to everybody, even to classmates who treated me like a doormat. I did have a few close friends, but I still felt alone, even when spending time with them. Gwynn was one such friend. We often played together after school, but I constantly worried that her next-door neighbor would come over to join us. I never understood that she could be good friends with me and with someone else: I thought someone had to lose out, and it would naturally be me.

By the eighth grade, I avoided joining cliques. Though I did this in part to stop worrying so much about what others thought of me, it differentiated me even more from my classmates. I got along well with everyone, but I did not feel I was part of a loop. I became wrapped up in trying to figure out where I did fit in, but this just made me an observer of everyone else's behavior. I began to focus almost entirely on academics, especially psychology. My studies in psychology helped me to realize that I was delayed in reaching adolescence. Knowing this helps me to understand the increasing number of arguments I've had with Mom and Dad since I've started dating and gone off to college. Mom admits that part of the problem is that she and Dad are very protective of me. "After all," she argues, "when you're dealing with someone whose childhood was so painful that you're not sure she has any intact self-esteem, you have to watch out for her!"

More a problem than my parents' overprotectiveness, however, is *my* unreadiness to assert my independence from them. I realize that I ask Mom and Dad's advice in a lot of arenas that most 20-year-olds wouldn't even mention to their parents, but I don't think it's fair to judge me by the standards of the average 20-year-old. Because I was born with an unusual set of circumstances that prevented my life experience from being average, it has been a lot harder for my parents to let me spread my own wounded little wings and fly. Maybe I am the one most afraid of falling if they let go, however.

With so many obstacles to overcome and so many new insights to consider, my first quarter at college was grueling. Although I felt sure that I would be doomed in all of my classes, my love for learning and my desire to know I was doing my best kept me getting up every morning for class. I had developed a labor-intensive work ethic over my high school years: I simply worked on something until I understood it, which meant I often worked a lot harder on my studies than others. Still, I didn't attribute my success to intelligence; a nagging inner voice told me I couldn't possibly be smart if I needed so much more time to understand what my classmates got almost immediately.

My nagging voice began to get louder at college where I was always surrounded by other students. I observed their casual study habits and easy comings and goings. I, on the other hand, sat in my room working, taking breaks for only food, bathroom, sleep, or class. This really did not bother me: I was motivated by fear of failure to work my hardest. I thought I was doing fine—until I got my first-quarter grades.

They arrived and I was devastated: a 3.0 GPA. Granted, this is a great GPA, especially at a selective college, but I had put absolutely all of my time, effort, and heart into my studies. Was this a gauge of how the next four years of my life would go? Even worse, I had gotten a "C+" in my Data Analysis class, my first "C" ever. Though I had spent hours with the professor outside of class and I had done and redone almost all of the assignments, it had all been for nothing. But it wasn't just the grades that upset me. It was that I now knew I was working harder than other people who were making the same or better grades than I was. It was the fact that the work ethic that I had labored so long and hard to perfect had failed me. It was also the fact that I felt I wasn't good enough for the college now, and never would be.

On the Saturday night after I returned to New England from Christmas break, as the others in the dorm headed out to have fun, I was ready to call it quits. I called Mom and Dad for what I thought would be a routine call, but as soon as Mom answered, I began to sob uncontrollably. All the frustration of not being rewarded for my hard work last term overwhelmed me, as did the thought of changing my now-discredited work habits. I feared if I modified my work ethic, I might return to the confusing world of childhood. I felt doomed to bang my head against the wall again by repeating last term: work ethic, failure, and all. I was so hysterical that my parents feared I might try to harm myself; Mom was prepared to make the 520-mile drive here in a severe snowstorm. But after a long conversation, I finally stabilized, exhausted from all the pain and tears. I fell asleep that night feeling that I had the love of my family, but definitely nothing else.

Although I never again hit a point that low, I spent the first few weeks of my winter term merely existing. I lost my appetite, my enjoyment of academia, and my faith that the world could be fair. I spent about a month in counseling, which I didn't find that helpful except that I started to talk out my feelings. The counselor couldn't grasp the extent to which my learning disabilities had affected and were still affecting me, which was the heart of my problem.

I found much more comfort talking with the woman whom I'd once thought of as a meddling troublemaker, who had now become a dear, understanding friend: Mary Fox. The time we spent together was extremely productive and meaningful. Mary has learning and hearing disabilities herself, which helped her get right to the heart of the things that were bothering me. She knew that just because I'd been able to compensate for my disabilities didn't mean I hadn't suffered in the process. She also realized that being at college meant a lot less to me than actually being happy with myself for one moment in my life, and she thought these values were in the right place. One might say that Mary and I couldn't help but bond because of our similarities, but people with learning disabilities are just as different from one another as those without. And no, the term *learning-disabled* doesn't bother me; I think if you make the term too euphemistic, people won't realize how hard you've had to work to achieve your goals. By talking with Mary, I gained such pride in myself in terms of dealing with my learning disabilities, and she will always be a pivotal person in my life.

I have often wondered what kind of person I would have become had my learning disabilities been diagnosed earlier. My first instinct is to think that an early diagnosis would have been detrimental because I would have known that I had a legitimate excuse not to excel academically, and I would likely not be so motivated to learn. It is, after all, this attribute that I take the most pride in. My motivation makes me my own hero, for I've never met anyone willing to struggle as long or hard on anything as I am. With an early diagnosis, I would also likely have been placed in special education classes. As it was, some of my teachers wanted to put me in special education, but Mom and Dad resisted the suggestion. I needed the push of a regular curriculum and later a gifted-and-talented program to achieve what I have today. Without the challenge of these classes, I could not possibly have qualified for the opportunity that I have at college today. Nevertheless, I can't deny the emotional cost of being diagnosed late. Mom often cries about the fact that it took us so long to recognize my learning disabilities, as well as the related psychological costs. Had we known earlier, a psychologist could have helped me combat some of the painful realities I'm facing now, which are much bigger and more impenetrable than they would have been as a child. Though it's so frustrating to think I might have been helped earlier, I simply have to exert myself to bring my self-esteem up to the point my success says it deserves to be.

I have known since the fifth grade that I wanted to be a clinical psychologist. I sometimes worry that my interest in psychology is a way to avoid dealing with my own emotional problems; it is certainly much less painful to deal with others' problems than my own. Still, I am actively engaged enough in helping myself and having others help me, and I feel I am ready to be a helper as well. My family and I only recently realized the emotional toll my learning disabilities have taken on me, and if I can prevent that pain from afflicting one other person, I will have done the job I feel destined to do.

I believe being intelligent and learning-disabled is one of the hardest predicaments a person can find herself in: to have trouble understanding, but also to *know* that you're not understanding. The worst part is that other people can't see that something is different about you. They can't understand why you're preoccupied with self-esteem and happiness. I have cried out many times to this world that may never understand me, "If I have to be learning-disabled, I'd rather be stupid!" In retrospect, however, I feel that I have been very lucky. Being learning-disabled and intelligent presents a precarious paradox. Well-intentioned experts who don't know the best way to help people struggling with such a paradox could destroy hopes and dreams. I hate to imagine how much less I would be without parents who refused to give up on me, even after so many doctors did. I thank God that each event in my life has occurred as it has, for I fear that one slight change in the decisions my family and I have made might have rendered me anything but a survivor. My confidence hasn't caught up yet, but with my motivation and the support of my family and friends, I believe I just might make it.

Case 17

HOLDING MY BREATH

ANDY PRESTON

DOI: 10.4324/9781003165378-21

Andy Preston

As a senior in college, Andy looks back on significant relationships with his friends and finds that they have helped him learn to be more comfortable with who he is. When he gives up his childhood love of theater and turns to sports in middle school, he assumes a masculine identity that remains important to him, even as he becomes more convinced of his homosexuality. In college, through friendships and romantic relationships, Andy learns to accept all aspects of who he is. He also finds that by being himself, he can contribute to change and the growth of others.

When I woke up that Tuesday morning and jumped down from the top bunk, my legs felt especially sore. The post-season lifting schedule is considerably more grueling than in-season. Lacrosse had gone on for four months. Once the season ended, we started lifting at full blast: front squats, back squats, single-leg squats, off-bench squats, cleans, pulls, jerks. As I landed on the ground, 6 feet down from my bed, my quadriceps felt the impact.

I showered, shaved, brushed my teeth, and put my contacts in like any normal morning. Except I went over the conversation I was about to have so many times in the shower that my fingers turned prune-like after half an hour and that made it more difficult to hold my contacts. My fingers were almost insensitive to the touch of the small plastic objects, and it took me a few extra minutes before I finally got them in my eyes and the fuzzy world became visible. Back in my room, I paced back and forth, repeating words and phrases in my head. None of them sounded right. So I cleaned up the common room as one of my roommates remained sleeping in the bedroom. I straightened up all of the papers on the desk. I put all of the clothes from the chair away in the closet. I put my books on the shelf. None of these mindless actions could take my brain away from the task at hand.

I had worried for the last five years of my life how I would ever tell my parents that I was gay. But when I finally got the words out of my mouth with my mother sitting 3 feet away from me, my breathing finally slowed down. It didn't matter what came of it—whether she came over and kissed me or got right back in her car and drove home. She did neither. In my imagination, she was supposed to break into tears and tremble and hold my hand and say, "I love you." In my mind we were going to sit together and cry out our feelings and emotions. My mother seemed to have neither at the moment. She simply sat on that couch and told me that she and my father would always love me no matter what.

I showed her a picture of my boyfriend, Adam, and she smiled. She told me that she was just glad I would not have to do this alone, and then she strayed from the topic of homosexuality. I was ready to talk. This was the morning I had chosen to open up to my mother, to tell her the secret burden I had been carrying for too long, and here she was, essentially telling me that it was silly for me to have kept the secret. Why did I think it would be so upsetting to her? Why did I choose to let this eat me up inside when there was nothing to fear on the outside? She acted as if this was any other day of my life.

We went out to lunch, and then I took her to meet Adam. In my mother's attempt to avoid any awkwardness, she gave him a big hug (a welcome to the family kind of thing) and blabbered on for a while about nothing of any importance. When she left, I felt changed. I tried to remember my last family phone call, so I could remember it as the last time I would ever have to lie about who I was dating. Adam hugged me and told me how proud of me he was for coming out to my mother. He felt relieved. I didn't. The worst is yet to come, I thought, when my father hears the news.

The next morning, I awoke to read this e-mail in my in-box:

Hi:
I have one million questions for you—and when you are ready to talk, I am ready to listen. Every night, after going to sleep, we wake up in the morning. As a father, husband, parent, educator, and health care professional, I can honestly say that it is my lifelong experience that one's sexual preference is not the issue—the central issue is that when you wake up you are excited with what you will be accomplishing during the upcoming day. Your dreams, goals, and enthusiasm for life are what really count. What we want to do with our precious and precarious lives and how we want to share the joy of living with others is really what this is all about. I am writing this note to tell you that I love you, am very proud of you, and look forward to some frank discussion with you when you come home soon.
—Dad x0x0x0x0x

I started to cry. I needed to read the note again to make sure that my brain was not playing tricks on me. There was no way that I had just received that note from my father. For ten years, I had thought about members of the same sex. For five years, I had actually thought about the reality of being gay. For the last three, I had wrestled with my life, staying up all night unable to fall asleep because I was worried about how my parents would react. Adam handed me a tissue. Part of me was shaking and the other part of me was completely at rest.

When I was younger, I used to wish for bad parents. I used to wish that my parents fought, or that they would get divorced, so that when I turned out to be really screwed up, everyone would know whom to blame. I hoped that they would stop loving me, so that I could pretend I was doing this to get back at them. But as I walked up toward class that morning, I knew how glad I was that my wish had not come true. My father had just told me that he loved me and was very proud of me. In class that morning, my friends asked me what was wrong, since my eyes looked red. I told them that I was just tired. It was true. I was tired of hiding my life from the ones who gave me life. I was tired of feeling guilty for something I never had control over, not a single day in my twenty years of existence. I was tired of worrying that nobody would accept me.

A week and a half later, my father took me out for a lobster dinner—my favorite meal—to open me up. As we drove out to the restaurant, I didn't worry about the things I used to worry about. Instead, I worried that my father would not be able to handle all the answers to his questions. How would he reconcile being blind to my sexuality for so long?

He grilled me about everything during our dinner. As we buttered our rolls, he asked me when I first knew that I was gay. "When I was 19 years old," I told him, "because I knew I would never love my current girlfriend. But really, it was when I was 13 years old, because I started to fantasize about the same sex. And I can trace it back to being aroused when I was 6 or 7. But actually, I remember when I was 4 years old, my friend Rod and I would lie on top of each other naked." My father gasped at this last remark. How could I claim to have known that I was gay at 4 years old?

By the time the clam chowders were served, we were well into my high-school experience. He asked what it was like to hide this from everyone and I told him how awful it really was. He sympathized with me, but he found it difficult to match my emotions. His life works scientifically. There is always an explanation and something that we can learn from everything. We talked about the importance of trust and communication. I saw something new in his eyes. Was this man, in his midfifties, trying to tear down all the walls I had built and find out who his son really was? Every once in a while, he would pause and look down, unable to understand how he had let me feel so badly about myself, or how he had not been there when his son needed him. I tried to console him, saying, "Dad, I spent my entire adolescence trying to hide this from you. I became a pretty good liar, even to myself. How could you have seen this coming when I did everything I could to paint a different picture for you?"

I was full after that meal. My father was still full of questions. He would never see the world in the same way again. He had to turn his world upside down in order to understand me and fit my life into it. The whole stigma of homosexuality was now part of his life, whether he liked it or not. In time, he could make adjustments to his world, to allow the current situation to make sense, but he could never go back to the way it was. That world no longer existed. He could never again look at a gay couple and wonder who made them turn out like that. When he heard a fellow doctor make an off-color joke about homosexuality, he had to speak up now, because it was my father's world that the doctor was making fun of.

Growing up I had every advantage that a Jewish kid from the suburbs would want, from private schools to youth sports to sleep-away camps. At the age of 5, I entered kindergarten in a private school where my sister and brother were in the fourth and sixth grades, respectively. In second grade I started attending Hebrew school three times a week, and that didn't stop until seventh grade when I had my Bar Mitzvah.

My early love was theater. By age 6, I was creating my own musicals, writing the scripts and the music, and recruiting friends to perform my plays. In third grade, I joined a theater troupe with my friend Evan; we were the two youngest members of the group made up of mostly fourth, fifth, and sixth graders. When some scouts from the Boston theater district came to watch us rehearse, I was asked to audition for the role of Tiny Tim in *A Christmas Carol*. I was chosen as an understudy for the character and later received roles as a child in two other professional plays. It seemed that my life was set; my goal was to grow up to be a Hollywood or Broadway actor.

Throughout my acting days, my sister and brother often tormented me for being too artistic. I learned to associate arts with something bad, something nobody wanted to be connected with. My sister and brother would throw around the term "gay" without really thinking about sexual orientation. To them it was just an insult, something that little boys are supposed to avoid. They knew that it was more "gay" to write plays than to play sports, so I was surrounded by these ideas at an early age. One afternoon, before an evening performance at a professional play in Boston, my father handed me the new issue of *Time*.

Andy Preston

The cover read "AIDS and the Arts." The discussion that followed left me horrified. He asked me repeatedly if the men with whom I performed had tried to touch me in strange places. If his intention was to turn me away from the stage, he succeeded—that was the final professional play of my life. I never believed that my father was insinuating anything about me, or that he meant to do me any harm. As a doctor, he spends his life trying to improve health, and as a father, he wants the best for his children. But in trying to protect me, he alienated me. I knew I could no longer feel proud of my accomplishments around him.

Starting the summer after third grade, I traveled up to East Falls, New Hampshire—a town too small for its own post office—for overnight camp: eight weeks of sports, campfires, and cabin fights, culminating in an event called "color war," which I had the misfortune to lose for four straight years. It was at camp where I first developed strong friendships with boys of completely different backgrounds. Each year, we would come back to see each other, one year older, and we would hope to be placed in the same cabin as our buddies.

The first time I can remember being sexually aroused was during the second summer at camp, when I was 10 years old, watching one of my bunkmates change out of his bathing suit. It was my first real erection, and I didn't know what it meant. A few weeks later, another bunkmate was given a *Playboy* from his older brother, and we all sat around a bed and flipped through the pages, noting how hairy some of the girls were and rating their breasts. When a buddy asked if I was getting hard looking at the girls, I told him I didn't know. I asked him if he was hard, and he said of course, that he always got hard looking at naked girls. I noted this, and also thought about my first erection earlier that summer. How funny that mine came from an undressing buddy while his came from a silly magazine.

My camp had a big teepee right in front of the main lodge, and the director said that on special occasions a few campers could have the privilege of sleeping in the teepee for a night. So during my third year at camp, five of us decided to drag our sleeping bags down to the lodge and spend a night under the stars. We didn't anticipate the rain soaking us, nor did we plan the events of that night. I can't remember how it started, but I do remember another boy and I coupling off into one sleeping bag. Two others boys followed along, both in the same bag. The fifth boy put his head inside his sleeping bag and pulled the string tight so that he could not see what was going on.

We decided to pretend that we were boy and girl, acting like lovers, since we were 11 and did not know exactly how everything worked. We

332

had our pants on during the entire scene, but our shirts were off and our hands were exploring each other's bodies. It felt so great to me, but I didn't know if I was supposed to enjoy it or not. My hand went up and down his back and I felt every bone and every bump from his shoulder blades down to his buttocks. One of the boys in the other two-man sleeping bag said that he was getting hard and asked if that made him gay. The other boy in his bag proclaimed that it meant nothing, that obviously we were all imitating having sex with women and that getting hard was just a consequence of this role-playing. We were just perfectly regular guys using each other to feel what older guys got to feel all the time.

When we woke up the next morning, we vowed not to mention what had happened the night before. We said we'd forget what happened, but I couldn't. I developed feelings for the other boy who shared my sleeping bag with me, and I think he felt the same way. We spent a lot of time together, but we never repeated what we had done in the teepee. Maybe we were in denial, or maybe we didn't understand our desires, but we were able to maintain a unique friendship without speaking directly about that night. You could argue that this was the first "homosexual" relationship of my life, but at that age we did what we enjoyed doing and didn't think much of it.

The summer after sixth grade my father again took me aside and told me that I was going to play football. He told me that I wanted to be tough, not a sissy, and that playing football would not only teach me to be tough, but it would show people exactly what type of person I was. "If you want to be cool," he told me, "you should play football and quit all of the acting business. You don't want to be a sissy, do you?"

When he told me not to be a sissy, we both knew what he was trying to say: acting would make me gay while football would be the answer to everyone's prayers. My older siblings had been calling me gay for years for all of the singing and acting I did, and here my dad was telling me that I could forget all of that and start a new identity in middle school as a football player. There was a part of me that hated my dad for telling me to give up something that I loved so much. To assume that he could change me by changing my after-school interests was naïve of him, but, at the same time, I understood that he loved me and wanted what was best for me. In his eyes, I would benefit from my peers approving of me.

My athletic career took off from there. We had been a sports family for as long as I could remember. I loved sports and they came naturally to me. I guess sports were just overshadowed by what seemed like my more natural talent: acting. I left the stage behind almost cold turkey and dove right into the athletic world.

I became best friends with Austin in eighth grade, my second year in middle school and my second year of football. Austin had a thin build, brown hair, and a boyish face, and was almost a foot taller than me. We bonded during the seventh-grade football season. That first year I was clueless on the field and almost never got into the game. I didn't even know all of the rules. But during the summer after seventh grade, Austin and I went to football camp and I learned how to be a receiver and a running back. By eighth grade I led the middle school team in touchdowns. Austin and I became inseparable for the next few years. For a 13-year-old who recognizes his interests in other boys, the ideal relationship is with your best friend. I figured we could be best friends, and in private we could be boyfriends. Nobody would question us since we spent so much time together anyway. What I didn't know was that he never shared this fantasy with me.

While on a vacation to the Caribbean with my family, Austin and I were playing tackle football in the pool. As the contact increased, so did my arousal level. As I pulled him down in the water, I made sure to brush by his waist and let him know of my interest. Later, when we were back in our room watching television, I decided to continue our little game. Without saying a word to each other, I brought Austin to climax. He could argue that he was imagining a female with him and that I was the only thing he had to get him off. But the truth is that we had taken part in homosexual activity without speaking. Incidents like this occurred on more than one occasion, but he never initiated any of them. Perhaps to him it was just messing around with a friend. We never once talked about the few incidents, but I thought it was all understood. I, the initiator, wanted to continue that part of our relationship; he didn't want to talk about it.

By early junior year in high school, Austin and his girlfriend started sleeping together and I knew that I had lost him for good. He pressured me to find a girl of my own and sleep with her, but I wasn't interested. The guy I fell for let me down; he switched over to the straight side and tried to drag me over with him. I couldn't change though. I was gay. While I may have been unable to say it out loud, I knew it then for sure.

I came to college with the intention of fitting in, being like everyone else, and graduating without attracting too much attention. I didn't envision life beyond college because, for me, there was no imaginable life. What gay role models did I have? My uncle and his boyfriend of twenty years? My family had made fun of them and their lifestyle since I was a baby. My understanding of grown-up gay men was that they were unhappy and disliked. This was hardly how I wanted to spend my life, so I blocked adulthood out of my mind. I imagined life until graduation and after that I figured I would disappear. I would go and live the life I wanted without worrying about how I would be judged. Thinking back, it's funny to even consider disappearing into obscurity. I have never been one to sit in the background and let others steal the show. That is not me.

As soon as I got to college, I met three of my future lacrosse teammates. We spent the first few weeks of school together while the rest of the class ran through orientation meetings and scavenger hunts and carnivals. I always knew that my teammates respected me for my abilities on the field, but I was worried about portraying the part of a heterosexual college athlete off the field. One night, early in our first term, a few of my teammates and I ended up in the dining hall on our way from one fraternity to another. When the first cute blonde girl walked by our table, each of my teammates followed her closely with their eyes. Did they notice that I forgot to pay particular attention to the blonde girl? Perhaps they were too distracted to see.

Driving to the fields one afternoon during fall practices a senior turned right to me and said, "Hey, what's your story? I never hear about you with the ladies. Do you get around?" I hesitated. A few seconds later, I managed a laugh. As I was about to respond with something like "I'm not quite the player that you are," my roommate and best friend Chris jumped in and saved me. "He holds his own." And just like that, it was done. All it took was one sentence, one claim from a reliable source, and my manhood was restored. I didn't have to provide evidence, names, and descriptions of each girl I had been with. I didn't even have to say a word. Chris saved me that time. I didn't know how much longer I could keep up the act.

When I later ended up telling Chris the truth, he shrugged his shoulders, smiled, and gave me a high-five. That was Chris in a nutshell. He had a way of simplifying everything. Maybe he had really known all along and didn't need to make a big deal of it. Maybe it just didn't matter to him. He confirmed his confidence in me as a friend with a simple high-five. Why did something like this stress me out so much when I had friends who responded by giving me a high-five and a pat on the back?

During my sophomore year, as I was coming out, I roomed with Chris and Shane. Shane, my roommate for most of freshman year, was a fairly good-looking guy with brown hair who came from San Francisco.

He was laid-back, he liked to party, and we spent a lot of time together. I think Shane trusted me, and he appreciated my ability to make friends. We joked together, listened to music together, and most importantly we enjoyed each other's company. I felt that I had accomplished something important my freshman year, finding a quality friend at college.

While I didn't see Shane as the ideal mate, I certainly saw more than just a good friend. Many times, we would be up late at night studying, and we would end up getting into a wrestling match. If he ever sensed that I had become aroused by the physical contact, he never pulled back. I don't think that Shane was aroused in the same way that I was, but I am sure that he also saw me as more than just a close friend.

During my first three terms at college, I had experienced kissing and other intimate activities with girls on a few occasions, but I always came away from these nights feeling guilt from being unable to enjoy these "normal" activities, fear that the girl would see my lack of desire and tell on me, and a strange pleasure from participating in something that is supposed to bring me joy. At a dance party one night, Shane, seeing me turn down girls who might have been potential hookups, told two female friends that he thought I must be gay. The girls soon told me that my roommate and supposed best friend had been spreading a rumor about me. Completely uncomfortable with this situation, I laughed it off, thinking that my relaxed attitude would show these girls that I was clearly straight.

For three months, Shane and I continued to hang out and eat meals together, and we pledged the same fraternity at the beginning of the winter term. But there was no longer any depth to our relationship. It was clear what had driven us apart: he assumed I was gay and not telling him, while I was offended that he had spread rumors about me. I wrestled with the thought of coming out every day that fall term.

For years, I had considered myself gay, and I hadn't really questioned it in recent memory. But believing something and saying it out loud are two totally different things. When my friend Caitlin was over at my room one afternoon, I leaned toward her and whispered to her through cupped hands, "I'm gay." In saying these two words, it was like I truly became a homosexual. Up until that point, I only thought my homosexuality was something that could come true. But once those words were out of my mouth, I could never take them back. Caitlin shook her head in disbelief and repeated to me numerous times, "That's not a funny joke. I know you are kidding and it isn't funny." I put her hand up against my chest and she felt how fast my heart was beating. It took her twenty minutes of head shaking before she apologized for making this so difficult and not believing me in the first place. Caitlin was the only one I told for quite some time, but eventually I was able to say the words out loud and not feel bad about what I was saying.

My relationship with Shane was still fairly weak, and I felt partially responsible. So one night, instead of going to bed early as was my custom, I decided I would make the effort and appeal to him by staying up and making something of our broken friendship.

"Uhh … this is pretty hard to say. I feel like you know what I'm going to say but here goes. All that stuff you said about me, what you thought about me, well, you were right."

"Yeah I know, dude. No worries."

"Ha. Well, it has been pretty difficult for me trying to deal with everything and it didn't help much that you were spreading shit around. I don't know why you would have done that to me." He seemed to understand where I was coming from, and he apologized for the way he had handled it. That night we reestablished a closeness that we hadn't felt since our freshman year, and maybe formed a deeper friendship than ever.

Adam, an older brother in the fraternity I had just joined, e-mailed me one night after a frat event and asked me if I wanted to get something to eat with him. Adam was about five-foot-ten, with a muscular build and gorgeous blue-green eyes. He was one of the better-looking seniors in school and he was openly gay. After a crazy night of drinking that next weekend, I awoke to read this e-mail in my in-box the next morning:

> Hey, here's the bottom line. I have a bit of a crush on you. I am really drunk tonight and I'm letting it all out. Sorry if this is not what you asked for by joining a fraternity. You seem like such a great guy and I don't want you to be unhappy …

Despite some of the drunken rambling, it appeared that he had made the first move. I wrote him back and explained to him that I understood his actions and that I was indeed gay. He asked me to meet up with him that night so we could talk.

I told my roommates that I was going to the library to meet a friend to go over some organic chemistry problems. I met Adam at his car; he suggested that I might feel more relaxed getting away from campus. Something about the comfort in his voice made me forget all about any sexual attraction I had for him. I thought, "Here is this guy who came out to his entire fraternity and even took a guy to his formal.

337

He knows what it is like and he can show me the ropes and help me along." When I looked over at this handsome guy, I saw a big brother, a mentor. He told me about coming out to his family, how difficult that had been for him, but how easy they had made it for him. Adam kept trying to get me to speak, to open up, but I preferred to listen.

We drove through back roads on a lightly snowing night, and the car went in and out of lighted areas, in and out of the shadows. I thought, "If my roommates knew I was driving around the dark areas of town with a homosexual, what would they think of me?" We drove by a familiar road that I remembered running once with my teammates in daylight. I thought about my teammates, seeing me now in this car. When other cars drove by, I turned to the side so they couldn't make out my identity.

Just before returning to my dorm, Adam pulled the car over in a shaded area. He started to breathe heavily and he started to babble something like, "Should I do it?" I asked him what was going on, and he just looked over and smiled. He reached his hand across my face. With this soft grip, he pulled my head toward his and we kissed. His heart was beating fast. I could feel his nervousness, but I did not share it. Perhaps I would have been more nervous if I had thought about it. But instead, I was thinking about the past, and how many kisses I had taken part in without feeling anything. The only kisses that I could remember were for show. In this car, I wanted to kiss him more. His lips, slightly chapped from the cold weather, met mine. His beard against my face was a new feeling. It was almost like I could feel his manliness rubbing against my face. My heart didn't start beating fast until he returned me to my dorm, when I thought of two things: how incredible that moment, my first kiss, was, and what I was going to tell my roommates.

After another evening in his car, I told Adam that we would have to choose a warmer spot. Those big winter jackets were ruining the moment. Adam and I agreed to meet in the library up in the stacks, an obscure area only inhabited during exams. Just being here with him was cause for concern, since he was openly gay. Someone who happened to go looking for an East Asian book at this time of night might stumble upon the two of us and piece things together. Sometimes I would close my eyes, clench my fists, and pray that I would not get caught. Other times I wished that somebody would just find me so I could end the whole charade and just bring Adam to my room like everyone else did with their girlfriends.

On Valentine's Day I told Adam that I wanted to spend the night with him more than anything. This was Valentine's Day, the day people spend with their special someone. I put on my khaki pants, a nice collared shirt, and I met Adam for dinner. On my way out the door, a few friends asked if I was going on a date, and I gave them a crazy look as if to say, "Me? Of course not. You guys know that I don't go on dates."

At dinner I told Adam that I wanted to get away from school with him, so that we could share this special night together. Each time I expressed this interest, he countered by reminding me that his room was only a five-minute walk down the path. I knew that. I also knew that he had three apartment-mates who were all in my fraternity. I couldn't bear to think that someone might see me walking into a room and immediately think "gay." Most of the older brothers in my fraternity thought of me first as the lacrosse player. I wanted them to get to know me before making judgments, but I didn't particularly mind the stereotype of the lacrosse player as it associated me with traditional masculine stereotypes. Being thought of as gay, however, evoked just the opposite stereotypes.

Eventually I gave in, willingly, but also feeling as though I was holding my breath under water and praying not to drown. I stood in the doorway at Adam's apartment unsure if I wanted to show my face. I took a deep breath and stepped around the corner. Bob, Adam's roommate and our fraternity brother, smiled and held out his hand to give me a high-five; Bob's girlfriend, Jennifer, said that it was good to see me again. Adam's eyes closed up just a bit as he smiled, one of those "I'm so proud of you and I don't want to forget this moment" type of smiles. Adam and I sat down next to each other on the couch, and I was sure that Bob and Jennifer would be completely conscious of every move that we made. I was wrong though. Holding hands, we watched television like any normal couple on Valentine's Day, and Bob and Jennifer couldn't have cared less about us. Bob was entranced by the show, laughing at every mildly funny joke. Jennifer, as self-conscious as anyone, was probably too worried about how she came off to notice me. As the evening went on, I began to undergo a transformation. I knew I wouldn't be instantly comfortable with this new self, but it was starting to grow on me.

After walking into his room Adam locked the door behind us, and I felt like we were alone, somewhere far off, like nobody could get to us now. He gave me a huge hug, as was his ritual, but this time our shirts were off and our chests met for the first time. He had a little bit of hair, but his chest was muscular, and you could feel the divisions of his abdominals. When we got into bed, everything felt so natural. It was one of those small college beds, wide enough for only one, so he slept on his back, and I slept on his chest. I turned my head to the side so that his shoulder became my pillow, and I lay down to sleep with my boyfriend, like lovers do on Valentine's Day.

We fell in love over the long, dark, cold winter at school. It happened on nights like our joy ride in the fogged-up car, or when we waltzed across the frozen pond at two in the morning one night in February, or as we sat inside with hot chocolate as the wind howled down the street toward the river. I looked at him and saw a beautiful human being. Beyond his looks, he was an incredible person who thought of others before himself. He spent his afternoons with under-privileged children in the area and wanted to teach in the Bronx public schools after graduation. Besides all of this, he always showed a great deal of faith in me. I saw him as a role model as well as a boyfriend, and I saw no reason to break up in June. We said "I love you" to each other after we got back from a two-week spring break period without each other, and we never stopped saying it. Soon we would say the words so often that it began to feel like a greeting. Adam was my first love, and for this reason, I will always vividly remember moments spent with him.

We decided that as long as we cared about each other this much and weren't hurting anybody, we should stay together after his graduation. I was off from school in the fall term, and being away from school was a much different experience than being a student. I went to work each morning, came home each afternoon, went to the gym, ate dinner, watched a little television, and went to bed to get some rest for work the next day. Every night before bed, Adam and I would talk on the phone and tell each other about how our days had gone. On weekends we would visit each other, and this became our motivation to get through the week.

All of this changed when I was back at school for winter term and Adam was still away. I no longer had a set schedule, and I wasn't always free at any point in the evening to call Adam. He got upset because he was used to stability, part of which was hearing my voice before he went to sleep. When he told me that he thought about me all day and couldn't wait to talk to me, I would have to be honest and tell him that he hadn't crossed my mind all day and that I couldn't really talk more than a few minutes.

Winter term was pledge term and one of the new pledges happened to be a boy on whom I had had my eye for over a year. Keith lived on my hall that year and something about him—maybe it was the way he looked at me—made me think that he could be gay as well. We had developed a friendship, and when he pledged my fraternity we got even closer. Many nights we drank together, and I always had a good time. Sometimes I would go home and start fantasizing about Keith, and I wouldn't stop to catch myself just because I was with Adam. I let the fantasies go because in my mind, they were just fantasies—there was no chance that they would come true. I was with Adam.

By March Adam and I both knew it wasn't working. He had emotional needs: someone to talk to on the phone, someone to visit him on weekends, someone to listen to him and care for him. I had little space for someone else in my life, and I resented Adam for making me feel guilty. While we both felt our relationship had deteriorated, we had separate solutions. He wanted us to find a way to make it work, while I found no need to do so. Something in my mind had changed, some critical connection, some brain synapse completely reversed. I felt like he was a lost soul, someone who had fallen into a mild depression with his job and life in a big city, and that I could not be the savior that he wanted or needed. I needed to take care of myself.

I had cut off emotionally from the relationship long before, and by Friday, less than a week after the breakup, I again saw Adam as a friend, a role model. I made a point to go drinking with Keith at the fraternity that night, and when the night was over, I took him back to my room. I had assumed that it would take some convincing, but it didn't. As we walked home from the fraternity, we were in constant physical contact. We elbowed and pushed each other as we walked past the library and up a slight hill to get to the other side of campus where we both lived, and it seemed like our hands were touching so closely that we could have been holding hands. When we reached the point where the paths diverged to his room or mine, I continued on the path to my dorm.

"Where are you going?" he asked.

"To my room. Come." He nodded with a slight smile and followed me to my room. As I unlocked the door and we sat down on my futon a few inches from each other, I realized that I had no prior evidence to suggest that Keith was in fact a homosexual. I had gone on gut instinct up until this point, choosing, unlike Adam, not to e-mail him with my feelings. When I leaned over to kiss him, making the first move as the older, more experienced guy, I recognized a somewhat confused but overjoyed look in his eyes. He had never before kissed a guy, and he had never even imagined this scenario happening in college. His blue hat sat atop his head at a slight angle, and I positioned myself in front of him. He closed his eyes, perhaps not wanting to see what was really happening, and I could feel his breath. It was heavy, and his heart was beating fast, just as Adam's had when he had tried to kiss me the first time. I was not nervous, though, just elated. I had this boy in my room, this boy on whom I had had a crush since I first saw him more than a year and a half before.

Keith has a youthful, boyish look. He swims competitively, and his upper body is strong. Hair covers his upper chest. When one of us lies down on top of the other, Keith is a few inches shorter than me. That night, when I took his lacrosse cap off of his head, I took comfort in the fact that I was in my room alone with the kind of guy who wears a lacrosse cap, the type of guy who nobody would ever imagine to be in my room. Keith doesn't fulfill any of the gay stereotypes. He is the type to take me to a sports bar where people would wonder if we are just buddies or if we are on a date, an aspect of mystery or ambiguity that I enjoy. He has an air of masculinity about him, and this is part of what attracts me to him. We can sit around and push each other and watch sports together. We are best friends, and yet we are so much more than that. This is what I had idealized since I was in seventh grade.

I have learned so much about myself, about the world, and about relationships from my two boyfriends in college. Adam was gay, everyone knew, and he wasn't ashamed. He told me that being gay was a blessing because he had the chance to change people's minds, and that he joined a fraternity because he wanted to teach tolerance to the Greek system. Keith, on the other hand, joined a fraternity because he wanted to meet new people, get closer with the members of his pledge class, and have a good time while at college. His reasons were much more like mine. We both like the party scene, the brother bonding activities, and the tight friendships that we have made.

I have always been a fairly public and social member of my fraternity, and when I came out, nothing changed. My brothers respected me for who I was, and we never had any problems. I never meant to change anyone's mind, as Adam did, but just my presence and my confidence as one of the guys changed the way people acted in a positive way. For instance, when our social chair tells us about our parties, he tells us to "feel free to invite all significant others to the pre-party," a subtle change from saying, "bring a girlfriend," something he said he did for me. Dating one of my fraternity brothers has been a touchy subject for some, but they were never vocal about it. Most of the guys were fine with it.

Being gay is a reality for me, something that was probably determined by the time I came out of my mother's womb. I haven't openly questioned why it happened to me in many years. At certain times, being gay has made me privileged. I have had the chance to affect many more people as an openly gay athlete or member of a fraternity than I would have otherwise. Being an athlete has always given me some sort of crutch in order to feel comfortable and secure with myself. Athletics are often associated with masculinity, and I have always used this conception to forge my identity. Perhaps I am a homosexual, but nobody perceives me as weak or feminine.

Coming into my senior year, I knew the younger members of the gay community at school would look up to me, and I thought that I should take a more active role in that community. I am now an officer in the Gay Straight Alliance, where we meet once a week and discuss important gay issues on the campus and beyond. It is a great chance to get to know guys a few years below me who are going through a lot of the same experiences I did. Now I see freshmen who have already come out to their friends and who contemplate joining a fraternity as an openly gay pledge, something I never imagined. At our weekly meetings, we often look at the state of gay rights in the country today. I have never been extremely interested in politics, but the Massachusetts Supreme Court ruling in 2003 inspired me, and I am not about to give up the right to equal marriage. Half a century ago, people said that interracial marriages were wrong and unnatural. Even though the courts saw this as discriminatory, it took another ten years for the country to recognize legal interracial marriages. Now that the courts have found discrimination in our current laws, how much longer must we wait while our country again holds back equal rights to its citizens?

As I look back at my college career, I am glad that I have figured things out in time to really enjoy myself. My original intention to leave college without making much noise, without impacting people or leaving my mark, failed, and I am extremely happy about that. Through college, I met a few people who convinced me to do my own thing, and I know that I benefited from this advice. Now when I get the chance to talk to younger guys, guys who still have important decisions to make in their college years, I tell them to be themselves, do what matters to them, and their friends will be there. I hope they listen to me, and I hope their time in college is as rewarding as mine has been.

For many years I worried about how I was going to come out to family. Now my mother, father, sister, and brother are the most supportive people in my life. My parents continue to love me; my mother brags about my accomplishments to her friends and my father keeps pictures from my athletic career in his office. This past winter, Keith came with me on a family ski trip, joining my sister and her boyfriend, and my brother and his wife. Both of my siblings are older than me, both are in serious relationships, and, for a few years, I had felt a distance between us. Part of me wanted to show them that my relationship is no different, that our relationship can last as long as theirs. On that ski trip, it was clear that the distance no longer remained. We treat each other like we always have, only now we respect each other as adults. In the end, I have learned that all romantic relationships are made up of the same components. There is intimacy. There is passion. There is love. Adam and I had all three of these. Keith and I are lucky because we are also best friends. Our relationship is not different from any other college relationship. We go on dates, go to dance parties together, go to formal occasions together, and we wake up in the morning after spending the night together. After college, we would like to share a life, a family. It might be a little more difficult to have children, but we will have them and they will be loved as much as any children on this earth. For the rest of my life, I know that I will encounter people who do not understand me. I also know that I will continue to affect others, because I can change people's minds simply by being honest and by being true to myself.

Follow-up

ANDY: FIVE YEARS LATER

DOI: 10.4324/9781003165378-22

I am one of the lucky ones. I don't say those words often enough, but I know how true they are. At age 27 I haven't yet acquired enough experience to lecture about life's lessons learned, but if I look back a decade at the frightened 17-year-old that I was, I can tell him confidently that I have made it out the other side. I like to think about my life the way it is now—stable and full of happiness. The major issues I faced at 17 have been figured out or reduced to minor problems by 27. But the painful reality is that it wasn't always so perfect. It is hard to go back there, but it is important to remember what it was really like. It was scary, but I know now it was not the end of the story. I still don't know the end, but I do know that things are really good—great, in fact. I never could have predicted being here at the time I had so many doubts and worries.

At 17, I was certain of only one thing—I was different. At that age, being different really makes you just like everyone else, but you feel as if you are completely alone. I kept my secret to myself for a few more thought-filled, painful years. I occasionally dreamed of telling my close friends; I even wrote a letter to one friend explaining everything, but I never had the courage to take it out of my dresser and was afraid my mother would somehow discover it. So I kept it all inside and thought about ways to escape.

Sports ruled my life at that time, and I constantly feared that my teammates would figure out my secret and reject me. Writing that sentence is so much easier than living through it was. My friends and I spent time together every day. We hung out in the locker room, practiced for several hours, grabbed dinner together. On weekends, we traveled to away games. We would sit together in a bus and then compete as a team. All of those shared experiences, all that trust necessary between teammates—and yet I was so afraid of what would happen if my teammates found out.

You know how guys are with girls that they like? They get a little nervous and their breathing is heavier—sometimes it is visibly noticeable. As I sat next to my teammates on the bus or in the locker room, I tried so hard to control my heart rate and my breathing because I feared they might somehow suspect my sexuality by the pace of my chest rising up and down. I acted as straight as humanly possible when I sensed any suspicion from my teammates. It was a ridiculous fear; each guy in that locker room probably had his own issues to worry about— whether it was about a girl, family, schoolwork, friends, etc.—but how could I have known that at the time? I lived in fear each moment.

I did not value my life. At first, taking my life was just a passing thought, but it became much more than that. It is no secret that gay and lesbian teenagers are the number-one risk group for committing suicide. Ending one's life becomes a realistic option for getting rid of the secret without having to go through the pain of coming out. It offers a way to avoid having to tell the truth to family, friends, the world. I shudder at the thought of suicide entering the discussion at any level. Sometimes people throw it out as a threat to someone else, as if they might end their life and leave the other person with the guilt. But actually contemplating suicide—that is something far different, far scarier. Nobody can go to that dark place with you and bring you back to reality. I have never really admitted how real that felt until now. But with the confidence gained from how my life has turned out, I can go there now and remember the pain I struggled with. The best decision that I ever made was to ignore those dark thoughts.

Although as a teenager I could not have believed it possible, I came out while still a competitive athlete. Afterwards I continued to play sports successfully and even had a brief professional career. My teammates' support was crucial during the coming-out process. They got past the gay issue so quickly that I never really had to deal with it. I came out one day, and the next time I saw them it was an accepted fact. They never resented me; instead, they appreciated and loved me for my honesty. After all, I exposed them to something new, something that forced them to question their assumptions. After coming out there was nothing holding us apart, and my sexuality actually ended up bringing me closer to my teammates. Would that 17-year-old believe me? I wish he could have known it would be okay, could have known that he would not have to give up any of his dreams in sports in order to be out. In fact, I eventually had the opportunity to make a huge impact on thousands of people by telling my story openly. I wish I had not worried so much that it would be revealed that I am gay and thus end my athletic career. Many people have taken the time to tell me that my courage in sharing my story made their life easier and relieved them of some of their own big worries.

Finding Happiness at Home and at Work

When I was 17, I was so afraid of not fitting in that I tried to date and hook up with girls. It took careful planning to feign interest without getting found out. I always had an excuse for avoiding sex. I complained about my sports injuries or being tired or intoxicated—or worse, I would blame the girl for not turning me on enough. Inevitably, you end up hurting the girls you pretend to go after and I know I caused a lot of pain by continuing with these efforts, but what was I supposed to do? I can remember having a girlfriend over to my house and being so relieved to find out that she was having her period—an easy excuse for keeping things non-sexual. But she deserved a guy who genuinely wanted to be with her, not someone using her as a cover. Over time, it became more difficult to fool the girls and each relationship had to end. I remember discussing life plans with one of my girlfriends who was probably smart enough to put all the pieces together, due to my continuous excuses for avoiding intimate moments. When I mentioned having kids—at some point in my life, not necessarily with her—she acted surprised that I saw them in my future. It struck me that she would question it, and it was something I never forgot. I still want kids, but I want to share them with a partner.

I have fallen in love, several times in fact. I have experienced the real emotions of love and jealousy and a broken heart. Keith and I continued to date for several years after I wrote my original story. Looking back at what I thought I wanted and what I liked about my relationship with Keith—the masculinity and the mystery—it couldn't be further from the way I now feel. Those things probably had more to do with my own insecurities. I enjoyed not being labeled gay and I loved being perceived as a masculine homosexual. Today I no longer want a boyfriend I can go to a sports bar with and "blend in." I want a partnership based on love, mutual respect, trust, and caring. Each of us determines our own level of comfort, and if I want to kiss my boyfriend in the most masculine sports bar in the world, I will do so happily.

Today I have found a level of happiness that I never thought possible—like what you think occurs only in the movies. Three years ago, I became friends with a wonderfully creative, caring man named Jamie. When the timing was right, we found ourselves in each other's arms and we haven't looked back. We support and love each other and we make decisions that benefit us as partners. We live together and we smile together and we experience the joys of life together. Jamie is not my boyfriend. He is my partner. I feel so completely fulfilled and I want everyone to experience this feeling. Most importantly, I want to tell that 17-year-old that he should not worry about love because he will have it. He will have it all.

It is somewhat ironic that I questioned the importance of life at 17 and now am in the business of trying to save lives. After college, I discovered a passion for cancer research. I have almost completed a PhD in biology with a specialty in prostate cancer. I get to use my brain every day to tackle important issues—to challenge and to question and to innovate. Finding something positive that keeps you up at night thinking is rare in life. I love what I am doing, and I want to be a professor with a research lab and teaching responsibilities. In the world of graduate school, I am completely open about my sexuality and Jamie attends lab events regularly. My friends at the school are proud of what I have accomplished in coming out.

Maybe things worked out the way they did for a reason. Maybe I had to experience what I did and reach a critical point inside of me before I could come out to the world. Maybe everything clicked at the right point for me. There is no way to know how my life would have turned out differently if I could have come out at 17. Each gay or lesbian teenager has different circumstances and different timing that works out for him or her. Some are able to come out early, and others wait until years after college to come to terms with being gay. Again, all I can say to my 17-year-old self is that things will work out. Things did work out!

Love and Support of Family

Whether the path is rocky or smooth, every coming-out story is by nature a success story. I know I am one of the lucky ones and that many aren't so lucky. Many never get to come out, never get to be themselves. Many don't get to come out in their own time or on their own terms. I am in the fortunate position of sitting here to reflect on my journey and draw from those factors that may be useful to others who are wondering how their story might turn out. Family is one such factor.

In my original story, I described coming out to my parents. It was difficult for me because, as all closeted people do, I feared being shunned by my family. At the very least, I worried that they would see me differently—not as the person I had always been but as the sexuality that would come to define me. This fear kept me up at night and caused me to be closed off from my parents and siblings. And yet, when it comes to family, I again am one of the lucky ones. Some of my friends have parents who do not believe in homosexuality and continue to set them up with the opposite sex or worse, send them to so-called ex-gay conversion therapists. At our college, the gay and lesbian alumni foundation has a scholarship fund to support students whose parents have refused to pay for their children's education after they come out. It is frightening that parents could be so misguided and completely fail to love and support their own children because of something beyond anyone's control.

This was certainly not the case for me. As I mentioned in the earlier story, my parents never wavered in their love and support. They only were interested in understanding where I was coming from and why I had hidden such a large part of myself from them. Today my mother is one of my biggest advocates. She emails me links about gay rights protests in her area, and she cried in front of my partner and his mother during the Jewish High Holidays when it was her turn to talk about what she was thankful for. She was so proud as a parent to watch her baby achieve the level of love and happiness I have with Jamie.

But in spite of their support, my family and I were not entirely comfortable around each other immediately after I came out. Eventually, however, when I talked to my siblings on the phone, we discussed my relationships openly. I took my various boyfriends home with me to meet the family and we all went on ski trips or beach vacations together. My family had to get to know me with a partner in my life. In some cases, I needed to educate them. My brother-in-law once asked at a family gathering, "Don't gay men want to be women and that's why they date men?" He had no hatred for me or for gay or lesbian people, he simply had no education about homosexuality. That same brother-in-law is now one of my closest friends and one of my biggest advocates. It is not important what his previous knowledge was but where his intentions lay. He has told me he could sense that I was closed off when he first met me and he just wanted to get to know the real me. We bonded over Wiffle ball games in the backyard, over our opposing sides of the Red Sox–Yankees rivalry each summer, and over our similar, easily excitable, always positive personalities. He watched me grow up into a confident young adult and I watched him become an amazing father and husband. We don't ignore my homosexuality now; we continue to discuss and learn about it in a supportive way, together. The same guy who once believed I wanted to be a woman now fully supports his wife, my sister, donating an egg to mix with my partner's sperm so we can create a child, through a surrogate, that has genes from both sides of the family. Most men would not be so giving or understanding. This is how far we all have come as a family. I know how truly fortunate I am.

Recently we had a mini-family reunion, and one of my cousin's sons, who is maybe 8 years old, said to me, "Why did you just kiss that man?" I responded, "Because he is my boyfriend." The boy asked, "Does that mean you are gay?" I said, "Yes, is that okay with you?" He replied "Yup" and got back to playing his game. Later he asked his mother, my cousin, "Did you know that there are two gay people in your family?" and she replied, "Yes, I know." Her son heard the sureness in her voice and quickly realized it was a non-issue. This story shows how casual my family and I are about my being gay, and how comfortable I have become in that I am able to calmly communicate with my young cousin about an issue that is clearly not typical in his life.

Another great family experience was finally getting to see my gay uncles married in Massachusetts. My mother's brother and his partner have lived together for thirty years. When I was growing up, they were always forced to tone down their private lives in public, and my family ridiculed them for their sexuality behind their backs. It taught me that it very clearly was not okay to be openly gay. After I finally came out, things started to change. It almost seemed like it became cool to be gay and my uncles suddenly received a great deal of interest. Everyone wanted to know about their lives and about their relationship. My family's earlier feelings about my uncles' sexuality kept everyone from really getting to know each other. Now that being gay no longer made someone an outcast, my family could begin to appreciate my uncles for who they really are—two wonderfully caring, colorful men with great taste. They are easy to talk to, throw the best parties, and seem a whole lot younger than my parents or anyone else in that generation. In June 2007, they shared an amazing evening with their families during which we celebrated their love—and the brave decision by the Massachusetts Supreme Court to allow loving couples like them to be legally married. After all they had to go through, it was a great feeling to watch them be the center of everyone's attention. The rest of us, including those who used to mock their "gay lifestyle," were just happy to see two people in love.

Having the support of my family was something I did not predict, but their support has allowed me to grow from where I was when I first came out to the person I am now. I also am extremely appreciative of the friends I have always surrounded myself with. So where do I see my life going from here? I hope to get married one day and enjoy the freedoms and rights that all humans deserve. The political climate is as unclear as ever. However, the simple fact is that as ever more people come out, their friends and families are realizing that denying basic rights to their loved ones is wrong. The world only moves in one direction, toward progress. As Dr. Martin Luther King Jr. said, "The arc of the moral universe is long but it bends towards justice." I believe that Dr. King knew what he was talking about.

Andy Preston

I hope that 17-year-olds in the future will not have to experience the fears I have described. Teenagers have enough to deal with already. Over the past five to ten years, I have heard about so many teenagers who have been able to come out in high school or even earlier. It warms my heart to know that they have the courage to be true to themselves, and I hope they also have the support of loved ones. But even if they aren't quite there yet, I know it will turn out okay for them. Everyone has a different path, and my story is just one of many. I am here to tell my 17-year-old self that all of the fears diminish over time, that he will get past it, that he will live his life the way it was meant to be lived.

Case 18

MULTIHUED

ANTHONY LUCKETT

DOI: 10.4324/9781003165378-23

Anthony Luckett

When at a tender age our half Korean, half African American writer is abandoned by his father, his mother is forced to place him in a series of foster homes where he remains until college. He longs to feel a sense of love and belonging, but his world does not allow for trust in others or the full expression of his feelings. With adolescence he begins to struggle without role models to reconcile his biracial identity as a double minority. Writing his story in his senior year of college, he is able to reflect on how the ways of coping that allowed him to navigate the cold emotional landscape of his childhood were now preventing him from building trust and love in intimate relationships. This insight about his challenges to finding happiness illuminates his path forward.

On Being Asian

They asked me to write about why choosing
    or choosing not to choose sides is relevant
    in my life.
    I told them that before my thoughts could travel from mind to mouth
    I heard the universe whisper life into my mother's womb.
    Lucky me.
    I might have survived the sound of fate mumbling destiny
    while reading a novel on a love unfilled.
    He bookmarked where love had been emptied
    and now I'm pessimistic.
    I'd give up but which way is up to me?
    Where is down to earth when I can't stop thinking about having left
heaven.
    I've danced with angels and solved multiracial differential equations
    in three dimensions. I stand in the fourth now speaking
    about the three axial frames of reference and not one of them
    described what it was to be Asian.
    Sometimes, when I'm not being Korean,
    I speak Konglish with my mother and eat Kimchee
    alone in my dorm so my roommates can't smell it …
    I hum Ah-Ri-Rhang to my dreams so they and sleep can be lovers.
    Under the covers in the dark I imagine myself with straight hair
    and a grandmother that cooks for me every night despite her own
desires.
    But when I close my double eyes in private I remember my
birthright

birthplace and inner fires.

If I had a log for every time I've been asked

whose side I would have taken in the Riots,

the earth would be a ball of flame and we'd wander lost in our lust to label everything

we see because for every sort of people you think I might be,

they all know they're not in me

and all I hear are voices in my head still asking questions that don't move me any more.

I'm black and Korean, devoid of sympathy for culture vultures that

circle over my head; a fateful halo reminds me that it's time to be free

of the thirty-eight parallels I've seen folks draw on me …

They asked me to write about why choosing

or choosing not to choose sides is relevant in my life.

I told them that before my mouth was informed by mind that

I piggybacked the universe's spine and tapped into my Chi …

Lucky Me.

I might not have survived nearly four years of fate's interpretation of destiny.

But.

Here I am.

On Being Black

I feel as if I am an interloper in a land where the packed snow smells of watermelon.

And I traverse the hills picking snowflakes and spitting seeds that plant themselves in my journey.

Walking in circles.

My racial profile eludes my facial style.

I don't look the part.

and I am black by association.

Misappropriate usage of my visage has been the ground on which I walk alone treading the Mason-Dixon poverty line.

Perforated like my spinal cordless phonetic Nile tones.

I'm light-skinned.

Where do I fit in next to "I've seen you befores" and "my cousin looks just like yous"? And, because I've got Seoul in the windows of my soul, I've also heard "He ain't just black I told you sos." So.

Sometimes when I'm not being black, I speak in Ebonics and quote Ca$h Money's Greatest Hits.

I purposely fail tests just to see … just to see if I'm keepin' it real. I walk slowly and strut, nod to say "what's up dogg, peace, ah-ight, that's tight, smoke? Nah, shit shorty and hey. My. Nigga."

I've got my finger on figuring it out but when I'm out of my mind what is insane?

My father gave me the greatest lesson on what a black man should be by not being around for me to follow his bad example.

Now Jazz is my mother and Hip Hop my sample of what daddies be like.

I feel as if I've intruded into a land where the snow smells of watermelons and I'm no longer picking cotton snowflakes but bad decisions.

Ones that spit the seeds of a freer future plantation.

Walking in circles encircled by miracle manacles I be dazzled and unfocused. Black by association.

And, I don't look the part that's played me.

Only.

Time isn't planted with watermelon seeds.

I felt the beat of my mother's chest against the side of my face. Drowsily I looked up and out of the taxicab window. I fell back to sleep against my mother's chest. I was snug and clinging to Mom as best I could. Finally, we stopped. Mom nudged me awake and brought me out of the car. There was a large wood house in front of me. There were two shadows in the doorway of this house. I walked into the house and sat down at a table and put my head down. My eyes were cracked open, and I caught sight of Mom talking with one of the shadows. They spoke and spoke. Then without warning, Mom started walking out the door and I ran after her. As I descended the steps in front of the house I saw Mom get back into the cab. The tailpipe exhaust made the red lights eerie at night as the cab drove off and I screamed, "Mommy! Where are you going? Mommy!" I couldn't say anything else. I was so shocked that she would just leave me. All I saw were the red taillights getting smaller and smaller and more and more blurry as my tears fell.

The lady escorted me back into the house. As I sat down at the table, the man and woman looked at me. She began to peel a tangerine and asked me if I wanted any. No, I didn't want any! I wanted my mom. I wanted my mom. The impact of my mother leaving left me speechless for a long, long time. I remember sitting at that table for what felt like hours—long enough for there to be veins of salt down my cheeks where the tears had tumbled. There were things running through my body and soul that I didn't have the words to fit to. All through my childhood, that image of the dwindling taillights haunted me because I still hadn't come to terms with being left in the care of strangers. The household that I was born into had fallen apart by the time I was 4 years old. This is how my story begins.

I was born in Suwon, Korea, to a Korean mother and African American father. In less than a year, my mother, father, and I moved to London, England, where my mother had a job as a model and teacher, and my father was still in the service of the United States Air Force. We somehow ended up in San Francisco, California, where we lived near an Air Force base. I don't remember moving, just being in different places and different feelings that come with it. I don't remember having friends, and I wasn't allowed to be in the same room as my father when he and his friends watched adult movies and smoked. He flickered in my mind until his presence disappeared.

When I was left with the tangerine family, each day was like awaking from one bad dream into another. They were a white family. Looking back, I cannot remember a time when I felt like I was a part of that family, perhaps because my recollection of the negative outweighs the occasional happy moments that I can only vaguely remember. My memory serves me tidbits of history salvaged after a tumultuous beginning to life. One of the most enduring memories I have of my time there was the way I spent a number of my weekend mornings on nice days. The funnies were handed to me by two of my foster parents, Jim and Marcy. A hand on my shoulder turned me toward the side door, and I was asked to go outside and read. Jim gave me a hasty nod and told me it was OK to go outside in my underwear. I was uncomfortable but didn't know what to say. I walked slowly out of the door and sat down on the picnic bench with the funnies. Before I started reading I carefully screened the surroundings for onlookers. I opened the pages slowly, hesitantly, and read at an even slower pace. Systematically, I scanned the premises for onlookers as I read the funnies. When I was done with the funnies, I thought it would be all right to go back inside the house; I felt as if my reading the comics was a punishment. I stood up and walked up to the screen door, and it was locked. When I finally got back inside it wasn't long before I was outside again; at least I was clothed on my return excursions. The words were usually, "It's nice out, so why don't you go outside?" Those innocuous words never really sparked any real thought until I heard them repeated over and over again. Nobody ever wanted me in the house. It wasn't as if I truly wanted to be inside so much as I wanted to belong. I just wanted to feel accepted, but nobody wanted to know what I wanted. I missed my mom, and I didn't like living with this tangerine family.

My unstable disposition was kept aflame by my anger and aggression. In school I was your typical problem child—the kid who doesn't keep quiet, who is always running around and won't listen. My rage would cause me to get into fistfights, and I can even recall throwing a chair across the classroom at another student and hitting the teacher by mistake. My tangerine family foster father, Jim, was called and that night he spanked contempt and embarrassment into my backside at the dinner table. It didn't hurt anything but my pride.

In retrospect, I suppose I should be grateful that a family would take me in and care for me for as long as they did. I suppose that I should thank them for providing a roof over my head and food for me to eat. I suppose that I would indeed be grateful if it were not for memories riddled with nightmares and a feeling of emptiness that fills my gut. Each day I was made to feel as if I wasn't wanted. The house was a large, beautifully crafted wood house with a basement, two floors, and an attic. They kept bees on the side of their house to collect honey to sell. The garage was a bottomless pit of baubles, toys, auto parts, and other things that families accumulate over years. The pond behind the house was connected to a creek that was filled with tadpoles. The woods were deep and magnificent. Unfortunately, there was no home for me in that picturesque niche down a quarter-of-a-mile driveway off of Whitney Road. When I think back, the darkness overshadows the light. There were things that happened in that niche that my mother does not know about to this day. The worst part about that tale is that Jim and Marcy knew—and did nothing to protect me.

Jim's father must have been in his sixties when I met him. He was a large, heavyset man with gray stubble, a dirty T-shirt, and a dirty odor. I didn't care much for him so I never understood why they ever left me alone with him. They knew what he did on those walks out in the woods at night. He would lead me around behind the pond, and we'd sit on the bench. In a gruff voice he'd ask me if I liked him. I was frozen because even the first time it happened didn't seem like the first time it happened. His coarse hands would find their way on to my back and the friction would rattle my tiny 6-year-old frame. His large body overwhelmed me as his large hands found their way off of my back and into my pants. I felt his stubble on my face and in my mouth. I wanted to scream but couldn't. Who would come? Jim and Marcy knew already, I was certain, and Mommy was not there. He touched me where I hadn't even discovered myself and asked again if I liked him. No, I did not like him! I wanted him to go away but I couldn't tell him that. I sat quiet and wished that it would end sooner and sooner each time. I hated walking with Jim's father.

Jim and Marcy were aware because one night after I had "taken a walk," they asked me what happened on the walk with Grandpa. "He touched me here," I said pointing to my groin. "And kissed me. Then he touched me here …" There was a pause as the two stood there. The sad truth is I don't remember that being the last night that he sapped, rubbed away, and swore to secrecy my childhood with his 60-plus-year-old mouth, disturbing hands, and five o'clock shadow.

Of all the bad things I remember, the most difficult to deal with was the fact that something bad was happening to me, and my foster parents knew. They knew, and they knew that I knew they knew, and still nothing. No protection, no nothing—except for more walks with Grandpa. I didn't feel as if it was my fault, but for some perverted reason I thought that I might have deserved treatment like that. If everybody knew, maybe it was normal, but part of me knew it couldn't have been. I don't remember too much else about the tangerine family; their faces are murky images of exaggerated features. Fortunately, life is very different for me now. But family secrets have to start somewhere. I had come to terms with what had happened during the summer after my senior year of high school, but I was 20 years old when I finally came around to writing about this incident.

> The night that cried for those
> Hands to stop
> That! Stop That! … Stops that Rock my brain,
> My pains to sleep in that
> Cradle made for one … I would still Kill the night that cried for Me.

There is a part of me that would commit murder to regain the innocence, security, and trust I had taken from me on those walks. Motherfuckers! I will never forget what I lost there. I often wonder what life would have been like had I not lived with that tangerine family: Jim, Marcy, and their children. It is difficult to think outside of the past because my history is documented in who I am as a person. Scholars say that a child's personality is shaped by the time he is 5 years of age.

I'm beginning to think there is some truth to that. I was dealt a pair of incompatible, strong-willed parents and confusion, chaos, and abandonment before the age of 5. I sometimes wonder how I got through four years with Jim and Marcy's family—misbehaving in school, missing my mother, and all the while feeling I didn't belong.

When my mom finally came to get me out of that tiny niche on Whitney Road when I was 8 years old, I didn't know then that I would move twice more before the fifth grade. I moved next to Astoria, Queens, in New York, where I lived with my mom's friend, Kyoung. I attended parochial school for the third grade and just as the school year ended, I moved back to Ohio.

This time Ohio was different. I stayed with a Korean woman named Young. She lived with a Tae Kwon Do instructor and her two sons, Tony, age 16, and Andy, age 14. The few months that I was with this family, a number of things came to light. I found out that my mother was paying for me to live there when Young became increasingly angry with me for no reason that I could see. Tony pulled me aside one day after I had been yelled at and told me that his mother wasn't angry with me but was angry with my mother because she hadn't paid. Hadn't paid? Why hadn't she paid? I wondered. I understood that raising someone costs money, but why hadn't she paid? Young once told me that she was raising me because my mom didn't know how to take care of me. She said that if my mom left me I would have nothing to worry about because she would take care of me. As hard as I found that to believe since the lady was always angry with me, I wanted to believe that I had nothing to worry about. Her offer, though strange and twisted to me, sounded somewhat inviting since I hated moving and I didn't know what to believe.

Young's words seared my ears, and the thought of Mom not returning haunted me. As it turned out, Mom also had paid Jim, Marcy, and Kyoung. This new information forced the connection in my mind between my mom's missed payments and the treatment I was receiving. I resented both my foster families and my mother. It was difficult enough to comprehend these families being paid for my care, but I really resented the thought that my mother would dare miss a payment. My resentment was twofold. First, the untainted perception I had of my mother began to soil. Then, when I began questioning my mother, I began losing faith in my own judgment and trusted no one. In a matter of months, Mom came back and moved me once again.

It was in the middle of the fourth grade that I arrived in New York City for the second time. This time it was the Woodside section of

Queens where I stayed with the Kims until I went away to college. At this house were the head of the family, "Uncle," his wife, and their two sons, James and John. The Kims had six other foster children in addition to me. All of the kids in Uncle's care attended Public School 11 only five blocks away. Most of the class dismissed me as the new kid dressed in hand-me-downs until people noticed that I was artistically inclined and athletically adept—which was at least a start and more than I had ever had before. School didn't mean much to me until I reached the sixth grade where I met Mr. Meadow. He was the first person to take a genuine interest in my abilities as a student, athlete, and scientist. His charisma would fill the room, and the amount of passion and energy he devoted to his students was peerless. Mr. Meadow motivated my curiosity, intelligence, and creativity. He changed my outlook on school and on myself.

Mr. Meadow was about 5 feet 10 inches and had what I can only describe as a white Afro, only his hair wasn't thick and he wasn't black. He looked a lot like pictures I had seen of Mark Twain. He let me sit in the back of class with the microscope. I would bring in samples of dirty water that I had retrieved from various sources in the neighborhood. When my face was in that microscope the world around me did not exist. I watched in awe the paramecia and other microorganisms swimming around in the water. The truth is that I was teacher's pet, and I liked it even if some other people didn't like it. Mr. Meadow's spirit was very apparent to me, and I basked in his presence. He used to tell me to train for the decathlon before I knew what one was. He always asked that I remain true to myself and taught me not to be influenced by others. One conversation we had shines above all others. We had been talking and then he looked into my eyes. "Tony, don't ever change. I'm serious. Don't ever change. OK?" I didn't know how to react to the solemnity behind his words, so all I could muster was a simple nod of affirmation. Don't change? I couldn't understand the full meaning of what he was trying to say or how to take it truly to heart. His investment in me was matched by my desire to learn from him and the genuine respect I had for this man who respected me and believed in me. He helped to erase a great deal of my self-doubt, and he built my confidence.

I wish my life at school were even remotely representative of my life in the Kim residence. Perhaps it would be asking too much of life to have things go well in both worlds. During my stay with the Kim family, I never once felt as if I was a part of the family. Aside from the mistrust they had of the world in general, the way in which they ran a family was not healthy. According to the Korean old school of thought, children were commodities and were to be seen and not heard.

I distanced myself from everything in the Kims' household except from Uncle's son James. He was the only member of that family with whom I felt I had any connection. The Kims owned two apartments on the same floor of the building. James and I stayed in apartment 4D with his grandmother while the rest of the family lived in apartment 4B. James and I would stay up late playing video games or watching television. Sometimes, we'd play basketball together and for about a year, he was one of my Tae Kwon Do instructors. James also tutored me in math. He was my older brother and I looked up to him. We never spoke about what I was truly feeling except for once.

> "You know bro, I've never really felt at home here," I said to James softly.
> "I know. I can understand that."
> "It's like … well, it's not like I'm very upset that I wasn't a part of this family because, well … you know."
> "Yeah," he said as he shook his head.
> "It's kind of sad, bro," I said.
> "It is. That it is," he said softly.

A moment of silence overtook the room and he gave me an understanding nod, as if to say he understood my discomfort of never feeling "at home" and my struggle to get away. I was sad that I had lived with a family for almost a decade and never felt truly welcome there. Beyond not feeling welcome, I was so uncomfortable I didn't like being in the physical presence or close vicinity of Uncle or Auntie. So that I could spend the least amount of time at home with the Kims I would go out as much as I could and stay out late, and I was as active as I possibly could be in high school. Looking back I can see the irony that at age 6 I was always upset at being made to stay out of Jim and Marcy's house; twelve years later I was doing everything I could to stay out of the house. "Men don't run from their problems." Who could have taught me this? Jim? The Tae Kwon Do instructor? Tony or Andy? Uncle? James? I wouldn't know. Though I picked up pieces of manhood from each of them along my path of development, I am unclear how to apportion to what extent these male foster figures have affected me.

With loneliness as my companion and introspection my bedfellow, I brooded over the questions that challenged my understanding of my circumstances, my mother, and the world around me. The changes happening to my body only contributed to my confusion and lack of understanding. While undergoing these changes in my life, Mom was still a sporadic beacon of light, and while I took her for granted, I resented my predicament and wanted more from her than just an escape from my current environment. I wanted attention and to belong. The difficulty of dealing with my loneliness was more than feeling I didn't belong in my various foster homes—it was complicated by my developing racial identity. I had lived with one white family, a single Korean woman, and two very different Korean families. But I am Korean and black. No one I lived with could fully understand what it was to be a mix of two separate minority worlds, and until later in my life, neither could I.

I always knew that I was different. With the tangerine family it was very obvious, especially when they would pick me up from school. Everywhere I went, including New York City, I managed to warrant a second look. This made me so terribly self-conscious that I was embarrassed by my heritage. I remember once, Mom and I were on the subway. I sat next to Mom who was dressed in a white linen outfit and sat reading the latest volume of *Korean Health Digest*. As I sat there, I stared around me and secretly hoped that no one was staring back. I don't know whether it was the book she was reading or the clothes she was wearing, but I felt like everyone on the train was looking at us. My uneasiness at her presence was displayed on my face. I was so unused to being in my mother's presence that it was as if she were some strange foreigner reading her magazine right next to me. Then she turned to me and began speaking Korean in front of everyone. As her native language entered my ears, perfectly intelligible, I wanted her to stop. My brusque responses to her were in English, my native language. But she was happy speaking to me that way, showing her affection, and I should have been too, but instead I was overwhelmed by feelings of embarrassment. I was certain that everyone on the train could see that I was not fully Korean and so was wondering why this woman was speaking to me in that tongue. Not coincidentally, that is exactly what I was wondering, too.

I will never forget that painful train ride with Mom in which the most important thing to me was not wanting a subway car full of strangers to know that I spoke or understood my mother's native language. I felt as if she were determined to make me fully Korean. The language barrier that exists between us has really hindered our relationship. On the one hand, Mom is this loving person, her caring and warmth just flowing over me. On the other hand, my mother is a person whom I've had very little time to get to know. My mom has been absent nearly all my life, yet strangely enough she knows me a lot better than

I have given her credit for. That day on the train she looked deep into my eyes as she was speaking to me and then stopped and went back to reading her magazine. It was as if she had sensed my innermost thoughts, the discomfort and conflict I sat with. So, for the rest of the journey we rode in silence.

I have always prided myself on being different, but for a long time, I felt funny. The type of "funny" that I felt the first time I heard someone call me a "Chink," an experience only matched by the first time I was called a "nigger." As the hapless victim of the synergy in being the biracial new guy, I have always been conscious of my differences, externally and internally. To my Korean friends I always felt like the token black guy. To those two black men who passed me on 43rd Avenue one indelible night, I was a "Chink." The powerful feelings of contempt and racism are vivid and lasting. So permanent, that I revisit them every now and again. What is it that people see when they look at me, and why do their furtive stares make me uncomfortable? As I attempt to answer these questions, I find myself caught in life's gauntlet of self-discovery.

During my years in high school I had not fully come to terms with my racial identity, but at least my relationship with my mother was getting better. It was no consolation that we couldn't be together, but I began to realize that she had really wanted the best for me all along. The sacrifice my mother made transcends human emotion and reason, at least to any American or any non-Korean way of thinking. My mother gave up her life so that I might have a better chance at success than she. In my selfish adolescence, I was unable to recognize her strength, humility, and sacrifice. After my freshman year at college, however, I was blessed with the opportunity to fully appreciate my mother's gift of life and my responsibility for it.

By the time I had finished my first year at college I had not seen my mother since my high school graduation. I spent the summer working to raise enough money to visit my mother in Houston, Texas. I had changed since I last saw her. My first year of college had filled my life with new academic and extracurricular experiences, and I had braided my hair in cornrows and put on fifteen pounds. What would she think? As I disembarked the plane my mother stood at the gate anticipating my arrival. I saw her radiant 5 foot 5 inch frame tiptoeing, almost hovering. Her caring eyes scanned each passenger with X-ray precision and surprisingly looked right through me. I nearly passed her before she recognized who I was. In an instant, her eyes lit up and her smile increased tenfold and her arms reached out for me. "Oh my goodness! I almost didn't recognize my Tony—so handsome and tall. Oh my goodness!" she exclaimed. It certainly had been a long time.

When we arrived at the apartment my mother had been living in for some time, I couldn't help but notice it looked like she had just moved in, because of the lack of any furnishings. In the living room there was a table on which was a small pewter picture frame with a picture of us on my 16th birthday. The kitchen had not been touched. My thoughts echoed off of the bare walls as I helped to put away the groceries we had bought for dinner. I asked my mother why there wasn't anything in her house. I could almost hear her response before she answered: she spent so much of her time working that she had no need for an apartment to look and feel comfortable. Before I could even enjoy having spent twelve hours with Mom, she had to go to help out at the store where she worked.

When she came home she began cooking. I helped her for a short while, then relaxed and sat watching her in action from the living room. We finally sat down to a feast, and I gorged myself and we spoke. It wasn't the kind of hapless chatter that you might expect two people to have after a long separation. Every gesture and word was a conversation in its own right. The synergy of mother and child contributed to the regenerative air in that humble room. We finished our meal, and I remember her teasing me about my hair. She didn't want me to have long hair, and she also didn't like my cornrow braids. Seeing through my snappy excuses she said, "You don't always have to wear your culture out like that." I spent all night thinking about her insight.

My last day in Houston came quickly. I packed quietly and wore a smile of satisfaction on my face. I was happy that I had the opportunity to see my mother. She offered her motherly words of wisdom as the taxi pulled up to her door. I asked the driver if he would take pictures of my mother and me together. He took a step back and aimed the camera at us. I told Mom to get on my back and when she did, I carried her around the parking lot. Her laughter was so pure I almost collapsed. When I let her down, I hugged her as the driver snapped another picture. After giving my mom the biggest hug and kiss any son could muster, I called on the Lord's strength to prevent my tears from surfacing. It wasn't that I was afraid of being unmanly, I just chose not to cry all the tears behind the ones on the surface. If I started, she would too, and I don't think the taxi driver was prepared to deal with a bawling mother and equally torn son, so I stared out of the taxi window and smiled. She stood there waving back with the same painful grin on her face. As the car pulled away I felt as if my brain was saturated from holding back all of the contentment and tears. I made small talk with the driver during the ride to the airport.

I thought about her meager living conditions and how blessed I was to have a mother who cared about me so much. I have been asked why she didn't keep me by her side. Other people have questioned her motives for placing me in the foster care of other families. This visit answered my own questions. It is difficult to put into words what my mother's burden is. Like many traditional Korean parents, she wanted for me all that she had missed in her own life. She dropped out of college to work to support me when I was 6 or 7. And although I moved many times to different foster families, I was uprooted less often than she was during that time. As the object of her love, I felt obligated to my Korean heritage and how important it is to her that I don't lose what little I know. I thought about her words of advice that I don't always have to "wear my culture out." I felt as if I did in order to remind myself of my own background. It was a constant struggle. The pride I had for my mother's heritage was countered by the overwhelming negative feeling I got when she would overemphasize my Korean-ness. At one point, she asked if I would change my last name from that of my father to her own. I was torn up by the powerful nature of that request. It was as if she wanted me to discard my blackness or to destroy the traces I had of my father's heritage. On one hand, my father was absent from my life, so why should I carry his name? On the other hand, my name has been my basic identity since I was born. In the end, I didn't change my name and my mother understood.

Race matters. And it doesn't. I cannot detach myself from the biracial aspects of my background. Though I state this obvious fact about my racial identity, I sometimes wonder how my life would have been different if I were just of a single race. I have been told that I have benefited by having received the best of both worlds. And while I have been exposed to both the ugliness and benefits of multiracial life, I have not felt the need to choose one side of my racial background over the other. I have reached a level of comfort where I am proud of all that I am. In some respects I would say that I am more of a New Yorker culturally than either Korean or black. For me, the distinction is important. Race and culture are synonymous when people with a similar history or genetic makeup share common life experiences unique to their heritage. There is no singular black experience in America that I can identify with. Neither is there any definitive Korean or multiracial experience. To say the very least, growing up multihued has never been dull. But my racial composition is deeply intertwined with all the important relationships in my life. My relationships with my mother, with friends, and with the opposite sex all reflect the intricate connections between different parts of my life.

An important illustration of this connectivity is how I have interacted with the opposite sex. I have not had much difficulty attracting women because of my physical appearance, which undoubtedly has to do with my multiracial look. But physical attractiveness has not been the only source of my appeal. Because I have craved the attention of women from the day my mother left me with the tangerine family, over the years I have developed a personality and demeanor that commands attention. Merely attracting women, however, has not solved my loneliness or other interpersonal problems. The obstacle to my having more meaningful and satisfying intimate relationships is rooted in all of the baggage I bring to the table when I get involved in a relationship. Since everything is connected, many of the ways in which I interact with my mother have carried over into my intimate relationships. It therefore makes sense to me that I am an emotionally difficult person to get to know. It seems reasonable and rational to me that I can love someone and then leave her in a heartbeat.

These patterns are a reality in my life. I believe that the lack of family and maternal stability while I was growing up has fostered my pick-up-and-go mentality when it comes to intimacy. I have had to be somewhat callous emotionally to avoid breaking down. My perspective has undergone a number of changes with each new relationship. In the past year I have made conscious efforts to dim the glowing lack of faith I have in womanhood. I feel betrayed in many ways by girls I date. Perhaps I am holding them accountable for my subconscious disappointment with my nomadic lifestyle, and because everything is so short-lived.

It is easier for me to become physically involved with a woman than to invest any serious emotions or real love. The few times that I have really trusted and loved, the relationship failed to survive long distances and miscommunications. Emotional self-preservation outshines my desire for true companionship and so I have closed off parts of myself. In addition to repressing parts of my personality, at the start of a new relationship I determine just how much feeling I am willing to put into a particular relationship, and I seldom deviate from that plan. Some people say that a person should love like they've never loved before, but what about hurting like never before? A guiding truth is that I don't want to hurt like I have before. Every time I grow close to someone, thoughts of long distances and miscommunications remind me of past pains. Many

Anthony Luckett

of my friends, past girlfriends, and sexual partners have questioned my dead-end response to them:

> Why don't you just let go of your past? Why can't you just enjoy us right now?
>
> Can you stop dwelling on what went wrong before? Why don't you want to be with me?
>
> Why don't you just open up?

How could they not know that, of course, I have asked myself the same questions a thousand times over.

"My future wife is not enrolled at this college" is how I euphemistically put the lack of companionship in my college experience. My desire to transcend my personal history and emotional limitations has been nullified, and I am presently torn between sexual attraction to multiple females and meaningful co-existence with one woman. College life is not conducive to long-distance relationships. Consequently, I am ill-prepared for what it is I am wishing for. I come to the relationship table with baggage. All of my unsolved and unanswered problems and questions stay packed up, and I expect these females to magically shed light on something they know nothing about—the deeper me. With each encounter I either find out something new about myself, or I am reminded of some undesirable quality in my personality. In short, I am still searching for myself. I am afraid of being hurt again.

My relationships with the opposite sex have left a stone in my heart. I have weathered self-induced loneliness because of my closed nature. And, through understanding, I have broken the stone in my heart. It's a healing process. I don't think that I will be able to have a meaningful and healthy relationship until I have rid myself of all of these smaller stones. Mistrust, fear, anger, and resentment must fade behind love for me to move on.

Even the longest journey begins with one step. Over the years the stride, pace, and frequency of these steps have all changed. Now, twenty-two years later, my journey continues. I feel as if I have revealed as much about the journey as I have about the traveler. The words and stories I have shared highlight the most powerful memories I have of people and experiences that helped determine my path in life. However, they are only fractions of my entire story. I have not mentioned my true friends who have been my surrogate family and support every step of the way. I am eternally grateful for having them in my life. Neither have I mentioned my involvement in student organizations, dance, my fraternity, or my academics. One can imagine the gamut of things I found to enhance my only child existence. My search for a complete me is undying. The motivation it generates is eternal.

For my narrative to be complete, I need to know the full story for myself. So, I have begun to search for my father, who was my age when my mother conceived me. The thought that a man out there somewhere is the provider of half my genetic code, and that his presence in my life before the age of 5 has influenced my growth, sparks insurmountable curiosity. My search has begun with the help and support of my mother and my friends. I have no expectations, but whether I find him or not, the search itself can only further my journey of self-discovery.

Index

Index